Why Do You Need This New Edition?

If you're wondering why you should buy this new edition of *The Writer's World*, here are 10 good reasons!

1 **Your World:** You spend your day texting friends and family, checking Facebook and Twitter, and listening to music on your iPod. New teaching suggestions help your instructors to incorporate more activities that include these cutting edge devices. For example, in Chapter 4, you are invited to compare and contrast two commercial Web sites made by car companies and in a Tech Tip you are asked to analyze the best features on your cell phone.

2 **New Editing Handbook Sections:** Two new themes appear in the Editing Handbook. Section 1 is now called Lifestyles, and it focuses on health, exercise, and food. Section 4, Trades and Technology, emphasizes information technologies, building industries, infrastructure, and health-care technology. Many practices in other grammar chapters have been updated or completely changed.

3 **New Grammar Chapter:** New to this edition is Chapter 23, Exact Language. This new chapter focuses on dictionary and thesaurus usage and precise vocabulary. You will learn to recognize and correct clichés and slang.

4 **Updated High-Interest Paragraph Models and Practices:** Throughout the book you will notice new examples, fresh sample paragraphs, innovative writing practices, novel Writer's Desk topics, and abundant grammar practice. In fact, to make the content more topical and appealing, roughly 30 percent of the book's content has been updated.

5 **Getting Motivated:** Cooperative Learning Teaching Tips appear throughout the book and can be used by your instructor to promote peer-to-peer interaction, share knowledge, solve a problem, negotiate, and reflect. These activities will help prepare you for the workplace!

6 **Fun Media:** The film writing prompts have been updated to include newer and more recent movies. The new movies include *Avatar* and *Precious*, among others.

7 **New Photos:** New opening photos and photo writing prompts appear throughout the book. Each grammar chapter has an opening photo that helps to show the thematic content. New photo writing prompts appear throughout the book.

8 **New Readings:** In Chapter 30, six new readings relate to the grammar themes. Bill Bryson, Juan Rodriquez, Dorothy Nixon, and Ellen Goodman are some of the new writers featured in the chapter. You will read about engaging and relevant topics such as the effective branding of Apple, shopping for religion, and the overeating epidemic.

9 **Nonnative Speakers & The Writer's World:** The authors have extensive experience with nonnative speakers, and have included more precise ESL tips to help teachers in and out of the classroom. You are in good hands!

10 **Chapter Objectives & MyWritingLab:** Each chapter in *The Writer's World: Sentences and Paragraphs* now opens with a list of chapter objectives and ties them into the most powerful online writing tool on the planet with Pearson's **MyWritingLab** (www.mywritinglab.com). Now you can truly grasp chapter content and test your understanding of that content with MyWritingLab in a more meaningful way!

PEA

W9-CHP-648

MyWritingLab™ has helped students like you from all over the country.

MyWritingLab™ can help you become a better writer and help you get a better grade.

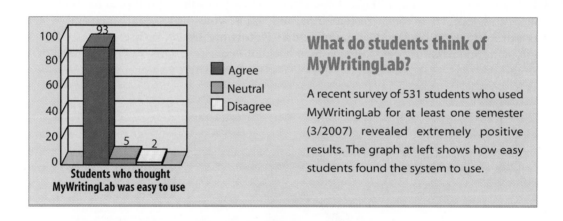

What do students think of MyWritingLab?

A recent survey of 531 students who used MyWritingLab for at least one semester (3/2007) revealed extremely positive results. The graph at left shows how easy students found the system to use.

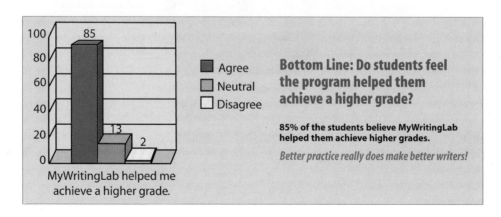

Bottom Line: Do students feel the program helped them achieve a higher grade?

85% of the students believe MyWritingLab helped them achieve higher grades.

Better practice really does make better writers!

www.mywritinglab.com

Registering for MyWritingLab™...

It is easy to get started! Simply follow these steps to get into your MyWritingLab course.

1. **Find Your Access Code** (it is either packaged with your textbook, or you purchased it separately). You will need this access code and your course ID to join your MyWritingLab course. Your instructor has your course ID number, so make sure you have that before logging in.

2. **Click on "Students"** under "First-Time Users." Here you will be prompted to enter your access code, enter your e-mail address, and choose your own Login Name and Password. After you register, you can **click on "Returning Users"** to use your new login name and password every time you go back into your course in MyWritingLab.

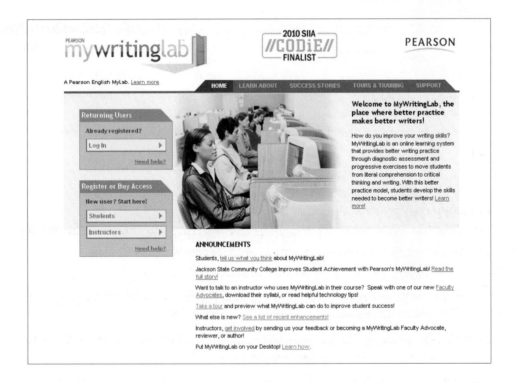

After logging in, you will see all the ways MyWritingLab can help you become a better writer.

www.mywritinglab.com

The Homepage . . .

Here is your MyWritingLab HomePage.
You get a bird's eye view of where you are in your course every time you log in.

Your **Course** box shows your class details.

Your **Study Plan** box shows what you last completed and what is next on your **To Do** list.

Your **Gradebook** box shows you a snapshot of how you are doing in the class.

Your **Other Resources** box supplies you with amazing tools such as:

- **Pearson Tutor Services**—click here to see how you can get help on your papers by qualified tutors ... before handing them in!

- **Research Navigator**—click here to see how this resembles your library with access to online journals for research paper assignments.

- **Study Skills**—extra help that includes tips and quizzes on how to improve your study skills

- **Pearson e-Text**—click here to read and reference the e-Text version of your textbook!

Now, let's start practicing to become better writers. Click on the Study Plan tab. This is where you will do all your course work.

www.mywritinglab.com

The Study Plan . . .

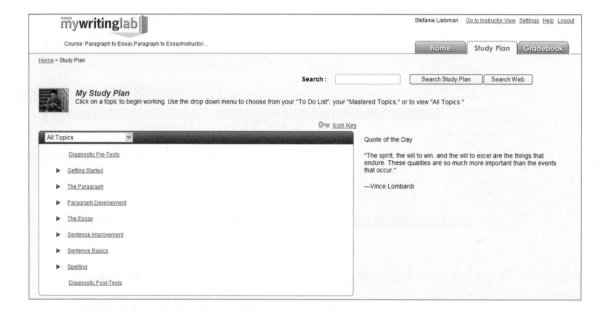

MyWritingLab provides you with a simple Study Plan of the writing skills that you need to master. You start from the top of the list and work your way down. You can start with the Diagnostic Pre-Tests.

The Diagnostic Pre-Tests . . .

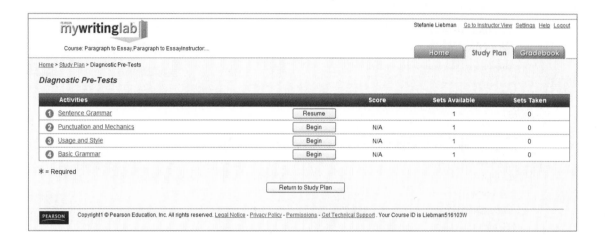

MyWritingLab's Diagnostic Pre-Tests are divided into four parts and cover all the major grammar, punctuation, and usage topics. After you complete these diagnostic tests, MyWritingLab will generate a personalized Study Plan for you, showing all the topics you have mastered and listing all the topics yet unmastered.

www.mywritinglab.com

The Diagnostic Pre-Tests . . .

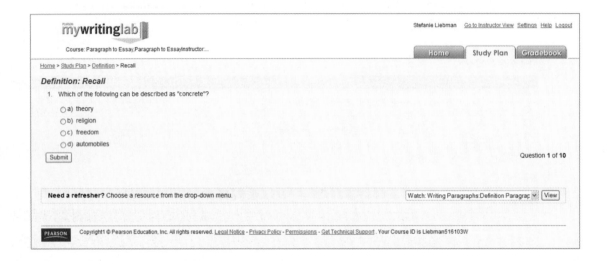

The Diagnostic Pre-Tests contain five exercises on each of the grammar, punctuation, and usage topics. You can achieve mastery of the topic in the Diagnostic Pre-Test by getting four of five or five of five correct within each topic.

After completing the Diagnostic Pre-Test, you can return to your Study Plan and enter any of the topics you have yet to master.

www.mywritinglab.com

Watch, Recall, Apply, Write . . .

Here is an example of a MyWritinglab Activity set that you will see once you enter into a topic. Take the time to briefly read the introductory paragraph, and then **watch** the engaging video clip by clicking on "Watch: Tense."

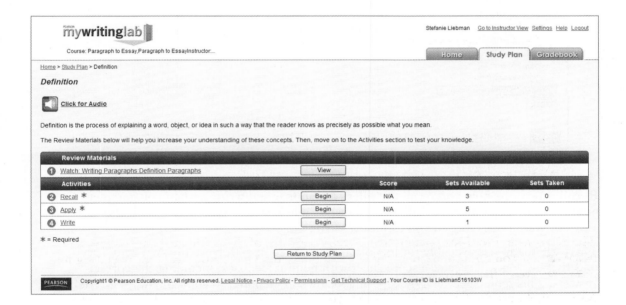

The video clip provides you with a helpful review.
Now you are ready to start the exercises. There are three types:

- Recall—activities that help you *recall* the rules of grammar
- Apply—activities that help you *apply* these rules to brief paragraphs or essays
- Write—activities that ask you to demonstrate these rules of grammar in your own writing

www.mywritinglab.com

Watch, Recall, Apply, Write . . .

Recall questions help you recall the rules of grammar and writing when you complete multiple-choice questions, usually with four possible answers. You get feedback after answering each question, so you can learn as you go!

There are many sets available for lots of practice. As soon as you are finished with a set of activities, you will receive a score sheet with helpful feedback, including the correct answers. This score sheet will be kept in your own gradebook, so you can always go back and review.

Watch, Recall, Apply, Write . . .

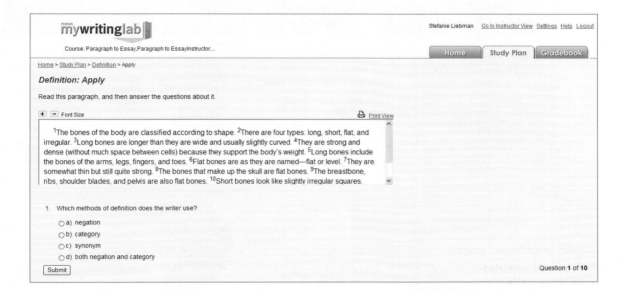

Apply exercises help you apply writing and grammar rules to brief paragraphs or essays. Sometimes these are multiple-choice questions, and other times you will be asked to identify and correct mistakes in existing paragraphs and essays.

Your instructor may also assign **Write exercises**, which allow you to demonstrate writing and grammar rules in your own writing.

Helping Students Succeed . . .

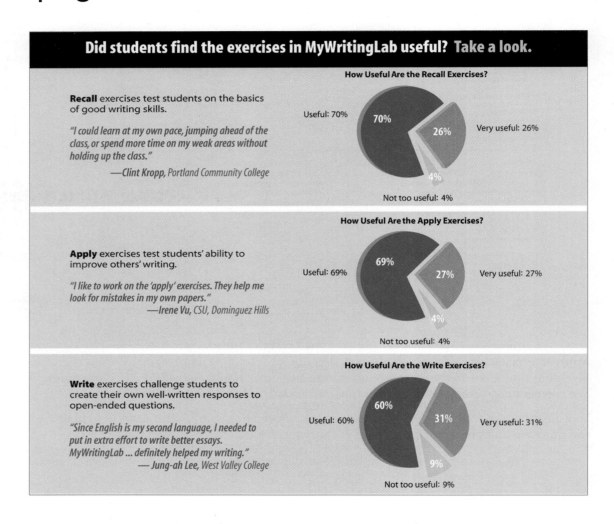

Did students find the exercises in MyWritingLab useful? Take a look.

Recall exercises test students on the basics of good writing skills.

"I could learn at my own pace, jumping ahead of the class, or spend more time on my weak areas without holding up the class."

—*Clint Kropp, Portland Community College*

How Useful Are the Recall Exercises?

Useful: 70% — 70%

26% — Very useful: 26%

4%

Not too useful: 4%

Apply exercises test students' ability to improve others' writing.

"I like to work on the 'apply' exercises. They help me look for mistakes in my own papers."

—*Irene Vu, CSU, Dominguez Hills*

How Useful Are the Apply Exercises?

Useful: 69% — 69%

27% — Very useful: 27%

4%

Not too useful: 4%

Write exercises challenge students to create their own well-written responses to open-ended questions.

"Since English is my second language, I needed to put in extra effort to write better essays. MyWritingLab ... definitely helped my writing."

—*Jung-ah Lee, West Valley College*

How Useful Are the Write Exercises?

Useful: 60% — 60%

31% — Very useful: 31%

9%

Not too useful: 9%

Students just like you are finding MyWritingLab's Recall, Apply, and Write exercises useful in their learning.

www.mywritinglab.com

The Gradebook . . .

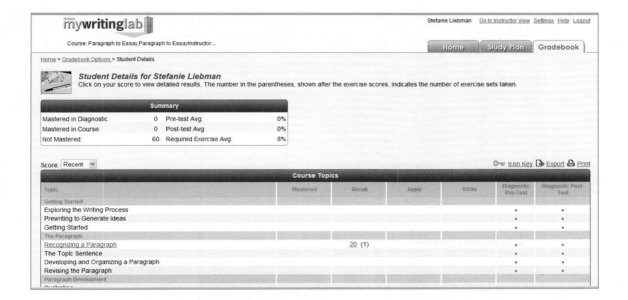

Let's look at how your own on-line gradebook will help you track your progress.

Click on the "Gradebook" tab and then the "Student Detail" report.

Here you are able to see how you are doing in each area. If you feel you need to go back and review, simply click on any score and your score sheet will appear.

You also have a Diagnostic Detail report so you can go back and review your diagnostic Pre-Test and see how much MyWritingLab has helped you improve!

Here to Help You . . .

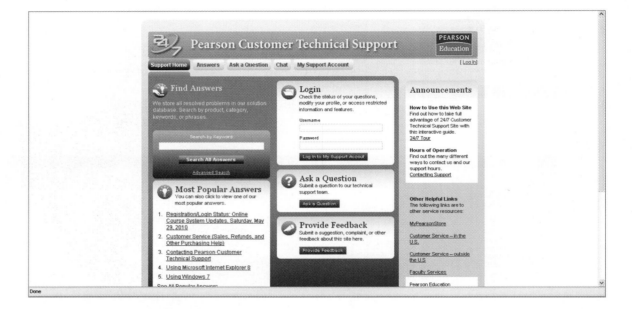

Our goal is to provide answers to your MyWritingLab questions as quickly as possible and deliver the highest level of support. By visiting www.mywritinglab.com/help.html, many questions can be resolved in just a few minutes. Here you will find help on the following:

- System Requirements
- How to Register for MyWritingLab
- How to Use MyWritingLab

For student support, we also invite you to contact Pearson Customer Technical Support (shown above). In addition, you can reach our Support Representatives online at http://247.pearsoned.com. Here you can do the following:

- Search Frequently Asked Questions About MyWritingLab
- E-mail a Question to Our Support Team
- Chat with a Support Representative

www.mywritinglab.com

LYNNE GAETZ   SUNEETI PHADKE
Lionel Groulx College   St. Jerome College

The Writer's World

Sentences and Paragraphs

THIRD EDITION

Prentice Hall

Boston   Columbus   Indianapolis   New York   San Francisco   Upper Saddle River
Amsterdam   Cape Town   Dubai   London   Madrid   Milan   Munich   Paris   Montreal
Toronto   Delhi   Mexico City   Sao Paulo   Sydney   Hong Kong   Seoul   Singapore   Taipei   Tokyo

Senior Acquisitions Editor: Matthew Wright
Senior Development Editor: Katharine Glynn
Senior Marketing Manager: Thomas DeMarco
Senior Supplements Editor: Donna Campion
Senior Media Producer: Stefanie Liebman
Project Coordination, Text Design, and Electronic Page Makeup: Laserwords Maine
Art Director: Anne Nieglos
Cover Designer: Ximena Tamvakopolous
Cover Illustrations: Sunglasses, Thorsten Rust/Shutterstock Images; left image, © MBI/Alamy; right image, © Purestock/Alamy
Photo Researcher: Katharine S. Cebik
Image Permissions: Lee Scher
Senior Manufacturing Buyer: Mary Ann Gloriande
Printer and Binder: Courier Corporation
Cover Printer: Lehigh-Phoenix Color Corporation

For permission to use copyrighted material, grateful acknowledgment is made to the copyright holders on pages 465–466, which are considered an extension of this copyright page.

Copyright © 2011, 2009, 2006 by Pearson Education, Inc.

All rights reserved. No part of this publication may be reproduced, stored in a retrieval system, or transmitted, in any form or by any means, electronic, mechanical, photocopying, recording, or otherwise, without the prior written permission of the publisher. Printed in the United States. To obtain permission to use material from this work, please submit a written request to Pearson Education, Inc., Permissions Department, 1900 E. Lake Ave., Glenview, IL 60025, or fax to (847) 486-3938, or e-mail glenview.permissions@pearsoned.com. For information regarding permissions, call (847) 486-2635.

Prentice Hall
is an imprint of

www.pearsonhighered.com

1 2 3 4 5 6 7 8 9 10—CRK—13 12 11 10

Student Edition ISBN-13: 978-0-205-78179-9
Student Edition ISBN-10: 0-205-78179-9
Annotated Instructor's Edition ISBN-13: 978-0-205-78183-6
Annotated Instructor's Edition ISBN-10: 0-205-78183-7

Brief Table of Contents

Contents

Inside Front Cover
  Sentences Checklist
  Revising and Editing Symbols

Preface   x

The Editing Handbook   112

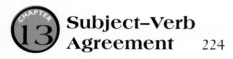

Reading Strategies and Selections   404

Reading Strategies and Selections   405

Appendices

Preface

About the Third Edition of *The Writer's World: Sentences and Paragraphs*

Thank you for making the second edition of *The Writer's World* a resounding success. We are delighted that the book has been able to help so many students across the country. The third edition of *The Writer's World* can also help students produce writing that is technically correct and rich in content. It is our goal for this preface to give you a deeper understanding of how we arranged the text and the key components you will find in this new edition of *The Writer's World: Sentences and Paragraphs*.

When we started the first edition, we set out to develop practical and pedagogically sound approaches to help students improve their writing skills. For those new to the book, here is some background information to give a more complete picture.

A Research-Based Approach

From the onset of the development process, we have comprehensively researched the needs and desires of current developmental writing instructors. We met with more than forty-five instructors from around the country, asking for their opinions and insights regarding (1) the challenges posed by the course, (2) the needs of today's ever-changing student population, and (3) the ideas and features we were proposing to provide them and you with a more effective learning and teaching tool. Prentice Hall also commissioned dozens of detailed manuscript reviews from instructors, asking them to analyze and evaluate each draft of the manuscript. These reviewers identified numerous ways in which we could refine and enhance our key features. Their invaluable feedback was incorporated throughout *The Writer's World*. The text you are seeing is truly the product of a successful partnership between the authors, the publisher, and well over one hundred developmental writing instructors.

How We Organized *The Writer's World*

The Writer's World is divided into three parts for ease of use, convenience, and ultimate flexibility.

Part I: The Writing Process teaches students how to formulate ideas (Exploring); how to expand, organize, and present those ideas in a piece of writing (Developing); and how to polish their writing so that they convey their message as clearly as possible (Revising and Editing). The result is that writing becomes far less daunting because students have specific steps to follow.

Chapter 4 of Part I gives students an overview of nine patterns of development. As they work through the practices and write their own paragraphs, students begin to see how using a writing pattern can help them fulfill their purpose for writing.

Chapter 5 of Part I covers the parts of the essay and explains how students can apply what they have learned about paragraph development to essay writing.

Part II: The Editing Handbook is a thematic grammar handbook. In each chapter, the examples correspond to a section theme, such as Lifestyles, Trades and Technology, or The Business World. As students work through the chapters, they hone their grammar and editing skills while gaining knowledge about a variety of topics. In addition to helping retain interest in the grammar practices, the thematic material provides sparks that ignite new ideas that students can apply to their writing.

Part III: Reading Strategies and Selections offers tips, readings, and follow-up questions. Students learn how to write by observing and dissecting what they read. The readings are arranged by the themes that are found in Part II: The Editing Handbook, thereby providing more fodder for generating writing ideas.

How *The Writer's World* Meets Students' Diverse Needs

We created *The Writer's World* to meet your students' diverse needs. To accomplish this goal, we asked both the instructors in our focus groups and the reviewers at every stage not only to critique our ideas but also to offer their suggestions and recommendations for features that would enhance the learning process of their students. The result has been the integration of many elements that are not found in other textbooks, including our visual program, coverage of nonnative speaker material, and strategies for addressing the varying skill levels students bring to the course.

The Visual Program

A stimulating, full-color book, *The Writer's World* recognizes that today's world is a visual one, and it encourages students to become better communicators by responding to images. **Chapter-opening visuals in Part I** help students think about the chapters' key concepts in new ways. For example, in the Chapter 5 opener, a photograph of a skyscraper sets the stage for essay writing. Both the skyscraper and an essay need specific types of support to make them sturdy structures.

Each chapter in Part II opens with a photo to help illustrate the theme of the examples and exercises in that chapter and section.

The visuals in Part III provide students with further opportunities to write in response to images. Students get additional writing practice through different activities such as looking at photos and watching films. These visual aids inspire students and give them varied and engaging topics for writing.

Seamless Coverage for Nonnative Speakers

Instructors in our focus groups noted the growing number of nonnative/ESL speakers enrolling in the developmental writing courses. Although some of these students have special needs relating to the writing process, many of you still have a large portion of native speakers in your courses whose more traditional needs must also be satisfied. To meet the challenge of this rapidly changing dynamic, we have carefully implemented and integrated content throughout to assist these students. *The Writer's World* does not have separate ESL boxes, ESL chapters, or tacked-on ESL appendices. Instead, information that traditionally poses challenges to nonnative speakers is woven seamlessly throughout the book. In our extensive experience teaching writing to both native and nonnative speakers of English, we have learned that both groups learn best when they are not distracted by ESL labels. With the seamless approach, nonnative speakers do not feel self-conscious and segregated, and native speakers do not tune out detailed explanations that may also benefit them. Many of these traditional problem areas receive more coverage than you would find in other textbooks, arming the instructor with the material to effectively meet the needs of nonnative speakers. Moreover, the Annotated Instructor's Edition provides over seventy-five ESL Teaching Tips designed specifically to help instructors better meet the needs of their nonnative speakers.

Issue-Focused Thematic Grammar

In our survey of instructors' needs, many of you indicated that one of the primary challenges in teaching your course is finding materials that are engaging to students in a contemporary context. This is especially true in grammar instruction. **Students come to the course with varying skill levels,** and many students are simply not interested in grammar. To address this challenge, we have introduced **issue-focused thematic grammar** in *The Writer's World*.

Each section in Part II revolves around a common theme. These themes include Lifestyles, Entertainment and Culture, Beliefs, Trades and Technology, The Earth and Beyond, Relationships, Creatures Large and Small, and The Business World. Each chapter within a section includes issues related to the theme. The thematic approach enables students to broaden their awareness of important subjects, allowing them to infuse their writing with reflection and insight. Also, we believe (and our reviewers concurred) that it makes grammar more engaging. And the more engaging grammar is, the more likely students will retain key concepts— raising their skill level in these important building blocks of writing.

We also feel that it is important not to isolate grammar from the writing process. Therefore, The Writer's Room at the end of each grammar section contains writing topics that are related to the theme of the section and that follow different writing patterns. To help students appreciate the relevance of their writing tasks, **each grammar chapter begins with a grammar snapshot**—a sample taken from an authentic piece of writing that highlights the grammar concept. There is also an editing checklist that is specific to the grammar concepts covered in that chapter. Finally, at the end of each grammar section, there is The Writers' Circle, a collaborative activity that is particularly helpful to nonnative speakers.

What Tools Can Help Students Get the Most from *The Writer's World*?

Overwhelmingly, focus group participants and reviewers asked that both a larger number and a greater diversity of exercises and activities be incorporated into the text. In response to this feedback, we have developed and tested the following items in *The Writer's World*. We are confident they will help your students become better writers.

Hints   In each chapter, **Hint** boxes highlight important writing and grammar points. Hints are useful for all students, but many will be particularly helpful for nonnative speakers. For example, in Chapter 3 (page 37) there is a hint about being direct and avoiding circular reasoning.

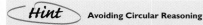

Hint   **Avoiding Circular Reasoning**

Circular reasoning means that a writer restates his or her main point in various ways but does not provide supporting details. The main idea goes in circles and never progresses-kind of like a dog chasing its tail. Avoid using circular reasoning by writing a concise topic sentence and by supporting the topic sentence with facts, examples, or anecdotes.

For example, the following paragraph has circular reasoning.

People should not drink and drive because it is too dangerous. They can hurt themselves. Drinking and driving causes accidents, and sometimes people die.

The Writer's Desk   Part I includes **The Writer's Desk** exercises that help students get used to practicing all stages and steps of the writing process. Students begin with prewriting and then progress to developing, organizing (using paragraph plans), drafting, and finally, revising and editing to

create a final draft. Turn to Chapter 3, page 42, for an example of The Writer's Desk.

The Writer's Desk **Revise and Edit Your Paragraph**

Choose a paragraph that you wrote for Chapter 2, or choose one that you have written for another assignment. Carefully revise and edit your paragraph.

Checklists   Each end-of-chapter checklist is a chapter review exercise. Questions prompt students to recall and review what they have learned in the chapter. Turn to Chapter 3, page 45, for an example of the Checklists feature.

REVISING AND EDITING CHECKLIST

When you revise and edit a paragraph, ask yourself the following questions.

☐ Does my paragraph have **unity?** Ensure that every sentence relates to the main idea.

☐ Does my paragraph have **adequate support?** Verify that there are enough details and examples to support your main point.

☐ Is my paragraph **coherent?** Try to use transitional expressions to link ideas.

☐ Does my paragraph have good **style?** Check for varied sentence patterns and exact language.

☐ Does my paragraph have any errors? **Edit** for errors in grammar, punctuation, spelling, and mechanics.

☐ Is my **final draft** error-free?

The Writer's Room   The Writer's Room contains writing activities that correspond to general, college, and workplace topics. Some prompts are brief to allow students to freely form ideas while others are expanded to give students more direction.

There is literally something for every student writer in this end-of-chapter feature. Students who respond well to visual cues will appreciate the photo writing exercises in **The Writer's Room** in Part II. Students who learn best by hearing through collaboration will appreciate the discussion and group work prompts in **The Writers' Circle** section of selected **The Writer's Rooms.** To help students see how grammar is not isolated from the writing process, there are also **The Writer's Room** activities at the end of sections 1 to 8 in Part II: The

Editing Handbook. Turn to Chapter 3, page 44, to see an example of The Writer's Room.

The Writer's Room

Writing Activity I

Choose a paragraph that you have written for this course. Revise and edit that paragraph, and then write a final draft.

Writing Activity 2

Choose one of the following topics, or choose your own topic and write a paragraph. You could try exploring strategies to generate ideas. The first sentence of your paragraph should make a point about your topic. Remember to revise and edit your paragraph before you write the final draft.

General Topics

1. an interesting dream
2. a family story
3. a wonderful view
4. littering
5. an accident

College or Work-Related Topics

6. an unusual experience at college
7. computer problems
8. reasons to stay in college
9. a personality conflict at work
10. working with your spouse

New to the Third Edition

New Editing Handbook Sections

Two new themes appear in the Editing Handbook. Section 1 is now called Lifestyles, and it focuses on health, exercise, and food. Section 4, Trades and Technology, emphasizes information technologies, building industries, infrastructure, and health-care technology. Many practices in other grammar chapters have been updated or completely changed.

New Grammar Chapter

New to this edition is Chapter 23, Exact Language. This chapter focuses on dictionary and thesaurus usage and precise vocabulary. Students learn to recognize and correct clichés and slang.

Updated High-Interest Paragraph Models and Practices

Throughout the book you will notice new examples, sample paragraphs, writing practices, Writer's Desk topics, and grammar practices. In fact, to make the content more topical and appealing, roughly 30 percent of the book's content has been updated.

Cooperative Learning Teaching Tips

Are your students sometimes lacking in motivation? Do they seem bored? Scattered throughout the book are cooperative learning teaching tips. Cooperative learning, which promotes peer interaction, helps students share knowledge, problem-solve, negotiate, and reflect. Students are responsible for their contribution to a team effort. Chapter 2 features a jigsaw activity. Groups of students focus on a specific organizational strategy and then collaborate to share information about time, space, and emphatic order. Other tips such as Roundtable Writing, Non-Stop Talking, and Pair & Share help make routine lessons far more interesting and enjoyable. These communicative and interactive activities are especially useful for nonnative speakers.

Tech Tips

New to this edition are some teaching tips that incorporate everyday technology. Students in this digital age spend their days texting, checking their Facebook page, and listening to music on their iPods. The Tech Tips help students learn while using the technology that they are familiar with. For example, in Chapter 4, students are invited to compare and contrast two commercial Web sites made by car companies and in another Tech Tip they are asked to analyze the best features on their cell phones.

New ESL and Regular Teaching Tips

Instructors will notice an abundance of updated teaching tips throughout the book. The authors have extensive experience with nonnative speakers, and have included more precise ESL tips to help teachers in the classroom.

New Readings and Updated Film Prompts

In Chapter 30, six new readings relate to the grammar themes. Bill Bryson, Juan Rodriquez, Dorothy Nixon, and Ellen Goodman are some of the new writers featured in the chapter. Students read about engaging and relevant topics such as the effective branding of Apple, shopping for religion, and the overeating epidemic. The film writing prompts have been updated to include more recent movies.

New Photos

New opening photos and photo writing prompts appear throughout the book. Each grammar chapter has an opening photo that helps to show the thematic content. New photo writing prompts appear throughout.

Acknowledgments

Many people have helped us produce *The Writer's World*. First and foremost, we would like to thank our students for inspiring us and providing us with extraordinary feedback. Their words and insights pervade this book.

We also benefited greatly from the insightful comments and suggestions from over one hundred instructors across the nation, all of whom are listed in the opening pages of the Annotated Instructor's Edition. Our colleagues' feedback was invaluable and helped shape *The Writer's World* series content, focus, and organization.

We are indebted to the team of dedicated professionals at Prentice Hall who have helped make this project a reality. They have boosted our spirits and have believed in us every step of the way. Special thanks to Katharine Glynn for her magnificent job in polishing this book and to Matthew Wright for trusting our instincts and enthusiastically propelling us forward. We owe a deep debt of gratitude to Yolanda de Rooy, whose encouraging words helped ignite this project. Karen Berry's attention to detail in the production process kept us motivated and on task and made *The Writer's World* a much better resource for both instructors and students.

Finally, we would like to dedicate this book to our husbands and children who supported us and who patiently put up with our long hours on the computer. Manu, Octavio, and Natalia continually encouraged us. We especially appreciate the help and sacrifices of Diego, Becky, Kiran, and Meghana.

A Note to Students

Your knowledge, ideas, and opinions are important. The ability to clearly communicate those ideas is invaluable in your personal, academic, and professional life. When your writing is error-free, readers will focus on your message, and you will be able to persuade, inform, entertain, or inspire them. *The Writer's World* includes strategies that will help you improve your written communication. Quite simply, when you become a better writer, you become a better communicator. It is our greatest wish for *The Writer's World* to make you excited about writing, communicating, and learning.

Enjoy!

Lynne Gaetz and Suneeti Phadke
writingrewards@pearson.com

Call for Student Writing!

Do you want to be published in *The Writer's World*? Send your paragraphs and essays to us along with your complete contact information. If your work is selected to appear in the next edition of *The Writer's World*, you will receive an honorarium, credit for your work, and a copy of the book!

Lynne Gaetz and Suneeti Phadke
writingrewards@pearson.com

Suneeti Phadke on Salt Spring Island, British Columbia.

Lynne Gaetz in the Rocky Mountains.

The Writing Process

The ability to express your ideas in written form is very useful in your personal, academic, and professional life. It does not take a special talent to write well. If you are willing to practice the writing process, you will be able to produce well-written sentences, paragraphs, and essays.

The Writing Process

The writing process involves exploring, expanding, and organizing ideas and then bringing them all together in sentences and paragraphs. Before you begin working through the chapters in Part I, review the main steps in the writing process.

Exploring

Step 1: Consider your topic.

Step 2: Consider your audience.

Step 3: Consider your purpose.

Step 4: Try exploring strategies.

Developing

Step 1: Narrow your topic.

Step 2: Express your main idea.

Step 3: Develop your supporting ideas.

Step 4: Make a plan or an outline.

Step 5: Write your first draft.

Revising and Editing

Step 1: Revise for unity.

Step 2: Revise for adequate support.

Step 3: Revise for coherence.

Step 4: Revise for style.

Step 5: Edit for technical errors.

Exploring

The exploring stage of the writing process is like trying out a new dish. You search for interesting recipes and ingredients.

> " *The greatest mistake you can make in life is to be continually fearing you will make one.* "
>
> —ELBERT HUBBARD (1856–1915)
> *American author*

What Is Exploring?

An explorer investigates a place to find new and interesting information. **Exploring** is also useful during the writing process. Whenever you have trouble finding a topic, you can use specific techniques to generate ideas.

There are four steps in the exploring stage of the writing process.

ESSAY LINK

When you plan an essay, you should follow the four exploring steps.

EXPLORING

STEP 1 ➤	**Consider your topic.** Think about whom or what you will write about.
STEP 2 ➤	**Consider your audience.** Determine who your intended readers will be.
STEP 3 ➤	**Consider your purpose.** Think about your reasons for writing.
STEP 4 ➤	**Try exploring strategies.** Practice using various techniques to find ideas.

Understanding Your Assignment

As soon as you are given an assignment, make sure that you understand your task. Answer the following questions about the assignment.

- How many words or pages should I write?
- What is the due date for the assignment?
- Are there any special qualities my writing should include?
- Will I write in class or at home?

After you have considered your task, think about your topic, purpose, and audience.

Topic

Your **topic** is what you are writing about. When your instructor gives you a topic for your writing, you can narrow it to suit your interests. For example, if your instructor asks you to write about relationships, you could write about marriage, divorce, children, family responsibilities, or traditions. You should focus on an aspect of the topic that you know about and find interesting.

When you think about the topic, ask yourself the following questions.

- What about the topic interests me?
- Do I have special knowledge about the topic?
- Does anything about the topic arouse my emotions?

Audience

Your **audience** is your intended reader. The reader might be your instructor, other students, your boss, your co-workers, and so on. When you write, remember to adapt your language and vocabulary for each specific audience. For example, in a formal report written for your business class, you might use specialized accounting terms, but in an e-mail to your best friend, you would probably use abbreviations or slang terms.

When you consider your audience, ask yourself the following questions.

- Who will read my assignment? Will it be my instructor, other students, or people outside my classroom?
- What do my readers probably know about the subject?
- What information will my readers expect?

 **Your Instructor as Your Audience**

For many college assignments, your audience is your instructor. When you write for him or her, use standard English. In other words, try to use correct grammar, sentence structure, and vocabulary.

Do not leave out information because you assume that your instructor knows a lot about the topic. When your instructor reads your work, he or she will expect you to reveal what you have learned or what you have understood about the topic.

Purpose

Your **purpose** is your reason for writing. Sometimes you may have more than one purpose. When you consider your purpose, ask yourself the following questions.

- Do I want to **entertain?** Is my goal to tell a story?
- Do I want to **persuade?** Is my goal to convince the reader that my point of view is the correct one?
- Do I want to **inform?** Is my goal to explain something or give information about a topic?

 **Purposes May Overlap**

Sometimes you may have more than one purpose. For example, in a paragraph about a childhood memory, your purpose could be to tell a story about your first trip to a new place. At the same time, you could inform your readers about the things to see in that area, or you could persuade readers that traveling is, or is not, worthwhile.

Exploring Strategies

After you determine your topic, audience, and purpose, try some **exploring strategies**—also known as **prewriting strategies**—to help get your ideas flowing. There are two types of prewriting strategies: general and focused. **General prewriting** will help you develop wide-ranging ideas to write about. **Focused prewriting** will help you narrow a broad topic so that the topic becomes more specific and therefore more manageable for your assignment. In this chapter, you will see examples of general prewriting.

The three most common strategies are *freewriting, brainstorming,* and *clustering.* It is not necessary to do all of the strategies explained in this chapter. Find the strategy that works best for you.

 **When to Use Exploring Strategies**

You can use the exploring strategies at any stage of the writing process.

- To find a topic
- To narrow a broad topic
- To generate ideas about your topic
- To generate supporting details

Freewriting

When you **freewrite,** you write without stopping for a limited period of time. You record whatever thoughts come into your mind without worrying about them. Even if you run out of ideas, you can just repeat a word or phrase, or you can write "I don't know what to say."

During freewriting, do not be concerned with your grammar or spelling. If you use a computer, let your ideas flow and do not worry about typing mistakes. Remember that the point is to generate ideas and not to create a perfect sample of writing.

ALFONZO'S FREEWRITING

College student Alfonzo Calderon jotted down some of his thoughts about friends. He wrote for five minutes without stopping.

> *Friends. They're important. I have a best friend, he's a good basketball player. I've known him since high school. I went on Facebook and joined my high school graduating class group. I get lots of information about old friends there. What else? Privacy issues. Users should be careful about personal information. Identity theft. Some people have hundreds of friends on Facebook. They are not real friends. Some people are lonely. They just communicate through the Internet. The Internet is useful. I don't know what else to write. . . . There are different types of friends.*

PRACTICE I

Underline topics from Alfonzo's freewriting that could be expanded into complete paragraphs.

The Writer's Desk Freewriting

Choose one of the following topics and do some freewriting. Remember to write without stopping.

TOPICS: Food   Stress   Fun

_____

_____

_____

_____

_____

_____

_____

_____

_____

_____

_____

_____

_____

_____

Brainstorming

When you **brainstorm,** you create a list of ideas. You can include opinions, details, images, questions, or anything else that comes to mind. If you need to, you can stop to think while you are creating your list. Do not worry about grammar or spelling. Remember that the point is to generate ideas.

JINSUK'S BRAINSTORMING

College student Jinsuk Suh brainstormed about the topic "neighborhoods." Her audience was her instructor and other students, and her purpose was to inform.

- large versus small neighborhoods
- flea markets
- crime
- ethnic neighborhoods
- my neighbors
- markets
- neighborhood friends

PRACTICE 2

Read Jinsuk's list about neigborhoods, and underline ideas that could be developed into complete paragraphs.

The Writer's Desk Brainstorming

Choose one of the following topics and brainstorm. Let your ideas flow when you create your list.

TOPICS: Celebrations   College   Fashion trends

_____

_____

_____

_____

_____

_____

_____

_____

_____

_____

Clustering

When you **cluster,** you draw a word map. To begin, write your topic in the middle of the page. Then, think of ideas that relate to the topic. Using lines or arrows, connect each idea to the central topic or to other ideas. Keep writing, circling, and connecting ideas until you have groups, or "clusters," of them on your page. When you finish, you will have a visual image of your ideas.

ANTON'S CLUSTERING

College student Anton Gromyko used clustering to explore ideas about movies.

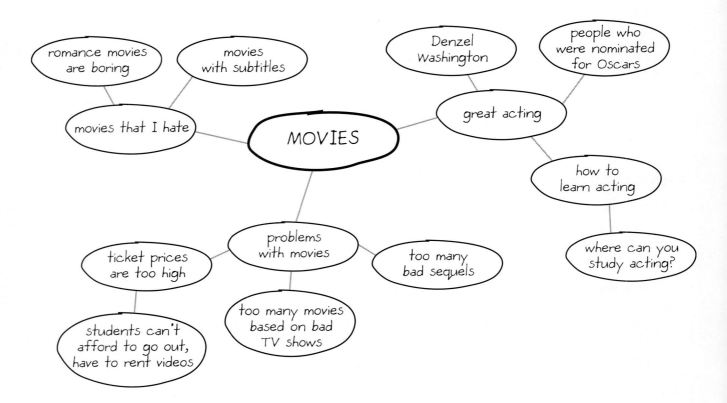

PRACTICE 3

Look at Anton's clustering. Circle one or more clusters that would make a good paragraph.

The Writer's Desk Clustering

Choose one of the following topics and try clustering on the next page. Let your ideas flow when you create your cluster.

TOPICS: Technology   Dating   Money

 **Questioning**

Another way to generate ideas about a topic is to ask yourself a series of questions and write responses to them. The questions can help you define and narrow your topic. One common way to do this is to ask yourself *who, what, when, where, why,* and *how* questions.

Question	Possible Answers
Why do people travel?	To escape, to learn about other cultures, to enjoy good weather
How can they travel?	Flying, taking a train or bus, taking walking tours, hiking, sailing, cycling
What are inexpensive ways to travel?	Find last-minute deals, go backpacking, stay with friends or in youth hostels, share gas expenses

Journal and Portfolio Writing

Keeping a Journal

American educator and writer Christina Baldwin once said, "Journal writing is like a voyage to the interior." One good way to practice your writing is to keep a journal. In a journal, you record your thoughts, opinions, ideas, and impressions. Journal writing provides you with a chance to practice your writing without worrying about the audience. It also gives you a source of material when you are asked to write about a topic of your choice.

You can write about any topic that appeals to you. Here are some suggestions.

- **College:** You can describe new things you have learned, express opinions about your courses, and list ideas for assignments.
- **Your personal life:** You can describe your feelings about your career goals. You can also write about personal problems and solutions, reflect about past and future decisions, express feelings about your job, and so on.
- **Controversial issues:** You can write about your reactions to controversies in the world, in your country, in your state, in your city, at your college, or even within your own family.
- **Interesting facts:** Perhaps you have discovered new and interesting information in a course, in a newspaper, or in some other way. You can record interesting facts in your journal.

 The Writer's Room

Writing Activity 1: Topics

Choose one of the following topics, or choose your own topic. Then generate ideas about the topic. You may want to try the suggested exploring strategy.

General Topics

1. Try freewriting about sports. Jot down any ideas that come to mind.
2. Try brainstorming about important ceremonies. List the first ideas that come to mind.
3. Try clustering about kindness. First, write the word *kindness* in the middle of the page. Then create clusters of ideas that relate to the topic.

College or Work-Related Topics

4. Try freewriting to come up with ideas about career choices.
5. Brainstorm about influential people. To get ideas, list anything that comes to mind when you think about people you admire.
6. Try clustering about competition. Write the word *competition* in the center of the page, and then create clusters of ideas about the topic.

Writing Activity 2: Photo Writing

View the following cartoon. What is the topic? Who is the audience? What is the purpose? Does the cartoon achieve its purpose? Brainstorm a list of ideas about any topics that come to mind after seeing the cartoon.

NO, I DON'T HAVE A SCANNER YOU CAN BORROW.

© Ralph Hagen/www.CartoonStock.com

EXPLORING CHECKLIST

When you explore a topic, ask yourself the following questions.

☐ What is my **topic?** Consider what you will write about.

☐ Who is my **audience?** Think about your intended readers.

☐ What is my **purpose?** Determine your reason for writing.

☐ Which exploring strategy will I use? You could try one of the next strategies or a combination of strategies.

    Freewriting is writing without stopping for a limited period of time.
    Brainstorming is making a list.
    Clustering is drawing a word map.
    Questioning is asking and answering questions.

mywritinglab   To check your progress in meeting this chapter's objectives, log in to **www.mywritinglab.com**, go to the **Study Plan** tab, click on **The Writing Process** and choose **Exploring** from the list of subtopics. Read and view the resources in the **Review Materials** section, and then complete the **Recall, Apply,** and **Write** sets in the **Activities** section.

Developing

The developing stage of the writing process is like cooking a meal. Combining a variety of ingredients, you develop the recipe.

> *Inspiration is wonderful when it happens, but the writer must develop an approach for the rest of the time.*
>
> —LEONARD BERNSTEIN (1918–1990)
> *American composer*

ESSAY LINK

You can follow similar steps when you develop an essay. See Chapter 5 for more details about essay writing.

What Is Developing?

Chapter 1 explained how you can explore ideas for writing. This chapter takes you, step by step, through the development of a paragraph. There are five key steps in the developing stage.

DEVELOPING

STEP 1	**Narrow your topic.** Find an aspect of the topic that interests you.
STEP 2	**Express your main idea.** Write a topic sentence that expresses the main idea of the piece of writing.
STEP 3	**Develop your supporting ideas.** Generate ideas that support your topic sentence.
STEP 4	**Make a plan.** Organize your main and supporting ideas, and place your ideas in a plan.
STEP 5	**Write your first draft.** Communicate your ideas in a single written piece.

Reviewing Paragraph Structure

A **paragraph** is a group of sentences focusing on one central idea. Paragraphs can stand alone, or they can be part of a longer work such as an essay, a letter, or a report.

The **topic sentence** expresses the main point of the paragraph and shows the writer's attitude toward the subject.

The **body sentences** provide details that support the main point.

The **concluding sentence** brings the paragraph to a satisfactory close.

Topic sentence _____
_____. Supporting detail _____
_____
_____. Supporting detail _____
_____
_____. Supporting detail _____
_____.
Concluding sentence _____
_____.

VEENA'S PARAGRAPH

College student Veena Thomas wrote the following paragraph. Read her paragraph, and then answer the questions.

> **As college students, we have a completely different culture than anyone else.** A few thousand students live together in what amounts to our own little city. Crowded into doubles and triples, we are brought together by our physical closeness, our similarities, and our differences. We share the bathrooms with strangers who soon become friends. We laugh together, cry together, and sleep through class together. Our dorm room becomes our refuge with its unmade beds, posters on the walls, and inflatable chairs. Money is a problem because we never have enough of it. When we get sick of cafeteria food, we subsist on 25-cent ramen noodles and boxes of oatmeal. We drink way too much coffee, and we order pizza at 1 a.m. We live on College Standard Time, which is about four hours behind everyone else. So while everyone else sleeps, we hang out with our music playing until the early hours of the morning. It's a different life, but it's our life, and we love it.

PRACTICE I

Look at the structure of Veena's paragraph. The topic sentence (a statement of a main idea) is in bold. List Veena's supporting ideas. The first one has been done for you.

We live in our own little city of students crowded together

We share the bathroom with strangers who soon become friends.
We laugh togather, cry togather, and sleep through class togather.
Money is a problem. because We never have enough of it.

_____

_____

Paragraph Form

Your paragraphs should have the following form.

- Always indent the first word of a paragraph. Move it about 1 inch, or five spaces, from the left-hand margin.
- Leave a 1- to 1½-inch margin on each side of your paragraph.
- Begin every sentence with a capital letter, and end each sentence with the proper punctuation.
- If the last sentence of the paragraph does not go to the margin, leave the rest of the row blank.

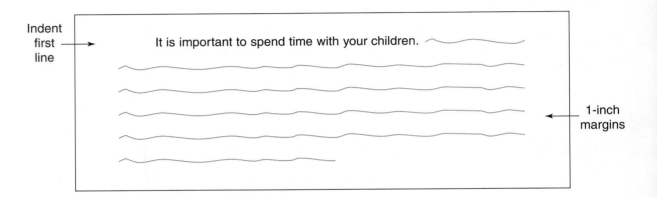

Narrow the Topic

Sometimes you may be given a topic that is too broad for one paragraph. In those situations, you need to make your topic fit the size of the assignment. When you **narrow your topic**, you make it more specific. To narrow your topic, you can use the exploring strategies (freewriting, brainstorming, clustering, or questioning) that you learned in Chapter 1.

DONOVAN'S LIST TO NARROW THE TOPIC

College student Donovan Lynch used brainstorming to narrow his broad topic, "food."

　　—good restaurants
　　—when I ate too much junk food
　　—labeling genetically modified food

The Writer's Desk Narrow the Topic

The next topics are very broad. Practice narrowing each topic.

EXAMPLE: Neighborhoods: *Community center*

　　　　　　　　　　　　　　Neighborhood markets

　　　　　　　　　　　　　　Neighborhood crime

1. Technology: _____
   _____
   _____

2. Fashion trends: _____
   _____
   _____

3. Dating: _____
   _____
   _____

4. Celebrations: _____
   _____
   _____

5. YouTube: _____
   _____
   _____

The Topic Sentence

The next step in the writing process is to write a sentence that expresses the main idea. In a paragraph, the statement of the main idea is called the **topic sentence.** The topic sentence of a paragraph has several features.

- It introduces the topic.
- It states the main (or controlling) idea.
- It is the most general sentence.
- It is supported by the other sentences.

The **controlling idea** is an essential part of the topic sentence because it makes a point about the topic. The controlling idea expresses the writer's opinion, attitude, or feeling. You can express different controlling ideas about the same topic. For example, the following topic sentences are about leaving the family home, but each sentence makes a different point about the topic.

narrowed topic   controlling idea
Leaving the family home is a difficult experience for some college students.

controlling idea   narrowed topic
The most exciting and important part of a youth's life is **leaving the family home**.

PRACTICE 2

Read each topic sentence. Underline the topic once and the controlling idea twice. To find the topic, ask yourself what the paragraph is about.

EXAMPLE:

College students should take their studies seriously.

1. Several interesting things happened when the probe landed on Mars.
2. Children without siblings tend to be self-reliant.
3. The bronze sculpture was truly original.
4. Become a better listener by following three simple steps.
5. The dorm room was an uncontrollable mess.
6. High blood pressure is caused by several factors.

ESSAY LINK

When you write a thesis statement for an essay, ask yourself questions 1–3 to check that your thesis statement is complete and valid.

Writing an Effective Topic Sentence

When you develop your topic sentence, avoid some common errors by asking yourself these four questions.

1. **Is my topic sentence a complete sentence?** Your topic sentence should always be a complete sentence that reveals a complete thought.

Incomplete:	Living alone.
	(This is a topic but *not* a topic sentence. It does not express a complete thought.)
Topic sentence:	There are many advantages to living alone.

2. **Does my topic sentence have a controlling idea?** Your topic sentence should make a point about your paragraph's topic. It should not simply announce the topic.

Announcement:	I will write about nursing.
	(This sentence announces the topic but says nothing relevant about it. Do not use expressions such as *My topic is* or *I will write about.*)
Topic sentence:	Nurses need to be in good physical and psychological health.

3. **Does my topic sentence make a valid and supportable point?** Your topic sentence should express a valid point that you can support with details and examples. It should not be a vaguely worded statement, and it should not be a highly questionable generalization.

Vague:	Today's students are too weak.
	(How are they weak?)
Invalid point:	Today's students have more responsibilities than those in the past.
	(Is this really true? This might be a hard assertion to prove.)
Topic sentence:	Some of the best students in this college juggle schoolwork, children, and part-time jobs.

4. **Can I support my topic sentence in a single paragraph?** Your topic sentence should express an idea that you can support in a paragraph. It should not be too broad or too narrow.

Too broad:	There are many good libraries.
	(It would be difficult to write only one paragraph about this topic.)
Too narrow:	The college library is located beside the student center.
	(What more is there to say?)
Topic sentence:	The college library, which is beside the student center, contains valuable resources for students.

Hint   **Write a Clear Topic Sentence**

Your topic sentence should not express an obvious or well-known fact. Write something that will interest your readers and make them want to continue reading.

Obvious:	Work is important.
	(Everybody knows this.)
Better:	When looking for a job, remember that some things are more important than having a good salary.

PRACTICE 3

Identify why each of the following topic sentences is not effective. Then, choose the word or words from the list that best describe the problem with each topic sentence. (A topic sentence may have more than one problem.) Finally, correct the problem by revising each sentence.

Incomplete	Vague	Announces
Invalid	Broad	Narrow

EXAMPLE:

I am going to write about athletes.

Problem: *Announces; broad*

Revised sentence: *The salaries in professional basketball are too high.*

1. Two reasons for the decline of the family farm.

Problem: _____

Revised statement: _____

  _____

2. Animals are becoming extinct.

Problem: _____

Revised statement: _____

_____

3. In this paper, I will give my opinion about tabloid newspapers.

Problem: _____

Revised statement: _____

_____

4. Adolescents are more reckless.

Problem: _____

Revised statement: _____

_____

5. Having a part-time job.

Problem: _____

Revised statement: _____

_____

6. Money is important.

Problem: _____

Revised statement: _____

_____

 **Placement of the Topic Sentence**

Because you are developing your writing skills, it is a good idea to place your topic sentence at the beginning of your paragraph. Then, follow it with supporting details. Opening your paragraph with a topic sentence helps your readers immediately identify what your paragraph is about.

PRACTICE 4

Choose the best topic sentence for each paragraph.

1. First, physical exercise builds muscle strength and increases stamina. Aerobic activities strengthen heart muscles. Running or cycling can also improve endurance. Furthermore, physical activity greatly benefits mental health. It reduces stress and helps people to relax. Also, individuals can make new friends by joining a gym or sports class. In addition, people can learn new skills when they practice a sport or activity.

Possible topic sentences:

_____ Many people join a gym or play a sport.

__✗__ When people participate in a physical activity, they gain many advantages.

_____ People should participate in sports that they like to keep their motivation.

2. In their book *Second Chances*, Blakeslee and Wallerstein cite studies showing that boys are more likely to have external behavior problems after a marital breakup. For example, boys may become more impulsive, aggressive, and antisocial. After divorce, girls generally internalize their anger and frustration. They may become anxious and depressed.

Possible topic sentences:

_____ Girls often become withdrawn after a divorce.

_____ Divorce is common in North America.

__✗__ Research suggests that male and female children react to divorce in different ways.

3. Whenever Americans send an e-mail, it leaves a footprint on more than one computer. The record allows employers and others to have access to employee correspondence. Also, most cities have a complex system of cameras in public places. For example, traffic cameras take pictures of drivers going through red lights or speeding. This information is automatically transmitted to the traffic police, who can then send traffic tickets to the offenders. Moreover, anytime an Internet user buys a product online, the consumer's profile is created. Profiles are often sold to marketing companies.

Possible topic sentences:

_____ The Internet has changed our lives in many ways.

_____ Technology gives humans the ability to control their lives.

__✗__ Modern computer technology has led to a loss of our privacy.

The Writer's Desk Write Topic Sentences

Narrow each topic. Then, write a topic sentence that contains a controlling idea. (You could refer to your ideas in The Writer's Desk: Narrow the Topic on pages 14–15.)

EXAMPLE: Families

Narrowed topic: *Neighborhood markets*

Topic sentence: *Zion market is one of the busiest and best Korean markets.*

1. Technology

   Narrowed topic: _Spaceflight to Mars (?)_

   Topic sentence: _A smart phone allows its user to do several things previously unimagined_

2. Fashion trends

   Narrowed topic: _Pants_

   Topic sentence: _Nowadays, many adolescents wear their pants below their waist._

3. Dating

   Narrowed topic: _Blind dates_

   Topic sentence: _Blind dates are embarrassing as well as expensive and you still don't get any_

4. Celebrations

   Narrowed topic: _New Years_

   Topic sentence: _New Years is the best time of the year to have a celebration_

5. YouTube

   Narrowed topic: _videos_

   Topic sentence: _Videos on youtube can be very helpful when you don't feel for a test_

ESSAY LINK

In an essay, you place the thesis statement in the introduction. Then each supporting idea becomes a distinct paragraph with its own topic sentence.

The Supporting Ideas

After you have written a clear topic sentence, you can focus on **supporting details,** which are the facts and examples that provide the reader with interesting information about the subject matter. There are three steps you can take to determine your paragraph's supporting details.

1. Generate supporting ideas.
2. Choose the best supporting ideas.
3. Organize your ideas.

Generating Supporting Ideas

You can use an exploring strategy—freewriting, brainstorming, clustering, or questioning—to generate supporting ideas.

JINSUK'S SUPPORTING IDEAS

Jinsuk Suh chose one of her narrowed topics related to "neighborhoods" and wrote her topic sentence. Then she listed ideas that could support the topic sentence.

TOPIC SENTENCE: <u>**Zion market is one of the busiest and best Korean markets.**</u>

- products are of good quality
- fruits and vegetables are fresh
- price of products are low
- many people
- sale each weekend
- no quarrels between customers and employees
- employees are kind
- very noisy

> **TECHNOLOGY LINK**
>
> If you write your paragraph on a computer, put your topic sentence in bold. Then you (and your instructor) can easily identify it.

The Writer's Desk List Supporting Ideas

Choose one of your topic sentences from the previous Writer's Desk, and make a list of ideas that could support it.

Topic sentence: _Videos on youtube can can be very helpful to study for a test.._

Supporting ideas: _- You can watch a variety of videos on the same topic._

2 * _- The videos are very helpfull._

1 * _- You can listen to the video and still be do other taskes._

- You can watch the same videos as much as you like.

- It's free

- It will be helpfull to get you an A on your teste..

3 * _- You can get different points of views on the same topic._

Choosing the Best Ideas

A paragraph should have **unity**, which means that all of its sentences relate directly to its topic sentence. To achieve unity, examine your prewriting carefully and then choose three or four ideas that are most compelling and that clearly support your topic sentence. You may notice that several items in your list are similar; therefore, you can group them together. Remove any ideas that do not support your topic sentence.

JINSUK'S SUPPORTING IDEAS

First, Jinsuk crossed out ideas that she did not want to develop. Then, she highlighted three of the most appealing ideas and labeled them A, B, and C. Finally, she regrouped other details from the list that best supported the most appealing ideas.

TOPIC SENTENCE: **Zion market is one of the busiest and best Korean markets.**

- **products are of good quality**   *A*
- fruits and vegetables are fresh
- **price of products are low**   *B*
- ~~many people~~
- sale each weekend
- no quarrels between customers and employees
- **employees are kind**   *C*
- ~~very noisy~~

TECHNOLOGY LINK

On a computer, you can cut (ctrl X) and paste (ctrl V) similar ideas together.

On a Mac, you can highlight and drag sentences.

Hint **Identifying the Best Ideas**

There are many ways to highlight your best ideas. You can circle the best supporting points and then use lines or arrows to link them with secondary ideas. You could also use highlighter pens or asterisks (*) to identify the best supporting points.

The Writer's Desk Choose the Best Ideas

For the Writer's Desk on page 21, you produced a list of ideas. Identify ideas that clearly support the topic sentence. If there are any related ideas, group them. You can cross out ideas that you do not want to develop.

ESSAY LINK

In an essay, you can also use time, space, or emphatic order to organize your ideas.

Organizing Your Ideas

The next step is to organize your ideas in a logical manner. There are three common organizational methods: time order, emphatic order, and space order. You can use **transitions**—words such as *first*, *then*, and *furthermore*—to guide readers from one idea to the next. You can find a more complete list of transitions on page 38 in Chapter 3, "Revising and Editing."

Time Order

When you use **time order,** you arrange the details according to the sequence in which they have occurred. Use time order to narrate a story, explain how to do something, or describe a historical event.

before   then   after that

Here are some transitional expressions you can use in time order paragraphs.

after that	first	later	next
eventually	in the beginning	meanwhile	then
finally	last	months after	while

The next paragraph uses time order.

> Throughout the history of music, financial backing has been needed to support the composition and production of musical performances. In Europe during the Middle Ages, the greatest patron of music was the church. Then, in the Renaissance, Baroque, and Classic eras, the foremost patrons were wealthy aristocrats who employed composers and performers in their courts. Later, in the nineteenth century, the main support for music gradually spread to the middle classes. Public concerts became common, and music was funded by ticket sales and by the sale of printed music for amateurs to perform at home. Finally, during the twentieth century, this reliance on wider support continued to grow. Now, the central driving force behind the production of most popular music is commercial gain. The profits are enormous.
>
> —Jeremy Yudkin, *Understanding Music*

PRACTICE 5

Use time order to organize the supporting details beneath each of the topic sentences. Number the details in order starting with 1.

1. If you win a large amount of money in a lottery, there are some things you should do to maintain your sanity.

   _____ Take a leave of absence from your job.

   _____ Keep enough money in your savings account to take a vacation.

   _____ Take a long vacation.

   _____ Collect the money and immediately deposit it in a secure bank fund.

   _____ Stay away until the publicity about your win dies down.

2. Greg Mortenson's incredible adventure led him to dedicate his life to a humanitarian cause.

   _____ Wanting to repay the villagers for their kindness, he returned to the United States and started a non-profit organization to fund schools in Pakistan.

   _____ In 1993, Greg Mortenson tried to climb K2, the world's second tallest mountain.

_____ By 2009, Mortenson had established 131 schools in Pakistan and Afghanistan.

_____ Residents from Korphe, a poor village in Pakistan, nursed him back to health.

_____ Completely lost, he wandered down the mountain in a state of exhaustion.

_____ The book *Three Cups of Tea*, written in 2006, publicized Mortenson's projects in Pakistan.

_____ During his stay in Korphe, he saw that the village lacked a school.

Emphatic Order

When you use **emphatic order,** you organize supporting details in a logical sequence. For example, you can arrange details from the least to the most important, from the best to the worst, from the least appealing to the most appealing, from general to specific, and so on. How you order the details often depends on your purpose for writing.

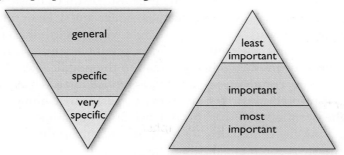

Here are some transitional expressions you can use in emphatic order paragraphs.

above all	first	moreover	particularly
clearly	furthermore	most important	principally
especially	least of all	most of all	therefore

The following paragraph uses emphatic order. The writer presents characteristics from the least to the most important.

> Psychologists have determined that people facing difficult circumstances have no single source of resilience. Rather, many factors come into play. First, those with developed social skills tend to be more resilient than other people. For example, Oprah Winfrey, a great communicator, survived traumatic events in her childhood. Furthermore, some people have a genetic predisposition toward higher self-esteem. But one character trait, above all others, seems to help people cope, and that is the ability to maintain an optimistic attitude. According to author Martin Seligman, positive thinkers tend to believe that problems are outside themselves and not permanent, and they generally rise above failure.

—Suzanne Moreau, student

 **Using Emphatic Order**

When you organize details using emphatic order, use your own values and opinions to determine what is most or least important, upsetting, remarkable, and so on. Another writer may organize the same ideas in a different way.

PRACTICE 6

Use emphatic order to organize the supporting details beneath each topic sentence. Number them in order from most important (1) to least important (5) or from least important (1) to most important (5).

1. Doing homework assignments can benefit schoolchildren in many ways.

   ___3___ Finishing homework assignments gives students a sense of accomplishment.

   ___5___ Children learn to follow directions.

   ___4___ Students learn the subject better by correcting mistakes or improving their work.

   ___2___ Pupils learn to manage their time.

   ___1___ Homework assignments allow parents to understand what their children are learning.

2. Our new mayor has made many mistakes.

   ___4___ He made negative comments about some religious minorities.

   ___1___ He wears unflattering suits that are too large.

   ___3___ He hired his own children as advisors.

   ___5___ He made a lot of money on a land flip, and citizens believe he is corrupt.

   ___2___ He doesn't smile for photographs.

Space Order

When you use **space order,** you describe an image in the sequence in which you see it. For example, you could describe something or someone from top to bottom or bottom to top, from left to right or right to left, or from far to near or near to far.

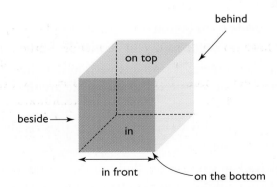

Here are some transitional expressions you can use in space order paragraphs.

above	closer in	near	on the top
at the back	farther out	next to	to the left
behind	in front	on the bottom	under

In the next paragraph, by taking the reader on a visual tour around his home, the writer describes the effects of a tornado.

> The house stopped trembling, and we knew that the tornado had passed. We jumped out of bed and did not know what we would find. We ran to the back of the house. What we found was our oldest daughter still asleep in a completely undisturbed room. We discovered our other two daughters also still asleep in another intact room. The storm did not touch the back portion of the house. Our section in the front of the home was less fortunate. Large pieces of the roof were in a tree. The rain was coming in and bringing globs of wet insulation with it. My wife began running around putting pots under the leaks, but I told her to forget it because the roof was gone.
>
> —Louis M. Tursi, *The Night Crawler*

PRACTICE 7

Read the next paragraph and answer the questions that follow.

unobstructed:
clear

crevices:
cracks

> We placed our tent in a clearing and had an **unobstructed** view of Mount Pilatus. The peak of the mountain was snow covered. Just below the snow, there were rows of pines cut by **crevices.** Under the pines there was a rocky cliff where several mountain goats wandered. At the bottom of the mountain was a village. We could see the church steeple and the red and black roofs of mining houses.
>
> —Carlo Tomasino

1. In what order does the writer describe the scene? Choose the best answer.

   a. top to bottom   b. left to right

2. Underline some transitional expressions used in this paragraph to indicate space order.

PRACTICE 8

Use spatial order—moving from bottom to top—to organize the supporting details beneath the topic sentence. Number the sentences from 1 to 5.

> Tourists and architectural students gasp in delight when they see the Casa Mila, the last completed avant-garde architectural work of Antoni Gaudí.

_____ Chimneys covered with broken ceramic tiles rise from the roof and seem to touch the sky.

_____ The sidewalk in front of the building is decorated with blue and green ceramic tiles designed in the form of starfish.

_____ The walls of the building are not straight but are in the shape of a gigantic wave.

_____ The roof, dotted with small windows, is sand-colored.

_____ Each balcony has curved black railings giving a further impression of waves on the ocean.

PRACTICE 9

Read the following topic sentences, which also appeared in Practice 2. Decide what type of order you could use to develop the paragraph details. Choose time, space, or emphatic order.

EXAMPLE:

College students should take their studies seriously.   *Emphatic*

1. Several interesting things happened when the probe landed on Mars.   _____

2. Children without siblings tend to be self-reliant.   _____

3. The bronze statue was truly original.   _____

4. Become a better listener by following three simple steps.   _____

5. The dorm room was an uncontrollable mess.   _____

6. High blood pressure is caused by several factors.   _____

The Writer's Desk Organize Your Ideas

Look at the list of ideas that you wrote for the Writer's Desk on page 21. Organize your ideas using space, time, or emphatic order by placing numbers beside the ideas.

The Paragraph Plan

A **paragraph plan**—or **outline**—is a map that shows the paragraph's main and supporting ideas. To make a plan, write your topic sentence. Then list supporting points and details in the order in which you wish to present them. You can use time, space, or emphatic order to organize the supporting points.

 **Adding Specific Details**

When you prepare your paragraph plan, ask yourself whether your supporting ideas are detailed enough. If not, then you can add details to make that supporting idea stronger. For example, in Jinsuk's list about Zion market, one of the points was about good-quality products. She added more details to make that point stronger and more complete.

        Products are of good quality

        – fruits and vegetables are fresh

Added: – clear colors of fruits

        – juicy and sweet

JINSUK'S PARAGRAPH PLAN

After she chose the best ideas and organized them, Jinsuk modified her topic sentence and wrote a paragraph plan.

TOPIC SENTENCE: Zion market is one of the busiest Korean markets because it has good-quality products, low prices, and kind employees.

Support 1:	I can find many products of good quality
Details:	— fruits and vegetables are fresh
	— clear colors of fruits
	— delicious, juicy, and sweet
Support 2:	The prices of many products are low.
Details:	— better prices than in other markets
	— sales every weekend
Support 3:	Employees are kind
Details:	— there are no quarrels between customers and employees
	— manager responds quickly to requests

The Writer's Desk Write a Paragraph Plan

Look at the topic sentence and the organized list of supporting ideas that you created for the previous Writer's Desks. Now, fill in the following paragraph plan. Remember to include details for each supporting idea.

Topic sentence: _____

_____

Support 1: _____

Details: _____

_____

Support 2: _____

Details: _____

_____

Support 3: _____

Details: _____

_____

The First Draft

The next step is to write the first draft. Take information from your paragraph plan and, using complete sentences, write a paragraph. Your first draft includes your topic sentence and supporting details.

JINSUK'S FIRST DRAFT

Jinsuk wrote the first draft of her paragraph about Zion market. You may notice that the paragraph contains mistakes. In Chapter 3, you will see how she revises and edits her paragraph.

> Zion market is one of the busiest Korean markets because it has three characteristics: good quality, low prices, and kind employees. Shopping in Zion market makes me excited because I can find many products of good quality. Especially, the fruits. They are all fresh. Their colors are clear. They are delicious, they are flavorful, juicy, and sweet. In addition, the prices of many products are lower than thoses in other markets. Every weekend, different kind of products are on sale. All the employees are very kind. I have never had uncomfortable situation or witnessed any quarrels between customers and employees. The manager keeps walking around the market and the head of each section respond quickly to the requests of the customers. The fruit section manager suggests which fruit is the tastiest. His happy face makes me feel good. These three characteristics make this market one of the busiest markets.

 **Writing the Concluding Sentence**

Some paragraphs end with a **concluding sentence,** which brings the paragraph to a satisfactory close. If you want to write a concluding sentence for your paragraph, here are three suggestions.

- Restate the topic sentence in a new, fresh way.
- Make an interesting final observation.
- End with a prediction, suggestion, or quotation.

ESSAY LINK

Essays end with a concluding paragraph. For more information about essay conclusions, see pages 106–107.

The Writer's Desk **Write Your First Draft**

In the previous Writer's Desk on page 28, you created a paragraph plan. Now, on a separate sheet of paper, write your first draft of that paragraph.

The Writer's Room

Writing Activity 1: Topics

In the Writer's Room in Chapter 1, "Exploring," you used various strategies to find ideas about the following topics. Select one of the topics and write a paragraph. Remember to follow the writing process.

General Topics

1. sports
2. ceremonies
3. kindness

College or Work-Related Topics

4. career choices
5. an influential person
6. competition

Writing Activity 2: Photo Writing

Describe your neighborhood. You could describe a person you frequently see or a place such as a park or building.

✔ DEVELOPING CHECKLIST

When you develop a paragraph, ask yourself the following questions.

☐ Does my **topic sentence** introduce the topic and state the controlling idea?

☐ Do I **support the topic sentence** with facts and examples?

☐ Do I **organize the details** using time, space, or emphatic order?

☐ Does my **paragraph plan** help me visualize the main and supporting ideas?

☐ Does my **first draft** use complete sentences?

PEARSON mywritinglab To check your progress in meeting this chapter's objectives, log in to **www.mywritinglab.com**, go to the **Study Plan** tab, click on **The Writing Process** and choose **Developing** from the list of subtopics. Read and view the resources in the **Review Materials** section, and then complete the **Recall, Apply,** and **Write** sets in the **Activities** section.

Revising and Editing

The revising and editing stages of the writing process are like adding the finishing touches to a meal. Small improvements can help a good meal become a great one.

> ❝ *Mistakes are the portals of discovery.* ❞
> —JAMES JOYCE (1882–1941)
> *Irish author*

What Are Revising and Editing?

Revising and editing are effective ways to improve your writing. When you **revise,** you modify your writing to make it more convincing and precise. You do this by looking for inadequate development and poor organization, and then you make any necessary changes. When you **edit,** you proofread your final draft. You look for errors in grammar, spelling, punctuation, and mechanics.

There are five key steps in the revising and editing stages.

REVISING AND EDITING

STEP 1 ➤ **Revise for unity.** Make sure that all parts of your work relate to the main idea.

STEP 2 ➤ **Revise for adequate support.** Ensure that you have enough details to effectively support the main idea.

STEP 3 ➤ **Revise for coherence.** Verify that your ideas flow smoothly and are logically linked.

STEP 4 ➤ **Revise for style.** Make sure that your sentences are varied and interesting.

STEP 5 ➤ **Edit for technical errors.** Proofread your work and correct errors in grammar, spelling, mechanics, and punctuation.

Revise for Unity

In a paragraph, every idea should move in the same direction just like this railroad track goes straight ahead.

When a paragraph has **unity,** all of the sentences support the topic sentence. If a paragraph lacks unity, then it is difficult for the reader to understand the main point. To check for unity, verify that every sentence relates to the main idea.

ESSAY LINK

When revising an essay, ensure that each body paragraph has unity.

DEVON'S PARAGRAPH WITHOUT UNITY

College student Devon Washington wrote the following paragraph, and he accidentally drifted away from his main idea. If he removed the highlighted sentences, then his paragraph would have unity.

> **Athletes who use steroids damage their reputations and their health.** Young children look up to their favorite sports stars, and they want to be like those stars. When someone famous such as Barry Bonds admits to using performance-enhancing drugs, young fans begin to think that steroid usage is acceptable. Bonds and others send a message that the only way to succeed in sports is to cheat. Steroids also hurt the athletes' bodies. The substances can damage the kidneys, the liver, and the heart. Some great athletes never took steroids, such as Lance Armstrong. Many people accused him, but he never had a positive drug test. So Armstrong shows people that they can succeed without drugs. Nobody should use drugs to have a better performance.

The writer took a detour here.

PRACTICE I

Read paragraphs A, B, and C. For each one, underline the topic sentence. Then indicate whether the paragraph has unity. If the paragraph lacks unity, remove the sentences that do not relate to the topic sentence.

A. In this computer age, electronic voting seems like a logical way to collect and count votes. However, paperless electronic voting is both unreliable and dangerous. First, the software in voting machines may be faulty. During the 2006 midterm elections, overseers in some states noted that machines switched votes from one candidate to another because of touch-screen problems. Additionally, voting machines can be easily manipulated. In 2004, Maryland hired RABA Technologies to try to hack the state's new voting machines. Computer whizzes were able to vote more than once and change voting outcomes, and they concluded that even high-school students could hack the machines. In Holland, hackers using telephone lines were able to manipulate and delete votes. However, electronic voting has some good points. The elimination of paper ballots is good for the environment. Also, votes can be counted more quickly by machine than they can by hand. Certainly, governments should think twice about implementing electronic voting machines.

Circle the correct answer. Does the paragraph have unity?
    a. yes   b. no

B. To minimize the problems associated with divorce, parents need to maintain a stable environment for their children. For example, any fighting over finances or child visitation should not occur in front of the children. Parents should try to live near each other so that the kids have easy access to both parents. To further stabilize children's lives after a divorce, many parents now opt for the "family home." The kids don't have to change houses to visit each parent; instead, the parents take turns living in the family home. If parents just remember to put children first, then the effects of divorce on the children can be minimized.

Circle the correct answer. Does the paragraph have unity?
    a. yes   b. no

C. It is extremely dangerous to send text messages while driving. In a poll commissioned by the American Automotive Association (AAA), 66 percent of people under twenty-four years of age admitted to sending or receiving a text while driving. In New York, five cheerleaders were killed in an auto accident after a driver became distracted while text messaging. According to a *New York Times* editorial, a University of Utah study showed that texting car drivers "are twenty-three times more likely to cause a crash than a non-texting driver." Another dangerous practice is racing. Sometimes, one person challenges another, and the drivers decide to see who is the fastest, but they do not consider other drivers or pedestrians. Racers can cause serious accidents. People should try to drive more carefully.

Circle the correct answer. Does the paragraph have unity?
a. yes   b. no

Revise for Adequate Support

A bridge is built using several well-placed support columns. Like a bridge, a paragraph requires adequate support to help it stand on its own.

ESSAY LINK

When you revise an essay, ensure that you have adequately supported the thesis statement. Also, verify that each body paragraph has sufficient supporting details.

When you revise for adequate support, ensure that your paragraph contains strong and convincing supporting details.

JINSUK'S REVISION FOR ADEQUATE SUPPORT

Jinsuk Suh wrote a paragraph about Zion market, but she needed some specific examples to back up some of her points. She added some details to strengthen her paragraph.

Zion market is one of the busiest Korean markets because it has

three characteristics: good quality, low prices, and kind employees.

Shopping in Zion market makes me excited because I can find many

products of good quality. Especially, the fruits. They are all fresh. Their

, and the fruits are not dried-up but moist
colors are clear. They are delicious, they are flavorful, juicy, and sweet.

In addition, the prices of many products are lower than thoses in other
            There are special discounts on fresh vegetables, bags of rice, and
                                        cartons filled with brown eggs.
markets. Every weekend, different kind of products are on sale. All the

employees are very kind. I have never had uncomfortable situation or

witnessed any quarrels between customers and employees. The

manager keeps walking around the market and the head of each

section respond quickly to the requests of the customers. The fruit

, a small chubby man who always smiles,
section manager suggests which fruit is the tastiest. His happy face

makes me feel good. These three characteristics make this market one

of the busiest markets.

PRACTICE 2

The following paragraph attempts to persuade, but it does not have any specific details that make strong points.

> Children should be taught about healthy eating from a young age. Toddlers can learn to enjoy a nutritious breakfast. Schoolchildren can have healthy lunch snacks. Also, parents should not buy fast food. In the evenings, instead of greasy food, parents can serve a healthy meal. Children can learn good eating habits.

When the preceding paragraph is expanded with specific details and examples, it becomes more convincing. Add details on the lines provided.

Children should be taught about healthy eating from a young age. Toddlers can learn to enjoy a nutritious breakfast. For instance, instead of _____,

_____

a young child might eat _____.

_____

Schoolchildren can have healthy lunch snacks, including _____.
Also, parents should not buy fast food such as _____

_____.

In the evenings, instead of greasy _____,

_____

parents can serve a healthy meal such as _____

_____.

Children can learn good eating habits.

 Avoiding Circular Reasoning

Circular reasoning means that a writer restates his or her main point in various ways but does not provide supporting details. The main idea goes in circles and never progresses-kind of like a dog chasing its tail. Avoid using circular reasoning by writing a concise topic sentence and by supporting the topic sentence with facts, examples, or anecdotes.

For example, the following paragraph has circular reasoning.

People should not drink and drive because it is too dangerous. They can hurt themselves. Drinking and driving causes accidents, and sometimes people die.

When a paragraph has circular reasoning, the main idea does not progress. The writer leads the reader in circles.

PRACTICE 3

The next passages do not have sufficient supporting examples. List examples for each paragraph. With numbers, indicate where you would place the supporting examples.

EXAMPLE:

(1)

My sister's apartment is a disaster zone. The entrance and the kitchen

(2)

are messy. So is the bathroom. There are things everywhere.

Add examples: *(1) The front hall is filled with shoes.*

The kitchen sink is filled with dirty dishes.

(2) There are wet towels on the bathroom floor.

1. Some smells are very beautiful. The odors in nature are nice. I like the smells in the forest. There are also wonderful food smells. Also, I have a favorite smell. It makes me have wonderful memories.

Add examples: _smell _____ Roste_ _____

_____

_____

2. When you build a birdhouse, there are a few things you need. Some supplies are necessary. You should shop for them.

Add examples: _____

_____

_____

3. Since 2000, reality television has invaded our homes. There are many types of reality shows. They all include ordinary people who participate in unusual contests. Sometimes the shows take place in unusual places.

Add examples: _____

_____

_____

Revise for Coherence

Just as couplings link train cars, transitional expressions link ideas in a paragraph.

ESSAY LINK

To create coherence in an essay, you can place transitional expressions at the beginning of each body paragraph.

When you revise for coherence, you ensure that your reader has a smooth voyage through your paragraph. **Coherence** means that the sentences flow and are logically organized.

Transitional Expressions

Transitional expressions are linking words or phrases, and they show the reader the connections between ideas in paragraphs and essays. Here are some common transitional expressions.

Function	Transitional Word or Expression			
Addition	again also besides	first (second, third) for one thing furthermore	in addition in fact moreover	next then	
Concession of a point	certainly	indeed	no doubt	of course	to be sure
Comparison	as well	equally	likewise	similarly	
Contrast	however in contrast	instead nevertheless	on the contrary on the other hand		
Effect or result	as a result	consequently	then	therefore	thus
Example	for example for instance	in other words namely	specifically to illustrate		
Emphasis	above all clearly	in fact in particular	indeed least of all	most important most of all	of course undoubtedly
Space	above at the back behind below	beside closer in farther out in front	in the middle inside nearby on the bottom	on the left/right on top outside under	
Summary or conclusion	generally in conclusion in other words	in short on the whole therefore	thus to conclude to summarize		
Time	after that at that time at the moment currently earlier eventually first (second, etc.)	gradually immediately in the future in the past later meanwhile now	one day presently so far subsequently suddenly then these days		

GRAMMAR LINK

For more practice using transitions in sentences, see Chapter 15, "Compound Sentences."

 **Use Transitional Expressions with Complete Sentences**

When you add a transitional expression to a sentence, ensure that your sentence is complete. Your sentence must have a subject and a verb, and it must express a complete thought.

Incomplete: First, the price of movie tickets.

Complete: First, the price of movie tickets <u>is too high</u>.

PRACTICE 4

Add the following transitional expressions to the next paragraph. Use each transitional word once. There may be more than one correct answer for each space.

also	furthermore	undoubtedly
first	however	

When you go backpacking in a foreign country, there are a few simple things you should pack for the trip. _____, bring clothing that is easy to wash. Leave items that need ironing or dry cleaning at home. _____, make sure you pack a small medical kit. It could be difficult and expensive to find things such as aspirin and bandages if you're on a beach in Thailand. _____, bring a comfortable money belt that you can wear under your clothing. _____, try not to overpack. After you've packed your bag, remove items so that there is a small empty space in your pack. _____, you will find and buy souvenirs during your trip.

Revise for Style

Just as a blend of colors makes a train interior more beautiful, varied sentence style makes a paragraph more compelling.

ESSAY LINK

Revise your essays for style, ensuring that sentences are varied and that your language is exact. To learn more about sentence variety and exact language, see Chapters 17 and 23.

Another important step in the revision process is to ensure that you have varied your sentences and that you have used concise wording. When you revise for sentence style, ask yourself the following questions.

- Have I used a variety of sentence patterns?
- Have I used exact language?
- Have I avoided using repetitious or vague language?

JINSUK'S REVISION FOR COHERENCE AND STYLE

Jinsuk Suh revised her paragraph about Zion market. To show connections between ideas, she added transitional words. She also changed some language to make it more exact.

Zion market is one of the busiest Korean markets because it has three characteristics: good quality, low prices, and kind employees. Shopping in Zion market makes me excited because I can find many products of good quality. Especially, the fruits. They are all fresh. Their colors are clear, and the *stalks and peels of all* fruits are not dried-up but moist. ~~They~~ *Also, they* are delicious, they are flavorful, juicy, and sweet. In addition, the prices of many products are lower than thoses in other markets. Every weekend, different kind of products are on sale. There are special discounts on fresh vegetables, bags of rice, and cartons filled with brown eggs. ~~All~~ *Furthermore, all* the employees are very kind. I have never had uncomfortable situation or witnessed any quarrels between customers and employees. The manager keeps walking around the market and the head of each section respond quickly to the requests of the customers. ~~The~~ *For example, the* fruit section manager, a small chubby man who always smiles, suggests which fruit is the tastiest. His happy face makes me feel good. These three characteristics make this market one of the busiest markets.

Added exact language. ➤

Added a transition. ➤

Added a transition. ➤

Added a transition. ➤

Edit for Errors

When you **edit,** you reread your writing and make sure that it is free of errors. Look for mistakes in grammar, punctuation, mechanics, and spelling. The editing guide on the inside front cover of this book contains some common editing codes that your teacher may use.

 **Spelling and Grammar Logs**

It is a good idea to put your text aside for a day or two before you edit it. You could also keep a spelling and grammar log.

- **Keep a spelling log.** In a notebook or binder, keep a list of all of your spelling mistakes. Then, you can refer to your list of spelling errors when you edit your writing.
- **Keep a grammar log.** After you receive each corrected assignment, choose an error. Write down the error and a rule about it in your grammar log.

See Appendix 5 for more information about the spelling and grammar logs.

JINSUK'S EDITING

Jinsuk edited her paragraph for spelling and grammar errors.

Zion market is one of the busiest Korean markets because it has three characteristics: good quality, low prices, and kind employees. Shopping in Zion market makes me excited because I can find many products of good quality. Especially, the fruits. *are tasty* They are all fresh. Their colors are clear, and the stalks and peels of all fruits are not dried-up but moist. Also, they are delicious, *. T* they are flavorful, juicy, and sweet. In addition, the prices of many products are lower than ~~thoses~~ *those* in other markets. Every weekend, different ~~kind~~ *kinds* of products are on sale. There are special discounts on fresh vegetables, bags of rice, milk, and cartons filled with brown eggs. Furthermore, all the employees are very kind. I have never had *an* uncomfortable situation or witnessed any quarrels between customers and employees. The manager keeps walking around the market *,* and the head of each section ~~respond~~ *responds* quickly to the requests of the customers. For example, the fruit section manager, a small chubby man who always smiles, suggests which fruit is the tastiest. His happy face makes me feel good. These three characteristics make this market one of the busiest markets.

TECHNOLOGY LINK

Word processors have spelling and grammar checkers. If the program suggests ways to correct errors, carefully verify that the computer's suggestions make sense before you accept them.

The Writer's Desk Revise and Edit Your Paragraph

Choose a paragraph that you wrote for Chapter 2, or choose one that you have written for another assignment. Carefully revise and edit your paragraph.

Peer Feedback

After you write a paragraph or an essay, it is useful to get peer feedback. Ask another person such as a friend, family member, or fellow student to read your work and give you comments and suggestions on its strengths and weaknesses.

 **Offer Constructive Criticism**

When you peer-edit someone else's writing, try to make constructive suggestions rather than destructive comments. Phrase your comments in a positive way. Look at the following examples.

Instead of saying . . .	You could say . . .
Your examples are dull.	Perhaps you could add more details to your examples.
Your paragraph is confusing.	Your topic sentence needs a controlling idea.

When you are editing someone else's work, try using a peer feedback form as a guideline. A sample form is on the next page.

Peer Feedback Form

Written by: _____   Feedback by: _____

Date: _____

1. Your main idea is _____

   _____

   _____

2. Your best supporting ideas are _____

   _____

   _____

   _____

3. I like _____

   _____

   _____

4. Perhaps you could change _____

   _____

   _____

   _____

5. My other comments are _____

   _____

   _____

   _____

   _____

   _____

The Final Draft

When you have finished making revisions on the first draft of your paragraph, write the final draft. Include all of the changes that you have made during the revising and editing phases. Before you hand in your final draft, proofread it one last time to ensure that you have caught any errors.

The Writer's Desk Writing Your Final Draft

You have developed, revised, and edited your paragraph. Now write the final draft. Before you hand it to your instructor, proofread it one last time to ensure that you have found all of your errors.

 The Writer's Room

Writing Activity 1

Choose a paragraph that you have written for this course. Revise and edit that paragraph, and then write a final draft.

Writing Activity 2

Choose one of the following topics, or choose your own topic and write a paragraph. You could try exploring strategies to generate ideas. The first sentence of your paragraph should make a point about your topic. Remember to revise and edit your paragraph before you write the final draft.

General Topics

1. an interesting dream
2. a family story
3. a wonderful view
4. littering
5. an accident

College or Work-Related Topics

6. an unusual experience at college
7. computer problems
8. reasons to stay in college
9. a personality conflict at work
10. working with your spouse

REVISING AND EDITING CHECKLIST

When you revise and edit a paragraph, ask yourself the following questions.

☐ Does my paragraph have **unity?** Ensure that every sentence relates to the main idea.

☐ Does my paragraph have **adequate support?** Verify that there are enough details and examples to support your main point.

☐ Is my paragraph **coherent?** Try to use transitional expressions to link ideas.

☐ Does my paragraph have good **style?** Check for varied sentence patterns and exact language.

☐ Does my paragraph have any errors? **Edit** for errors in grammar, punctuation, spelling, and mechanics.

☐ Is my **final draft** error-free?

mywritinglab To check your progress in meeting this chapter's objectives, log in to **www.mywritinglab.com**, go to the **Study Plan** tab, click on **The Writing Process** and choose **Revising and Editing** from the list of subtopics. Read and view the resources in the **Review Materials** section, and then complete the **Recall, Apply,** and **Write** sets in the **Activities** section.

Paragraph Patterns

A fashion designer uses diverse patterns to create coats for different purposes. In this chapter, you will learn about nine writing patterns.

" *Art is the imposing of a pattern on experience.* "

—ALFRED NORTH WHITEHEAD (1861–1947)
Mathematician and philosopher

What Are Paragraph Patterns?

Paragraph patterns, or **modes**, are methods writers can use to develop a piece of writing. Each pattern has a specific purpose. For example, if you want to entertain your audience by telling a story about your recent adventure, you might write a narrative paragraph. If your purpose is to explain the steps needed to complete an activity, you might write a process paragraph. Sometimes, more than one pattern can fulfill your purpose. Take a moment to review nine different writing patterns.

Pattern	Purpose
Illustration	To illustrate or prove a point using specific examples
Narration	To narrate or tell a story about a sequence of events that happened
Description	To describe using vivid details and images that appeal to the reader's senses

(continued)

Pattern	Purpose
Process	To inform the reader about how to do something, how something works, or how something happened
Definition	To define or explain what a term or concept means by providing relevant examples
Comparison and Contrast	To present information about similarities (compare) or differences (contrast)
Cause and Effect	To explain why an event happened (the cause) or what the consequences of the event were (the effects)
Classification	To sort a topic into different categories
Argument	To argue or to take a position on an issue and offer reasons for your position

A) The Illustration Paragraph

An **illustration paragraph** uses specific examples to **illustrate** or clarify the main point. For example, if you are writing a paragraph about your most valuable possessions, you might list your grandmother's ring, your photo album, your family videos, and so on.

Illustration writing is a pattern that you frequently use in college writing because you must support your main idea with examples.

PRACTICE I

Read the paragraph and answer the questions that follow.

> In recent visits to Canada, Mexico, Costa Rica, and Ecuador, I saw adolescents routinely behaving in ways American experts condemn as horrifying. **Ontario** nineteen-year-olds queued in liquor stores and drank in pubs alongside elders. Teens in **Quito**, **Riobamba**, and **San José** thronged to late-night discos. Unchaperoned **Ensenada** middle-schoolers strolled hand-in-hand along late-night downtown streets after emerging from unrated movies. Latin American cybercafés (often managed by teens or children) overflowed with unsupervised youths clicking unfiltered computers. Laughed a **Mountie** when I asked if Toronto had a youth curfew, "Maybe for six-year-olds." By American expert thinking, European, Canadian, and Latin American adolescents should be developmentally damaged alcoholic felons.
>
> —Mike Males, "Freedom: For Adults Only"

Ontario: a province in Canada

Quito: the capital of Ecuador

Riobamba: a city in Ecuador

San José: a city in Costa Rica

Ensenada: a city in Mexico

Mountie: a Canadian federal police officer; the name derives from the word *Mounted* in Royal Canadian Mounted Police.

1. What is the subject? _____

2. Underline the topic sentence of this paragraph.

3. List five supporting examples.

_____

_____

_____

_____

_____

_____

4. What is the author's point of view about the treatment of teens in the United States?

_____

_____

The Writer's Desk Exploring

Think about the following questions, and write down the first ideas that come to mind. Try to write two or three ideas for each topic.

EXAMPLE: What clutter do you have in your home?

kitchen cupboard filled with junk, letters on hall table, shoes piled in

closet, basement filled with boxes

1. What are some examples of objects that you value?

   _____

   _____

   _____

2. What are some creative gift ideas?

   _____

   _____

   _____

3. What are some traits of an effective boss?

   _____

   _____

   _____

The Topic Sentence

The topic sentence in an illustration paragraph controls the direction of the paragraph. It includes the topic and a controlling idea about the topic.

controlling idea   topic

There are <u>several good reasons</u> **to save money.**

The Writer's Desk **Write Topic Sentences**

Write a topic sentence for each of the following topics. Your sentence should have a controlling idea that expresses the direction of the paragraph. Remember that the goal of the paragraph is to give examples.

EXAMPLE:

Topic: Clutter in the home

Topic sentence: *Several places in my home are magnets for clutter.*

_____

1. Topic: Objects that you value

Topic sentence: _____

_____

2. Topic: Creative gift ideas

Topic sentence: _____

_____

3. Topic: An effective boss

Topic sentence: _____

_____

The Supporting Ideas

In an illustration paragraph, the examples support the topic sentence. A paragraph plan helps you organize your topic sentence and supporting details.

An Illustration Paragraph Plan

When you write an illustration paragraph plan, make sure that your examples are valid and that they relate to the topic sentence. In the following plan, the topic sentence is supported by three examples. Then, each example is supported with details.

TOPIC SENTENCE: **Several places in my home are magnets for clutter.**

Support 1: The front closet is a mess.
 Details: — shoes piled on top of one another
 — scarves, umbrellas, hats, gloves heaped at top of closet

Support 2: The hallway table is never clear.
 Details: — covered with letters, newspapers, opened bills

Support 3: A kitchen cupboard attracts junk.
 Details: — coupons, pens, screwdriver, twist ties, and other odds and ends piled in it

The Writer's Desk Develop Supporting Ideas

Choose one of the topic sentences that you wrote for the previous Writer's Desk, and write a detailed paragraph plan. List at least three examples that could support the topic sentence, and then give details for each.

Topic sentence: _____

_____

Support 1: _____

Details: _____

_____

Support 2: _____

Details: _____

_____

Support 3: _____

Details: _____

_____

Support 4: _____

Details: _____

_____

The Writer's Desk Write an Illustration Paragraph

You have made a list of supporting ideas and details for a topic. Now write an illustration paragraph. After you finish writing, remember to revise and edit your paragraph.

The Writer's Room

Writing Activity 1: Topics

Write an illustration paragraph about one of the following topics.

General Topics

1. mistakes
2. favorite clothing
3. inexpensive decorating solutions
4. annoying habits
5. inexpensive activities

College and Work-Related Topics

6. inappropriate workplace clothing
7. qualities of a good or bad coworker
8. undesirable or difficult jobs
9. useful objects in my workplace
10. excuses for not finishing something

Writing Activity 2: Photo Writing

Examine the photo. As you look at it, think about things that frustrate you or drive you crazy. Then write an illustration paragraph.

WRITING LINK

See the Writer's Rooms in the following grammar chapters for more illustration writing topics.

Chapter 8, Writer's Room topic 1 (page 161)
Chapter 12, Writer's Room topic 1 (page 222)
Chapter 15, Writer's Room topic 1 (page 257)
Chapter 21, Writer's Room topic 1 (page 316)
Chapter 22, Writer's Room topic 1 (page 326)

READING LINK

The following readings use examples to support the main idea.
"A Cultural Minefield" by William Ecenbarger (page 420)
"The Rewards of Dirty Work" by Linda L. Lindsey and Stephen Beach (page 449)

✔ ILLUSTRATION PARAGRAPH CHECKLIST

As you write your illustration paragraph, review the paragraph checklist on the inside back cover. Also, ask yourself the following questions.

☐ Does my topic sentence include a controlling idea that can be supported with examples?

☐ Do my supporting ideas contain sufficient examples that clearly support the topic sentence?

☐ Are the examples smoothly and logically connected?

B) The Narrative Paragraph

A **narrative** paragraph tells a story about what happened and generally explains events in the order in which they occurred.

There are two main types of narrative writing. When you use **first-person narration**, you describe a personal experience using *I* or *we* (first-person pronouns). When you use **third-person narration**, you describe what happened to somebody else using *he*, *she*, or *they* (third-person pronouns). Most news reports use third-person narration. Review the following examples.

First person: When I was a child, I played a terrible prank on my sister.

Third person: The mayor denied reports that he had misappropriated funds.

PRACTICE 2

Read the paragraph and answer the questions that follow.

> When I was in seventh grade, one of the big ninth-grade girls began bullying me. She didn't shake me down for lunch money or even touch me. But she stalked me in the halls, on the playground, and in the girls' lavatory. The way that **buffarilla** rolled her eyes and worked her neck in my direction, I could feel her fingers yanking out every hair on my head—and I didn't have that much. In class, instead of paying attention, I began to envision the after-school crowd that would gather to watch me get stomped into the ground. Every day, my adversary seemed to grow bigger, meaner, and stronger. In my mind she evolved from a menacing older girl into a monster. By the time I realized that she wasn't really interested in fighting me—just intimidating me with dirty looks— I was already bruised from kicking my own butt.
>
> —Bebe Moore Campbell, "Dancing with Fear"

buffarilla: an invented word that is a combination of buffalo and gorilla

1. What type of narration is this selection?
   a. First person   b. Third person

2. Underline the topic sentence.

3. What organizational method does the author use?
   a. Time order   b. Space order   c. Emphatic order

4. List what happens in the paragraph. (List only the main events.)

   _____

   _____

   _____

   _____

5. What did the author learn?

   _____

   _____

The Writer's Desk Exploring

Think about the following questions, and write down the first ideas that come to mind. Try to write two or three ideas for each topic.

EXAMPLE:

What are some bad purchases that you have made?

Bought black dress that is really too small

Bought a used car that was a lemon

Spent too much on a horrible haircut

_____

1. What interesting place have you visited? What did you do in that place?

_____

_____

_____

2. Think about an accident or injury that you, or someone you know, had. What happened?

_____

_____

_____

3. Think of a moment when you felt very proud. What happened?

_____

_____

_____

_____

The Topic Sentence

The **topic sentence** controls the direction of the paragraph and includes the topic and a controlling idea. To create a meaningful topic sentence for a narrative paragraph, you could ask yourself these questions: What did I learn? How did I change? How is the event important?

            topic   controlling idea

Our high school graduation ceremony was a disaster.

The Writer's Desk **Write Topic Sentences**

Write a topic sentence for each of the following topics. Your sentence should make a point about the topic. Remember that the goal of the paragraph is to tell a story.

EXAMPLE:

Topic: A bad purchase

Topic sentence: My problems began the moment I paid for my used car.

1. Topic: A place I have visited

   Topic sentence: *My family and I visited the Cancun, last year.*

2. Topic: An accident or injury

   Topic sentence: *I was driving my new car when I was hit from behind.*

3. Topic: A proud moment

   Topic sentence: *The day my friends and I graduated Highschool*

The Supporting Ideas

A narrative paragraph should contain details that explain what happened. To be as complete as possible, a good narrative paragraph should provide answers to most of the following questions.

- *Who* is the paragraph about?
- *What* happened?
- *When* did it happen?
- *Where* did it happen?
- *Why* did it happen?
- *How* did it happen?

WRITING LINK

Writing Link

For more information about organizing ideas using time, space, and emphatic order, see pages 22 to 25 of Chapter 2, "Developing."

A Narrative Paragraph Plan

When you write a narrative paragraph plan, make sure that your details are valid and that they relate to the topic sentence. Also, think about how you can organize your ideas. In the following plan, each detail explains what happened by using time order.

TOPIC SENTENCE: **My problems began the moment I paid for my used car.**

> Support 1:   When I paid the $500, the seller expressed relief.
> Details: — actually said "Whew"
>   — exchanged knowing glances with his buddy

Support 2: The drive home was filled with anxiety.
    Details: — became concerned that the car wouldn't make it
           — car seemed to gain and lose power
           — twice had to stop the car because it was overheating

Support 3: I parked the car in my apartment parking space and noticed
           something dripping.
    Details: — smelled burning oil
           — black liquid dripped and stained the pavement
           — landlord, with a scowl, peered out her window at my car

The Writer's Desk Develop Supporting Ideas

Choose one of the topic sentences that you wrote for the previous
Writer's Desk, and write a detailed paragraph plan. List the events in
the order in which they occurred.

Topic sentence: _____

_____

Support 1: _____

  Details: _____

_____

_____

Support 2: _____

  Details: _____

_____

_____

Support 3: _____

  Details: _____

_____

_____

The Writer's Desk Write a Narrative Paragraph

You have made a list of supporting ideas for a topic. Now write a
narrative paragraph. After you finish writing, remember to revise and
edit your paragraph.

WRITING LINK

See the Writer's Rooms in the following grammar chapters for more narrative writing topics.

Chapter 9, Writer's Room topic 1 (page 179)

Chapter 14, Writer's Room topic 1 (page 245)

Chapter 15, Writer's Room topic 2 (page 257)

Chapter 21, Writer's Room topic 1 (page 316)

Chapter 23, Writer's Room topic 1 (page 337)

READING LINK

Narrative Essays

The following readings use examples to support the main idea.

"Birth" by Maya Angelou (page 410)

"The Fire Below" by Bill Bryson (page 432)

The Writer's Room

Writing Activity 1: Topics

Write a narrative paragraph about one of the following topics.

General Topics

1. a scandal
2. a bad hair experience
3. a wedding
4. a good or bad financial decision
5. something you learned from a parent or relative

College and Work-Related Topics

6. a mistake at work
7. a smart career decision
8. a positive college experience
9. when you were first hired
10. when you lost or quit a job

Writing Activity 2: Photo Writing

Examine the photo. As you look at it, think about a journey you have taken. Write a narrative paragraph about a spiritual or physical journey.

✔ NARRATIVE PARAGRAPH CHECKLIST

As you write your narrative paragraph, review the paragraph checklist on the inside back cover. Also, ask yourself the following questions.

☐ Does my topic sentence clearly express the topic of the narration, and does it make a point about that topic?

☐ Does my paragraph answer most of the following questions: who, what, when, where, why, how?

☐ Do I use transitional expressions to help clarify the order of events?

☐ Do I include details to make my narration more interesting?

C) The Descriptive Paragraph

When writing a **descriptive** paragraph, use words to create a vivid impression of a subject. Descriptive writing often contains details that appeal to the five senses: seeing, smelling, hearing, tasting, and touching. You want readers to be able to imagine that they are experiencing what you are describing. For example, you might describe a frightening experience or a stunning landscape.

PRACTICE 3

Read the paragraph and answer the questions that follow.

> The last **portage** of my canoe trip was the hardest. I had been traveling through the back country of Algonquin Park for four straight days, and my shoulders were killing me. To transport my heavy red canoe, I had to lift it over my head and rest the wooden cross bar on my shoulders. New canoes are designed with molded cross bars, but my canoe had a straight bar that dug into my muscles. I felt as though pins were being driven into my shoulders and back. As I walked, my breathing was deep, and the stench of my own sweat overpowered the freshness of the northern air. I clenched my teeth as I tried, unsuccessfully, to avoid thinking of my aching muscles. I focused on each step, my boots crunching the pine needles that covered the winding path. Occasionally, as I marched through the forest, I would try to adjust the canoe in a vain effort to lessen the pain it was inflicting. Throughout it all, I anticipated the relief that would come with the sound of the lapping water at the end of the path. I imagined the rocky edge of the lake where I could set down my burden and lay down to recover my strength for the long journey ahead. But until that gentle babbling of the water reached my ears, I could only focus on forgetting the pain.
>
> —Stephen Laing, student

portage: the act of carrying a boat and goods overland from one body of water to another

1. Underline the topic sentence.

2. The writer uses words and phrases that appeal to sight, hearing, smell, and touch. Write some words or phrases that appeal to each sense.

   Sight: _____

   _____

   Hearing: _____

   _____

   Smell: _____

   _____

   Touch: _____

   _____

The Writer's Desk Exploring

Think about the following questions, and write down the first ideas that come to mind. Try to write two or three ideas for each topic.

EXAMPLE: What do you remember about a difficult moment?

blackout, stuck in elevator, time I broke up with my girlfriend, when my

mom caught me smoking, when I was accused of cheating

1. Where do you go when you want to relax? Think of two or three places.

2. What did you look like in the past? What fashions did you wear? What hairstyles did you have? (You might look at old photographs for inspiration.)

3. When you were a child, what interesting home did you visit? Think about the home of a friend or relative.

The Topic Sentence

In the **topic sentence** of a descriptive paragraph, you should convey a dominant impression about the subject. The dominant impression is the overall mood that you wish to convey. For example, the paragraph could convey an impression of tension, joy, nervousness, or anger.

topic   controlling idea

When I arrived at the secluded cabin, <u>I felt relieved.</u>

The Writer's Desk **Write Topic Sentences**

Write a topic sentence for each of the following topics. Your sentence should state what you are describing and express a dominant impression.

EXAMPLE:

Topic: A difficult moment

Topic sentence: *When the power went out in the elevator, I panicked.*

_____

1. Topic: A relaxing place

   Topic sentence: _____

   _____

2. Topic: Yourself in the past

   Topic sentence: _____

   _____

3. Topic: An interesting home

   Topic sentence: _____

   _____

The Supporting Ideas

To create a dominant impression, think about your topic and make a list of your feelings and impressions. These details can include things that you saw, heard, smelled, tasted, or touched.

 **Use Interesting and Detailed Vocabulary**

In your paragraph, use interesting descriptive vocabulary. Avoid overused words such as *nice, bad, mean,* and *hot.* For example, instead of writing "He was mean," you might write "He was as nasty as a raging pit bull." For more information about specific and vivid language, refer to Chapter 23, Exact Language.

The Writer's Desk List Images and Impressions

Think about images, impressions, and feelings that the following topics inspire in you. Make a list under each topic.

EXAMPLE:

A difficult moment: *Stuck in*

elevator

pitch black

no sound

perspiration trickling down my back

scared and alone

stuffy air

my heart pounded

1. A relaxing place: _____

_____

_____

_____

_____

_____

_____

2. Yourself in the past: _____

_____

_____

_____

_____

_____

_____

_____

3. An interesting home: _____

_____

_____

_____

_____

_____

_____

_____

WRITING LINK

For more Information about organizing ideas using time, space, and emphatic order, see pages 22–25 in Chapter 2, "Developing."

A Descriptive Paragraph Plan

When you write a descriptive paragraph plan, make sure that your details are valid and that they relate to the topic sentence. You could place your details in space order, time order, or emphatic order. The order that you use depends on the topic of your paragraph. In the following plan, the details, which are in time order, appeal to the senses and develop the dominant impression.

TOPIC SENTENCE: **When the elevator jolted to a stop, I panicked.**

Support 1:   The light in the elevator went out.
Details: —was pitch black

Support 2: I was alone.
   Details: — scared
             — complete silence

Support 3: I began to panic.
   Details: — heart raced
             — pounding sounds in my ears
             — began pacing and touching the walls

Support 4: I heard a loud banging noise.
   Details: — elevator lights came on
             — elevator began to move

The Writer's Desk Develop Supporting Ideas

Choose one of the topic sentences that you developed in the previous Writer's Desks, and write a detailed paragraph plan. Remember to develop a dominant impression.

Topic sentence: _____

_____

  Support 1: _____
    Details: _____

_____

  Support 2: _____
    Details: _____

_____

  Support 3: _____
    Details: _____

_____

  Support 4: _____
    Details: _____

The Writer's Desk Write a Descriptive Paragraph

You have made a list of supporting ideas for a topic. Now write a descriptive paragraph. After you finish writing, remember to revise and edit your paragraph.

WRITING LINK

See the Writer's Rooms in the following grammar chapters for more descriptive writing topics.

Chapter 9, Writer's Room topic 2 (page 179)

Chapter 11, Writer's Room topics 1 and 2 (page 207)

Chapter 17, Writer's Room topic 1 (page 276)

Chapter 19, Writer's Room topic 1 (page 291)

Chapter 26, Writer's Room topic 1 (page 374)

READING LINK

The following readings use descriptive writing.

"Fish Cheeks" by Amy Tan (page 408)

"What It Feels Like to Walk on the Moon" by Buzz Aldrin (page 429)

The Writer's Room

Writing Activity 1: Topics

Write a descriptive paragraph about one of the following topics.

General Topics

1. a movie theater
2. a fad or fashion trend
3. a shocking experience
4. an eccentric family member
5. a messy place

College and Work-Related Topics

6. a good meeting place on campus
7. an unusual teacher from your past
8. the place where you study
9. a bad day at work
10. the style of clothing you wear to work

Writing Activity 2: Photo Writing

Describe a celebration or ceremony that you participated in. Use words that appeal to the senses.

✔ DESCRIPTIVE PARAGRAPH CHECKLIST

As you write your descriptive paragraph, review the paragraph checklist on the inside back cover. Also, ask yourself the following questions.

☐ Does my topic sentence clearly show what I will describe?

☐ Does my topic sentence make a point about the topic?

☐ Does my paragraph have a dominant impression?

☐ Does each body paragraph contain supporting details that may appeal to the reader's senses?

D) The Process Paragraph

A **process** is a series of steps done in chronological or emphatic order. In a **process paragraph,** you explain how to do something. For example, you might explain how to change the oil in your car, how to plan a party, or how to write a résumé. The reader should be able to follow the directions and do the process.

PRACTICE 4

Read the paragraph and answer the questions that follow.

> Safety in welding is essential. Welders need to wear the proper safety gear to avoid potentially dangerous events. First, they must wear gauntlet gloves to protect their hands and skin from the intense heat and the electric arc rays, which can burn skin worse than the sun in a fraction of a second. Second, they must wear a welding helmet with a filter lens, which shades their eyes from the bright rays of the electric arc or the combustible gas flame. The effect experienced after eyeball exposure, even when indirect, is called arc flash. Arc flash causes eyes to redden, burn, and itch, and can leave a person temporarily and possibly permanently blind. Trained welders know the possibility of getting a lighter scale arc flash from simple things like reflective stripes on coveralls or from a partner welding nearby. Furthermore, welders must never wear clothing made of synthetics because it can melt and burn the skin. Also, plastic shoes and jewelry should be avoided. These items can cause serious burns, and they can smolder or ignite into flames.
>
> —Kelly Bruce, student and professional welder

1. Underline the topic sentence. Remember that the topic sentence may not be the first sentence in the paragraph.

2. In process paragraphs, the support is generally a series of steps. List the steps a person should take to be safe when welding.

    _____

    _____

    _____

    _____

3. Circle the transitional expressions that introduce each point.

4. This paragraph does not have a concluding sentence. Write a concluding sentence.

    _____

    _____

The Writer's Desk Exploring

Think about the following questions, and write down the first ideas that come to mind. Try to write two or three ideas for each topic.

EXAMPLE: What are some ways to find a mate?

join a club, ask your friends, be open and receptive, don't act desperate,

be yourself, use an Internet dating service

1. What are some things you should do when you prepare for a move to a new place?

2. What should you do if you want to plan a surprise party?

3. What steps can you take to impress a date?

The Topic Sentence

The topic sentence in a process paragraph includes the process you are describing and a controlling idea.

topic (process)   controlling idea

When you make a mosaic, there are several precautions you should take.

It is also possible to make a topic sentence that contains a map, or guide, to the details that you will present in your paragraph. To guide your readers, you can mention the main steps in your topic sentence.

topic   controlling idea

When you build a ceramic tile mosaic, have the proper safety equipment, tools, and workspace.

The Writer's Desk **Write Topic Sentences**

Write a topic sentence for each of the following topics. Your sentence should have a controlling idea that expresses the direction of the paragraph. Remember that the goal of the paragraph is to explain how to do something.

EXAMPLE:

Topic: How to find a mate

Topic sentence: *With careful preparation and screening, you can find a mate on the Internet.*

1. Topic: How to prepare for a move

   Topic sentence: _____

   _____

2. Topic: How to plan a surprise party

   Topic sentence: _____

   _____

3. Topic: How to impress a date

   Topic sentence: _____

   _____

The Supporting Ideas

When you write the supporting ideas, decide which steps your reader needs to take to complete the process. Explain each step in detail. Organize your steps chronologically. Remember to mention any necessary tools or supplies.

 **Give Steps, Not Examples**

When you explain how to do a process, describe each step. Do not simply list examples of the process.

How to Relax

List of Examples	Steps in the Process
Read a book.	Change into comfortable clothing.
Take a bath.	Do some deep breathing.
Go for a long walk.	Choose a good book.
Listen to soothing music.	Find a relaxing place to read.

A Process Paragraph Plan

When you write a process paragraph plan, decide how you will organize your plan, and make sure that you explain each step clearly. In the following paragraph plan, the writer uses emphatic order to describe the process.

TOPIC SENTENCE: **With careful preparation and screening, you can find a mate on the Internet.**

Step 1: Prepare by finding a viable dating site.
Details: — Ask friends about possible sites.
— Make sure the site targets people in your area.

Step 2: Write an interesting profile.
Details: — Use positive terms to describe yourself, such as *dynamic* and *energetic*.
— Get a friend or a professional to look over your profile.

Step 3: Screen replies carefully.
Details: — Choose your favorite responses.
— Invite friends to help you sort potential dates.

Step 4: Meet only in public places.
Details: — Consider meeting in the daytime, maybe in a coffee shop.
— Avoid alcohol as it can cloud judgment.

The Writer's Desk Develop Supporting Ideas

Choose one of the topic sentences that you wrote for the previous Writer's Desk, and write a detailed paragraph plan.

Topic sentence: _____

_____

Support 1: _____
Details: _____
_____

Support 2: _____
Details: _____
_____

Support 3: _____
Details: _____
_____

Support 4: _____
Details: _____
_____

The Writer's Desk **Write a Process Paragraph**

You have made a list of supporting ideas for a topic. Now write a process paragraph. After you finish writing, remember to revise and edit your paragraph.

The Writer's Room

Writing Activity 1: Topics

Write a process paragraph about one of the following topics.

General Topics

1. how to play a specific sport
2. how to discipline a small child
3. how to find an apartment
4. how to make friends
5. how to make a great cup of coffee

College and Work-Related Topics

6. how to use a particular machine
7. how to choose a college
8. how to dress for success
9. how to do a task in your workplace
10. how to keep a job

WRITING LINK

See the Writer's Rooms in the following grammar chapters for more process writing topics.

Chapter 6, Writer's Room topic 1 (page 129)
Chapter 10, Writer's Room topic 1 (page 197)
Chapter 22, Writer's Room topic 2 (page 326)
Chapter 28, Writer's Room topic 1 (page 395)

Writing Activity 2: Photo Writing

Examine the photo and think about processes that you can describe. For example, you might explain how to get along with coworkers, neighbors, or family members. Other ideas include how to make friends or how to do team work.

READING LINK

The following readings contain examples of process writing.

"How to Handle Conflict" by P. Gregory Smith (page 442)
"How to Remember Names" by Roger Seit (page 444)

> ✔ **PROCESS PARAGRAPH CHECKLIST**
>
> As you write your process paragraph, review the paragraph checklist on the inside back cover. Also, ask yourself the following questions.
>
> ☐ Does my topic sentence make a point about the process?
>
> ☐ Does my paragraph explain how to do something?
>
> ☐ Do I clearly explain each step in the process?
>
> ☐ Do I mention any supplies that my reader needs to complete the process?
>
> ☐ Do I use transitions to connect the steps in the process?

E) The Definition Paragraph

A **definition** tells you what something means. When you write a **definition paragraph,** you give your personal definition of a term or concept. Although you can define most terms in a few sentences, you may need to offer extended definitions for words that are particularly complex. For example, you can write a paragraph or even an entire book about the term *happiness.* The way that you interpret the term is unique, and you would bring your own opinions, experiences, and impressions to your definition paragraph.

PRACTICE 5

Read the paragraph and answer the questions that follow.

furtively: secretly and sneakily

Susan Boyle: a 2009 contestant on the reality TV program *Britain's Got Talent.*

We have moved from a pop culture to a peep culture. In pop culture, we turn on the TV, and celebrities entertain us with their performances. In peep culture, we **furtively** observe people's lives. Peep culture is reality TV, YouTube, MySpace, Facebook, Twitter, blogs, chat rooms, amateur porn, surveillance technology, cell phone texts, and more. Instead of getting our entertainment from scripted performances, we get our entertainment from unscripted, supposedly spontaneous peeping into other people's lives, including those of friends and family. **Susan Boyle** became an overnight celebrity because of peep culture. The entire world became obsessed with her after her transformation from a resident of a small Scottish town to a global celebrity. We liked her story and we peeped into her life. In many ways, her struggles and her breakdown will keep her story going. We have turned the spotlight on random regular people, and their lives fascinate us.

— Merril Mascarenhas

1. Underline the topic sentence. Be careful because it might not be the first sentence.

2. What is the writer defining? _____

3. Write your own definition of the term by summarizing the information in the paragraph.

   _____

   _____

4. The paragraph mentions Susan Boyle. Think of another example that could be added to the paragraph.

   _____

   _____

The Writer's Desk Exploring

Think about the following questions, and write down the first ideas that come to mind. Try to write two or three ideas for each topic.

EXAMPLE: What is *leet speak?*

   Computer language; uses numbers; hackers use it _____

1. What is *peer pressure?* _____

   _____

2. What is a *slob?* _____

   _____

3. What is a *gas guzzler?* _____

   _____

The Topic Sentence

In your **topic sentence,** indicate what you are defining and include a definition of the term. Look at the three ways to define a term.

- **Definition by synonym.** You can give a word that means the same thing as the term.

      term   +   synonyms
   Gratuitous means unnecessary or uncalled for.

- **Definition by negation.** Explain what the term is not, and then explain what it is.

        term   +   what it is not   +   what it is
   Sexual harassment is not harmless banter; it is intimidating and unwanted sexual attention.

- **Definition by category.** Decide what larger group the term belongs to, and then determine the unique characteristics that set the term apart from others in that category.

  term + category + detail

  A blogger is a writer who expresses his or her opinions in an Internet journal.

The Writer's Desk Write Topic Sentences

Write a topic sentence for each of the following topics. Your sentence should have a controlling idea that expresses the direction of the paragraph. Remember that the goal of the paragraph is to define something.

EXAMPLE:

    Topic: Leet speak

    Topic sentence: *Leet speak is not just a passing fad; it is a unique language used by computer users.*

1. Topic: Peer pressure

    Topic sentence: _____

    _____

2. Topic: A slob

    Topic sentence: _____

    _____

3. Topic: A gas guzzler

    Topic sentence: _____

    _____

The Supporting Ideas

A definition paragraph should include a complete definition of a term, and it should have adequate examples that support the definition. Remember to provide various types of support. Do not simply repeat the definition.

A Definition Paragraph Plan

When you write a definition paragraph plan, make sure that your details are valid and that they relate to the topic sentence.

TOPIC SENTENCE: **Leet speak is not just a passing fad; it is a unique language used by computer users.**

    Support 1: Leet speak is not a traditional language.
      Details: — not spoken or handwritten
            — needs a keyboard

Support 2: Like all languages, leet speak reflects the culture of the user.
    Details: — created by hackers to avoid detection
        — replaces letters with numbers
        — makes communicating on the Net faster

Support 3: Leet speak has pervaded cyberspace.
    Details: — A Web comic, *Megatokyo*, popularized leet speak.
        — Web site communities use leet speak to express excitement.
        — Web sites have dictionaries to translate between normal script and leet speak.

The Writer's Desk **Develop Supporting Ideas**

Choose one of the topic sentences that you wrote for the previous Writer's Desk, and write a detailed paragraph plan.

Topic sentence: _____

_____

Support 1: _____
   Details: _____

           _____

Support 2: _____
   Details: _____

           _____

Support 3: _____
   Details: _____

           _____

The Writer's Desk **Write a Definition Paragraph**

You have made a list of supporting ideas for a topic. Now write a definition paragraph. After you finish writing, remember to revise and edit your paragraph.

WRITING LINK

See the Writer's Rooms in the following grammar chapters for more definition writing topics.

Chapter 6, Writer's Room topic 2 (page 129)

Chapter 10, Writer's Room topic 2 (page 197)

Chapter 16, Writer's Room topic 1 (page 269)

Chapter 19, Writer's Room topic 2 (page 291)

Chapter 24, Writer's Room topic 2 (page 351)

Chapter 27, Writer's Room topic 2 (page 383)

READING LINK

Definition Essays
The following readings contain examples of definition writing.

"The Allure of Apple" by Juan Rodriquez (page 440)

"Meet the Zippies" by Thomas L. Friedman (page 446)

The Writer's Room

Writing Activity 1: Topics

Write a definition paragraph about one of the following topics.

General Topics

1. common sense
2. mall rats
3. road rage
4. a couch potato
5. a drama queen

College and Work-Related Topics

6. a golden handshake
7. hero worship
8. burnout
9. materialistic
10. an effective boss

Writing Activity 2: Photo Writing

What is a *nest egg?* Write a paragraph explaining the term.

✔ DEFINITION PARAGRAPH CHECKLIST

As you write your definition paragraph, review the paragraph checklist on the inside back cover. Also, ask yourself the following questions.

☐ Does my topic sentence contain a definition by synonym, negation, or category?

☐ Do all of my supporting sentences relate to the topic sentence?

☐ Do I use concise language in my definition?

☐ Do I include enough examples to help define the term?

F) The Comparison and Contrast Paragraph

You **compare** when you want to find similarities, and you **contrast** when you want to find differences. When writing a comparison and contrast paragraph, you prove a specific point by explaining how people, places, things, or ideas are the same or different. For example, you might compare two jobs that you have had, two different ways of disciplining, or two ideas about how to stimulate the national economy.

Before you write, you must make a decision about whether you will focus on similarities, differences, or both. As you explore your topic, it is a good idea to make a list of both similarities and differences. Later, you can use some of the ideas in your paragraph plan.

PRACTICE 6

Read the paragraph and answer the questions that follow.

> In the restaurant business, cooks and servers have the main positions, and some people say that cooks have a difficult job. <u>However, cooks have several advantages over servers.</u> First, cooks can get paid up to $15 an hour whereas servers earn the minimum wage and must depend on tips. If the cook has a bad day, he or she can snap at others. The server, on the other hand, has to remain polite and make sure that the guests are welcomed and treated warmly. When cooks mess up, their checks won't suffer, but servers cannot show stress or impatience because it directly affects their tips. Furthermore, the cleaning schedule is easier for a cook. At the end of the shift, the chef has to clean up only his or her work station. The server has to wait until the customers have all left and then clean the section and the side station. Sometimes the server has to clean a shelving area, which can take up to an hour. Most of the time, the silverware has to be rolled in a special napkin for the next day, which is the server's responsibility. Finally, after a long shift, cooks can keep their entire income and do not have to share with the others who helped them accomplish their job. Servers, however, have to give a percentage of their tips to the bartender and the busboy or busgirl. So although the cook is considered to be the harder worker in the restaurant business, it is the server who really deserves respect.
>
> — Tiffany Hines, student

1. Underline the topic sentence. Be careful because it may not be the first sentence.

2. List the key differences between the job of a cook and a server.

Cook	Server
_____	_____
_____	_____
_____	_____
_____	_____
_____	_____

The Writer's Desk Exploring

Think about the following questions, and write down the first ideas that come to mind. Try to write two or three ideas for each topic.

EXAMPLE: Compare two beautiful seasons.

Autumn	**Spring**
red and gold colors	*budding leaves and flowers*
days get shorter	*days get longer*
trees lose leaves	*trees turn green*

1. Compare two friends or family members.

Type 1: _____   Type 2: _____

_____   _____

_____   _____

_____   _____

2. Compare two different jobs that you have had.

Job 1: _____   Job 2: _____

_____   _____

_____   _____

_____   _____

3. Compare what you do on two different holidays. For example, you could compare Thanksgiving and Halloween.

Holiday 1: _____   Holiday 2: _____

_____   _____

_____   _____

_____   _____

The Topic Sentence

The topic sentence in a comparison and contrast paragraph indicates whether you are making comparisons, contrasts, or both. When you write a topic sentence, indicate what you are comparing or contrasting, and express a controlling idea. The following are examples of topic sentences for comparison and contrast paragraphs.

My brother and father argue a lot, but they have very similar personalities.

Topic (what is being compared):	father and brother
Controlling idea:	similar personalities

A cat is much easier to care for than a dog.

Topic:	cats and dogs
Controlling idea:	cats are easier to care for

The Writer's Desk **Write Topic Sentences**

Write a topic sentence for each of the following topics. Your sentence should have a controlling idea that expresses the direction of the paragraph.

EXAMPLE:

> Topic: Two seasons
>
> Topic sentence: *Although both seasons are beautiful, the spring is a more hopeful time than the fall.*

1. Topic: Two friends or family members

   Topic sentence: _____

   _____

2. Topic: Two jobs

   Topic sentence: _____

   _____

3. Topic: Two holidays

   Topic sentence: _____

   _____

The Supporting Ideas

In a comparison and contrast paragraph, you can develop your supporting ideas in two different ways.

Point-by-Point Development

To develop a topic point by point, you look at similarities or differences by going back and forth from one side to the other.

Topic-by-Topic Development

To develop your ideas topic by topic, you discuss one topic in detail, and then you discuss the other topic in detail. The next plans are for a paragraph comparing two dogs.

TOPIC SENTENCE: **My two dogs are different in every way.**

Point-by-Point Comparison
- **Support 1:** Appearance
  - — Dog A
  - — Dog B
- **Support 2:** Skills
  - — Dog A
  - — Dog B
- **Support 3:** Temperament
  - — Dog A
  - — Dog B

Topic-by-Topic Comparison
- **Dog A:** — Appearance
  - — Skills
  - — Temperament
- **Dog B:** — Appearance
  - — Skills
  - — Temperament

A Comparison and Contrast Paragraph Plan

When you write a comparison and contrast paragraph plan, decide which pattern you will follow: point by point or topic by topic. Then add some details.

TOPIC SENTENCE: **Although both seasons are beautiful, spring is a more hopeful time than fall.**

Support 1:   Fall is beautiful.
Details: — crisp fresh air
          — gold, orange, and red leaves

Support 2:   Autumn becomes a depressing period.
Details: — colder winds and bare tree branches
          — awareness of winter's arrival

Support 3:   Spring is also a lovely time.
Details: — budding flowers and leaves
          — squirrels and birds return

Support 4:   Spring is a time of hope and renewal.
Details: — nature comes back to life
          — knowledge of warmer days to come

The Writer's Desk Develop Supporting Ideas

Choose one of the topic sentences that you wrote for the previous Writer's Desk, and write a detailed paragraph plan.

Topic sentence: _____

_____

Support 1: _____

Details: _____

_____

Support 2: _____

Details: _____

_____

Support 3: _____

Details: _____

_____

Support 4: _____

Details: _____

_____

The Writer's Desk **Write a Comparison and Contrast Paragraph**

You have made a list of supporting ideas for a topic. Now write a comparison and contrast paragraph. After you finish writing, remember to revise and edit your paragraph.

 The Writer's Room

Writing Activity 1: Topics

Write a comparison and contrast paragraph about one of the following topics.

General Topics

1. parental discipline in the past versus discipline today
2. two television shows
3. two neighborhoods
4. two famous people
5. two youth subcultures

College and Work-Related Topics

6. expectations about college and the reality of college
7. a small school or college and a large school or college
8. two different coworkers
9. working alone and working with others
10. two different bosses

WRITING LINK

See the Writer's Rooms in the following grammar chapters for more comparison and contrast writing topics.

Chapter 8, Writer's Room topic 2 (page 161)
Chapter 12, Writer's Room topic 2 (page 222)
Chapter 14, Writer's Room topic 2 (page 245)
Chapter 18, Writer's Room topic 1 (page 285)
Chapter 20, Writer's Room topic 2 (page 301)
Chapter 28, Writer's Room topic 2 (page 395)

Writing Activity 2: Photo Writing

Examine the photo, and think about things that you could compare and contrast. Some ideas might be fast food versus healthy food, street vendors versus restaurants, two restaurants, or two meals. Then write a comparison and contrast paragraph.

READING LINK

The following readings use comparison and contrast writing.

"The New Addiction" by Josh Freed (page 412)
"The Zoo Life" by Yann Martel (page 434)

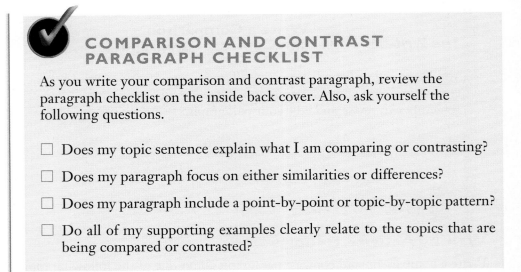

COMPARISON AND CONTRAST PARAGRAPH CHECKLIST

As you write your comparison and contrast paragraph, review the paragraph checklist on the inside back cover. Also, ask yourself the following questions.

☐ Does my topic sentence explain what I am comparing or contrasting?

☐ Does my paragraph focus on either similarities or differences?

☐ Does my paragraph include a point-by-point or topic-by-topic pattern?

☐ Do all of my supporting examples clearly relate to the topics that are being compared or contrasted?

G) The Cause and Effect Paragraph

Cause and effect writing explains why an event happened or what the consequences of such an event were. You often analyze the causes or effects of something. You may worry about what causes your mate to behave in a certain manner, or you may wonder about the effects of fast food on your health.

Because a paragraph is not very long, it is best to focus on either causes or effects. If you do decide to focus on both causes and effects, make sure that your topic sentence expresses your purpose to the reader.

PRACTICE 7

Read the paragraph and answer the questions that follow.

It is quite common to find university students who wait until the last minute to write a term paper or to study for an exam. However, procrastination should be avoided because it has detrimental effects on students' health and well being. First, students who procrastinate are doomed to suffer lower marks. Instead of taking the time to carefully research the subject, go over written notes, draft an outline, write a draft, and revise and edit it, students do **cursory** research and do not bother preparing an outline. The draft that results from this process is sloppy and filled with logical and grammatical errors, which leads to a poor grade. Furthermore, there are emotional **hindrances** generated by the pressured nature of rushed work. The sense of a looming deadline causes increased feelings of stress in the procrastinating student, which affects his or her ability to concentrate. Consistent procrastinating over schoolwork combined with other everyday stresses can cause a student to break down. Finally, procrastinating students can damage their physical health. For example, many students stay up all night cramming for exams. They do not get adequate sleep, which impairs judgment and harms the body. Therefore, procrastinating can diminish a student's work, physical condition, mental condition, and academic future.

—Arthur Carlyle, student

cursory: superficial, brief

hindrances: obstacles

1. Underline the topic sentence. Be careful as it may not be the first sentence in the paragraph.

2. Does the paragraph focus on causes or effects? _____

3. Who is the audience? _____

4. Circle three transitional words or phrases that lead the reader from one point to the next.

5. Using your own words, list the three causes or effects.

_____

_____

_____

The Writer's Desk **Exploring**

Write some possible causes and effects for the following topics. Think of two or three ideas for each topic. Then choose whether you would rather write about causes or effects.

EXAMPLE: Why do some parents spoil their children, and how does being spoiled affect the children?

Causes	Effects
want child to like them	*children don't appreciate material*
don't have parenting skills	*goods*
can't say no	*hurts parent-child relationship*
	children have no patience

Focus on: *Causes*

1. Why do people marry, and how does marriage affect people's lives?

Cause	Effects
_____	_____
_____	_____
_____	_____
_____	_____

Focus on: _____

2. What are some of the causes and effects of credit card debt?

Causes	Effects
_____	_____
_____	_____
_____	_____
_____	_____

Focus on: _____

3. Why do people litter? What are the effects of littering?

Causes   **Effects**

_____   _____

_____   _____

_____   _____

_____   _____

Focus on: _____

The Topic Sentence

The topic sentence in a cause and effect paragraph must clearly demonstrate whether the focus is on causes, effects, or both.

topic   controlling idea (causes)
I buy fast food for many reasons.

topic   controlling idea (effects)
Fast food has had negative effects on my health.

topic   controlling idea (causes and effects)
Fast food, which I eat for many reasons, has had some negative effects on my health.

> ### Hint   Do Not Confuse *Affect* and *Effect*
>
> *Affect* is a verb, and *effect* is a noun. *Affect* (verb) means "to influence or change," and *effect* (noun) means "the result."
>
> verb
> Secondhand smoke can affect children's health.
>
> noun
> Secondhand smoke has many negative effects on children's health.

The Writer's Desk   Write Topic Sentences

Write a topic sentence for each of the following topics. Your sentence should have a controlling idea that expresses the direction of the paragraph.

EXAMPLE:

Topic: Spoiled children

Topic sentence: *Parents spoil their children for several reasons.*

1. Topic: Marriage

   Topic sentence: _____

   _____

2. Topic: Credit card debt

   Topic sentence: _____

   _____

3. Topic: Littering

   Topic sentence: _____

   _____

The Supporting Ideas

After you have developed an effective topic sentence, generate supporting ideas. For a cause and effect paragraph, think of examples that clearly show the causes or effects. Then arrange your examples in emphatic order. Emphatic order means that you can place your examples from the most to the least important or from the least to the most important.

A Cause and Effect Paragraph Plan

When you write a cause and effect paragraph plan, think about the order of your ideas. List details under each supporting idea.

TOPIC SENTENCE:	<u>Parents spoil their children for many reasons.</u>
Support 1:	People are not educated about good parenting skills.
Details:	— Schools do not teach how to be a good parent.
	— Some people may follow the habits of their own parents.
Support 2:	They want to be the child's friend instead of an authority figure.
Details:	— Parents won't say no.
	— Parents want to be liked.
Support 3:	They believe that children should have the best things in life.
Details:	— Parents think they are doing their children a favor by buying toys, video games, and so on.
	— They feel that there is nothing wrong with instant gratification.
Support 4:	Some parents are motivated by guilt to overspend on their children.
Details:	— They spend very little time with their children.
	— Parents buy gifts, unnecessary clothing, and so on.

The Writer's Desk **Develop Supporting Ideas**

Choose one of the topic sentences that you wrote for the previous Writer's Desk, and write a detailed paragraph plan.

Topic sentence: _____

_____

Support 1: _____

Details: _____

_____

Support 2: _____

Details: _____

_____

Support 3: _____

Details: _____

_____

Support 4: _____

Details: _____

_____

The Writer's Desk **Write a Cause and Effect Paragraph**

You have made a list of supporting ideas for a topic. Now write a cause and effect paragraph. After you finish writing, remember to revise and edit your paragraph.

The Writer's Room

Writing Activity 1: Topics

Write a cause and effect paragraph about one of the following topics. As you consider each topic, think about both causes and effects.

WRITING LINK

See the Writer's Rooms in the following grammar chapters for more cause and effect writing topics.

Chapter 7, Writer's Room topic 1 (page 148)
Chapter 13, Writer's Room topic 1 (page 238)
Chapter 22, Writer's Room topic 3 (page 326)
Chapter 24, Writer's Room topic 1 (page 350)
Chapter 25, Writer's Room topic 1 (page 361)

General Topics

1. losing a good friend
2. driving too fast
3. having a pet
4. having plastic surgery
5. moving to a new country

College and Work-Related Topics

6. participating in team sports
7. having workplace stress
8. achieving good grades
9. working with a friend, mate, or spouse
10. working nights

Writing Activity 2: Photo Writing

Examine the photo. Consider how your clothing choices affect the way that others judge you.

READING LINK

The following readings use cause and effect writing.

"Fat Chance" by Dorothy Nixon (page 414)
"Is It Love or a Trick?" by Jon Katz (page 436)

CAUSE AND EFFECT PARAGRAPH CHECKLIST

As you write your cause and effect paragraph, review the paragraph checklist on the inside back cover. Also, ask yourself the following questions.

☐ Does my topic sentence indicate clearly that my paragraph focuses on causes, effects, or both?

☐ Do I have adequate supporting examples for causes and/or effects?

☐ Do I make logical and valid points?

☐ Do I use the terms *effect* and *affect* correctly?

H) The Classification Paragraph

In a **classification paragraph**, you sort a subject into more understandable categories. Each of the categories must be part of a larger group, yet they must also be distinct. For example, you might write a paragraph about different categories of housework that must be done in the kitchen, bathroom, and living room, or you could divide the topic into chores done by the children, parents, and grandparents.

To find a topic for a classification paragraph, think of something that can be sorted into different groups. Also, determine a reason for classifying the items. When you are planning your ideas for a classification paragraph, remember two points:

1. **Use a common classification principle. A classification principle** is the overall method that you use to sort the subject into categories. To find the classification principle, think about one common characteristic that unites

the different categories. For example, if your subject is "relationships," your classification principle might be any of the following:

- types of annoying dates
- ways to meet people
- dating alone, with another couple, or in groups
- types of couples

2. **Sort the subject into distinct categories.** A classification paragraph should have two or more categories.

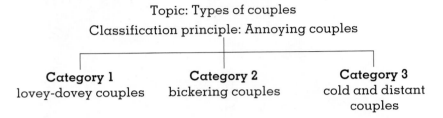

Topic: Types of couples

Classification principle: Annoying couples

Category 1	Category 2	Category 3
lovey-dovey couples	bickering couples	cold and distant couples

PRACTICE 8

Read the paragraph and answer the questions that follow.

> Violations of the criminal law can be of many different types and can vary in severity. Felonies are the most serious crimes. This category includes acts such as murder, rape, aggravated assault, robbery involving a weapon, and arson. Felons can be sentenced to death or have their property confiscated. A misdemeanor is a less serious crime and consists of an offense such as petty theft, disorderly conduct, or disturbing the peace. It also includes simple assault, in which the victim suffers no serious injury and in which none was intended. In general, misdemeanors can be thought of as a crime punishable by a year or less in prison. A third category of crime is the inchoate offense. Inchoate means "incomplete or partial," so inchoate offenses are those that have not yet been fully carried out. Sometimes an offender is not able to complete a crime. A burglar, for instance, may drop his tools and run if interrupted. Conspiracies are another type of inchoate offense. For example, a woman who intends to kill her husband may make a phone call to find a hit man. The call is evidence of her intent and can result in her imprisonment.
>
> —Frank Schmalleger, excerpt from *Criminal Justice Today*

1. Underline the topic sentence.

2. What are the three categories?

   _____ _____ _____

3. What is the classification principle? In other words, how are the three categories of crime distinct?

   _____

4. The writer uses emphatic order. How are the crimes listed?
   a. most to least serious   b. least to most serious

The Writer's Desk **Exploring**

Think about the following questions, and write down the first ideas that come to mind. Try to write two or three ideas for each topic.

EXAMPLE:

What are some types of financial personalities?

cheapskates, binge spenders, sensible spenders, and squanderers

1. What are some types of pleasant smells?

_____

_____

2. What are some categories of eaters?

_____

_____

3. What are some different types of service workers?

_____

_____

The Topic Sentence

The topic sentence in a classification paragraph clearly indicates what a writer will classify. It also includes the controlling idea, which is the classification principle that the writer will use.

Several types of reality shows try to manipulate viewers.

Topic: reality shows
Classification principle: types that manipulate viewers

You can also mention the types of categories in your topic sentence.

The most beautiful scenes in nature are waterfalls, pine forests, and desert landscapes.

Topic: scenes in nature
Classification principle: types of beautiful scenes

The Writer's Desk **Write Topic Sentences**

Write a topic sentence for each of the following topics (on page 86). Your sentence should have a controlling idea that expresses the categories you will develop.

EXAMPLE:

Topic: Financial personalities

Topic Sentence: *The three types of people with irrational spending habits are cheapskates, binge spenders, and squanderers.*

1. Topic: Pleasant smells

   Topic sentence: _____

   _____

2. Topic: Eaters

   Topic sentence: _____

   _____

3. Topic: Service workers

   Topic sentence: _____

   _____

The Supporting Ideas

After you have developed an effective topic sentence, generate supporting ideas. In a classification paragraph, you can list details about each of your categories.

 **Categories Should Not Overlap**

When sorting a topic into categories, make sure that the categories do not overlap. For example, you would not classify *healthy snacks* into vegetables, cheese, and carrots because carrots fall into the vegetable category. Each category should be distinct.

A Classification Paragraph Plan

When you write a classification plan, think of how you will organize your categories. Include different examples in each category.

TOPIC SENTENCE: **The three types of people with irrational spending habits are cheapskates, binge spenders, and squanderers.**

Support 1: Cheapskates deprive themselves and others.
Details: — never buy nice clothing
— skimp on quality of food
— never treat others

Support 2: Binge spenders save most of the time but then overspend on crazy items.
Details: — don't make logical choices
— might skimp on meals but then pay a lot for a car
— buy cheap suits but spend too much on shoes

Support 3: The most self-destructive spender is the squanderer.
Details: — might use up entire paycheck on entertainment
— can't make it to the end of the month without going broke
— constantly pays interest on loans and credit cards

Make a Classification Chart

Another way to visualize your categories and your supporting ideas is to make a detailed classification chart. Break down the main topic into several categories, and then give details about each category. A classification chart is a visual representation of your plan.

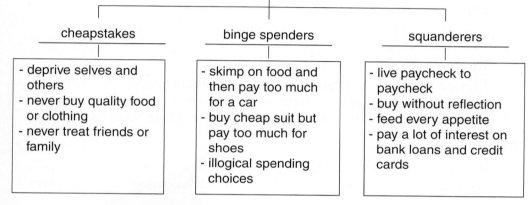

Topic sentence: The three types of people with irriational spending habits are cheapskates, binge spenders, and squanderers.

cheapstakes	binge spenders	squanderers
- deprive selves and others - never buy quality food or clothing - never treat friends or family	- skimp on food and then pay too much for a car - buy cheap suit but pay too much for shoes - illogical spending choices	- live paycheck to paycheck - buy without reflection - feed every appetite - pay a lot of interest on bank loans and credit cards

The Writer's Desk Develop Supporting Ideas

Choose one of the topic sentences that you wrote for the previous Writer's Desk, and write a detailed paragraph plan. Or, if you prefer, you could make a visual classification chart on a separate sheet of paper.

Topic sentence: _____

_____

Support 1: _____
Details: _____

_____

Support 2: _____
Details: _____

_____

Support 3: _____
Details: _____

_____

The Writer's Room

Writing Activity 1: Topics

Choose any of the following topics, or choose your own topic, and write a classification paragraph.

General Topics

Types of . . .

1. collectors
2. problems in a relationship
3. unhealthy foods
4. purses
5. inexpensive hobbies

College and Work-Related Topics

Types of . . .

6. uniforms
7. college students
8. workplaces
9. communicators
10. stress-coping strategies

Writing Activity 2: Photo Writing

Examine this photo, and think about some classification topics. For example, you might discuss types of pets, types of pet owners, or types of entertainment involving animals. Then write a classification paragraph about the photo..

WRITING LINK

See the Writer's Room in the following grammar chapters for more classification writing topics.

Chapter 8, Writer's Room topic 1 (page 161)
Chapter 26, Writer's Room topic 2 (page 374)
Chapter 27, Writer's Room topic 1 (page 383)

READING LINK

Classification

The following reading uses classification writing.

"What's Your Humor Style?" by Louise Dobson (page 418)

✔ CLASSIFICATION PARAGRAPH CHECKLIST

As you write your classification paragraph, review the checklist on the inside back cover. Also, ask yourself the following questions.

☐ Does my topic sentence explain the categories that will be discussed?

☐ Do I use a common classification principle to unite the various items?

☐ Do I offer sufficient details to explain each category?

☐ Do I arrange the categories in a logical manner?

☐ Does all of the supporting information relate to the categories that are being discussed?

☐ Do I include categories that do not overlap?

I) The Argument Paragraph

In an **argument paragraph**, you take a position on an issue, and you try to defend your position. For example, you might argue that taxes are too high, that a restaurant is excellent, or that a certain breed of dog should be banned.

Although some people may disagree with you, try to be direct in argument writing. State your point of view clearly and unapologetically.

PRACTICE 9

Read the next paragraph and answer the questions that follow.

According to the Children's Defense Fund Action Council, about 3,300 children and teens are killed by gunfire in the United States every year, and close to 15,000 children are injured by firearms. To stem the tide of gun-related deaths and injuries, public schools should teach gun-safety courses. First, guns are **prevalent** in our society, and we cannot stop children from being fascinated with them. Even if parents have no guns in their homes, their children could come across a gun in a friend's home or on the street. Second, children who understand the danger of guns will not be so attracted to weapons. If a child is permitted to hold a gun, feel its kick, hear its deafening blast, and witness its destructiveness, he or she will realize how hazardous a gun is. Furthermore, if children know how to use guns responsibly, there will be fewer gun accidents. An uninformed child may not realize that a gun is loaded or that the safety catch is off. After taking a gun-safety course, that same child would immediately recognize that a gun is ready to fire and extremely dangerous. If children are not properly educated about gun use, the numbers of accidental deaths and injuries will rise.

—Dean Cochrane, student

prevalent: widespread

1. Underline the topic sentence.

2. How does the author prove that there is a problem? _____
   _____
   _____
   _____

3. What are the three main arguments? _____
   _____
   _____
   _____
   _____

4. What are some transitional expressions that the writer uses? _____
   _____

5. How does the writer conclude his paragraph?
   a. A prediction   b. A quotation   c. A suggestion

The Writer's Desk **Exploring**

Think about the following questions, and write down the first ideas that come to mind. Try to write two or three ideas for each topic.

EXAMPLE: What are the benefits or disadvantages of daycare?

I don't know. Bad things are kids get more viruses. But many parents

have no choice and must work.

1. Should the custom of tipping for service be abolished? Why or why not?

_____

_____

_____

2. Did your high school have adequate supplies and equipment? Evaluate a school that you went to.

_____

_____

_____

3. Are social networking sites helpful or harmful? Explain your answer.

_____

_____

_____

The Topic Sentence

The **topic sentence** in an argument paragraph mentions the subject and a debatable point of view about the subject. You can use *should, must,* or *ought to* in your topic sentence.

<u>Our police forces should not use</u> **racial profiling.**

controlling idea — topic (issue)

Your topic sentence can further guide your readers by listing the specific arguments you will make in the paragraph.

<u>Parents should not</u> **spank their children** because spanking is a violent act,

controlling idea — topic (issue) — argument 1

it scares children, and it teaches children to become violent.

argument 2 — argument 3

 **Write a Debatable Topic Sentence**

Your topic sentence should be a debatable statement. It should not be a fact or a statement of opinion.

Fact:	Some breeds of dogs can be aggressive.
	(Who can argue with that point?)
Opinion:	I think that pit bulls should be banned.
	(This is a statement of opinion. Nobody can deny that you want pit bulls to be banned. Do not use phrases such as *In my opinion, I think,* or *I believe* in your topic sentence.)
Argument:	Pit bulls should be banned.
	(This statement is debatable.)

The Writer's Desk **Write Topic Sentences**

Write a topic sentence for each of the following topics. Your sentence should have a controlling idea that expresses the direction of the paragraph. Remember that the goal of the paragraph is to express your viewpoint.

EXAMPLE:

Topic: Value of daycare

Topic sentence: *Daycare has benefits for both parents and children.*

1. Topic: Tipping for service

   Topic sentence: _____

   _____

2. Topic: Your high school's resources

   Topic sentence: _____

   _____

3. Topic: The value of social networking sites

   Topic sentence: _____

   _____

The Supporting Ideas

In the body of your paragraph, give convincing supporting arguments. Try to use several types of supporting evidence such as anecdotes, facts and statistics, and answers to the opposition.

- **Anecdotes** are specific experiences or stories that support your point of view.
- **Facts** are statements that can be verified in some way. **Statistics** are a type of fact. When you use a fact, make sure that your source is reliable.
- Think about your opponents' arguments, and provide **answers to the opposition** in response to their arguments.

 **Avoid Circular Reasoning**

Circular reasoning means that a paragraph restates its main point in various ways but does not provide supporting details. Avoid it by offering separate supporting ideas and precise examples.

Circular

Film actors, who lead decadent lives, should not earn huge salaries because so many average people struggle. Many ordinary folks work long hours and have trouble making ends meet. Some actors work only a few months, earn millions, and then buy ridiculous luxury items. They lose touch with reality. Film studios should cut actors' high salaries and then disburse the remaining amount to people who really need the money.

Improved

Film actors, who often lead decadent lives, should not earn huge salaries while so many average people struggle. Many ordinary folks, **such as teachers and nurses,** work long hours and have trouble making ends meet. **Yet, the actor Brad Pitt's $20-million-per-movie salary is more than the combined wages of a small city's police department.** Also, some actors lose touch with reality. **Consider the difference between John Travolta, who flies a private jet, and a caregiver like Luisa Moreno, who spends $18.40 a day commuting on public buses. And, in a nation with so much homelessness, the actor Johnny Depp owns an entire island in addition to several houses.** Film studios should cut actors' high salaries and then disburse the remaining amount to people who really need the money.

An Argument Paragraph Plan

When you write an argument paragraph plan, think about how you will organize your arguments. If possible, include different types of supporting evidence: facts, statistics, anecdotes, and answers to the opposition.

TOPIC SENTENCE: **Daycare has benefits for both parents and children.**

Support 1: Many parents need to work while their children are young.
Details:
— poor economy
— must pay for necessities like food and shelter
— daycare workers watch the children while parents earn a living

Support 2: Children learn some basic skills.
Details:
— learn the alphabet
— learn to count and learn numbers
— get good preparation for school

Support 3: Daycare can help children's mental and physical development.
Details:
— early exposure to viruses results in stronger immune systems
— learn to share and develop self-control
— overcome separation anxiety and become more independent

The Writer's Desk **Develop Supporting Ideas**

Choose one of the topic sentences that you wrote for the previous Writer's Desk, and write a paragraph plan. Include supporting arguments, and list a detail for each argument.

Topic sentence: _____

_____

Support 1: _____

Details: _____

_____

Support 2: _____

Details: _____

_____

Support 3: _____

Details: _____

_____

Support 4: _____

Details: _____

_____

The Writer's Desk **Write an Argument Paragraph**

You have made a list of supporting ideas for a topic. Now write an argument paragraph. After you finish writing, remember to revise and edit your paragraph.

 The Writer's Room

Writing Activity 1: Topics

Write an argument paragraph about one of the following topics. Remember to narrow your topic and to follow the writing process.

WRITING LINK

See the Writer's Rooms in the following grammar chapters for more argument writing topics.

Chapter 7, Writer's Room topic 2 (page 148)
Chapter 13, Writer's Room topic 2 (page 238)
Chapter 16, Writer's Room topic 2 (page 270)
Chapter 17, Writer's Room topic 2 (page 276)
Chapter 18, Writer's Room topic 2 (page 285)
Chapter 20, Writer's Room topic 2 (page 301)
Chapter 23, Writer's Room topic 2 (page 337)
Chapter 25, Writer's Room topic 2 (page 361)

READING LINK

The following readings use argument writing.

"The Cult of Emaciation" by Ben Barry (page 423)
"Shopping for Religion" by Ellen Goodman (page 426)

General Topics

1. length of compulsory schooling
2. watching too much television
3. overscheduling children
4. right to privacy for politicians or celebrities
5. teenage curfew

College and Work-Related Topics

6. an unfair college rule
7. work that is not appreciated
8. compulsory art courses in college
9. vending machines in schools
10. compulsory voting

Writing Activity 2: Photo Writing

Write an argument paragraph explaining your views about dieting.

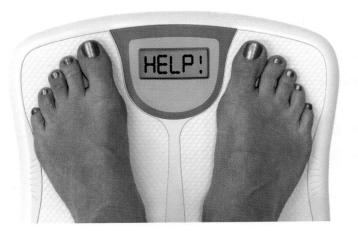

✔ ARGUMENT PARAGRAPH CHECKLIST

As you write your argument paragraph, review the paragraph checklist on the inside back cover. Also, ask yourself the following questions.

☐ Does my topic sentence clearly state my position on the issue?

☐ Do I support my position with facts, statistics, anecdotes, or answers to the opposition?

☐ Do my supporting arguments provide evidence that directly supports the topic sentence?

mywritinglab   To check your progress in meeting this chapter's objectives, log in to **www.mywritinglab.com**, go to the **Study Plan** tab, click on **The Writing Process** and choose **Paragraph Patterns** from the list of subtopics. Read and view the resources in the **Review Materials** section, and then complete the **Recall, Apply,** and **Write** sets in the **Activities** section.

Writing the Essay

A skyscraper is supported by columns of steel and concrete. In the same way, an essay is a sturdy structure that is supported by a strong thesis statement and solid body paragraphs.

> *Words are tools that automatically carve concepts out of experience.*
>
> —Julian Sorrell Huxley (1887–1975)
> *British biologist*

EXPLORING

Exploring the Essay

An **essay** is a series of paragraphs that supports one central idea. It is divided into three parts: an **introduction**, a **body**, and a **conclusion**. There is no perfect length for an essay. Some instructors prefer five-paragraph essays, and others may ask for two- or three-page essays. The important thing to remember is that all essays, regardless of length, have certain features: the introductory paragraph introduces the essay's thesis, the body paragraphs provide support for the thesis, and the concluding paragraph brings the essay to a satisfactory close.

Review the examples on pages 96 and 97 to see how different types of sentences and paragraphs can form an essay.

The Sentence

A **sentence** always has a subject and a verb and expresses a complete thought.

> People with bad habits make a negative impression on others.

The Paragraph

A **topic sentence** introduces the subject of a paragraph and shows the writer's attitude toward its subject.

The **body** of a paragraph contains details that support its topic sentence.

A paragraph ends with a **concluding sentence.**

> People with bad habits make a negative impression on others. Some individuals display bad habits when interacting with others, such as swearing constantly. Moreover, a person with bad personal hygiene does not win many friends. Also, a person who does not take care of his health has a serious bad habit. Everybody should work toward a little self-improvement.

The Essay

An **introduction** engages the reader's interest and contains a **thesis statement.**

> People with bad habits make a negative impression on others.

Body paragraphs support the main idea of an essay.

> First, some people repeatedly do inconsiderate actions.

> Moreover, a person who has bad personal hygiene does not win many friends.

> Furthermore, a person who does not take care of his or her health has a serious bad habit.

A **conclusion** reemphasizes the main idea (thesis) and restates the main points of an essay. It brings an essay to a satisfactory close.

A concluding paragraph in the essay ends with a **concluding statement.**

> Everybody should work toward a little self-improvement.

The Essay's Structure

Each body paragraph begins with a topic sentence.

The introductory paragraph presents the essay's topic and contains its thesis statement.

The title gives a hint about the essay's topic.

The thesis statement contains the essay's topic and its controlling idea.

Bad Habits

Who in the world doesn't have any bad habits? It is part of every human being in the world. Habits are actions that people are so used to doing that they keep on doing them again and again, sometimes without noticing. Bad habits are automatic actions that are undesirable; people should avoid doing them. People with bad habits make a negative impression on others.

First, some people repeatedly do inconsiderate actions. For instance, those who constantly swear do not think about the effects of their words on others. My brother Mike uses four-letter words which make me uncomfortable. Also, those who interrupt are disrespectful. They do not value the opinions of others. Finally, people who are late for appointments show a lack of consideration. My best friend Terrel often makes me wait for him, and it hurts our relationship. By being discourteous, a person can lose friends.

Moreover, a person who has bad personal hygiene does not win many friends. People who never wash their hands after going to the bathroom are a good case in point. A person who drinks directly from the milk or juice carton instead of using a glass sets a poor example. It is also very unpleasant to be around people who do not shower regularly or brush their teeth twice a day.

Furthermore, a person who does not take care of his or her health has a serious bad habit. Many teenagers spend too much time in front of their computer screen; they don't move. They certainly don't practice sports. Some people don't take care of their bodies because they smoke or take drugs. Also, some people don't eat nutritious foods or get enough sleep, both of which are essential for good health.

The more people display bad habits, the more they create a negative image of themselves. They also set a bad example for family and friends. Of course, nobody is perfect. But that does not mean that people should maintain negative characteristics. The best way to get rid of a bad habit is to have the will to make a change in lifestyle. Everybody should work towards a little self-improvement.

—*Renaud Allard, student*

The concluding paragraph brings the essay to a satisfactory close.

Each body paragraph contains details that support the thesis statement.

Explore Topics

When you are planning your essay, consider your topic, audience, and purpose. Your **topic** is whom or what you are writing about. Your **audience** is your intended reader, and your **purpose** is your reason for writing. Do you hope to entertain, inform, or persuade the reader?

Narrowing the Topic

You may need to narrow your topic (make it more specific) to ensure that it suits your purpose for writing and fits the size of the assignment. To narrow your topic, you can use some exploring methods, such as questioning (asking and answering questions) or brainstorming (jotting a rough list of ideas that come to mind). These strategies are explained in more detail in Chapter 1.

WILLIAM'S LIST TO NARROW THE TOPIC

Student writer William Sing used brainstorming and questioning to narrow his broad topic, "education."

- Coed schools versus single-sex schools
- Qualities of a good teacher
- Extracurricular activities
- Prayer in public schools
- Year-round schooling
- Should private schools be abolished?
- Bullying
- Is there too much emphasis on high school sports?
- Why do students drop out?

The Writer's Desk **Narrow the Topic**

Each of the following topics is very broad. Practice narrowing each topic.

EXAMPLE:

Foreign cultures: *traveling to another country*

learning a foreign language

multiculturalism in the United States

1. Work: _____

_____

_____

_____

2. Entertainment: _____

_____

_____

3. Housing: _____

_____

_____

_____

DEVELOPING

The Thesis Statement

Once you have narrowed the topic of your essay, it is important to state your topic clearly in one sentence. Like the topic sentence in a paragraph, the **thesis statement** introduces what the essay is about and arouses the interest of the reader by making a point about the topic.

Characteristics of a Good Thesis Statement

A thesis statement has the following characteristics.

- It expresses the main topic of the essay.
- It contains a controlling idea.
- It is a complete sentence that usually appears in an essay's introductory paragraph.

       topic   controlling idea

Credit card fraud is a serious problem.

      controlling idea   topic

The public has the right to know about **the scandalous private lives of politicians.**

Writing an Effective Thesis Statement

When you develop your thesis statement, ask yourself the following questions.

1. **Is my thesis statement a complete statement that has a controlling idea?**

   Your thesis statement should always reveal a complete thought and make a point about the topic. It should not simply announce the topic.

Incomplete:	Campus drinking.
	(This is not a complete statement. A complete sentence has both a subject and a verb.)
Announcement:	I will write about campus drinking.
	(This announces the topic but says nothing relevant about the topic. Do not use expressions such as *I will write about* or *My topic is.*)
Thesis statement:	Binge drinking is a serious problem on college campuses.

2. **Does my thesis statement make a valid and supportable point?**

Your thesis statement should express a valid point that you can support with details. It should not be a vaguely worded statement, and it should not be a highly questionable generalization.

Vague:	Politicians spend too much money.
	(Which politicians? What do they spend it on?)
Invalid point:	Politicians are liars.
	(Is this really true for all politicians? This generalization might be difficult to prove.)
Thesis statement:	Our mayor has spent too much money on renovations to his office.

> ⟨*Hint*⟩ **Give Specific Details**
>
> Make sure that your thesis statement is very clear. You should give enough details to make it interesting. Your instructor may want you to guide the reader through your main points. You can do this by including specific points that you will later argue in the body of your essay.
>
> My years in high school taught me to stand up for myself, to focus on my goals, and to be an open-minded person.

PRACTICE I

Identify why each of the following thesis statements is not effective. There may be more than one reason. Then revise each statement.

Announces   Incomplete   Invalid   Vague

EXAMPLE:

In this essay, I will discuss hazing in colleges.

Problem:	*Announces*
Revised sentence:	*Colleges should severely punish students who organize or participate in hazing events.*

1. Our government is good.
   Problem: _____
   Revised statement: _____
   _____

2. Road rage.
   Problem: _____
   Revised statement: _____
   _____

3. I am going to write about beauty pageants.
   Problem: _____
   Revised statement: _____
   _____

4. Traditional marriage is outdated.
   Problem: _____
   Revised statement: _____
   _____

5. Compensation for victims of crime.
   Problem: _____
   Revised statement: _____
   _____

The Writer's Desk Write Thesis Statements

For each item, choose a narrowed topic from the previous Writer's Desk on pages 98–99. Then write an interesting thesis statement. Remember that each thesis statement should contain a controlling idea.

EXAMPLE:

Topic: **Foreign cultures**

Narrowed topic: *Learning a foreign language*

Thesis statement: *People have many advantages when they learn a foreign language.*

1. Topic: Work
   Narrowed topic: _____
   Thesis statement: _____
   _____

2. Topic: Entertainment

   Narrowed topic: _____

   Thesis statement: _____

   _____

3. Topic: Housing

   Narrowed topic: _____

   Thesis statement: _____

   _____

The Supporting Ideas

The thesis statement expresses the main idea of the entire essay. In the illustration below, you can see how topic sentences relate to the thesis statement and how details support the topic sentences. Every idea in the essay is unified and supports the thesis.

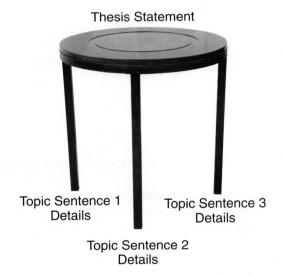

Thesis Statement

Topic Sentence 1
Details

Topic Sentence 2
Details

Topic Sentence 3
Details

Generating Supporting Ideas

To generate ideas for the body paragraphs, you can use exploring strategies such as brainstorming, clustering, or freewriting. Come up with any ideas that can support your thesis statement.

BEATRICE'S SUPPORTING IDEAS

Student writer Beatrice Hammond created a list to support her thesis statement. Then she reread her supporting points and removed ideas that she did not want to develop in her essay.

THESIS STATEMENT: <u>People have many advantages when they learn a foreign</u>
<u>language.</u>

Supporting points:

— feel comfortable in another country
— easier to develop friendships
— work in different places
— communicate with international clients
— increases flexibility
— creates tolerance for different cultures
— easier to travel
— able to read menus and signs
— ~~increases understanding of your own language~~
— ~~increases vocabulary~~

The Writer's Desk List Supporting Ideas

Choose one of your thesis statements from the previous Writer's Desk,
and create a list of possible supporting ideas. Then review your
supporting points and select the best ideas.

Thesis statement: _____

_____

Supporting ideas: _____

_____

_____

_____

_____

_____

_____

_____

The Essay Plan

When you write an **essay plan** or **outline,** organize your ideas logically by using
time, space, or emphatic order. To create an essay plan, do the following:

- Look at your list of ideas and identify the best supporting ideas.
- Write topic sentences that express the main supporting ideas.
- Add details under each topic sentence.

WRITING LINK

For more information about
organizing ideas using time, space,
and emphatic order, see pages 22–24
in Chapter 2, "Developing."

BEATRICE'S ESSAY PLAN

Beatrice wrote topic sentences and supporting examples and organized her ideas into a plan. Notice that her plan begins with a thesis statement, and she indents her supporting ideas.

THESIS STATEMENT: <u>People have many advantages when they learn a foreign language.</u>

    I. People who speak a foreign language find it very useful in the workplace.
       — They can work in a foreign country.
       — They can communicate with international clients.

    II. Understanding another language makes it easier for people who like to travel.
       — They find it easier to develop friendships while traveling.
       — They can read menus and signs in a foreign country.

    III. People who speak another language improve their understanding of different cultures.
       — They can analyze cultural values firsthand.
       — They get valuable insight into cultural differences by seeing or reading original versions of films or literature.

The Writer's Desk **Write an Essay Plan**

Write an essay plan using your thesis statement and topic sentences that express the supporting details you came up with in the previous Writer's Desk. Organize those ideas, and then write them in the essay plan below.

Thesis statement: _____

_____

I. _____

_____

Details: _____

_____

II. _____

_____

Details: _____

_____

III. _____

_____

Details: _____

_____

Concluding idea: _____

_____

The Introduction

After you have made an essay plan, develop the sections of your essay by creating an effective introduction, linking body paragraphs, and forming a conclusion.

The **introductory paragraph** presents the subject of your essay and contains the thesis statement. A strong introduction will capture the reader's attention and make him or her want to read on.

Introduction Styles

You can develop the sentences in the introduction in several different ways. To attract the reader's attention, your introduction can include various types of material.

- General background information
- Historical background information
- An interesting anecdote or a vivid description
- A contrasting position (an idea that is the opposite of the one you will develop)

 **Placement of the Thesis Statement**

Most introductions begin with sentences that present the topic and lead the reader to the main point of the essay. Generally, the thesis statement is the last sentence in the introduction.

PRACTICE 2

In the following introductions, the thesis statements are in bold print. Read each introduction, and circle the letter of the introduction style that each writer has used.

BEATRICE'S INTRODUCTION

In the era of globalization, the world is getting smaller. People travel more, businesses expand internationally, and many citizens emigrate to a different country. In today's world, groups of people are no longer isolated. They come into contact with many different cultures. **Thus, people have many advantages if they learn a foreign language.**

Style: a. Anecdote   b. General   c. Historical   d. Contrasting Position

1.   A few years ago, Brazilian police arrested an illegal alien. When they questioned him, he started speaking in a foreign language. So they hired Ziad Fazah to translate what the man was saying. Fazah claims to be the world's greatest polyglot. Fazah was born in Liberia but now lives in Brazil. He states that he is fluent in fifty-nine different languages. Fazah uses his linguistic abilities to communicate with people from around the world. Like Fazah, people see that it is advantageous in the modern world to know many languages.

Style: a. Anecdote   b. General   c. Historical   d. Contrasting Position

2.   Everybody speaks English. It is the international language of communication. Why should an English speaker go to all the trouble of learning a foreign language? Learning another language takes a lot of time and effort. So is the effort really worth it? Of course it is. **People gain many advantages when they learn a foreign language.**

Style: a. Anecdote   b. General   c. Historical   d. Contrasting Position

3.   The origins of human language are controversial. However, scholars have been studying the origins of languages spoken today. There are more than five thousand living languages in the world. Linguists group them into families of languages, each with a common ancestor. Sadly, many spoken languages today are dying rapidly. **Be that as it may, people have many advantages when they learn different languages.**

Style: a. Anecdote   b. General   c. Historical   d. Contrasting Position

The Conclusion

Every essay ends with a **conclusion.** The concluding paragraph rephrases the thesis statement and summarizes the main points in the essay.

BEATRICE'S CONCLUSION

Beatrice concluded her essay by restating her main points.

> People who speak another language find it advantageous in the workplace. Being able to communicate in a foreign language makes it easier for people to travel. Becoming proficient in a second language helps people to understand different cultures.

To make her conclusion more interesting and original, Beatrice could incorporate a prediction, a suggestion, or a quotation.

Prediction: As the world becomes smaller through increased technological communication, people will clearly see the advantages of learning a foreign language.

Suggestion: To gain all the advantages of learning a foreign language, sign up for a language course now.

Quotation: As American modernist poet Ezra Pound stated, "The sum of human wisdom is not contained in any one language."

 **Avoiding Problems in the Conclusion**

In your conclusion, do not contradict your main point, and do not introduce new or irrelevant information.

PRACTICE 3

The following essay is missing an introduction and a conclusion. Read the essay's body paragraphs, and underline the topic sentence in each. Then, on a separate sheet of paper, write an interesting introduction and an effective conclusion to make this a complete essay.

Write an introduction

Body Paragraph 1

The primary rationale for an arranged marriage is to achieve a secure link between two people. The couple shares the same values and upbringing. Since the families arrange the marital contract, the man and woman will most likely belong to the same ethnicity, class, and religion, and they will have a similar upbringing. Therefore, it is easy for the couple to share common principles or ideals. For example, John and Nisha understood each other from the start of their relationship. Both came from a similar background and had the same goals.

Body Paragraph 2

Moreover, the couple in the arranged marriage has the support of both extended families, which is important for the future success of the relationship. Marriages are considered to be an agreement between families and not just between two individuals. Therefore, the extended families have an interest in the success of the matrimonial alliance. If the newlyweds face an economic crisis, the extended family is there to lend a helping hand. If the young couple needs help coping with children, there is usually an aunt, uncle, or grandparent who will come to their aid. In this way, a lot of pressure on the marriage is relieved, and the husband and wife can concentrate on getting to know each other. Nisha explains the invaluable contribution of the extended family: "My mother-in-law looks after our daughter each afternoon. It frees up some of my time."

Body Paragraph 3

In addition, love can grow in an arranged marriage. Because the two people who are marrying are not blinded by infatuation or lust, they enter the marriage with their eyes wide open. The future husband and wife discuss personal and career goals, as well as family, religious, and financial values, before agreeing to marry. Knowing each other's opinions about such crucial issues gives the relationship a good start. It also clears the way for the young couple to get to know each other and appreciate each other, and it is not unusual for love to grow slowly but deeply. Many married couples who have been together for a long time will state enthusiastically that, over the years, they have come to understand, respect, and love their partners.

Write a conclusion

The Writer's Desk **Write an Introduction and a Conclusion**

In previous Writer's Desks in this chapter, you wrote an essay plan. Now write an introduction and a conclusion for your essay on a separate sheet of paper.

The First Draft

After creating an introduction and conclusion, and after arranging the supporting ideas in a logical order, you are ready to write your first draft. The first draft includes your introduction, several body paragraphs, and your concluding paragraph. Also, think of a title for your first draft.

The Writer's Desk **Write the First Draft**

Using the introduction, conclusion, and essay plan that you created in the previous Writer's Desk exercises, write the first draft of your essay.

REVISING AND EDITING

Revising and Editing the Essay

Revising and editing are extremely important steps in the writing process. When you revise your essay, you modify it to make it stronger and more convincing. You do this by reading the essay critically, looking for faulty logic, poor organization, or poor sentence style. Then you reorganize and rewrite it, making any necessary changes.

- **Revise for unity.** Verify that all of your body paragraphs support the essay's thesis statement. Also look carefully at each body paragraph to make sure that the sentences support the topic sentence.
- **Revise for adequate support.** Make sure that there are enough details and examples to make your essay strong and convincing.
- **Revise for coherence.** Make sure that your paragraphs flow smoothly and logically. To guide the reader from one idea to the next, or from one paragraph to the next, try using transitional words or expressions. Here are some examples.

finally	first	furthermore
in conclusion	moreover	second

- **Edit for errors.** Proofread your essay to check for errors in punctuation, spelling, grammar, and mechanics. There is an editing guide on the inside front cover of this book. It contains some common editing codes that your instructor may use.

WRITING LINK

For more information about revising, you may wish to review Chapter 3.

GRAMMAR LINK

To practice your editing skills, try the exercises in Chapter 29, "Editing Practice."

The Writer's Desk Revising and Editing Your Essay

In previous Writer's Desks, you developed an essay and wrote the first draft. Now revise and edit your essay.

The Final Draft

When you have finished revising the first draft of your essay, write the final version. This version should include all the changes that you have made during the revision phase of your work. You should proofread the final copy of your work to check for mistakes in grammar, spelling, mechanics, and punctuation.

The Writer's Desk Writing Your Final Draft

You have developed, revised, and edited your essay. Now write the final draft. Before you give it to your instructor, proofread it one last time to ensure that you have found as many errors as possible.

The Writer's Room

Writing Activity 1: Topics

Choose any of the following topics, or choose your own topic. Then, write an essay. Remember to follow the writing process.

General Topics

1. moving out of the family home
2. lotteries
3. reasons to stay single
4. financial mistakes
5. superstitions

College and Work-Related Topics

6. college politics
7. the value of work
8. feeling pressure
9. future goals
10. positive thinking

Writing Activity 2: Photo Writing

How are traditional parenting roles changing in contemporary times? Use specific examples to support your point of view.

 ESSAY CHECKLIST

Exploring

☐ Think about your topic, audience, and purpose.

☐ Try exploring strategies such as brainstorming or clustering to find and narrow your topic.

Developing

☐ Write a thesis statement that introduces the topic and states the controlling idea.

☐ Support the thesis statement with facts and examples.

☐ Organize your ideas using time, space, or emphatic order.

☐ Write an essay plan to help you visualize the main and supporting ideas.

☐ Write the first draft.

Revising and Editing

☐ Revise for unity.

☐ Revise for adequate support.

☐ Revise for coherence. Use transitional expressions to link ideas.

☐ Edit for errors in spelling, punctuation, grammar, and mechanics.

☐ Write the final draft.

mywritinglab To check your progress in meeting this chapter's objectives, log in to **www.mywritinglab.com**, go to the **Study Plan** tab, click on **The Writing Process** and choose **Writing the Essay** from the list of subtopics. Read and view the resources in the **Review Materials** section, and then complete the **Recall, Apply,** and **Write** sets in the **Activities** section.

PART II

The Editing Handbook

Why Grammar Is Important

Clear writing begins with a well-developed sentence. At the very least, a sentence needs a noun or pronoun and a verb. However, a sentence can become richer when it also includes adjectives, adverbs, conjunctions, interjections, or prepositions.

Clear writing also requires grammatically correct sentences. If your writing contains errors in grammar, you may distract readers from your message, and they may focus, instead, on your inability to communicate clearly. To improve your writing skills, it is useful to understand how the English language works. As your knowledge of grammar conventions increases, you will be more and more able to identify and correct errors in your writing.

In the Editing Handbook, you will learn to spot errors and you will also learn about the underlying rule that applies to each error.

Nouns, Determiners, and Prepositions

Section Theme: **LIFESTYLES**

*In this chapter, you will read about topics
related to lifestyles.*

Grammar Snapshot

Looking at Nouns, Determiners, and Prepositions

In her essay, "Yoga Y'all," Elizabeth Gilbert recounts her experiences in her yoga class. Certain parts of speech are in bold or are underlined. Identify which words are nouns, determiners, and prepositions.

> While it is true that I have had <u>some</u> fancy yoga **experiences** lately (including <u>a</u> recent **period** <u>in</u> an ancient **ashram** <u>in</u> **India**), my yoga **background** is actually quite long and gritty. My **mom** taught **yoga** <u>in</u> the early 1970s <u>to</u> **housewives** <u>at</u> the **Y.M.C.A.** <u>in</u> our blue-collar New England **town**.

In this chapter, you will identify and write about nouns, determiners, and prepositions.

1/24/11

CHAPTER 6

Nouns

Nouns are words that refer to people, places, or things. Nouns are divided into common nouns and proper nouns.

- **Common nouns** refer to general people, places, or things. Each begins with a lowercase letter. For example, *books, computer,* and *village* are common nouns.
- **Proper nouns** refer to particular people, places, or things. Each begins with a capital letter. For example, *Margaret Mead, the Amazon,* and *Thanksgiving* are proper nouns.

Singular and Plural Nouns

Nouns are either singular or plural. A **singular noun** refers to one of something, while a **plural noun** refers to more than one of something. Regular plural nouns end in *-s* or *-es*.

	Singular	**Plural**
People:	father	fathers
	sister	sisters
Places:	town	towns
	room	rooms
Things:	dish	dishes
	chair	chairs

449 ad
(english started)

 **Hint** ▷ **Adding -es**

When a noun ends in *-s, -x, -ch, -sh,* or *-z,* add *-es* to form the plural.

wish–wish**es**   box–box**es**   batch–batch**es**

Irregular Plural Nouns

Irregular plural nouns do not end in *-s* or *-es.* Here are some common irregular nouns.

Singular	**Plural**	**Singular**	**Plural**
child	children	mouse	mice
foot	feet	person	people
goose	geese	tooth	teeth
man	men	woman	women

Other Plural Noun Forms

Some nouns use other rules to form the plural. It is a good idea to memorize both the rules and the exceptions.

1. For nouns ending in *f,* or *fe,* change the *f* to *v* and add *-es.*

Singular	**Plural**	**Singular**	**Plural**
life	li**ves**	self	sel**ves**
thief	thie**ves**	shelf	shel**ves**

Some exceptions: belief, beliefs; roof, roofs.

2. For nouns ending in a consonant + *y*, change the *y* to *i* and add *-es*.

Singular	Plural	Singular	Plural
baby	bab**ies**	cherry	cherr**ies**
berry	berr**ies**	lady	lad**ies**

If a vowel comes before the final *y*, simply add *-s*.

Singular	Plural	Singular	Plural
boy	boy**s**	key	key**s**

3. Some nouns remain the same in both singular and plural forms.

Singular	Plural	Singular	Plural
deer	deer	moose	moose
fish	fish	sheep	sheep

4. Some nouns are thought of as being only plural and therefore have no singular form.

Only Plural			
clothes	goods	proceeds	scissors
eyeglasses	pants	savings	tweezers

5. Some nouns are **compound nouns,** or nouns with two or more words. To form the plural of compound nouns, add *-s* or *-es* to the last word of the compound noun.

Singular	Plural	Singular	Plural
graphic art	graphic art**s**	test tube	test tube**s**
human being	human being**s**	water pump	water pump**s**

If the first word in a hyphenated compound noun is a noun, add *-s* to the noun.

Singular	Plural	Singular	Plural
attorney-at-law	attorney**s**-at-law	passer-by	passer**s**-by
brother-in-law	brother**s**-in-law	runner-up	runner**s**-up

6. Some nouns that are borrowed from other languages keep the plural form of the original language.

Singular	Plural	Singular	Plural
alumnus	alumn**i**	medium	medi**a**
datum	dat**a**	phenomenon	phenomen**a**

 **Persons Versus People**

There are two plural forms of *person*. *People* is the common plural form.

Some **people** go to spas to relax. Many **people** like to get a massage.

Persons is used only in a legal or official context.

The Green Water Spa was broken into by **persons** unknown.

PRACTICE 1

Fill in each blank with either the singular or plural form of the noun. If both the singular and the plural forms are the same, put an *X* in the space.

Singular	**Plural**
EXAMPLES:	
lottery	*lotteries*
X	pants
1. child	Children
2. shelf	Shelves
3. phenomenon	phenomena
4. sister-in-law	Sisters-in-law *CP*
5. community	communities
6. medium	media
7. goggle X	goggles
8. tooth	teeth
9. life	lives
10. sunglass	sunglasses
11. high school	high schools
12. credit card	credit cards
13. factory	factories
14. scarf	scarves
15. person	people

PRACTICE 2

Each sentence contains an incorrect plural noun form. Correct the errors.

EXAMPLE:

　　　　　　　　　　　　　　　　　　　bookshelves
　　Bookstores stock many eco-lifestyle books on ~~bookshelfs~~.

1. Lifestyle is defined by how ~~peoples~~ live. *people*

2. It is determined by how human beings view ~~themselfs~~ and others. *themselves*

3. Personal ~~believes~~ and behaviors reflect lifestyle choices. *belief*

4. Green lifestyle supporters choose ~~activitys~~ that do not harm the environment. *activities*

5. Such proponents walk their ~~childs~~ to school and recycle garbage. *children*

6. Sociologists conduct many ~~studys~~ *studies* of lifestyles in different cultures.

7. Advertisers target ~~mens~~ *men* and women to promote products for different lifestyles.

8. Nowadays, there is a lot of discussion in the ~~medium~~ *media* about lifestyle.

 **Hint** > **Key Words for Singular and Plural Nouns**

• Use a singular noun after words such as *a, an, one, each, every,* and *another.*

   A **person** should exercise each **day**.

• Use a plural noun after words such as *two, all, both, many, few, several,* and *some.*

   Some **people** do many different **exercises**.

PRACTICE 3

Underline the key words that help to determine whether the noun in each sentence is singular or plural. Then, correct the errors in singular and plural nouns.

EXAMPLE:

children
Around the world, <u>many</u> ~~child~~ drink unsafe water.

1. Many person in the developing world are not able to live healthy lifestyles.

2. According to the World Health Organization (WHO), around one billion human being cannot access clean water.

3. In numerous developing country, drinking water is contaminated.

4. Sewage causes water contamination in several region around the world.

5. A major reasons for contaminated water is the inadequate funding of sewer systems.

6. Some third-world nation cannot finance and maintain water treatment facilities.

7. Multiple project exist to help third world states acquire drinking water.

8. Each years, scientists find ways to supply people with safe drinking water.

> ## *Hint* Plural Nouns Follow *"of the"* Expressions
>
> Use a plural noun after expressions such as *one of the, all of the, each of the,* and so on.
>
> Martha Stewart hosts <u>one of the</u> most popular television **shows** about home and lifestyle.

PRACTICE 4

Correct ten errors with singular and plural nouns.

EXAMPLE:

San Pellegrino is one of the most interesting ~~place~~ *places* in Italy.

1. Some American prefer to drink mineral water instead of regular water.
   One of the most famous ~~brand~~ *brands* is San Pellegrino. The naturally carbonated water is found in a mountainous ~~areas~~ *area* of Italy. It emerges from three spring at around 69.8 degrees Fahrenheit.

2. Italians have been drinking the water for hundreds of ~~year~~ *years*. The town of San Pellegrino started marketing its water in 1395. Famous artists praised the water for its restorative ~~qualityes~~ *qualities*. In 1509, Leonardo da Vinci wrote that each ~~glasses~~ *glass* was beneficial to one's health.

3. By the early 1900s, San Pellegrino water was exported to numerous ~~citys~~ *cities* around the world. By 1988, it was even exported to France. San Pellegrino water is an important product in the ~~lifes~~ *lives* of many ~~consumer~~ *consumers*. They think they are not only drinking mineral water but are also choosing a lifestyle.

Count Nouns and Noncount Nouns

In English, nouns are grouped into two types: count nouns and noncount nouns.

- **Count nouns** refer to people or things that can be counted, such as *car, book,* or *boy.* Count nouns have both a singular and a plural form.

    There is <u>one</u> **spa** in our town but <u>three</u> **spas** in the city.

- **Noncount nouns** refer to things that cannot be counted because they cannot be divided, such as *education* or *paint.* Noncount nouns generally have only the singular form.

    Music can often lead to a feeling of **serenity**.

To express a noncount noun as a count noun, you would have to refer to it in terms of *types*, *varieties*, or *amounts*.

People can practice different <u>types of</u> **meditation**.

The next table shows some common noncount nouns.

Abstract Nouns				
advice	effort	information	peace	research
attention	evidence	knowledge	progress	serenity
behavior	health	luck	proof	violence

PRACTICE 5

Change each word in italics to the plural form, if necessary. If you cannot use the plural form, write an *X* in the space.

EXAMPLE:

Today's modern spa originated in ancient socie~~ty~~ ___ies___ .

1. Since earliest times, people have believed that bathing in hot spring *water* ___X___ is a means of attaining good *health* ___X___ .

2. In the Roman Empire, soldiers marched long distances carrying heavy *equipment* ___X___ .

3. After long *march* ___marches___ , they bathed in mineral springs to heal aching *muscle* ___muscles___ .

4. Throughout the empire, bathing became a popular *ritual* ___X___ for all social *class* ___classes___

5. Romans would go to the public baths for several *hour* ___hours___ to exercise and socialize.

6. The baths would include *library* ___libraries___ , *restaurant* ___restaurants___ , and *garden* ___gardens___ .

7. Each *room* ___X___ would have comfortable *furniture* ___X___ and soft *music* ___X___ to help bathers relax.

8. The ruling class could gather important *information* ___X___ at the public baths.

9. Archaeological *evidence* ___X___ shows that in the year 300, the Romans had built more than nine hundred *bath* ___baths___

10. In subsequent *century* ___centuries___ , people continued to visit the Roman baths to treat different types of *illness* ___illnesses___ and maintain a healthy *lifestyle* ~~lifestyles~~ ___X___

Determiners

Determiners are words that identify whether a noun is specific or general.

> <u>The</u> motivational **speaker**, Leo Buscaglia, was also <u>an</u> **author**.

You can use many words from different parts of speech as determiners.

Articles:	a, an, the
Indefinite pronouns:	any, all, both, each, either, every, few, little, many, several
Demonstrative pronouns:	this, that, these, those
Numbers:	one, two, three

A, An, The

Some determiners can be confusing because you can use them only in specific circumstances. *A* and *an* are general determiners, and *the* is a specific determiner.

general   specific

> I want to watch <u>a</u> new film. <u>The</u> films in that collection are fascinating.

- Use *a* and *an* before singular count nouns but not before plural or noncount nouns.

singular count noun   noncount noun

> Buscaglia wrote <u>a</u> **book** on love. His clients made quick **progress** to overcome their fears.

 **A or An**

- Use *a* before words that begin with a consonant (*a* man, *a* house).

   Exception: When *u* sounds like *you*, put *a* before it (*a* uniform, *a* university).

- Use *an* before words that begin with a vowel (*an* exhibit, *an* umbrella.)

   Exception: When *h* is silent, put *an* before it (*an* hour, *an* honest man).

- Use *the* before nouns that refer to a specific person, place, or thing.

> <u>The</u> **writer** Zack Bugovsky also started <u>the</u> **company** Lovelife.

 **Avoid Overusing *The***

Do not use *the* before nouns that refer to certain types of things or places.

Languages:	He studies ~~the~~ Swahili.
Sports:	We played ~~the~~ football.
Most cities and countries:	Leo lived near ~~the~~ Lake Tahoe.
Exceptions:	*the* United States, *the* Netherlands

PRACTICE 6

Write either *a*, *an*, or *the* in the space provided. If no determiner is necessary, write *X* in the space.

EXAMPLE:

There are many different types of ____X____ yoga positions.

1. Yoga is __*a*__ spiritual way of life that combines mental and physical disciplines. It originated in __X__ India more than 5,000 years ago. __*The*__ earliest written descriptions of yoga are found in __*an*__ ancient text. __*The*__ text is called *Yoga Sutras of Patanjali.*

2. The West became acquainted with yoga initially in __*the*__ nineteenth century. At that time, British scholars translated many Indian books into __X__ English. In 1893, __*The*__ Hindu missionary traveled to __X__ America. Swami Vivekananda attended __*a*__ religious conference in __X__ Chicago. In __*the*__ following years, he journeyed around __*the*__ country lecturing on Hinduism and yoga. In the early 1900s, more yoga masters came to __*the*__ United States and attracted numerous disciples.

3. Today, yoga is extremely popular in __X__ Western countries, but it has become __*a*__ commodity. Many people practice yoga only as part of __*a*__ regime of physical exercise. They do not think of it as __*a*__ spiritual way of life.

Many, Few, Much, Little

Use *many* and *few* with count nouns.

Many **writers** have produced self-help books, but few **readers** have completely changed their lives.

Use *much* and *little* with noncount nouns.

Dr. Meghana Kale spent much **time** but very little **money** doing important research.

This, That, These, Those

Both *this* and *these* refer to things that are physically close to the speaker in time or place. Use *this* before singular nouns and *these* before plural nouns.

These **days**, many articles are written about theories of self-improvement. This **article** on my desk is on the power of positive thinking.

Use *that* and *those* to refer to things that are physically distant from the speaker in time or place. Use *that* before singular nouns and *those* before plural nouns.

> In the 1970s, many psychologists did research on happiness. In those **years**, scientists tried to develop useful tests to evaluate happiness. In that **building**, there is a library with many books on happiness.

Near the speaker:
this (singular)
these (plural)

Far from the speaker:
that (singular)
those (plural)

PRACTICE 7

Underline the best determiner in each set of parentheses. If no determiner is needed, underline the *X*.

EXAMPLE:

(<u>Many</u> / Much) physical activities increase fitness.

1. (<u>Many</u> / Much) people exercise regularly, but (<u>few</u> / little) individuals know about the man who popularized aerobic activities. Dr. Kenneth H. Cooper worked for (<u>the</u> / X) Air Force in (<u>the</u> / X) 1960s. In (these / <u>those</u>) days, scientists did not know why some Air Force recruits had strong muscles but no stamina. (Few / <u>Little</u>) research had been done on (a / <u>the</u>) cardiovascular system. Dr. Cooper found (<u>a</u> / X) link between (a / <u>an</u>) individual's athletic performance and his or her body's ability to use oxygen.

2. Cooper wrote (<u>a</u> / the) book in (the / <u>X</u>) 1968. It was called *Aerobics*. At (this / <u>that</u>) time, the public was becoming interested in (the / <u>X</u>) information about diet and exercise. Dr. Cooper's book revealed how (the / <u>X</u>) individuals could become physically fit. His method became (<u>the</u> / X) basis for modern aerobic programs.

3. (<u>These</u> / Those) days, people complain that they do not have (many / <u>much</u>) time for exercise. Doctors recommend regular (a / the / <u>X</u>) physical activity to maintain (the / <u>X</u>) good health.

PRACTICE 8 REVIEW

Correct fifteen errors with singular nouns, plural nouns, and determiners.

EXAMPLE:

John Harvey Kellogg was ~~the~~ *a* vegetarian.

1. John Harvey Kellogg and his brother Will were two of the most interesting personality in the food industry. John Harvey was a advocate of physical fitness. He was born in 1852 and studied medicine. In these days, few information was known about the relationship between the health and nutrition. He was one of the first person to see a connection between proper diet and well-being. He became the director of a health spa where he practiced his believes.

2. John Harvey and Will made the important discovery that changed what persons ate for breakfast. By using special machineries, the brothers developed flaked cereal. Will wanted to market the cereal to grocery stores, but John Harvey was against an idea. Therefore, John Harvey and Will parted ways, and in 1906, Will started the Kellogg Company. Since this time, Kellogg has been a world leader in producing breakfast cereals.

3. Will Kellogg became the rich man, but he was uncomfortable with his wealth. He also worried that too many wealth could corrupt his children. Thus, he did not leave his sons a large inheritance. Instead, he donated money to various charities. This days, very few people know about the Kelloggs.

Prepositions

Prepositions are words that show concepts such as time, place, direction, and manner. They show connections or relationships between ideas. Some common prepositions are *about, around, at, before, behind, beside, between, for, in, of, on, to, toward,* and *with.*

People go **to** many different spas **for** rest and relaxation.

In the spring, my sister will go **to** a spiritual retreat.

Prepositions of Time and Place

Generally, as a description of a place or time becomes more precise, you move from *in* to *on* to *at.*

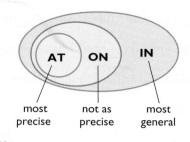

Preposition	Prepositions of Time	Prepositions of Place
in	in a year (in 2011) in a month (in October) in the morning, afternoon, evening in the spring, summer, fall, winter	in a city, country, etc. (in New Orleans, in China, in Central America)
on	on a day of the week (on Tuesday) on a specific date (on March 19) on a specific holiday (on Memorial Day) on my birthday on time ("punctual")	on a specific street (on Main Street) on a planet (on Venus) on certain technological devices (on TV, on the radio, on the phone, on the computer) on top
at	at a specific time of day (at 1:30) at night at breakfast, lunch, dinner	at a specific address (at 32 Cardinal Crescent) at a specific building (at the hotel)
from . . . to	from one time to another (from 10 am to 6 pm)	from one place to another (from New York to Miami)
for	for a period of time (for two hours)	for a distance (for five miles)

 **To Versus At**

• Use *to* after verbs that indicate movement from one place to another.

> go to   walk to   run to   move to   return to

Exception: Do not put *to* directly before *home*.

> I'll go ~~to~~ home with you. I won't go to his home.

• Use *at* after verbs that indicate being in one place (and not moving from one place to another).

> wait at   stay at   sit at   look at   work at

PRACTICE 9

Underline the correct prepositions in the parentheses.

EXAMPLE:

> I take Pilates classes (on / <u>at</u>) my school.

1. Joseph Pilates was born (<u>in</u> / at / X) Germany (<u>in</u> / on) 1880.

2. As a boy, Pilates mostly stayed (<u>at</u> / on) home because he had asthma.

3. (In / <u>On</u> /At) his fourteenth birthday, Pilates started to practice yoga to build up his strength.

4. (<u>In</u> / On) 1925, (in / <u>on</u>) November 2, he moved (<u>from</u> / in) Germany (at / <u>to</u>) England.

5. One day, while walking (at / in / <u>X</u>) home, he got an idea for an exercise method.

6. Eventually, Pilates moved (at / <u>to</u>) New York and opened an exercise studio (<u>in</u> / at) Manhattan (in / <u>on</u>) Eighth Avenue.

7. Pilates and his wife taught classes early (at/ <u>in</u> / on) the morning.

8. Initially, dancers went (at / in / <u>to</u>) the Pilates Studio to train (<u>for</u> / in) a couple of hours every week.

9. (<u>In</u> / At) 1960, the method started to become popular among celebrities.

10. Presently, there are exercise programs (in / <u>on</u>) television that teach audiences the Pilates method.

> ## Hint — *for, during, since*
>
> Sometimes people confuse the prepositions *for*, *during*, and *since*. Use *during* to explain when something happens, *for* to explain how long it takes to happen, and *since* to indicate the start of an activity.
>
> **During** <u>the blackout</u>, the meditation center closed **for** <u>two hours</u>.
>
> **Since** <u>2008</u>, I have been going to the meditation center.

PRACTICE 10

Correct six errors with prepositions.

EXAMPLE:

> *During*
> ~~In~~ my vacation, I went swimming ~~since~~ two hours each day.
>   *for*

Recently, I attended a conference on work–life balance. The keynote

speech lasted ~~during~~  two hours. One of the experts reported that many

Americans do not take their annual vacation. My company encourages

employees to take holidays ~~during~~ *for* a few weeks each year to avoid

burnout. Last year, ~~on~~ *in* the winter, I went ~~at~~ *to* Hawaii during ten days, and

I practiced tai chi. ~~Since~~ *For* three years, I have been taking tai chi lessons.

Common Prepositional Expressions

Many common expressions contain prepositions. A preposition can follow an adjective or a verb. These types of expressions usually express a particular meaning.

EXAMPLE: This morning, I <u>listened</u> **to** the radio.

The next list contains some of the most common prepositional expressions.

accuse (somebody) of	dream of	prepared for
acquainted with	escape from	prevent (someone) from
add to	excited about	protect (someone) from
afraid of	familiar with	proud of
agree with	feel like	provide (someone) with
angry about	fond of	qualify for
angry with	forget about	realistic about
apologize for	forgive (someone) for	refer to
apply for	friendly with	related to
approve of	good for	rely on
argue with	grateful for	rescue from
ask for	happy about	responsible for
associate with	hear about	sad about
aware of	hope for	satisfied with
believe in	hopeful about	scared of
belong to	innocent of	search for
capable of	insist on	similar to
care about	insulted by	specialize in
care for	interested in	stop (something) from
commit to	introduce to	succeed in
comply with	jealous of	take advantage of
concerned about	keep from	take care of
confronted with	located in	thank (someone) for
consist of	long for	think about
count on	look forward to	think of
deal with	opposed to	tired of
decide on	participate in	upset about
decide to	patient with	upset with
depend on	pay attention to	willing to
disappointed about	pay for	wish for
disappointed with	pray for	worry about

PRACTICE 11

Write the correct prepositions in the following sentences. Use the preceding list of common prepositional expressions to help you.

EXAMPLE:

Some people hope ___*for*___ good energy by following the tradition of Feng Shui.

1.   Many people are familiar ___*with*___ Feng Shui. The method teaches individuals how to live in harmony with nature. Feng Shui complies ___*with*___ ancient Chinese laws to help improve a person's quality of life.

2.   Feng Shui developed from Taoist philosophy. Followers believe _____ the idea that nature is filled with Qi, or energy. The ancient Chinese wished _____ favorable Qi to ensure their good fortune. They felt that Qi was responsible _____ the flow of positive energy. They insisted _____ building cities using Feng Shui principles.

3.   In the West, people became acquainted _____ the essentials of Feng Shui when China encouraged tourism. Americans developed an interest _____ Chinese culture. Since the 1970s, Feng Shui masters have specialized _____ arranging living environments for followers in the West. Critics say that Westerners are not practicing the entire tradition of Feng Shui but are only paying attention _____ parts of the philosophy.

FINAL REVIEW

A. Correct fourteen errors in singular and plural nouns and determiners.

EXAMPLE:

Bottled water is one of the fastest growing commercial ~~beverage~~ *beverages* in the world.

1.   One of the latest ~~trend~~ *trends* in American culture is drinking bottled ~~waters~~ *water*. Americans bring bottled water to football ~~matchs~~ *matches*, put it in their ~~lunch~~ ~~boxs~~ *boxes*, and drink it during business meetings. Many ~~familys~~ *families* choose to drink bottled water rather than tap water. They don't have ~~many~~ *much* confidence in tap water. In fact, in *the* United States, people spend more than fifteen billion dollars on bottled water every ~~years~~ *year*.

2. Americans consume bottled water for ~~much~~ *many* reasons. First, it is very

convenient because it can be transported everywhere. Second, ~~a~~ *an* individual

may believe that bottled water is healthier than tap water. ~~Those~~ *these* days,

marketers bombard consumers with the message that bottled water is a

healthier product than tap water. Some ~~companys~~ *companies* add unnecessary vitamins

or flavors to it. Most importantly, the industry influences ~~persons~~ *people* to believe

that buying ~~the~~ bottled water is a good lifestyle choice.

B. Correct six preposition errors.

EXAMPLE:

Activists worry ~~of~~ *about* the effects of bottled water on the environment.

3. Activists participated ~~on~~ *in* a discussion about bottled water. Americans should

be concerned ~~of~~ *about* the environmental effects of bottled water. ~~On~~ *IN* one year,

Americans use about 50 billion plastic bottles. To manufacture plastic

bottles, companies require billions of gallons of oil. Moreover, around 85

percent of plastic bottles are not recycled. ~~Since~~ *For* twenty years, they have

filled up landfills and leaked pollutants into the ground water. Also, people

should be aware ~~at~~ *of* the expense of transporting bottled water over long

distances. For example, bringing water from Fiji ~~at~~ *to* the United States uses

fossil fuels.

The Writer's Room

Write about one of the following topics. After you finish writing, circle any
plural nouns and underline any determiners.

1. What do you do to reduce stress? Explain some steps you take.
2. What does the term *healthy lifestyle* mean to you? Write a paragraph
   defining this term.

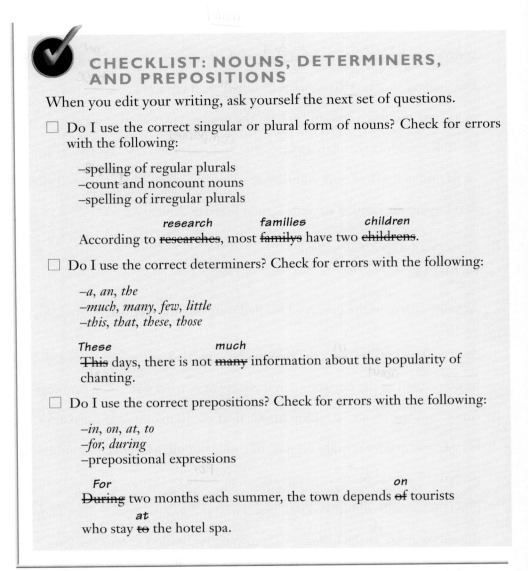

CHECKLIST: NOUNS, DETERMINERS, AND PREPOSITIONS

When you edit your writing, ask yourself the next set of questions.

☐ Do I use the correct singular or plural form of nouns? Check for errors with the following:

–spelling of regular plurals
–count and noncount nouns
–spelling of irregular plurals

According to ~~researches~~ *research*, most ~~familys~~ *families* have two ~~childrens~~ *children*.

☐ Do I use the correct determiners? Check for errors with the following:

–*a, an, the*
–*much, many, few, little*
–*this, that, these, those*

~~This~~ *These* days, there is not ~~many~~ *much* information about the popularity of chanting.

☐ Do I use the correct prepositions? Check for errors with the following:

–*in, on, at, to*
–*for, during*
–prepositional expressions

~~During~~ *For* two months each summer, the town depends ~~of~~ *on* tourists who stay ~~to~~ *at* the hotel spa.

mywritinglab   To check your progress in meeting this chapter's objectives, log in to **www.mywritinglab.com**, go to the **Study Plan** tab, click on **The Editing Handbook—Section 1 Some Parts of Speech** and choose **Nouns, Determiners, and Prepositions** from the list of subtopics. Read and view the resources in the **Review Materials** section, and then complete the **Recall, Apply,** and **Write** sets in the **Activities** section.

Pronouns

Section Theme: LIFESTYLES

In this chapter, you will read about issues related to food.

Grammar Snapshot

Looking at Pronouns

Catherine Pigott is a freelance writer. In this excerpt, Pigott shows how Western societies' attitude toward food differs from that of African societies. The pronouns are underlined.

> I tried desperately, but I could not eat enough to please them. It was hard for me to explain that I come from a culture in which it is almost unseemly for a woman to eat too heartily. It's considered unattractive. It was even harder to explain that to me thin is beautiful, and in my country, we deny ourselves food in our pursuit of perfect slenderness.

In this chapter, you will identify and write pronouns.

Pronoun-Antecedent Agreement

Pronouns are words that replace nouns (people, places, or things), other pronouns, and phrases. A pronoun must agree with its **antecedent,** which is the word to which the pronoun refers. Pronouns must agree in person and number with their antecedents.

> The <u>nutritionist</u> was frustrated because **she** did not receive enough recognition for **her** work.
> (*Nutritionist* is the antecedent of *she* and *her.*)

> <u>Farmers</u> are lobbying the government. **They** want better prices for crops.
> (*Farmers* is the antecedent of *they.*)

 **Hint**   **Compound Antecedents**

Compound antecedents consist of two or more nouns joined by *and* or *or*. When the nouns are joined by *and,* you must use a plural pronoun to refer to them.

> <u>Susan Brown and Alan Booth</u> published **their** book in 1997.

When the nouns are joined by *or,* you may need a singular or plural pronoun. If both nouns are singular, then use a singular pronoun. If both nouns are plural, use a plural pronoun.

> Does <u>California or Florida</u> have **its** own farming association?

> Have more <u>men or women</u> completed **their** degrees in agriculture?

PRACTICE I

The pronouns in the following sentences are in bold print. Underline each antecedent.

EXAMPLE:

> Early <u>agriculture</u> began around eight thousand years ago, and **it** was a milestone in human development.

1. <u>Early humans</u> hunted, so **they** had to follow animal migrations to get food.

2. At some point, hunters realized that it was easier to kill <u>an animal</u> if **it** was contained in a small area.

3. <u>Dr. Russell Fisch</u> believes that agriculture started more than seven thousand years ago, but **he** says that the domestication of animals started even earlier.

4. The first domesticated animal was probably <u>the dog</u>, and **it** helped early humans to hunt.

5. The growth of farming helped <u>early cities</u> to develop because **their** populations increased quickly.

6. Around 4,000 years ago, farmers first used irrigation in the Euphrates Valley, and **its** agricultural output grew enormously.

7. Ling-Mei Chang is an expert on agriculture, and **she** is researching early technology in the Nile Valley.

8. Does China or India have **its** own agricultural associations?

 **Using Collective Nouns**

Collective nouns refer to a group of people or things. The group acts as a unit; therefore, it is singular. For example, *family, army, crowd, group,* and *organization* are collective nouns.

> The food company advertises **its** products.
>
> The club meets every Thursday. **It** is for overeaters.

GRAMMAR LINK

For a list of collective nouns, see page 233 in Chapter 13.

PRACTICE 2

Underline the antecedents, and write the appropriate pronoun in each blank.

EXAMPLE:

Plows were invented in Mesopotamia around 5000 years ago, and _____*they*_____ improved agricultural productivity.

1. John Deere was an American blacksmith, and ____he____ vastly improved the design of the plow.

2. His wife believed in him, and ____She____ supported Deere in his business ventures.

3. American farmers experimented with Deere's new plow, and ____they____ were greatly impressed.

4. Deere sold thousands of plows when he first started to manufacture ____them____.

5. In 1855, to help his business, Deere moved to Moline, Illinois, because ____it____ is near the Mississippi River.

6. In 1861, Deere incorporated his company, and _____ continues to manufacture agriculture equipment today.

7. The agricultural association in our state is large and _____ recommends John Deere equipment.

Indefinite Pronouns

Most pronouns refer to a specific person, place, or thing. You can use **indefinite pronouns** when you talk about people or things whose identity is not known or is unimportant. The following table shows some common singular and plural indefinite pronouns.

Indefinite Pronouns

Singular:	another	each	nobody	other
	anybody	everybody	no one	somebody
	anyone	everyone	nothing	someone
	anything	everything	one	something
Plural:	both, few, many, others, several			
Either singular or plural:	all, any, some, half (and other fractions), more, most, none			

Singular Pronouns

When you use a singular indefinite antecedent, also use a singular pronoun to refer to it.

> Everyone wonders if **he** or **she** should eat better.

> No one wants to reduce **his** or **her** quality of life.

Plural Pronouns

When you use a plural indefinite antecedent, also use a plural pronoun to refer to it.

> Our town has many economic problems, and several of **them** are difficult to overcome.

> Although small farmers contribute to the economy, many must sell **their** farms.

Pronouns That Can Be Singular or Plural

Some indefinite pronouns can be either singular or plural, depending on the noun to which they refer.

> Many food inspectors came to the conference. All were experts in **their** fields.
> (*All* refers to food inspectors; therefore, the pronoun is plural.)

> We read all of the report and agreed with **its** recommendations.
> (*All* refers to the report; therefore, the pronoun is singular.)

 **Hint** **Using "of the" Expressions**

The subject of a sentence appears before the words *of the*. For example, in sentences containing the expression *one of the* or *each of the*, the subject is the indefinite pronoun *one* or *each*. You must use a singular pronoun to refer to the subject.

> One of the cookbooks is missing **its** cover.

If the subject could be either male or female, then use *his or her* to refer to it.

> Each of the students has **his or her** own copy of the book.

CHAPTER 7

PRACTICE 3

Underline the correct pronouns.

EXAMPLE:

Everybody is concerned about (<u>his or her</u> / their) health.

1.   Almost everyone at some point has eaten (<u>his or her</u> / their) lunch
   at a fast-food restaurant. But fast food is not only a modern American
   phenomenon. Every culture has (his or her / <u>its</u> / their) own examples of
   fast food. In Italy, most people eat (his or her / <u>their</u>) pizza slices at food
   stalls. In India, fast food is very popular. Few can avoid the temptation of
   eating (his or her / <u>their</u>) papri chaat or bhelpuri at food stands. In China,
   no one can resist buying (<u>his or her</u> / their) dumplings while cycling by the
   food vendors. Lebanon has contributed (<u>its</u> / their) great gift of fast food—
   the falafel sandwich—to North American cuisine.

2.   Fast food is popular with North Americans. McDonald's and (<u>its</u> /their)
   competitors are very successful businesses. For example, McDonald's is the
   largest fast-food chain in the world. Presently, <u>health care workers</u> and
   (his or her / its / <u>their</u>) government colleagues are closely scrutinizing the
   effects of fast food on North Americans. Health care workers believe that
   the popularity of fast food and (<u>its</u> / their) reliance on highly caloric
   ingredients is one reason for the growing obesity among young people.
   Each of the fast-food companies has made (<u>its</u> / their) own response to this
   criticism by offering lower calorie choices such as salads. However, critics
   do not think the response is adequate.

Vague Pronouns

Avoid using pronouns that could refer to more than one antecedent.

> **Vague:**   Manolo introduced me to his friend and <u>his</u> sister.
>   (Whose sister is it: Manolo's or his friend's?)
>
> **Clearer:**   Manolo introduced me to his friend and **his friend's** sister.

Avoid using the pronouns *it* and *they* if the word has no clear antecedent.

> **Vague:**   <u>They</u> say that farmers should receive more tax breaks.
>   (Who are *they?*)
>
> **Clearer:**   **Critics of government policy** say that farmers should receive
>   more tax breaks.

CHAPTER 7

Vague: It stated in the newspaper that many farmers are declaring bankruptcy.

(Who or what is *it?*)

Clearer: **The newspaper article** stated that many farmers are declaring bankruptcy.

Use *this, that,* and *which* only to refer to a specific antecedent.

Vague: The price of cattle feed was raised. This caused many ranchers to panic.

(What is *this?*)

Clearer: The price of cattle feed was raised. **This information** caused many ranchers to panic.

Hint   Avoid Repeating the Subject

When you clearly mention a subject, do not repeat the subject in pronoun form.

Dr. MacKenzie, he is more than eighty years old.

His course on food science, it is really interesting.

PRACTICE 4

Correct any vague pronoun or repeated subject errors.

EXAMPLE:

Doctors say
~~They say~~ that people should eat food from all food groups.

1. It says that some Americans are following a raw food diet.

2. The raw food diet it is supposed to have health benefits.

3. Sara told Roxanne that her energy level seemed to increase since starting the diet. *UNCLEAR PRONOUN*

4. They say that cooking food destroys many enzymes.

5. Followers of the diet ~~they~~ eat at least 75 percent of their food raw.

6. I could never try ~~this.~~ *EATING A RAW FOOD DIET*

7. It says that some foods, like kidney beans, should never be consumed raw.

8. This can cause food poisoning when eaten.

Pronoun Shifts

Making Pronouns Consistent in Person

Person is the writer's perspective. In some writing assignments, you may use the first person (*I, we*). For other assignments, you may use the second person (*you*) or the third person (*he, she, it, they*). Make sure that your pronouns are consistent in person. Therefore, if you begin writing from one point of view, do not shift unnecessarily to another point of view.

> *we*
> If we had studied, ~~one~~ would have passed the exam.

> *we*
> We visited every library, but ~~you~~ could not find the book.

Making Pronouns Consistent in Number

Pronouns and antecedents must agree in **number.** If the antecedent is singular, then the pronoun must be singular. If the antecedent is plural, then the pronoun must be plural.

> *his or her*
> Each nutritionist encouraged ~~their~~ clients to talk openly.

> *he or she*
> If a chef wants to reduce a restaurant's carbon footprint, ~~they~~ should buy locally grown food.

Hint   **Avoiding Pronoun Shifts in Paragraphs**

Sometimes it is easier to use pronouns consistently in individual sentences than in larger paragraphs or essays. When you write paragraphs and essays, always check that the pronouns agree with the antecedents in person.

In the next example, the pronouns are consistent in the first two sentences. However, they shift in person in the third sentence.

> **I** am studying food sciences, and **I** want to be a nutritionist. In **my** program,
> *I*
> there are so many courses that ~~you~~ cannot decide which ones to take.

PRACTICE 5

Correct the sentences that have pronoun shift errors. Write *C* beside any sentences that are correct.

EXAMPLE:

_____ I have seen so many memorable documentaries
> *I*
that ~~you~~ don't know which one is the most interesting.

1. <u>WE</u>   We went to see the documentary *Supersize Me* by
   Morgan Spurlock, and *we* ~~you~~ were amazed by the
   information.

2. _____ Spurlock conducted an experiment in which *he* ~~you~~
   ate three McDonald's meals each day.

SUPER SIZE ME

A Film of Epic Portions

3. _____ Spurlock started his experiment because ~~one~~ he had heard about rising rates of obesity in America.

4. _____ As I watched the film, ~~you~~ I could see the effects on Spurlock's body.

5. C As time went on, we saw Spurlock gaining weight, and we were shocked at how easily Spurlock's size changed.

6. _____ I read that McDonald's no longer sells supersized meals, and ~~you~~ I know that Spurlock's documentary influenced the decision.

7. C I heard that McDonald's is very critical of the documentary, so I am going to the McDonald's website to read about it.

8. _____ My friends and I like to eat fast food, but ~~you~~ we should really cut back.

Pronoun Case

Pronouns are formed according to the role they play in a sentence. A pronoun can be the subject or object of the sentence, or it can show possession. This chart shows the three main pronoun cases: subjective, objective, and possessive.

Pronoun Case

Singular	Subjective	Objective	Possessive Possessive Adjective	Possessive Pronoun
First person:	I	me	my	mine
Second person:	you	you	your	yours
Third person:	he, she, it, who, whoever	him, her, it, whom, whomever	his, her, its, whose	his, hers
Plural				
First person:	we	us	our	ours
Second person:	you	you	your	yours
Third person:	they	them	their	theirs

Subjective Case

A **subject** performs an action in a sentence. When a pronoun is the subject of the sentence, use the subjective form of the pronoun. In the following sentences, *she* and *we* are the subjects.

> **She** was a chef for about twenty-five years.

> **We** listened to a lecture on food safety yesterday.

Objective Case

An **object** receives an action in a sentence. When a pronoun is the object in the sentence, use the objective form of the pronoun. In the following sentences, *him* and *us* are objects.

> My horticulture class sent **him** an invitation to speak at the ceremony.

> My sister told **us** about the farmer's market.

Possessive Case

A possessive pronoun shows ownership.

- **Possessive adjectives** are always placed before the noun that they modify. In the next sentences, *his* and *her* are possessive adjectives.

    He finished **his** <u>essay</u> about fast food, but she did not finish **her** <u>essay</u>.

- **Possessive pronouns** replace the possessive adjective and noun. In the next sentence, *her* is a possessive adjective and *theirs* is a possessive pronoun.

    She finished **her** <u>essay</u> about fast food, but they did not finish **theirs.**

PRACTICE 6

Underline the pronouns in each sentence. Then identify the case of each pronoun. Write *S* for subjective case, *O* for objective case, and *P* for possessive case.

EXAMPLE:

                P

Celebrity chef Rachel Ray has <u>her</u> own television show.

1. Recently, celebrity chefs have acquired cult status, and <u>they</u> can influence many people.

2. Some chefs have acquired multimillion-dollar empires by promoting <u>their</u> own cookbooks, television shows, and kitchen products.

3. Julia Child learned how to cook when <u>she</u> moved to Paris with <u>her</u> husband.

4. Child became the first celebrity chef when <u>she</u> showed Americans the secret of French cuisine on <u>her</u> television show.

5. Child wrote easy-to-follow recipes, and <u>her</u> fans gained the self-confidence to cook French food in <u>their</u> homes.

6. Martha Stewart, another celebrity chef, is popular with fans because <u>she</u> gives <u>them</u> tips on how to improve <u>their</u> lifestyle.

7. More recently, Jaime Oliver has become famous, and the public admires <u>him</u> for improving menus in school cafeterias.

8. Nigella Lawson flirts while cooking on television, and many people enjoy watching <u>her</u>.

Problems with Possessive Pronouns

When using the possessive pronouns *hers* and *theirs*, be careful that you do not add an apostrophe before the *-s*.

hers	*theirs*

The recipe book is ~~her's~~. The food magazine is ~~their's~~.

Some possessive adjectives sound like certain contractions. Review these examples of commonly confused words.

Possessive adjective: **Their** field trip was canceled.

Contraction: **They're** going to go next week.   (*They're = they are.*)

Possessive adjective: **Your** nutritionist will help you choose the right food.

Contraction: **You're** going to enjoy the trip to the agricultural fair.   (*You're = you are.*)

Possessive adjective: **Its** theme is about the influence of technology on farming practices.

Contraction: **It's** a book that you should read.   (*It's = it is.*)

GRAMMAR LINK

See Chapter 27 for more detailed information about apostrophes.

Hint   **His or Her?**

To choose the correct possessive adjective, think about the possessor, *not* the object that is possessed.

• If something belongs to or is a relative of a female, use *her* + noun.

    Allison and **her** father both work as chefs.

• If something belongs to or is a relative of a male, use *his* + noun.

    John Deere wanted **his** workers to build solid plows.

PRACTICE 7

Underline the correct word in each set of parentheses.

EXAMPLE:

    The tomatoes are (her / <u>hers</u>), but the corn is (my / <u>mine</u>).

1.   Wycliffe Brown has been a farmer since (<u>his</u> / her/ their) father retired and gave (he / <u>him</u>) the family farm. He and (<u>his</u> / her) wife, Michelle, grow organic vegetables on (they're / <u>their</u> / theirs) farm. Michelle also grows organic herbs on (his / <u>her</u> / hers) own plot of land. The herd of sheep is also (they're / their / <u>theirs</u>). The farm is quite successful, but (<u>they're</u> / their / theirs) worried about (they're / <u>their</u> / theirs) competitors. In the United States, more and more large corporations are involved in agricultural production.

2.   Critics say that corporate farming concentrates agriculture production, distribution, and sales in one business source. As a result, the family farm is losing (it's / <u>its</u> / his) competitive edge and often goes bankrupt. A small farmer may be forced into doing business with a corporation. Proponents of corporate farming claim that mass food production is positive because of (it's / <u>its</u>) cost efficiency. The corporate farm is beneficial for everybody because (<u>it's</u> / its) able to provide cheaper food to more people all year around.

3.   My sister and I grew up on a farm where (<u>our</u> / ours) parents practiced organic farming methods, and (<u>we</u> / us) grew up eating only organic produce. My sister and I now have completely different shopping habits. I buy (<u>my</u> / mine) groceries anywhere convenient, but (<u>my</u> / mine) sister buys (her / <u>hers</u>) only at an organic market. Where do (<u>you</u> / your) buy (you / <u>your</u> / you're) food? Maybe (you / your / <u>you're</u>) also an organic food lover?

Pronouns in Comparisons with *Than* or *As*

Avoid making errors in pronoun case when the pronoun follows *than* or *as*. If the pronoun is a subject, use the subjective case. If the pronoun is an object, use the objective case.

If you use the incorrect case, your sentence may have a meaning that you do not intend it to have. Look at the differences in the meanings of the next sentences.

Objective case: I like pizza as much as **him.**
        (I like pizza *as much as I like him.*)

Subjective case: I like pizza as much as **he.**
        (I like pizza *as much as he likes pizza* or *I like pizza as much as he does.*)

 **Complete the Thought**

If you are unsure which pronoun case to use, test by completing the thought.
    He likes salty snacks more than **I** [like salty snacks].
    He likes salty snacks more than [he likes] **me.**

Pronouns in Prepositional Phrases

A **prepositional phrase** is made up of a preposition and its object. Therefore, always use the objective case of the pronoun after a preposition.

<u>To</u> **him,** Will Kellogg was a man with great ideas.

<u>Between</u> **you** and **me,** that breakfast cereal is too sweet.

CHAPTER 7

Pronouns with *And* or *Or*

Use the correct case when nouns and pronouns are joined by *and* or *or*. If the pronouns are the subject, use the subjective case. If the pronouns are the object, use the objective case.

He and I
~~Him and me~~ had to do a presentation on fusion cuisine.

                             him and me
The instructor asked ~~he and I~~ to present first.

> ### Hint   Finding the Correct Case
>
> An easy way to determine that your case is correct is to say the sentence with just one pronoun.
>
>   The teacher asked her and (**I, me**) to do the presentation.
>
> **Possible choices:** The teacher asked **I** . . . *or* The teacher asked **me** . . .
>
> **Correct answer:** The teacher asked her and **me** to do the presentation.

PRACTICE 8

Correct any errors with pronoun case. Write *C* in the space if the sentence is correct.

EXAMPLE:

    My friend likes this course more than ~~me~~.   <u>*I (do)*</u>

1. Sanjay and me are in the same economics class.   <u> I </u>

2. Him and I have to write a paper on the Green Revolution, a term applied to agriculture changes in the Third World in the 1960s.   <u>   </u>

3. Professor King informed our class that the term Green Revolution described the export of American farming techniques to third world nations.   <u>   </u>

4. My professor told we students that the Green Revolution increased agricultural productivity in the Third World.   <u>   </u>

5. Sanjay told my friend Gael and I that the Green Revolution also had negative effects.   <u>   </u>

6. The United States supplied seeds to third world farmers, but they encountered problems.   <u>   </u>

7. Prakash Gosh was a poor farmer, and wealthier farmers benefited more than him.   <u>   </u>

8. Him and his wife could not afford to buy seeds because they were too expensive.   <u>   </u>

9. Also, poorer farmers could not afford to buy expensive farm machinery, so them and their families suffered.   <u>   </u>

10. Between you and I, I think I might change my major from
    agricultural economics to computer science. _____

PRACTICE 9 REVIEW

Correct ten pronoun errors in the next paragraphs.

EXAMPLE:

Consumers should read food labels when they buy ~~they're~~ *their* groceries.

1.   Everyone wants his or hers food to taste good. But are consumers

equally concerned about the nutritional quality of they're food? A recent

focus group indicated that Americans would rather have one's food be tasty

than nutritious. The food industry has responded to this consumer

preference by adding flavors to packaged foods.

2.   The average American family eats approximately 25 percent of it's

meals at restaurants. Fast food contains a lot of artificial flavors, but so

does food at other types of restaurants. Macy Robards is a chef at an

expensive restaurant in Chicago. Although clients eat fresh ingredients at

her restaurant, their also getting a dose of artificial flavors. For example,

just as a fast-food chain may use artificial flavor for it's sauces and

dressings, she also uses such flavoring in her's.

3.   In his book, *Fast Food Nation*, Eric Schlosser writes that approximately ten

thousand new processed food products are marketed every year. Most

packaged food contains added flavors and colors. Schlosser is a well-known

personality, although some people find he a controversial figure. My friend

Lindsey is more influenced by Schlosser's book than me. Lindsey and me

discuss his book a lot.

Relative Pronouns

Relative pronouns can join two short sentences. Here is a list of relative pronouns.

who	whom	which	that	whose
whoever	whomever			

- *Who* (or *whoever*) and *whom* (or *whomever*) always refer to people. *Who* is the subject of the clause, and *whom* is the object of the clause.

  The <u>chef</u> **who** specializes in Japanese cuisine is speaking today.

  The <u>restaurant critic</u> **whom** you met is my sister.

- *Which* always refers to things. *Which* clauses are set off with commas.

  The Irish potato <u>famine</u>, **which** led to mass emigration, was caused by a disease.

- *That* refers to things.

  The history <u>book</u> **that** was about the Irish potato famine was a bestseller.

- *Whose* always shows that something belongs to or is connected with someone or something. It usually replaces the possessive pronoun *his*, *her*, or *their*. Do not confuse *whose* with *who's*, which means "who is."

  The food activist was selling fair-trade coffee when <u>his</u> car got towed.

  The food activist, **whose** car got towed, was selling fair-trade coffee.

GRAMMAR LINK

Clauses with *which* are set off with commas. For more information, see Chapter 26, "Commas."

> *Hint* **Who or Whom?**

If you are unsure whether to use *who* or *whom*, test yourself in the following way. Replace *who* or *whom* with another pronoun. If the replacement is a subject such as *he* or *she*, use *who*. If the replacement is an object such as *her* or *him*, use *whom*.

I know a pastry chef **who** makes excellent croissants.
(He makes excellent croissants.)

The man to **whom** you gave a recipe is a restaurant critic.
(You gave your recipe to <u>him</u>.)

PRACTICE 10

Underline the correct relative pronoun in each set of parentheses.

EXAMPLE:

Shoppers (<u>who</u> / which) are concerned about food sources buy organically grown produce.

1. People (<u>who</u> / whom) are concerned about the state of the world have a new method of expressing their views.

2. They can influence economic policy by buying food products (who / <u>that</u>) promote social equity.

3. Xing Feng and his wife are consumers for (<u>who</u> / whom) equitable trade is an important issue.

4. Therefore, they buy food (who / <u>that</u>) is labeled "fair trade."

5. Like the Fengs, other food activists (who / whom) believe in social causes also make political statements through consumer choices.

6. The food activism movement, (which / that) is growing rapidly, is a relatively new phenomenon.

7. In the past, consumers would boycott products of companies (which / that) used unfair business practices.

8. Nowadays, business people, for (who / whom) profits are important, look at customer buying trends.

9. Hugo Ricci, (who / whose) company sells fair trade products, says that his business is thriving.

10. The organic food and fair trade industry, (which / that) consumers are heartily supporting, made a profit of more than $30 billion last year.

PRACTICE 11

Write the correct relative pronoun from the list below in each blank. Remember that you cannot use *which* unless the clause is set off with commas.

| who | whom | whose | which | that |

EXAMPLE:

Consumers _____*who*_____ strongly support environmental causes often buy organic food.

1.   Organic food has many definitions. Food ___*that*___ has been grown using little or no synthetic pesticide or fertilizer is generally labeled organic. Farmers ___*whom*___ crops are labeled organic do not use genetically modified seeds. Many people ___*that*___ buy organic food think that such food is better for their health. However, food ___*which*___ has been grown organically is not nutritionally superior to non-organically grown food.

2.   Most consumers ___*who*___ buy organic food also believe that it is better for the environment. However, not everyone agrees. Dr. Norman Borlaug is considered to be the father of the Green Revolution. He believes that organic farming produces lower crop yields, requiring more land use. Synthetic fertilizers ___*that*___ contribute to greater crop production help the environment significantly more than organic methods.

3.   Consumers for ___*whom*___ health and environment are important should consider both sides of the issue. Certainly, the organic food industry, ___*which*___ is very profitable, will continue to grow in popularity in the near future.

Reflexive Pronouns (*-self, -selves*)

Use **reflexive pronouns** when you want to emphasize that the subject does an action to him- or herself.

> We ask **ourselves** many questions.

> The book sells **itself** because it is so good.

It is not typical to use reflexive pronouns for personal care activities, such as washing or shaving. However, you can use reflexive pronouns to draw attention to a surprising or an unusual action.

> My three-year-old **sister** fed **herself**.
>
> (The girl probably could not feed herself at a previous time.)

The next chart shows subjective pronouns and the reflexive pronouns that relate to them.

Pronouns That End with *-self* or *-selves*

Singular	Antecedent	Reflexive Pronouns
First person:	I	myself
Second person:	you	yourself
Third person:	he, she, it	himself, herself, itself
Plural		
First person:	we	ourselves
Second person:	you	yourselves
Third person:	they	themselves

Hint **Common Errors with Reflexive Pronouns**

Hisself and *theirselves* do not exist in English. These are incorrect ways to say *himself* and *themselves*.

> *themselves*
> The students went by ~~theirselves~~ to the lecture.

> *himself*
> The pastry chef worked by ~~hisself~~.

PRACTICE 12

Fill in the blanks with the correct reflexive pronouns.

EXAMPLE:

> I do not like to eat by _____*myself*_____.

1. Many times I wish that our dinner would get ready by
   _____itself_____.

2. I often cook meals by _____myself_____.

3. Sometimes my children start preparing dinner by _themselves_.

4. My son Alex goes grocery shopping by _himself_.

5. My daughter plans some meals by _herself_.

6. When my children make a fabulous dinner, I always say, "Congratulate _yourselves_ on a job well done."

7. If my husband is late coming home from work, my children and I eat by _ourselves_.

8. On such occasions, he humbly offers to clean the kitchen by _himself_.

9. Do you eat dinner with others or by _yourself_?

FINAL REVIEW

Read the following paragraphs and correct twenty pronoun errors.

EXAMPLE:

                        its

The Slow Food movement and ~~it's~~ supporters are getting publicity.

1.   In Italy, everybody loves ~~their~~ *his or her* food. Italians ~~they~~ take the time to enjoy long and delicious meals. In 1986, Carlo Petrini, ~~which~~ *who* was enjoying a coffee, read that McDonald's was opening an outlet in downtown Rome. To protest the growing presence of the fast-food culture, he started the Slow Food movement. This has been growing in popularity since that time.

2.   Although Petrini started the movement by ~~hisself~~ *himself*, he soon had many supporters. Those people, ~~who's~~ *whose* aim was to slow the increasingly hurried pace of daily life, developed a set of objectives. Their objectives, ~~who~~ *which* are quite diverse, are published on the group's website. The organization and ~~it's~~ *its* members preserve seed variety and educate the public on farming issues.

3.   Mr. Khalil Isoke and ~~her~~ *his* wife, Farah, are members of the Slow Food movement. They took my friend Miriam and ~~I~~ *me* to a cooking class. The chef, ~~which~~ *whose* skill was evident, was a good teacher. The other students ~~they~~ were all

better cooks than me. But I congratulated me when my dish turned out as well as them. At the end of the class, each of the participants shared their favorite recipes with the other students. The students for who the Slow Food philosophy is a lifestyle choice liked the cooking class very much.

4.   I am beginning to appreciate the philosophy of the Slow Food group. Sometimes I become so busy during the day that you don't have time to breathe. Between you and I, I could start to like cooking. Do you and you're friends know about the Slow Food movement?

 The Writer's Room

Write about one of the following topics. After you finish writing, circle any pronouns and check for pronoun–antecedent agreement, pronoun case, and pronoun shift.

1.   What causes people to eat junk food?
2.   Should fast-food companies be held responsible for some of the health problems in our society? Explain your point of view.

✔ CHECKLIST: PRONOUNS

When you edit your writing, ask yourself the next set of questions.

☐   Do I use the correct pronoun case? Check for errors with the following:

–subjective, objective, and possessive case
–comparisons with *than* or *as*
–prepositional phrases
–pronouns after *and* or *or*

Between you and ~~I~~ *me*, my parents were stricter with my brother than ~~I~~ *me*.

☐   Do I use the correct relative pronouns? Check for errors with *who*, *whom*, or *whose*.

My husband, ~~who~~ *whom* you have met, is a coffee salesman.

☐ Do my pronouns and antecedents agree in number and person?
Check for errors with indefinite pronouns and collective nouns.

The government announced ~~their~~ *its* new policy: everyone will have
~~their~~ *his or her* own identity card.

☐ Are my pronoun references clear? Check for vague pronouns and
inconsistent points of view.

~~They~~ *Policy makers* say that family farms are suffering. I read the report, and ~~you~~ *I*

could not believe what it said.

 The Writers' Circle **Collaborative Activity**

Work with a partner to write a short paragraph about what your partner has
in his or her purse, backpack, pencil case, or locker. Describe the items and
what the person does with those items. Then exchange paragraphs with your
partner and check that nouns and pronouns are used correctly.

READING LINK

Lifestyles
To read more about issues related to lifestyles, see the next essays.
"Fish Cheeks" by Amy Tan (page 408)
"The New Addiction by Josh Freed (page 412)
"Fat Chance" by Dorothy Nixon (page 414)

mywritinglab To check your progress in meeting this chapter's objectives,
log in to **www.mywritinglab.com**, go to the **Study Plan**
tab, click on **The Editing Handbook—Section 1 Some Parts of Speech** and
choose **Pronouns** from the list of subtopics. Read and view the resources in the
Review Materials section, and then complete the **Recall, Apply,** and **Write** sets
in the **Activities** section.

CHAPTER 8

Subjects and Verbs

Section Theme: **ENTERTAINMENT AND CULTURE**

In this chapter, you will read about music and musicians.

Grammar Snapshot

Looking at Subjects and Verbs

Sonia Margossian teaches singing. In the next excerpt from a speech, she discusses proper breathing techniques. Notice that subjects are in bold type and the verbs are underlined. Also observe that some sentences have no visible subjects.

> Stand straight, and place your hands on your stomach, just below the ribs. Then take a long, deep breath and carry the air to the bottom of your lungs. Your **shoulders** should not move as you breathe. As **you** continue to inhale, your **chest** will inflate.

In this chapter, you will identify subjects and verbs.

Identifying Subjects

A **sentence** has a subject and a verb, and it expresses a complete thought. The **subject** tells you who or what the sentence is about. The **verb** expresses an action or state. If a sentence is missing a subject or a verb, it is incomplete.

subject   verb

Prehistoric **humans** <u>banged</u> on hollow logs to make music.

Singular or Plural Subjects

Subjects may be singular or plural. To determine the subject of a sentence, ask yourself who or what the sentence is about.

A **singular subject** is one person, place, or thing.

Mozart learned to play piano at an early age.

The **violin** is difficult to master.

A **plural subject** is more than one person, place, or thing.

People still listen to Mozart's music.

Some **instruments** are easy to learn.

Pronouns as Subjects

A **subject pronoun** (*he, she, it, you, we, they*) can act as the subject of a sentence.

Greg wants that guitar, but **it** is very expensive.

Louisa has a great voice. **She** should sing more often.

Gerunds (*-ing* Words) as Subjects

Sometimes a **gerund** (the *-ing* form of a verb, acting as a noun) is the subject of a sentence.

Listening is an important skill.

Dancing can improve your cardiovascular health.

 **Simple Versus Complete Subject**

In a sentence, the **simple subject** is the noun or pronoun. The complete name of a person, place, or organization is a simple subject.

   she   guitar   Keyshia Cole   Sony Music Corporation

The **complete subject** is the noun, plus the words that describe the noun. In these examples, the descriptive words are underlined.

   <u>new acoustic</u> guitar   <u>Jazmine's upright</u> piano   <u>the tiny</u> microphone

simple subject

The expensive old **violin** is very fragile.

complete subject

PRACTICE I

Underline the complete subject in each sentence. (Remember to underline the subject and the words that describe the subject.) Then circle the simple subject.

EXAMPLE:

A famous recording (artist) is Beyoncé Knowles.

1. (Beyoncé Giselle Knowles) was born on September 4, 1981.
2. Singing became (her) greatest talent.
3. Seven-year-old (Beyoncé) entered her first music competition.
4. The talented young (girl) sang (John Lennon's) "Imagine."
5. Her best (friend) created a group called Girl's Tyme.
6. The six-member (group) traveled across the (nation).
7. (Beyoncé's family) was extremely supportive.
8. The group's (name) was changed to (Destiny's Child).
9. Their (songs) became extremely popular.
10. Beyoncé's supportive (father) quit his sales job to become the group's manager.

Compound Subjects

Many sentences have more than one subject. These are called compound subjects. Notice that *and* is not part of the compound subject.

> **Guitars**, **lutes**, and **banjos** are stringed instruments.

> **Reporters** and **photographers** crowded around the singer.

PRACTICE 2

Complete each sentence by adding one or more logical subjects.

EXAMPLE:

_____Rihanna_____ sings and dances.

1. In my opinion, _____R & B_____ is the most interesting type of music.

2. _____Gymnastics_____ is not one of my greatest talents.

3. _____Usher_____, _____Chris Brown_____, and _____Trey Songz_____ are great musicians.

4. The _____Guitar_____ is missing a string.

5. The _____harp_____ and _____piano_____ are my least favorite instruments.

Special Subject Problems
Unstated Subjects (Commands)

In a sentence that expresses a command, the subject is unstated, but it is still understood. <u>The unstated subject is *you*.</u> (The word *should* is implied.)

> Practice every day.   *→ will be on test*

> Do not judge the musician harshly.

Here, There

Here and *there* are not subjects. In sentences that begin with *here* or *there*, the subject follows the verb.

> verb   subject
> There <u>are</u> five **<u>ways</u>** to improve your voice.

> verb   subject
> Here <u>is</u> my **<u>iPod.</u>**

Hint   **Ask Who or What**

When you are trying to determine the subject, read the sentence carefully and ask yourself who or what the sentence is about. Do not presume that all nouns are the subjects in a sentence. For example, in the next sentence, *music, dance,* and *occasions* are nouns, but they are not the subject.

Most **<u>cultures</u>** use music and dance to celebrate special occasions.

PRACTICE 3

Underline one or more simple subjects in these sentences. If the subject is unstated, write *you.*

EXAMPLE:

> *You listen*
> ~~Listen~~ to music as often as possible.

1. Every known human <u>society</u> has a form of music.   *Simple subject*

2. <u>Music</u> stimulates many parts of the brain.

3. There are various musical <u>styles</u> in North America.

4. Some <u>cultures</u> do not distinguish between musicians and ordinary people.

5. For example, <u>music</u> is as natural as breathing in Indonesia.

6. Some animal <u>species</u> use musical sounds to communicate.

7. There are many exotic <u>birds</u> that are unable to sing.

8. <u>Douglas Nelson</u> taught songs to some sparrows.

9. If possible, try to learn a musical instrument.   *you*

Identifying Prepositional Phrases

A **preposition** is a word that links nouns, pronouns, and phrases to other words in a sentence. It expresses a relationship based on movement or position.

Common Prepositions

about	before	during	of	toward
above	behind	except	off	under
across	below	for	on	until
after	beside	from	onto	up
against	between	in	out	with
along	beyond	inside	outside	within
among	by	into	over	
around	despite	like	through	
at	down	near	to	

A **phrase** is a group of words that is missing a subject, a verb, or both, and it is not a complete sentence. A **prepositional phrase** is made up of a preposition and its object (a noun or a pronoun).

Preposition	**+**	**Object**
in		the morning
among		the shadows
over		the rainbow
with		some friends

> ### Hint Nouns Are Not Always Subjects
>
> Because the object of a preposition is a noun, it may look like a subject. However, the object in a prepositional phrase is never the subject of the sentence.
>
>   subject
> With her husband, **Carly** composed a hit song.

To help you identify the subject of a sentence, it is a good idea to put parentheses around prepositional phrases, cross them out, or identify them in some other way. In each of the following sentences, the subject is in bold type and the prepositional phrase is in parentheses.

(In most countries,) particular **musical styles** exist.

The **studio** (on Slater Street) is closed.

The **information** (in that magazine) is true.

PRACTICE 4

In each sentence, place parentheses around one or more prepositional phrases.
Then circle the simple subject.

EXAMPLE:

(According to Kristin Leutwyler of *Scientific American*,)prehistoric⟨humans⟩
listened to music.

1. In the past, Neanderthals may have had a musical tradition.

2. In 1996, Slovenian archeologist Ivan Turk discovered a small bone flute.

3. Over 50,000 years ago, the sweet-sounding flute was carved from the thigh
   of a cave bear.

4. With four nearly perfect holes in a row, the wind instrument was quite
   sophisticated.

5. In a speech, Boston biologist Jelle Atema discussed the technical skills of
   the ancient people.

6. Early humans, with their friends and family, probably played music together.

7. In other places such as Africa, South America, and China, scientists have
   found very old wind and stringed instruments.

8. Perhaps ancient people without a common language could communicate
   with musical sounds.

PRACTICE 5

If the underlined word is the subject, write *C* (for "correct") in the space. If the
underlined word is not the subject, then circle the correct subject(s).

EXAMPLES:

In 1959,⟨Michael Jackson⟩was born.   _____

The music <u>star</u> worked throughout his childhood.   *C*

1. Some young⟨children⟩demonstrate exceptional musical <u>gifts</u>.   _____

2. An amazing child <u>prodigy</u> is pianist Emily Bear.   _____

3. With intense <u>concentration</u>, seven-year-old Emily plays beautifully.   _____

4. The <u>child's</u> father and mother do not force her to perform.   _____

5. However, without a <u>doubt</u>, some talented children are exploited.   _____

6. At the <u>age</u> of five, Michael Jackson became a part of his family's
   musical act.   _____

7. His <u>days</u> were spent studying and then rehearsing.   _____

8. As a <u>child</u>, Jackson had the confidence and poise of an adult. _____

9. As an <u>adult</u>, the musical legend searched for his lost childhood.   _____

I always get nervous before taking a test.

CHAPTER 8

Identifying Verbs

Every sentence must contain a verb. The **verb** either expresses what the subject does or links the subject to other descriptive words.

Action Verbs

Action verbs describe the actions that the subject performs.

> The musicians <u>performed</u> in Carnegie Hall.

> The Irish dancers <u>stamped</u> their heels in time to the music.

Compound Verbs

When a subject performs more than one action, the verbs are called **compound verbs.**

> Mr. Gibson <u>makes</u>, <u>polishes</u>, and <u>sells</u> good-quality guitars.

PRACTICE 6

Fill in each space with an appropriate and interesting action verb.

EXAMPLE:

> The Petersons _____*paid*_____ for their tickets and _____*entered*_____ the theater.

1. Adam, the pianist, _____ the audience.

2. He then _____ beautifully.

3. At the end of the performance, the audience _*clapped*_ _*cried*_ and _*Cheered*_ _*screamed*_.

4. The performer _____ to his dressing room.

5. He _____ on his sofa, exhausted.

6. Somebody _____ on the door and _____.

Linking Verbs

Linking verbs (or state verbs) do not describe an action; instead, they describe a state of being or give information about the subject. The most common linking verb is *be* (*am, are, is, was, were*).

> The harp <u>is</u> a lovely instrument.

> Those sound systems <u>are</u> unreliable.

Other linking verbs link the subject with descriptive words.

        subject   linking verb   descriptive word
That **music**   sounds   *good.*

       subject   linking verb descriptive words
Felicia   seems   *quite eccentric.*

Here are some common linking verbs:

act	feel	seem
appear	get	smell
be (am, is, are, was, were)	look	sound
become	remain	taste

[handwritten marginal notes:] Particle is a verb form used as an adjective
ing → ending as an adjective

CHAPTER 8

PRACTICE 7

Underline the linking verb in each sentence.

EXAMPLE:

   In some cultures, musicians <u>are</u> important people in the community.

1. Among the Mandiki of Senegal, the jali <u>is</u> a highly specialized musician.

2. The jali <u>acts</u> as the official singer of the tribe.

3. His songs <u>sound</u> haunting and powerful.

4. The tribe's history <u>becomes</u> part of the jali's repertoire.

5. The music <u>seems</u> simple.

6. However, it <u>is</u> actually quite complex.

7. The jali <u>appears</u> confident during his performance.

8. The tribe members <u>are</u> ready for the jali to commemorate important events.

 Infinitives Are Not the Main Verb

Infinitives are verbs preceded by *to,* such as *to sing, to play,* and *to run.* An infinitive is never the main verb in a sentence.

              verb infinitive   verb   infinitive
Chuck Berry <u>wanted</u> to be famous. He <u>hoped</u> to become a music legend.

PRACTICE 8

Circle the simple subjects and underline the verbs in the following sentences. Some sentences have more than one verb. Write *L* beside any sentence that contains a linking verb.

EXAMPLE:

In the nineteenth century, (music) was a local activity.

1. Nowadays, with the Internet, talented amateur (musicians) are able to find an audience.

2. Lily Allen posted her own songs on her MySpace page.

3. Some singers become famous after appearing on talent shows.

4. In 2009, Susan Boyle appeared in a British talent show.

5. The frumpy Scottish woman seemed unattractive and comical.

6. Audience members snickered and rolled their eyes.

7. Then Boyle opened her mouth and sang.

8. The woman with bushy eyebrows became an Internet sensation.

9. During a two-week period, over 100 million people watched her on YouTube.

10. In 2010, the busy Scottish singer released her first album.

Susan Boyle

Helping Verbs

Many verbs contain two or more words: a main verb and a helping verb. The **main verb** expresses what the subject does or links the subject to descriptive words. The **helping verb** combines with the main verb to indicate tense, negative structure, or question structure.

Be, Have, Do

The common helping verbs *be*, *have*, and *do* combine with the main verb to indicate a tense, negative structure, or question structure.

Some songs <u>have been</u> <u>banned</u> from radio station play lists.

Modals

A modal is another type of helping verb. It indicates ability (*can*), obligation (*must*), possibility (*may, might, could*), advice (*should*), and so on.

Violent lyrics <u>can</u> <u>influence</u> children.

Questions

In question forms, the first helping verb usually appears before the subject.

> HV   subject   V
>
> <u>Should</u> radio **stations** <u>censor</u> song lyrics?

> HV   subject   V
>
> <u>Do</u> violent, sexist, or racist **songs** <u>influence</u> young listeners?

Hint   **Interrupting Words and Phrases**

Interrupting words may appear between verbs, but they are *not* part of the verb. Some interrupting words are *always, easily, ever, never, not, often, sometimes,* and *usually.*

> HV interrupter V
>
> Blues music <u>can</u> **sometimes** <u>be</u> sorrowful.

PRACTICE 9

Underline each complete verb once. Then underline each main verb twice.

EXAMPLE:

    Musicians with perfect pitch <u>are</u> <u>envied</u>.

1. According to an article in *Scientific American*, very few people <u>have</u> <u>achieved</u> perfect pitch.

2. Human beings with absolute pitch <u>will</u> easily <u>sing</u> an F sharp.

3. Most people <u>do</u> not <u>have</u> this ability.

4. Only one person in ten thousand <u>can</u> <u>identify</u> a note perfectly.

5. <u>Do</u> people from some cultures <u>have</u> a superior ability to recognize tones?

6. In languages such as Vietnamese and Mandarin, people can pronounce one word in several different ways.

7. The meaning of each word may depend on the tone of the word.

8. Diana Deutsch of the University of California has discussed the topic in her lectures.

9. According to Deutch, native speakers of tonal languages, even those with no musical training, can recognize and repeat notes perfectly.

10. Perhaps tonal words should be used to teach children about pitch.

FINAL REVIEW

Circle each simple subject and underline each complete verb. Underline each main verb twice. If prepositional phrases confuse you, you can cross them out or put them in parentheses.

EXAMPLE:

A <u>university</u> in Maryland <u>studied</u> the effects of music on health. The <u>study</u> <u>was published</u> in 2009.

1. Across the nation, citizens hope to become famous singers. Television programs have capitalized on this deep-seated desire. There are long line-ups at every *American Idol* audition. The popular program is watched by millions of viewers.

2. Of course, good singing is not a universal skill. Many people do not sing well. For instance, Jamie Orchard and Ryan Woo claim to have horrible voices. But singing may actually be beneficial for our bodies and our overall health. Everybody should sing sometimes.

3. A prominent researcher from George Washington University has published studies about singing and health. Dr. Gene D. Cohen did not expect singing to have a noticeable effect on human bodies. He decided to study two groups of seniors. One group was required to sing every day. The elderly men and women in the singing group felt better and had higher energy than those in the non-singing group. A University of Frankfurt study revealed similar results. Regular singing can stimulate blood circulation and reduce blood pressure.

4. Do you have some musical talent? Are you a good singer? Clearly, there are many good reasons to sing. You should not worry about the quality of your voice. You can always find a private place to create music. Daily singing can become part of your health regime.

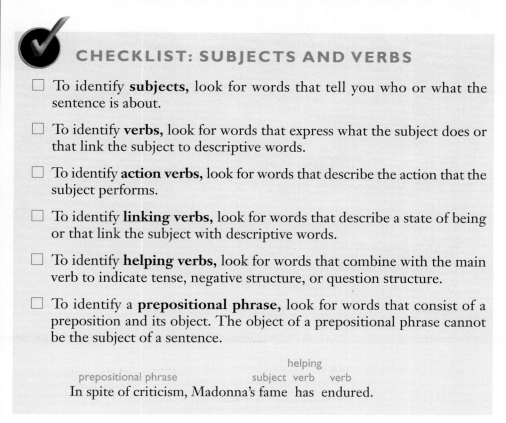

The Writer's Room

Write about one of the following topics. After you finish writing, circle your subjects and underline your verbs. Underline main verbs twice.

1. What qualities does a professional singer need? List at least five qualities.
2. Compare two different singers. How are they similar or different?

CHAPTER 8

✔ CHECKLIST: SUBJECTS AND VERBS

☐ To identify **subjects,** look for words that tell you who or what the sentence is about.

☐ To identify **verbs,** look for words that express what the subject does or that link the subject to descriptive words.

☐ To identify **action verbs,** look for words that describe the action that the subject performs.

☐ To identify **linking verbs,** look for words that describe a state of being or that link the subject with descriptive words.

☐ To identify **helping verbs,** look for words that combine with the main verb to indicate tense, negative structure, or question structure.

☐ To identify a **prepositional phrase,** look for words that consist of a preposition and its object. The object of a prepositional phrase cannot be the subject of a sentence.

                                                   helping
prepositional phrase   subject verb   verb
In spite of criticism, Madonna's fame has endured.

mywriting**lab** To check your progress in meeting this chapter's objectives, log in to **www.mywritinglab.com,** go to the **Study Plan** tab, click on **The Editing Handbook—Section 2 Problems with Verbs** and choose **Subjects and Verbs** from the list of subtopics. Read and view the resources in the **Review Materials** section, and then complete the **Recall, Apply,** and **Write** sets in the **Activities** section.

CHAPTER 9

Present and Past Tenses

Section Theme: **ENTERTAINMENT AND CULTURE**

LEARNING OBJECTIVES

1. Understanding Verb Tense (p. 163)
2. The Simple Present Tense (p. 163)
3. The Simple Past Tense (p. 169)
4. Avoiding Double Negatives (p. 176)

In this chapter, you will read about literature and the media.

Grammar Snapshot

Looking at Present and Past Tenses

In 1902, W. W. Jacobs wrote one of the most frightening tales in literature, "The Monkey's Paw." In this excerpt, the past tense verbs are underlined. Which past tense verbs are irregular?

> She <u>noticed</u> that the stranger <u>was</u> well dressed and <u>wore</u> a silk hat of glossy newness. Three times he <u>paused</u> at the gate, and then <u>walked</u> on again. The fourth time he <u>stood</u> with his hand upon it, and then with sudden resolution <u>flung</u> it open and <u>walked</u> up the path.

In this chapter, you will identify and write present and past tense verbs.

Understanding Verb Tense

A verb shows an action or a state of being. A **verb tense** indicates when an action occurred. For example, review the various tenses of the verb *write*.

Past time: J. K. Rowling <u>wrote</u> parts of her first book in a coffee shop.

Present time: She <u>writes</u> every morning.

Future: Perhaps she <u>will write</u> a new book next year.

 **Use Standard Verb Forms**

Nonstandard English is used in everyday conversation and may differ according to the region in which you live. **Standard American English** is the common language generally used and expected in schools, businesses, and government institutions in the United States. Most of your instructors will want you to write using standard American English.

Nonstandard: She **be** busy. She **don't** have **no** time to talk.

She **ain't** finished with her work.

Standard: She **is** busy. She **doesn't** have **any** time to talk.

She <u>isn't</u> finished with her work.

[handwritten note in margin: infinitive verb begins → (to) with the word]

The Simple Present Tense

The **simple present tense** shows that an action is a general fact or habitual activity.

Fact: Harry Potter bo<u>oks</u> <u>sell</u> in countries throughout the world.

Habitual activity: J. K. Rowling <u>writes</u> every morning.

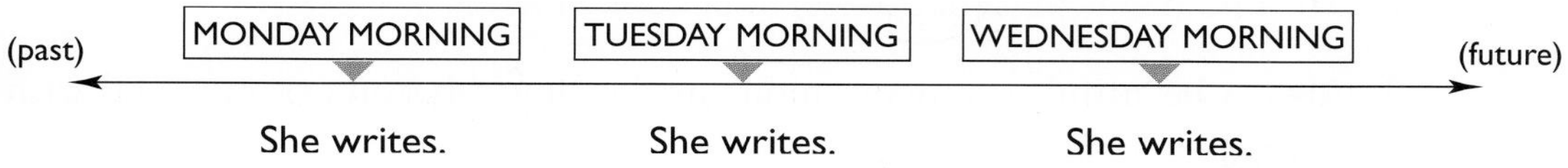

(past) ⟵ | MONDAY MORNING | | TUESDAY MORNING | | WEDNESDAY MORNING | ⟶ (future)

She writes.   She writes.   She writes.

Simple present tense verbs (except *be*) have two forms.

- **Base form.** When the subject is *I*, *you*, *we*, or *they*, do not add an ending to the verb.

  They <u>read</u> magazines. We often <u>borrow</u> their magazines.

- **Third-person singular form.** When the subject is *he*, *she*, *it*, or the equivalent (*Joe*, *Anne*, *New York*), add an *-s* or *-es* ending to the verb.

  The story <u>end</u>**s** badly. The main character <u>leaves</u> his family.

Look at the two forms of the verb *eat*. Notice the *-s* in bold print in the third-person singular form.

Present Tense of *Eat*

	Singular	Plural
First person:	I eat	We eat
Second person:	You eat	You eat
Third person:	He eats	They eat
	She eats	
	It eats	

CHAPTER 9

GRAMMAR LINK

See Chapter 13 for more detailed information about subject–verb agreement.

S = plural
P = singular

Subject–Verb Agreement

In the present tense, the subject and verb must **agree** in number. If the subject is third-person singular (*he, she, it*), the corresponding verb must have the singular form, too.

Although plural nouns usually end in -*s*, plural verbs do not. Instead, singular verbs have the -*s* or -*es* ending. Read the following sentences and notice the errors in subject–verb agreement.

       writes   *appear*
Jan Freeman ~~write~~ for the *Boston Globe*. Her columns ~~appears~~ every Sunday.

PRACTICE I

George Orwell, the author of *Animal Farm* and *1984*, wrote an essay called "Why I Write." The following sentences summarize his ideas. Underline the correct present tense form of each verb in parentheses.

EXAMPLE:

    Authors (<u>write</u>, writes) for several reasons.

1. Every writer (want, (wants)) to seem clever, according to George Orwell.

2. Most human beings ((like), likes) to be remembered.

3. Also, a beautiful or moving moment (become / becomes) immortal with writing.

4. A good writer (attempt, attempts) to show others the beauty of certain places.

5. People also (write, writes) to create a historical record of events.

6. Some writers (hope, hopes) to persuade others with their words.

7. Great novels (need, needs) to document political events.

8. Some lies (need / needs) to be exposed.

9. George Orwell's book *Animal Farm* (show, shows) certain injustices, and it (criticize, criticizes) Soviet-style communism.

10. Art (enjoy, (enjoys)) a relationship with politics.

Irregular Present Tense Verbs: *Be, Have*

Two common present tense verbs are irregular and do not follow the usual pattern for endings. Review the forms of the verbs *be* and *have*.

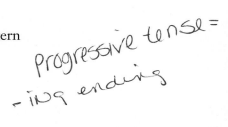

Progressive tense = -ing ending

Present Tense of *Be* and *Have*		
Singular	***Be***	***Have***
First person:	I am	I have
Second person:	You are	You have
Third person:	He is	He has
	She is	She has
	It is	It has
Plural		
First person:	We are	We have
Second person:	You are	You have
Third person:	They are	They have

> ## Hint
> ### Using the Irregular Verb *Be*
>
> Use the verb *be* to identify age, hunger, thirst, feelings, height, and temperature. Remember that the form of the verb must also agree with the subject of the sentence.
>
> **Age:** He ~~has~~ *is* forty years old.
>
> **Hunger and thirst:** He ~~has~~ *is* thirsty, and I ~~have~~ *am* hungry.
>
> **Temperature:** It ~~be~~ *is* cold outside.
>
> Do not use *be* to express agreement.
>
> I ~~am~~ agree.

PRACTICE 2

Write present tense verbs in the spaces provided. Use the correct forms of *be* and *have*.

EXAMPLE:

Stephenie Meyer _____*is*_____ the author of a successful series.

1. Meyer's book, *Twilight*, _____*is*_____ a romantic vampire tale. Over 40 million young adults _____*have*_____ the novel. In *Twilight*, Bella Swan _____*is*_____ seventeen years old. She moves to Forks, Washington. At school, the other students _____ not very friendly. However, one quiet boy with pale skin _____ very sweet to the newcomer. He _____ a loner. The other students _____ nothing nice to say about him. He _____ odd. For instance, at school he _____ never hungry. Soon, Bella _____ a crush on the quiet outsider.

2. Over time, Bella discovers that Edward _____ a vampire. He _____ thirsty for the taste of blood. However, he and his family _____ strong values and will not drink human blood. Small animals _____ to be careful, though. The novel _____ some surprising twists and turns.

3. *Twilight* _____ a huge online fan community. Meyer's book follows a Gothic literary tradition. Many horror novels _____ about a pale creature who drinks human blood. Usually, the vampire _____ extremely attractive. The vampire _____ always very old, yet he remains young and beautiful forever. The books appeal to our human desire for eternal youth and immortality. And of course, the romance _____ an attractive part of the story.

Question Forms: *Do* or *Does*

To create present tense questions, begin each question with *do* or *does*.

He complains a lot.	**Does** he complain a lot?
They read each night.	**Do** they read each night?

In the following chart, notice when to use the third-person singular form *does*.

Question Forms Using *Do* or *Does*		
	Singular	**Plural**
First person:	Do I work?	Do we work?
Second person:	Do you work?	Do you work?
Third person:	Does he work?	Do they work?
	Does she work?	
	Does it work?	

Exception: When the main verb is *be* (*is*, *am*, *are*), just move *be* before the subject to form a question.

The story is suspenseful.	**Is** the story suspenseful?
They are safe.	**Are** they safe?

PRACTICE 3

Fill in each blank with the correct present tense form of the verb *do* or *be*. Then underline the subject in each question.

EXAMPLES:

_____*Does*_____ it have a happy ending? _____*Is*_____ it interesting?

1. _____DO_____ we have time to discuss the novel?

2. _____Are_____ you a fan of murder mysteries?

3. _____DO_____ you want to read something else?

4. _____ the main character about forty years old?

5. _____ you like the author's writing style?

6. _____ he a good storyteller?

7. _____ the characters interesting?

8. _____ you know what the critics think?

9. _____ the newspaper critic fair?

Negative Forms: *Do Not, Does Not*

To form the negative of present tense verbs, place *do* or *does* and the word *not* between the subject and the verb.

We **do not** read her novels.   (Contraction: **don't** read)

Simon **does not** write every day.   (Contraction: **doesn't** write)

Negative Forms of *Do* and *Does*

	Singular Forms	Contraction
First person:	I do not work.	don't
Second person:	You do not work.	don't
Third person:	He does not work.	
	She does not work.	doesn't
	It does not work.	
	Plural Forms	
First person:	You do not work.	don't
Second person:	We do not work.	don't
Third person:	They do not work.	don't

Exception: When the main verb is *be* (*is, am, are*), just add *not*.

The story **is not** suspenseful.   (Contraction: **isn't**)

They **are not** happy with the ending.   (Contraction: **aren't**)

PRACTICE 4

A. Add *-s* or *-es* to each italicized verb, if necessary. Then, write the negative form and contraction in the spaces provided.

EXAMPLE:

	Negative Form	Contraction
Frodo *do* __es__ many strange things.	*does not do*	*doesn't do*

1. In *The Lord of the Rings*, a little hobbit *make*__s__ friends with a wizard.   does not make   doesn't do

2. He *live*__s__ in a small house.   does not live   doesn't live

3. His best friend, Sam, *eat* _____ a lot of greasy food.

_____ _____

4. They *leave* _____ their village to go on a journey.

_____ _____

5. Frodo *own* _____ a special ring.

_____ _____

6. The hobbits *meet* _____ some elves.

_____ _____

B. Write the correct form of the verb *be* in each blank. Then, write the negative form and contraction.

EXAMPLE:

	Negative Form	**Contraction**
Frodo's feet __are__ very large.	are not	aren't

7. Their journey _____ dangerous.

_____ _____

8. The hobbits _____ brave.

_____ _____

9. J. R. R. Tolkien's books _____ expensive.

_____ _____

 Hint   **Correcting Question and Negative Forms**

In question and negative forms, always use the base form of the main verb even when the subject is third-person singular. Put the -s or -es ending only on the helping verb (*does*).

have
Why does the magazine ~~has~~ so many subscribers?

contain
The magazine does not ~~contains~~ many advertisements.

PRACTICE 5

Correct errors in present tense verb forms.

EXAMPLE:

are
Romance novels ~~be~~ extremely popular.

1. Four Harlequin romance novels ~~sells~~ every second.
   sell

2. Romance novels are translated into many languages, but most of the writers *are* ~~be~~ from the United States, Canada, or Britain.

3. A typical romance novel follow a formula.

4. Initially, the heroine do not like the hero, and she struggles against her growing attraction.

5. Romance novels does not have sad endings.

6. Be chick lit and romance novels the same thing?

7. In so-called "chick lit," the heroine do not always fall in love.

8. Why do Heather Graham write romance novels?

9. According to Graham, each novel express a universal human emotion.

10. Stories about exciting relationships provides readers with an escape from reality.

The Simple Past Tense

The **simple past tense** shows that an action occurred at a specific past time. In the past tense, there are regular and irregular verbs.

Regular Past Tense Verbs

Regular past tense verbs have a standard *-d* or *-ed* ending (*talked, ended, watched*). Use the same form for both singular and plural past tense verbs.

Singular subject: F. Scott Fitzerald **published** his stories in several languages.

Plural subject: Last Friday, we **talked** about the novel.

LAST FRIDAY		TODAY

Last Friday. we **talked** about the novel.

 **Spelling of Regular Verbs**

Most regular past tense verbs are formed by adding -ed to the base form of the verb.

    talk–talk**ed**   mention–mention**ed**

Exceptions

• When the regular verb ends in -e, add just -d.

    hope–hope**d**   bake–bake**d**

• When the regular verb ends in a consonant + y, change the y to i and add -ed.

    fry–fr**ied**   apply–appl**ied**

Note: if the regular verb ends in a vowel + y, add just -ed.

    play–play**ed**   destroy–destroy**ed**

• When the regular verb ends in a consonant-vowel-consonant combination, double the last consonant and add -ed.

    stop–stop**ped**   jog–jog**ged**

GRAMMAR LINK

See Chapter 24, "Spelling," for more spelling tips.

PRACTICE 6

Write the past tense forms of the following verbs.

EXAMPLE:

watch   *watched*

1. care   _____   6. plan   _____

2. try   _____   7. rain   _____

3. stay   _____   8. rest   _____

4. employ _____   9. deny   _____

5. study   _____   10. ban   _____

> **Hint**   **Past Versus *Passed***
>
> Some people confuse *past* and *passed*. *Past* is a noun that means "in a previous time; before now."
>
>   She has many secrets in her <u>past</u>. Her mistakes are in the <u>past</u>.
>
> *Passed* is the past tense of the verb *pass*, which has many meanings. In the first example, it means "went by"; in the second example, it means "to successfully complete."
>
>   Many days <u>passed</u>, and the nights got shorter.

PRACTICE 7

Write the simple past form of each verb in parentheses. Make sure that you have spelled your past tense verbs correctly.

EXAMPLE:

In 1925, two boys (wonder) ____*wondered*____ how to enter the comic book industry.

1. In 1933, teenagers Jerry Seigel and Joe Shuster (create) _____ a story about an evil, power-hungry man.

2. Their short story, "The Reign of Superman," (describe) _____ a bald-headed villain who (aim) _____ to take over the world.

3. Nobody (want) _____ to buy their story.

4. Seigel and Shuster (change) _____ their lead character into a noble hero with super powers.

5. Four years later, DC Comics (agree) _____ to publish the first Superman comic.

6. In 1941, Seigel and Shuster (earn) _____ $75,000 for their Superman comics.

7. The pair (battle) _____ their publisher to get a larger share of the immense profits from Superman.

8. The angry publisher then (fire) _____ Seigel and Shuster.

9. In 1948, the writers (accept) _____ a small cash settlement.

10. They (sign) _____ away their rights to any future earnings from the Superman franchise.

11. In the 1950s, both men (watch) _____ the Superman TV series, and they (receive) _____ nothing for the series.

12. In 1978, Warner Communications, the makers of *Superman: The Movie*, (offer) _____ to pay the Superman creators a yearly pension.

Irregular Past Tense Verbs

Irregular verbs do not end in any specific letter. Because their spellings can change from the present to the past forms, these verbs can be challenging to remember.

Irregular Verbs

Base Form	Simple Past	Base Form	Simple Past	Base Form	Simple Past
be	was, were	cling	clung	forget	forgot
beat	beat	come	came	forgive	forgave
become	became	cost	cost	freeze	froze
begin	began	cut	cut	get	got
bend	bent	deal	dealt	give	gave
bet	bet	dig	dug	go	went
bind	bound	do	did	grind	ground
bite	bit	draw	drew	grow	grew
bleed	bled	drink	drank	hang	hung
blow	blew	drive	drove	have	had
break	broke	eat	ate	hear	heard
breed	bred	fall	fell	hide	hid
bring	brought	feed	fed	hit	hit
build	built	feel	felt	hold	held
burst	burst	fight	fought	hurt	hurt
buy	bought	find	found	keep	kept
catch	caught	flee	fled	kneel	knelt
choose	chose	fly	flew	know	knew

CHAPTER 9

Base Form	Simple Past	Base Form	Simple Past	Base Form	Simple Past
lay	laid	sell	sold	sting	stung
lead	led	send	sent	stink	stank
leave	left	set	set	strike	struck
lend	lent	shake	shook	swear	swore
let	let	shoot	shot	sweep	swept
lie*	lay	shrink	shrank	swim	swam
light	lit	shut	shut	swing	swung
lose	lost	sing	sang	take	took
make	made	sink	sank	teach	taught
mean	meant	sit	sat	tear	tore
meet	met	sleep	slept	tell	told
mistake	mistook	slide	slid	think	thought
pay	paid	slit	slit	throw	threw
put	put	speak	spoke	thrust	thrust
quit	quit	speed	sped	understand	understood
read	read	spend	spent	upset	upset
rid	rid	spin	spun	wake	woke
ride	rode	split	split	wear	wore
ring	rang	spread	spread	weep	wept
rise	rose	spring	sprang	win	won
run	ran	stand	stood	wind	wound
say	said	steal	stole	withdraw	withdrew
see	saw	stick	stuck	write	wrote

Lie means "to rest," for example, on a sofa or bed. When *lie* means "tell a false statement," it is a regular verb: *lie, lied, lied.*

PRACTICE 8

Write the correct past form of each verb in parentheses. Some verbs are regular, and some are irregular.

EXAMPLE:

In the 1950s, journalists at *The Confidential* (write) ____wrote____ about show-business scandals.

1. In 1833, the first American tabloid, the *New York Sun*, (hit) _____ the streets. Boys (sell) _____ the tabloids on street corners. Journalists (give) _____ readers stories about political scandals, murders, and other crimes.

2. In the 1952, a new tabloid (rise) _____ to prominence. An Italian publisher, Generoso Pope, Jr., (buy) _____ a newspaper called the *Enquirer.* It (be) _____ full of horse-racing tips.

3.　Pope (pay) _____ about $70,000 for the *Enquirer*. The paper's

focus (change) _____ from horse racing to bizarre and gory

stories about cannibalism and other crimes. The *Enquirer*'s staff (make)

_____ up incredible stories. Readers usually (think)

_____ that the stories were true.

The Past Form of *Be* (*Was* or *Were*)

The verb *be* has two past forms: *was* and *were*.

Past Tense of *Be*		
	Singular	**Plural**
First person:	I was	We were
Second person:	You were	You were
Third person:	He was She was It was	They were

PRACTICE 9

Fill in each blank with *was* or *were*.

EXAMPLE:

During the early years of Hollywood, people _____*were*_____ curious about
celebrities.

1.　In the early 1950s, there _____ many hoax stories in the *National*

Enquirer. However, in the late 1950s, that situation changed. Each

journalist _____ careful to include true stories about celebrities. The

friends and employees of the famous _____ often greedy. They

_____ ready to sell information to the tabloids.

2.　Some popular celebrities _____ on the front covers of the tabloids

each week. For example, during the 1960s, Elizabeth Taylor's love life

_____ front-page news. By wearing disguises, reporters _____

able to get close to the actress. For example, a photographer _____

able to take photographs of Taylor by posing as a waiter.

Negative Forms of Past Tense Verbs

To form the negative of past tense verbs, place *did* and the word *not* between the
subject and the verb.

The actress **did not** want to appear in tabloids.　(Contraction: **didn't**)

We **did not** buy that newspaper.　(Contraction: **didn't**)

Exception: When the main verb is *be* (*was, were*), just add *not*.

The story **was not** suspenseful.　(Contraction: **wasn't**)

They **were not** happy with the ending.　(Contraction: **weren't**)

PRACTICE 10

Write the negative forms of the underlined verbs. Use contractions.

EXAMPLE:

He <u>worked</u>. _____*didn't work*_____   They <u>were</u> hungry. _____*weren't*_____

1. She <u>was</u> busy. _____   6. I <u>did</u> it. _____

2. Joe <u>ate</u> a lot. _____   7. We <u>washed</u> up. _____

3. You <u>made</u> it. _____   8. They <u>were</u> late. _____

4. We <u>spoke</u>. _____   9. Kay <u>went</u> out. _____

5. I <u>lied</u>. _____   10. He <u>opened</u> it. _____

Question Forms of Past Tense Verbs

To create past tense questions, add the helping verb *did* before the subject and change the past tense verb to its base form.

Shuster drew Superman.   **Did** Shuster draw Superman?
They liked the story.   **Did** they like the story?

Exception: When the main verb is *be* (*was, were*), just move *be* before the subject to form a question.

The story was exciting.   **Was** the story exciting?
They were ready.   **Were** they ready?

> **Hint** **Use the Base Form After *Did***
>
> In question and negative forms, remember to use the base form—not the past form—of the main verb.
>
>   *use*
> Did he ~~used~~ a computer to write his book?

PRACTICE 11

Correct the errors with question or negative forms.

EXAMPLE:

    did he seem
Why ~~he seem~~ so surprised by his success?

1. J. R. R. Tolkien  ~~don't be~~ born in England.

2. He did not remained in South Africa.

3. When he moved to Birmingham, England?

4. Why did Tolkien wrote about hobbits?

5. His friends not believed in the value of myths.

6. Tolkien wasn't agree with his friends.

7. *The Lord of the Rings* didn't be popular at first.

8. Why the book became popular ten years after its release?

9. Why did the book sold more than 100 million copies?

Common Errors with *Be* and *Have*

Some writers find it particularly difficult to remember how to use the irregular verbs *be* and *have*.

- Use *were*, not *was*, when the subject is plural.

    were
    The photographers ~~was~~ extremely persistent.

- Use the standard form of the verb (*is* or *was*), not *be*.

    was
    The story about the movie star ~~be~~ shocking.

- Use the past form of the verb (*had*), not the present form (*have* or *has*), when speaking about a past event.

    had
    Mike Wallace ~~has~~ to work in dangerous war zones during his early days as a reporter.

PRACTICE 12 REVIEW

If the underlined past tense verb is incorrectly formed or in the wrong tense, write the correct form above it. There are twenty errors.

EXAMPLE:

                    wrote
In the past, many people <u>writed</u> memoirs.

1.   *bought*
        In 2005, I <u>buyed</u> a book called *A Million Little Pieces*, by James Frey. It

only <u>costed</u> 12 dollars. Later, Oprah Winfrey <u>choosed</u> Frey's novel for her

televised book club. According to Winfrey, the book <u>gived</u> hope to people

with addictions. The book <u>selled</u> more than 2 million copies.

2.   Some investigative reporters <u>be</u> skeptical. According to *The Smoking Gun*, Frey's book <u>was</u> not about true events. The author <u>maked</u> up many details. For example, Frey never <u>spended</u> eighty-seven days in jail. Soon, everybody <u>knowed</u> about the scandal.

3.   In 2006, Frey <u>taked</u> a big risk and appeared on another episode of *Oprah*. The popular host <u>be</u> very angry with Frey. After the show, Frey <u>thinked</u> that his career was over. Over the next year, he <u>losed</u> many friends. He <u>refunded</u> money to many book buyers.

4.   In 2008, another writer <u>called</u> her novel a memoir. Margaret B. Jones <u>wrote</u> about her life as a mixed-race girl from South Central Los Angeles. In the book, the main character <u>becomed</u> a gang member. However, Margaret Jones <u>haved</u> a middle-class life in San Fernando Valley. She never <u>grewed</u> up in South Central Los Angeles.

5.   Before his death in 2007, author Normal Mailer <u>speaked</u> about the "memoir" controversies. Frey and Jones never <u>hurted</u> others. They just <u>bended</u> the truth. People <u>readed</u> their books and enjoyed them. According to Mailer, all memoirs <u>are</u> full of lies because writers <u>want</u> to "create an ideal self."

Avoiding Double Negatives

A **double negative** occurs when a writer combines a negative word such as *no, nothing, nobody,* or *nowhere* with a negative adverb such as *not, never, rarely,* or *seldom.* The result is a sentence that has a double negative. Such sentences can be confusing because the negative words cancel each other.

Double negative: She <u>doesn't</u> give <u>no</u> interviews.

He <u>never</u> received <u>no</u> royalties.

How to Correct Double Negatives

There are two ways to correct double negatives.

- Completely remove *one* of the negative forms.

Incorrect	**Correct**
She **doesn't** give **no** interviews.	She **doesn't** give interviews.
	She gives **no** interviews.
He **never** received **no** royalties.	He **never** received royalties.
	He received **no** royalties.

- Change *no* to *any* (*anybody, anything, anywhere*).

Incorrect	**Correct**
She **doesn't** give **no** interviews.	She doesn't give **any** interviews.
He **never** received **no** royalties.	He never received **any** royalties.

PRACTICE 13

Underline and correct four errors with double negatives. You can correct each error in more than one way.

EXAMPLE:

> *have nothing or don't have anything*
> I don't have nothing on my Kindle.

1. In 2009, Amazon introduced a new product. The Kindle is an electronic gadget that can hold over 1,500 books. Readers don't need no heavy book bag. Instead, the Kindle fits into a pocket or purse. In 2009, Apple launched the iPad, which can also hold thousands of books.

2. Most reviewers don't say nothing bad about the Kindle or iPad. But will those products help or hurt the publishing industry? Downloaded books cost much less than paper books. A lot of people don't want to pay nothing for their books and newspapers.

3. Book publishers have to adapt to the new technologies. They can't do nothing to stop the changes in the industry.

FINAL REVIEW

Correct fifteen errors. There are present tense, past tense, and double negative errors.

EXAMPLE:

        were
The books ~~was~~ offensive.

1.   The Federal Anti-Obscenity Act past in 1873. After that, citizens was not able to buy certain novels. For example, in 1915, the U.S. government did not permitted Americans to import James Joyce's classic novel *Ulysses*. Officials called the book obscene. Some activists fighted the government, and in 1930, they winned the right to publish the book in the United States. In 2000, the Modern Library choosed *Ulysses* as the best book of the twentieth century.

2.   Between 1873 and 2008, school districts and libraries in the United States banned hundreds of novels for a variety of reasons. For example, in 1939, administrators at the St. Louis Public Library stoped lending John Steinbeck's classic *The Grapes of Wrath* because they thought that the novel's language was vulgar. In the 1960s, some people buyed the American classic *The Catcher in the Rye* in Canada because many states banned the novel. In the 1990s, some officials didn't want to stock no copies of Mark Twain's *Huckleberry Finn*. People were upset about the book's negative portrayal of African Americans. In 2008, a Florida parent feeled upset after she read *The Kite Runner*. She asked her local school board to ban the book.

3.   Generally, book banners wants to safeguard the values of their communities. They don't see no problem with book banning. Others believes that people should have the freedom to choose their own reading material. They feels that books give insight into the social attitudes of different eras. Book banning is an emotional issue, and people will continue to debate the subject.

The Writer's Room

Write about one of the following topics. After you finish writing, underline your verbs. Verify that you have formed your present and past tense verbs correctly.

1. What happened in a story, poem, play, or article that you read? Use the past tense in your narration.

2. What was your major source of entertainment during your childhood? Did you read, watch television, or play outside? Describe the main activities that you did.

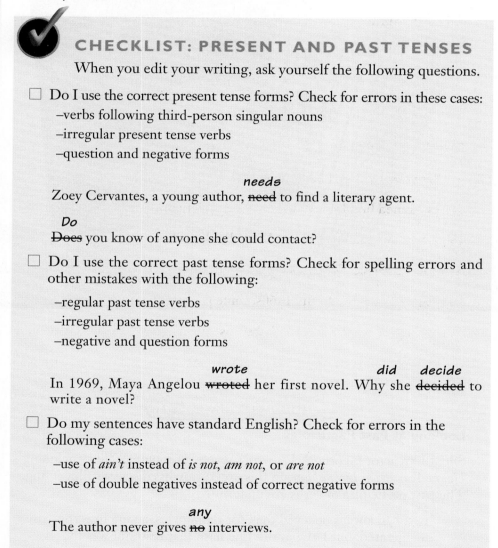

✔ CHECKLIST: PRESENT AND PAST TENSES

When you edit your writing, ask yourself the following questions.

☐ Do I use the correct present tense forms? Check for errors in these cases:
   –verbs following third-person singular nouns
   –irregular present tense verbs
   –question and negative forms

                                    needs
Zoey Cervantes, a young author, ~~need~~ to find a literary agent.

   Do
~~Does~~ you know of anyone she could contact?

☐ Do I use the correct past tense forms? Check for spelling errors and other mistakes with the following:

   –regular past tense verbs
   –irregular past tense verbs
   –negative and question forms

                        wrote   *did   decide*
In 1969, Maya Angelou ~~wroted~~ her first novel. Why she ~~decided~~ to write a novel?

☐ Do my sentences have standard English? Check for errors in the following cases:

   –use of *ain't* instead of *is not*, *am not*, or *are not*
   –use of double negatives instead of correct negative forms

                        any
The author never gives ~~no~~ interviews.

PEARSON **mywritinglab** ▶ To check your progress in meeting this chapter's objectives, log in to **www.mywritinglab.com**, go to the **Study Plan** tab, click on **The Editing Handbook—Section 2 Problems with Verbs** and choose **Present and Past Tenses** from the list of subtopics. Read and view the resources in the **Review Materials** section, and then complete the **Recall, Apply,** and **Write** sets in the **Activities** section.

CHAPTER 10

Past Participles

Section Theme: **ENTERTAINMENT AND CULTURE**

In this chapter, you will read about topics related to television and film.

Grammar Snapshot

Looking at Past Participles

Silent film actor George Arliss wrote several autobiographies, including *Up the Years from Bloomsbury*. In this excerpt, Arliss discusses film acting. The past participles of verbs are underlined.

> I had always believed that, for the movies, acting must be exaggerated, but I saw in this one flash that restraint was the chief thing that the actor had to learn in transferring art from the stage to the screen. The art of restraint and suggestion on the screen may any time be studied by watching the acting of the inimitable Charlie Chaplin.

In this chapter, you will identify and write past participles.

Past Participles

A **past participle** is a verb form, not a verb tense. You cannot use a past participle as the only verb in a sentence. Instead, you must use it with a helping verb. The most common helping verbs are forms of *have* or *be* (*have, has, had*, or *is, am, are, was, were*).

helping   past
verb   participle

My sister and I **were** <u>raised</u> in New York City.

Many movies **have been** <u>filmed</u> there.

Regular Verbs

Regular verbs end in *-d* or *-ed*. The past tense and the past participle of regular verbs are the same. Here are some examples.

Base Form	Past Tense	Past Participle
talk	talked	talked
cry	cried	cried
hope	hoped	hoped

PRACTICE I

Underline each helping verb that appears before the word in parentheses. Then write the past participle of the verb in parentheses.

EXAMPLE:

Some consumers <u>have</u> (complain) _____*complained*_____ about reality programs.

1. Many viewers <u>have</u> (develop) ____*DEVELOPED*____ a taste for reality shows.

2. Reality programming is not new, though. It <u>has</u> (appear) _____*APPEARED*_____ on network television since the 1940s.

3. *Wanted*, a show that <u>was</u> (produce) ____*PRODUCED*____ in 1955 by CBS television, contained interviews with fugitives and their families.

4. *Candid Camera*, which <u>was</u> (create) _____*CREATED*_____ by its host Alan Funt in 1948, showed regular people reacting to surprising events.

5. Many other producers have (copy) _____ Funt's ideas.

6. Ashton Kutcher's *Punk'd* was (base) _____ on Funt's show.

7. In 2003, many viewers were (attract) _____ to shows about finding the perfect mate.

8. For example, *The Bachelor* was (view) _____ by millions of people.

9. However, dating reality shows have (decline) _____ in the ratings.

10. Some reality shows have (remain) _____ popular.

Irregular Verbs

Certain verbs have irregular past forms and can be challenging to remember. Review the next list of common irregular verbs. Put an *X* next to verbs that you commonly misspell.

Irregular Verbs

Base Form	Simple Past	Past Participle	Base Form	Simple Past	Past Participle
arise	arose	arisen	feel	felt	felt
be	was, were	been	fight	fought	fought
beat	beat	beat, beaten	find	found	found
become	became	become	flee	fled	fled
begin	began	begun	fly	flew	flown
bend	bent	bent	forbid	forbade	forbidden
bet	bet	bet	forget	forgot	forgotten
bind	bound	bound	forgive	forgave	forgiven
bite	bit	bitten	freeze	froze	frozen
bleed	bled	bled	get	got	got, gotten
blow	blew	blown	give	gave	given
break	broke	broken	go	went	gone
breed	bred	bred	grind	ground	ground
bring	brought	brought	grow	grew	grown
build	built	built	hang	hung	hung
burst	burst	burst	have	had	had
buy	bought	bought	hear	heard	heard
catch	caught	caught	hide	hid	hidden
choose	chose	chosen	hit	hit	hit
cling	clung	clung	hold	held	held
come	came	come	hurt	hurt	hurt
cost	cost	cost	keep	kept	kept
cut	cut	cut	kneel	knelt	knelt
deal	dealt	dealt	know	knew	known
dig	dug	dug	lay	laid	laid
do	did	done	lead	led	led
draw	drew	drawn	leave	left	left
drink	drank	drunk	lend	lent	lent
drive	drove	driven	let	let	let
eat	ate	eaten	lie	lay	lain
fall	fell	fallen	light	lit	lit
feed	fed	fed	lose	lost	lost

Base Form	Simple Past	Past Participle	Base Form	Simple Past	Past Participle
make	made	made	spin	spun	spun
split	split	split	mean	meant	meant
meet	met	met	spread	spread	spread
mistake	mistook	mistaken	spring	sprang	sprung
pay	paid	paid	stand	stood	stood
put	put	put	steal	stole	stolen
quit	quit	quit	stick	stuck	stuck
read	read	read	sting	stung	stung
rid	rid	rid	stink	stank	stunk
ride	rode	ridden	strike	struck	struck
ring	rang	rung	swear	swore	sworn
rise	rose	risen	sweep	swept	swept
run	ran	run	swell	swelled	swollen
say	said	said	swim	swam	swum
see	saw	seen	swing	swung	swung
sell	sold	sold	take	took	taken
send	sent	sent	teach	taught	taught
set	set	set	tear	tore	torn
shake	shook	shaken	tell	told	told
shoot	shot	shot	think	thought	thought
show	showed	shown	throw	threw	thrown
shut	shut	shut	thrust	thrust	thrust
sing	sang	sung	understand	understood	understood
sink	sank	sunk	upset	upset	upset
sit	sat	sat	wake	woke	woken
sleep	slept	slept	wear	wore	worn
slide	slid	slid	weep	wept	wept
slit	slit	slit	win	won	won
speak	spoke	spoken	wind	wound	wound
speed	sped	sped	withdraw	withdrew	withdrawn
spend	spent	spent	write	wrote	written

PRACTICE 2

Write the simple past and the past participle of the following verbs.

Base Form	Past Tense	Past Participle
EXAMPLE:		
lose	*lost*	*lost*
1. cost	_____	_____
2. choose	_____	_____
3. drive	_____	_____
4. break	_____	_____

5. ring   _____   _____

6. bring   _____   _____

7. drink   _____   _____

8. think   _____   _____

9. build   _____   _____

10. become   _____   _____

11. grow   _____   _____

12. hit   _____   _____

13. sit   _____   _____

14. go   _____   _____

15. do   _____   _____

PRACTICE 3

The irregular past participles are underlined. Correct the twelve past participle errors, and write *C* above five correct verbs.

EXAMPLE:

learned

Many acting students have <u>learn</u> the Stanislavsky method.

1.   Most people have <u>thinked</u> about becoming famous actors. Acting seems like an easy thing to do; however, most successful actors have <u>spend</u> years developing their craft.

2.   If you want to be an actor, take some acting classes. Acting is <u>teached</u> in many colleges and private institutes. In acting classes, students are <u>given</u> the basic techniques. Acting students are often <u>telled</u> to read novels and plays as well as reference books and biographies. Most actors have <u>readed</u> many classic works.

3.   According to talent agent Myra Daly, after you have <u>took</u> your classes, you should develop your "persona." An actor is like a product; his or her persona is <u>selled</u>. Perhaps you have <u>became</u> the femme fatale, the bitter comic, the nice guy, the menacing criminal, or the girl next door. If you have <u>finded</u> a persona, it is easy for your agent to promote you. Although good actors can play many types of roles, even

many well-known actors have <u>falled</u> into a "type." For example, some people say Reese Witherspoon has not <u>shaken</u> her "girl next door" persona even though she has <u>been</u> in a variety of different roles. Some actors have <u>feeled</u> upset and frustrated when they have <u>been</u> typecast.

4.   The last step is to prepare your résumé and get references from teachers and other influential people who have <u>saw</u> your work. Traditionally, good acting jobs have <u>been</u> hard to find. If you persevere, and if you believe in your abilities, you have a chance at succeeding.

The Present Perfect Tense: *Have/Has* + Past Participle

A past participle combines with *have* or *has* to form the **present perfect tense**. You can use this tense in two different circumstances.

- Use the present perfect to show that an action began in the past and continues to the present time. Some key words and expressions to look for are *since, for, ever, not yet, so far,* and *up to now.*

PAST	PRESENT PERFECT	NOW

Makeup artist Ella Chu **has lived** in Los Angeles since 2006.

- Use the present perfect to show that one or more completed actions occurred at unimportant and unspecified past times. Some key words and expressions to look for are *already, once, twice, several times,* and *many times.*

PAST (unspecified past times)   NOW
   ?   ?   ?   ?

Ella Chu **has returned** to her hometown in Canada many times.

Look at the difference between the past tense and the present perfect tense in the following examples.

Simple past: In August 2005, three friends <u>launched</u> the Internet site YouTube.
(This event occurred at a known past time.)

Present perfect: Since 2005, the YouTube founders <u>have earned</u> a fortune.
(The action began in the past and continues to the present moment.)

J. Junkala <u>has made</u> more than twenty videos.
(The repeated past actions have occurred at unspecified past times.)

PRACTICE 4

Write the present perfect form of each verb in parentheses.

EXAMPLE:

Horror movies (be) _____*have*_____ _____*been*_____ around for almost a century.

1. Since its beginning, the Internet (change) _____
   _____ people's lives in various ways. Recently, with
   the introduction of video-sharing Web sites, people (have)
   _____ _____ the chance to flirt with fame.
   In fact, since 2005, thousands of ordinary men and women (make)
   _____ _____ videos for YouTube, MySpace,
   or other video-sharing sites.

2. Some of the videos (become) _____
   _____ extremely popular. For example, more than 30 million
   people (see) _____ _____ the amazing
   performance of Greyson Michael Chance, a twelve-year-old boy from
   Oklahoma. In 2010, he participated in a talent competition. His schoolmates
   looked on in wonder as he played piano and sang Lady Gaga's song,
   "Paparazzi." Since the video first appeared on YouTube, Chance's life
   (change) _____ . Many journalists (speak) _____
   with him, and some record producers (contact) _____ him. Lady
   Gaga (give) _____ him some advice. During an August 2010
   taping of the show *Ellen*, Gaga told the boy to focus on music, not on girls.

3. Sometimes, an online homemade video can contribute to enduring
   fame. For example, British singer Lily Allen (post) _____
   _____ several music videos on MySpace. Many times, she
   (thank) _____ _____ MySpace for giving her
   a large fan base.

4. For the last few years, some corporations (be) _____
   _____ upset with the spread of file-sharing Internet sites.
   Entertainment industry officials object to unauthorized use of film clips
   or songs. However, they (not, stop) _____
   _____ the video-sharing Web sites.

Hint   Time Markers

Time markers are words that indicate when an action occurred.

Simple Past Tense
To refer to an incident that occurred at a specific past time, use the following time markers.

yesterday	ago	when I was . . .	last (week, month, year . . .)
in the past	in 1925	during the 1990s	in the early days of . . .

<u>In 1989</u>, Spike Lee **directed** the film *Do the Right Thing*.

Present Perfect Tense
To refer to an action that began in the past and is still continuing, use the following time markers.

since	ever, never	so far	up to now
not yet	for (a period of time up to now)	lately	recently

I **have been** a Spike Lee fan <u>since 1990</u>.

To refer to an action that occurred at an unspecified past time or past times, use the following time markers.

many	several times	repeatedly	once, twice, three times

I **have watched** *Jungle Fever* <u>once</u> and *Malcolm X* <u>twice</u>.

PRACTICE 5

Underline the correct past tense or present perfect tense of each verb in parentheses.

EXAMPLE:

In 2010, *Avatar* (<u>won</u> / have won / has won) an Oscar for Best Visual Effects.

1. In 1934, the movie *King Kong* (contained / has contained / have contained) sets with miniature skyscrapers and model airplanes.

2. To make the ape movie back then, *King Kong* artists (created / have created / has created) a model of the giant ape and then (moved / have moved / has moved) the model slightly every few frames of film.

3. Since 1934, audiences (appreciated / have appreciated / has appreciated) special effects.

4. Since the 1980s, computerized animation (became / have become / has become) more sophisticated.

5. In recent years, film studios (developed / have developed / has developed) new animation techniques.

6. In 1995, *Toy Story* (was / has been / have been) the first completely computer-animated film.

7. Since then, many other computer-animated films (hit / have hit / has hit) movie screens.

8. In 2009, James Cameron (revolutionized / have revolutionized / has revolutionized) visual techniques in his film *Avatar*.

PRACTICE 6 REVIEW

Fill in the blanks with either the simple past tense or the present perfect tense.

EXAMPLE:

I (watch) _____*have watched*_____ *General Hospital* since I was seven years old.

1. Daytime soap operas (change) _____ a lot since they began. In the 1930s, soap companies (sponsor) _____ daytime radio dramas. For example, the program *The Guiding Light* (begin) _____ in the 1930s as a radio show. Then, in the 1940s, the television network CBS (film) _____*The Guiding Light.* It (be) _____ a popular daytime drama since then.

2. Soap operas are popular in many nations. Since 1980, Mexican producers (sell) _____ soap operas to nations around the world. Actress Salma Hayek (have) _____ the lead role in the Mexican soap opera *Teresa* in 1989. Her career (take) _____ off since then. Since the late 1990s, Mexican soap operas (be) _____ very popular in Russia.

3. For many years, critics (complain) _____ that the actors in soap operas are too beautiful. However, since the 1960s, British studios (bring) _____ regular-looking people to television screens. Since its debut, the long-running soap opera *Coronation Street* (star) _____ a variety of ordinary-looking actors. For more than fifty years, daytime soap operas (be) _____ an essential part of afternoon television schedules.

The Past Perfect Tense: *Had* + Past Participle

The **past perfect tense** indicates that one or more past actions happened before another past action. To form the past perfect, use *had* plus the past participle.

```
      PAST PERFECT              PAST              NOW
◄─────────▼──────────────────────▼──────────────────▼──────────►
```

The movie **had started** when Vladimir arrived.

Notice the differences between the simple past, the present perfect, and the past perfect tenses.

Simple past:	Last night I <u>rented</u> the video *No Country for Old Men*. (The action occurred at a known past time: *last night*.)
Present perfect:	I <u>have seen</u> most of Javier Bardem's movies. (The actions have occurred at unspecified past times.)
Past perfect:	When Denzel Washington appeared in *American Gangster*, he <u>had</u> already <u>acted</u> in several successful films. (All of the actions happened in the past, but Washington had acted in good movies before he appeared in *American Gangster*.)

PRACTICE 7

Underline the correct verb tense. Choose either the simple past or the past perfect verb.

EXAMPLE:

When Charlie Chaplin left England, he (already acted / <u>had already acted</u>) in many productions.

1. Charles Spencer Chaplin was born into a London slum on April 16, 1889, and in 1910, he (arrived / had arrived) in America.

2. Because Chaplin (accumulated / had accumulated) a lot of acting experience in England, Mack Sennett hired him to work in Sennett comedies.

3. In 1920, Chaplin earned $10,000 per week, which was more than he (ever earned / had ever earned) in his life!

4. About this time, he (developed / had developed) his Tramp character, which was inspired by the poverty that he (experienced / had experienced).

5. When he turned twenty-six years old, he fulfilled a dream that he (had / had had) for several years.

6. Chaplin (directed / had directed) his own movies, and, in his films, he expressed sympathy for the poor.

7. FBI agents investigated Chaplin because they thought that he (joined / had joined) the Communist party.

8. At that time, Chaplin didn't have American citizenship even though he (spent / had spent) most of his professional life in the United States.

9. In 1952, the U.S. immigration authorities revoked Chaplin's re-entry permit after he (sailed / had sailed) for England.

10. When Chaplin passed away in 1977, his children knew that he (lived / had lived) an extremely full and rewarding life.

PRACTICE 8   REVIEW

Underline the correct tense of each verb in parentheses. You may choose the simple past, the present perfect, or the past perfect tense.

EXAMPLE:

> In 2009, Bollywood (<u>released</u> / had released) over one thousand films.

1.   Since 2004, Americans (have become / had become) acquainted with Bollywood films. Before that time, most Americans (never saw / had never seen) an Indian film. The Indian film industry, however, (has been / had been) around since the early 1900s. The word *Bollywood*, from a mix of Bombay and Hollywood, first (appeared / had appeared) in 1975. Bollywood (has produced / had produced) many superstars. For example, Raj Kapoor was the Charlie Chaplin of Indian cinema. By the time Kapoor died in 1988, he (has already starred / had already starred) in almost one hundred films.

2.   Film director Danny Boyle (has already seen / had already seen) some Bollywood movies when he (began / had begun) filming *Slumdog Millionaire* in 2006. The film, which has many Bollywood elements, (won / had won) the Oscar for best picture in 2009. Even though Bollywood films may seem extremely melodramatic, international audiences appear to be enjoying them.

The Past Participle as an Adjective

A past participle can function as an adjective by modifying or describing the noun that follows it.

> He sat near the **broken** window.
>
> (*Broken* modifies *window*.)

PRACTICE 9

Write a logical past participle in each blank. Use the past participle form of the following verbs. Do not use the same verb more than once. Then write *adj* in the blank beside each sentence where the participle is used as an adjective.

depress	know	respect	see	torment
inspire	~~misunderstand~~	release	steal	

EXAMPLE:

The unforgettable Joker played a ___*misunderstood*___ villain.

1. The recently _____ film *The Dark Knight* was based on the comic book character Batman.

2. Director Christopher Nolan was a fan of the well- _____ comic book hero.

3. Heath Ledger played the Joker, a _____ psychopath.

4. With _____ money, the Joker financed his dark deeds of violence.

5. Ledger prepared many months for the role and gave an _____ performance.

6. A few months after he finished filming, the _____ actor accidently took an overdose of prescription drugs.

7. The _____ performer won the Academy Award for Best Supporting Actor posthumously.

8. The much- _____ *Batman* films have grown into a successful movie franchise.

The Passive Voice: *Be* + Past Participle

In sentences with the **passive voice,** the subject receives the action and does not perform the action. To form the passive voice, use the appropriate tense of the verb *be* + the past participle. The helping verb shows the verb tense.

passive
Acting is the art of lying well. I <u>am **paid**</u> to tell elaborate lies.

—Mel Gibson, actor

Look carefully at the following two sentences. Notice the differences between the active and the passive voice.

Active: Alejandro González Iñárritu **released** *Babel* in 2006.

(This sentence is active because the subject, Iñárritu, performed the action.)

Passive: The movie **was filmed** in 2005.
(This sentence is passive because the subject, the movie, did not perform the action.)

Active and Passive Voice

Verb Tenses	Active	Passive: *Be* + Past Participle
	The subject performs the action.	The subject receives the action.
Simple present:	They produce movies.	Movies <u>are</u> produced by them.
Present progressive:	are producing	<u>are being</u> produced
Simple past:	produced	<u>were</u> produced
Present perfect:	have produced	<u>have been</u> produced
Future:	will produce	<u>will be</u> produced
Modals:	can produce	<u>can be</u> produced
	could produce	<u>could be</u> produced
	should produce	<u>should be</u> produced

 **Avoid Overusing the Passive Voice**

Generally, try to use the active voice instead of the passive voice. The active voice is more direct and friendly than the passive voice. For example, read the next two versions of the same message.

Passive voice: Your questions about our cable service have been received by us. You will be contacted by our sales representative.

Active voice: We have received your questions about our cable service. Our sales representative will contact you.

PRACTICE 10

Decide whether each underlined verb is active or passive, and write *A* (for "active") or *P* (for "passive") above each verb.

EXAMPLE:

                                    P
The story <u>is based</u> on a fictional event.

1.   In the early 1940s, a radio <u>was owned</u> by almost every American

family. Then, in 1941, the first television show <u>was broadcast</u>. In 1942,

some veteran radio performers <u>predicted</u> that television would never

catch on. However, television <u>has been</u> a permanent fixture in

American homes since then.

2.   It is hard for us to imagine the excitement that <u>was felt</u> in the

1940s. In those years, one television <u>was watched</u> by many people,

including friends and relatives of the owners. In fact, TV watching <u>was</u> a

social event. For example, in 1946, the first TV sports extravaganza

<u>was staged</u> by NBC. The program <u>featured</u> boxing great Joe Louis. The

match <u>was seen</u> by about 150,000 people, or about thirty viewers per

television. Today, the average television <u>is watched</u> by only three people.

 **The by . . . Phrase**

In many passive sentences, it is not necessary to write the *by . . .* phrase.

The film was released in 2005 ~~by United Artists~~.

The costumes were made in France ~~by costume designers~~.

PRACTICE 11

A. Complete the following sentences by changing each italicized verb to the passive form. Do not alter the verb tense. In some sentences, you do not have to include the *by . . .* phrase.

EXAMPLE:

Producers make movies all over the world.

*Movies are made all over the world (by producers).*_____

1. Fame *attracts* many ordinary people.

   Many ordinary people _____

2. People *view* movie stars as happy, exciting people.

   Movie stars _____

3. In 2005, a producer *offered* Maria Figuera a job in a movie.

   In 2005, Maria Figuera _____

4. The director *filmed* the movie in Boston.

   The movie _____

5. Perhaps people *will recognize* Maria in the future.

   Perhaps Maria _____

B. The following sentences are in the passive voice. Change the verbs in italics to the active voice, but do not alter the verb tense.

EXAMPLE:

Some actors *are paid* too much money by the studios.

Studios <u>pay some actors too much money.</u>

6. Famous actors *have been stalked* by overzealous fans.

   Overzealous fans _____

7. A few years ago, Zac Efron's privacy *was invaded* by journalists.

   A few years ago, journalists _____

8. Many complaints *are made* by actors about their lack of privacy.

   Many actors _____

9. Perhaps actors *should not be chased* by paparazzi.

   Perhaps paparazzi _____

10. Tabloids *are enjoyed* by some ordinary people.

    Some ordinary people _____

Hint ▷ **Using the Passive Form**

In the passive voice, sometimes a form of the verb *be* is suggested but not written. The following sentence contains the passive voice.

Be is suggested:	Many movies **made** in the 1970s have become classics.
Be is written:	Many movies **that were** made in the 1970s have become classics.

PRACTICE 12 REVIEW

Correct fifteen errors with past participles.

EXAMPLE:

> *seen*
> I have ~~saw~~ *X-Men Origins: Wolverine* two times.

1. Comic book series, such as *Spiderman*, have been turn into movies. Other films, such as *The Green Hornet*, took from radio serials of the 1930s, have become successful films. Of course, great works of literature have also influence screenwriters.

2. William Shakespeare is the most well-knowed writer of all time. Many movies have been based on his plays. *Othello*, for example, was

transform into the urban drama *O.* The movie starred Mekhi Phifer as Odin, a talented black athlete who is envy by his peers. Odin falls in love with the headmaster's daughter. Hugo, the coach's son, is consume with jealousy, and he eventually causes Odin's downfall.

3.   In addition, exceptional books aimed at youths have also been maked into films. Melissa Rosenberg wrote a screenplay base on the novel *Twilight* by Stephenie Meyer. The novel is about a teenage girl who falls in love with a vampire. C.S. Lewis authored seven books for children in the 1950s, call *The Chronicles of Narnia.* The first two in the series, *The Lion, the Witch and the Wardrobe* and *Prince Caspian*, have been develop into films. In addition, *The Golden Compass*, from Philip Pullman's *Dark Materials* trilogy, was also turned into a movie. The two main characters, Mrs. Coulter and Lord Asriel, are play by Nicole Kidman and Daniel Craig.

4.   The rights to many best-sellers are hold by film studios. In fact, as soon as a new book is embrace by the public, producers try to determine whether the book should become a movie. Definitely, many great novels will be adapt by screenwriters.

FINAL REVIEW

Correct fifteen errors with past participles or the passive voice.

EXAMPLE:

paid
Many companies have ~~payed~~ producers to place products in films and on television.

1.   Advertisers display products in films, on television, and in videos to boost sales. Product placement was around since the 1930s. More

recently, brands show in films and on television have became pervasive. For example, *The Matrix Reloaded* was release in 2003 and featured only General Motors automobiles. Apple computers and iPods have appear in numerous films and television shows such as *The Office*.

2.   Tobacco is the most controversial product placement. By 1984, audiences had saw tobacco product placements in more than five hundred film productions. Health groups have consistently raise concerns about the impact of movie smoking on teen smoking rates. In fact, according to *CBS News*, films have greatly influence teenage smoking. Tobacco companies promised Congress in 1990 that they would not promote smoking in films. But films have continue to show characters smoking cigarettes. For example, the American Medical Association was anger by scenes from the 2009 movie *He's Just Not That Into You* because the film exhibited tobacco products.

3.   Recently, another trend has develop. It is product displacement. Some companies have decline to grant permission for their products to be connected to certain images. For example, in the movie *Slumdog Millionaire*, some scenes were film in a Mumbai slum. Mercedes-Benz cars could not be shown in shantytown scenes. However, the cars could be use whenever a scene was filmed in a rich neighborhood. Clearly, business and the entertainment industry have a relationship that is base on image and profit.

The Writer's Room

Write about one of the following topics. Identify all verbs, and verify that you have used and formed each verb correctly.

1. Some people spend more than four hours a day in front of the television. What steps can a television addict take to reduce his or her dependence on television?

2. Examine this photo. What are some terms that come to mind? Some ideas might be *reality television*, *talk show*, *couch potato*, or *sitcom*. Define a term or expression that relates to the photo.

CHIPS

CHECKLIST: PAST PARTICIPLES

When you edit your writing, ask yourself the next questions.

☐ Do I use the correct form of past participles? Check for spelling errors in the following:

–regular past participles
–irregular past participles

               turned   *written*
Novels are often ~~turn~~ into films, and the screenplays are ~~wrote~~ by the author.

CHAPTER 10

☐ Do I use the present perfect tense correctly?

have refused
Since 2004, I ~~refused~~ to watch television.

☐ Do I use the past perfect tense correctly?

had already seen
Ursula did not watch the movie because she ~~already saw~~ it.

☐ Do I use the active and passive voice correctly? Check for overuse of the passive voice and errors with verb form and usage.

many people watched the documentary.
Last month, ~~the documentary was watched by many people.~~

mywritinglab To check your progress in meeting this chapter's objectives, log in to **www.mywritinglab.com**, go to the **Study Plan** tab, click on **The Editing Handbook—Section 2 Problems with Verbs** and choose **Past Participles** from the list of subtopics. Read and view the resources in the **Review Materials** section, and then complete the **Recall, Apply,** and **Write** sets in the **Activities** section.

Progressive Tenses

Section Theme: **ENTERTAINMENT AND CULTURE**

*In this chapter, you will read about
well-known artists and issues in the art
world.*

Grammar Snapshot

Looking at Progressive Tenses

In this excerpt from one of his letters, Impressionist artist Vincent
van Gogh explains his progress in drawing. Notice the underlined
progressive verbs.

> Recently I have been drawing from the model a good
> deal. And I have all kinds of studies of diggers and sowers,
> both male and female. At present I am working with charcoal
> and black crayon, and I have also tried sepia and watercolor.
> Well, I cannot say that you will see progress in my drawings,
> but most certainly you will see a change.

In this chapter, you will identify and write progressive verb tenses.

Understanding Progressive Tenses

A **progressive tense** indicates that an action was, is, or will be in progress. Progressive verb tenses always include a form of the verb *be* and the present participle (or *-ing* form of the verb).

Past progressive:	She <u>was trying</u> to finish her painting when the phone rang.
Present progressive:	Right now, Marg <u>is visiting</u> the Louvre.
Present perfect progressive::	She <u>has been working</u> as a painter for twelve years.
Future progressive:	Tomorrow morning, at eleven o'clock, she <u>will be working</u>.

Present Progressive

The **present progressive** shows that an action is happening now or for a temporary period of time. Use this tense with key words such as *now, currently, at this moment, this week,* and *this month*.

> This month, Tamayo <u>is exhibiting</u> several paintings in an art gallery.

> Right now, Tamayo <u>is painting</u> a portrait.

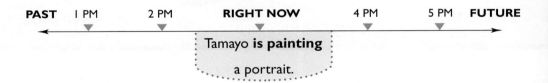

PAST	I PM	2 PM	**RIGHT NOW**	4 PM	5 PM	**FUTURE**

Tamayo **is painting** a portrait.

Affirmative, Question, and Negative Forms

Review the present progressive forms of the verb *work*.

Affirmative		Question Form Move *be* before the subject.		Negative Form Add *not.*		
I	am	Am	I	I	am	
She	is	Am	I	I	am	
He	is	Is	he	He	is	
It	is	working.	Is	it	working?	It	is	not working.
We	are	Are	we	We	are	
You	are	Are	you	You	are	
They	are	Are	they	They	are	

 **Spelling of Present Participles (-*ing* Verbs)**

To form most regular present participles, add -*ing* to the base form of the verb.

try–try**ing**   question–question**ing**

Exceptions

• When the regular verb ends in e, remove the e and add -*ing*.

realize–realiz**ing**   appreciate–appreciat**ing**

• When the regular verb ends in a consonant + *ie*, change the *ie* to *y* and add -*ing*.

lie–**ly**ing   die–**dy**ing

• When the regular verb ends in a consonant–vowel–consonant combination, double the last consonant and add -*ing*.

stop–stop**ping**   jog–jog**ging**

• When a verb of two or more syllables ends in a stressed consonant–vowel–consonant combination, double the last consonant and add -*ing*.

refer–refer**ring**   begin–begin**ning**

Note: If the two-syllable verb ends in an unstressed syllable, add just -*ing*.

offer–offer**ing**   open–open**ing**

PRACTICE I

Change each verb to the present progressive form.

EXAMPLE:

He runs. _____*is running*_____

1. We fly. _____
2. She studies. _____
3. You worry. _____
4. He writes. _____
5. I drive. _____

6. She plans. _____
7. We open. _____
8. He shops. _____
9. It happens. _____
10. It begins. _____

Compare the Simple Present and the Present Progressive

Use the present progressive when an action is happening right now or for a temporary period of time. Use the simple present tense when the action happens habitually or when the action is a fact.

Ellen is cleaning her brushes.   (Action is in progress.)

Ellen cleans her brushes.   (Action is habitual or factual.)

CHAPTER II

> ⟨*Hint*⟩ **A Common Tense Error**
>
> Sometimes people overuse the progressive tense. If an action happens on a regular basis, do not use the progressive tense.
>
> $\qquad\qquad\qquad\qquad\qquad$ *complain*
> Every week, Tamayo's students ~~are complaining~~ about the number of assignments.

PRACTICE 2

In each sentence, underline the correct verb tense. Then identify the action by writing *G* if it is a general fact or habit or *N* if it is happening now.

EXAMPLE:

This month, the Museum of Modern Art (exhibits, <u>is exhibiting</u>) the work of Jackson Pollock.   _N_

1. The Barth Gallery usually (changes, is changing) exhibits each month. _____

2. Right now, the gallery owner (negotiates, is negotiating) with a hot young artist. _____

3. Usually, Fandra Chang (combines, is combining) photography, silkscreening, and painting. _____

4. These days, she (works, is working) on a large cityscape photograph. _____

5. Currently, she (tries, is trying) to sell her photos at the gallery. _____

6. She (develops, is developing) new art techniques each year. _____

7. Another artist, Barri Kumar, (experiments, is experimenting) with European and Asian images these days. _____

8. He (doesn't want, isn't wanting) to give up his art career. _____

9. Right now, he (works, is working) on a new piece. _____

10. Both artists (are, are being) successful. _____

Past Progressive

The **past progressive** indicates that an action was in progress at a specific past time. It can also indicate that an action in progress was interrupted.

> Yesterday at 1:00 P.M., Tamayo <u>was cleaning</u> his studio.

> Tamayo <u>was cleaning</u> his studio when the fire started.

The fire started.   NOW

He **was cleaning** his studio.

Affirmative, Question, and Negative Forms

Review the past progressive forms of the verb *work*.

Affirmative			Question Form Move *be* before the subject.			Negative Form Add *not*.		
I	was		Was	I		I	was	
She	was		Was	she		She	was	
He	was		Was	he		He	was	
It	was	working.	Was	it	working?	It	was	not working.
We	were		Were	we		We	were	
You	were		Were	you		You	were	
They	were		Were	they		They	were	

PRACTICE 3

Fill in the blanks with the past progressive forms of the verbs in parentheses.

EXAMPLE:

Michelangelo (sculpt) ___*was sculpting*___ when he hurt his thumb.

1. Ludovico and Francesca Buonarroti (live) _____ in Florence when their son, Michelangelo, was born in 1475.

2. While Michelangelo and his classmates (draw) _____ sketches of churches, the teacher realized that the young boy had a great gift.

3. The painter Domenico Ghirlandaio (search) _____ for an apprentice when he heard about Michelangelo.

4. While he (work) _____ for Ghirlandaio, Michelangelo noticed the beauty of some statues.

5. Michelangelo (earn) _____ very little when he bought his first piece of marble.

6. In 1496, while the French ambassador and his wife (visit) _____ the Vatican, he commissioned Michelangelo to create a statue.

7. Romans came to see Michelangelo while he (sculpt) _____ *La Pièta*.

8. Spectators realized that the artist (create) _____ a magnificent statue.

Using Complete Verbs

In progressive forms, always include the complete form of the helping verb *be*. Also make sure that the main verb ends in *-ing*.

is
Right now, the photographer examining the scene.

taking
Adam was ~~take~~ a picture when I entered the room.

Hint   **A Past Progressive Pitfall**

Do *not* use the past progressive to talk about past habits or about a series of past actions.

drew
Renoir ~~was drawing~~ pictures of his friends when he was younger.

PRACTICE 4 REVIEW

Correct ten past progressive errors.

EXAMPLE:

listening
Pablo Picasso was ~~listen~~ to the radio when he heard about the attack on Guernica.

1.   The Spanish Civil War was fought from 1936 to 1939. Soon after the war was beginning, General Francisco Franco was making a pact with Germany and Italy. On April 26, 1937, German aircraft were destroying Guernica, a small village in the Basque region of Spain, killing many people.

2.   At that time, Pablo Picasso living in Paris. The Spanish government asked him to paint a mural for the Spanish Pavilion at the 1937 World Fair. While he contemplating what to paint, he heard about the bomb attack on Guernica. He was deciding to paint a mural to protest the inhumanity of war. While the painting, *Guernica*, was hang in the Spanish Pavilion, many people came to see it and disliked it. The public wanted to see a clearer denunciation of Franco. But Picasso responded by saying that as an artist, he was only follow his own vision.

3. After the fair, New York's Museum of Modern Art displayed the painting. Picasso was stating that the painting must return to Spain only after the death of Franco. Unfortunately, Franco still ruling Spain when Picasso died in 1973. However, in 1981, *Guernica* was returned to Spain and presently hangs in the Reina Sofia Museum in Madrid.

Other Progressive Forms

Many other tenses also have progressive forms. Review the information about the future progressive and the present perfect progressive.

Future Progressive

The future progressive indicates that an action will be in progress at a future time.

> Tomorrow morning, do not disturb Tamayo because he <u>will be working</u> in his studio.

Present Perfect Progressive

The present perfect progressive indicates that an action has been in progress, without interruption, from a past time up to the present.

> Tamayo <u>has been painting</u> for eight hours, so he is very tired.

 **Nonprogressive Verbs**

Some verbs do not take the progressive form because they indicate an ongoing state or a perception rather than a temporary action.

Perception Verbs	Preference Verbs	State Verbs	Possession
hear	care*	believe	have*
feel*	desire	know	own
look*	hate	mean	possess
smell*	like	realize	
see	love	suppose	
seem	prefer	think*	
taste*	want	understand	

*Some verbs have more than one meaning and can be used in the progressive tense. Compare the following pairs of sentences to see how these verbs are used.

Nonprogressive:	**Progressive:**
He **has** two Picassos. (Expresses ownership)	He **is having** a bad day.
I **think** it is expensive. (Expresses an opinion)	I **am thinking** about it.
The photo **looks** good. (Expresses an observation)	He **is looking** at the photo.

PRACTICE 5

Examine each underlined verb. Write *C* above correct verbs, and fix any verb errors. Some verbs may be incomplete or nonprogressive.

has
Miguel <u>been living</u> in Austin, Texas, for several years.

1. Currently, Miguel <u>working</u> in a contemporary art gallery.

2. Generally, he <u>is loving</u> his job, but this morning something strange happened.

3. Sharon, an installation artist, entered and dropped paper and envelopes on the floor while Miguel <u>was cleaning</u> the gallery.

4. Sharon <u>been working</u> as an artist for twelve years.

5. This week, she <u>is exhibit</u> an art project called *Lost Mail*.

6. Miguel <u>is wanting</u> to understand what a work of art is.

7. He <u>is liking</u> abstract paintings, and he <u>sees</u> the value in a lot of contemporary art.

8. However, he <u>is not understanding</u> what Sharon <u>is trying</u> to do.

9. According to Miguel, some contemporary artists <u>are preferring</u> to create art for each other rather than for the general public.

10. Sharon, however, <u>is believing</u> in the value of her art, and she <u>treats</u> each exhibit seriously.

FINAL REVIEW

Correct fifteen errors with progressive verbs.

EXAMPLE:

has
Artist Kittiwat Unarrom ̬ been making sculptures of grotesque body parts from bread since 2006.

1. When Judy Chicago was begin her career as an artist in the 1960s, an art critic was telling her that women cannot be artists. She was wanting to prove the critic wrong. Chicago making minimalist paintings when she became acquainted with feminism. While she creating an art piece, she decided to include feminist symbols in her artwork. In 1974, she was having an inspiration. She fashioned an installation artwork, *The Dinner Party*, to honor great women in history.

2. The sculpture was controversial. While Chicago was design the installation, she realized she could not make the entire piece by herself. So she was hiring about 400 volunteers to assemble the piece. One day, while one contributor viewing Chicago's installation, he noticed that the contributors' names were not mentioned. The museum director promised to add the contributors' names to a Web site.

3. Many artists regularly are hiring assistants to help make large art pieces. For example, Andy Warhol used assistants while he assembling large installations. Contemporary artists like Jeff Koons and Anish Kapoor often use an assembly line of workers to construct large-scale art projects. Art student Lewis Carey is thinking that artists who design large sculptures should get sole credit for the concept. Presently, Carey planning a ten-foot sculpture for his art class. He is knowing that he be hiring a few helpers to complete his project. However, some of his classmates disagree with him. An artist should give credit to helpers.

The Writer's Room

Write about one of the following topics. Make sure that you have used and formed your verbs correctly.

1. Describe your favorite work of art. It could be a painting, a sculpture, a piece of architecture, or an illustration.

2. Choose a place on campus. You could go to the cafeteria, the lawn outside, a student center, the library, the hallway, or anywhere else on campus. Then, sit and observe what is going on around you. Use your five senses. Write a paragraph describing the things that are happening.

CHECKLIST: PROGRESSIVE VERBS

When you edit your writing, ask yourself the next questions.

☐ Do I use the correct verb tenses? Check for the overuse or misuse of progressive forms.

created
Every year, Picasso ~~was creating~~ new types of paintings.

☐ Are my progressive verbs complete? Check for errors in the following:

–the verb *be*
–incomplete *-ing* forms

am posing   *taking*
Right now, I ~~posing~~ beside a fountain, and Christa is ~~take~~ a picture of me.

 To check your progress in meeting this chapter's objectives, log in to **www.mywritinglab.com**, go to the **Study Plan** tab, click on **The Editing Handbook—Section 2 Problems with Verbs** and choose **Progressive Tenses** from the list of subtopics. Read and view the resources in the **Review Materials** section, and then complete the **Recall, Apply,** and **Write** sets in the **Activities** section.

Other Verb Forms

CHAPTER
12

Section Theme: **ENTERTAINMENT AND CULTURE**

LEARNING OBJECTIVES

1. Modals (p. 210)
2. Nonstandard Forms: *gonna, gotta, wanna* (p. 214)
3. Conditional Forms (p. 215)
4. Gerunds and Infinitives (p. 219)

In this chapter, you will read about cultural differences.

Grammar Snapshot

Looking at Other Verb Forms

In this excerpt from their book *Cultural Anthropology*, Carol R. Ember and Melvin Ember discuss body types. Notice the modals in bold print.

> There is a tendency in our society to view "taller" and "more muscled" as better, which **may reflect** the bias toward males in our culture. Natural selection **may have favored** these traits in males but different ones in females. For example, because females bear children, selection **may have favored** earlier cessation of growth, and therefore less ultimate height in females so that the nutritional needs of a fetus **would** not **compete** with the growing mother's needs.

In this chapter, you will identify and write modals, conditionals, gerunds, and infinitives.

Modals

Modals are helping verbs that express possibility, advice, and so on. Review the list of some common modals and their meanings.

Common Modal Forms

Modal	Meaning	Present Form	Past Form
can	Ability	Amir **can draw** very well.	**could draw**
could	Possibility	He **could sell** his work.	**could have sold**
may		Amir **may become** famous.	**may have become**
might		Amir **might become** famous.	**might have become**
must	Obligation	We **must work** late.	**had to work***
	Probability	The buyers **must be** impatient.	**must have been**
should	Advice	He **should see** a lawyer.	**should have seen**
ought to		He **ought to see** a lawyer.	**ought to have seen**
will	Future action or willingness	They **will buy** his products.	**would buy**
would	Desire	I **would like** to see his designs.	**would have liked**

*Exception: To show the past tense of *must* (meaning "obligation"), use the past tense of the regular verb *have to*.

> ## Hint   Modal Forms Are Consistent
>
> Each modal has a fixed form. When the subject changes, the verb remains the same. In the example, *can* is the modal.
>
> I **can** go.   You **can** go.   She **can** go.
> We **can** go.   They **can** go.

PRACTICE 1

Read the following sentences. In the space, indicate the function of each underlined modal.

Ability   Possibility   Advice   Obligation   Desire

EXAMPLE:

People <u>ought to learn</u> about cultural differences.   *Advice*

1. You <u>could say</u> that culture is learned behavior that involves shared language, gestures, arts, attitudes, beliefs, and values.   _____

2. In the United States, people <u>may call</u> you by your first name.   _____

3. Many Americans <u>can speak</u> both English and Spanish.   _____

4. You <u>ought to remove</u> your shoes when you enter a home in India.   _____

5. In Japan, you <u>should bow</u> when you greet someone. _____

6. In Australia, instead of saying "Good day," you <u>could say</u> "G'day." _____

7. Many people <u>would like</u> to visit Australia. _____

8. In Great Britain, you <u>must drive</u> on the left side of the road. _____

9. In England, some people <u>might say</u> "I shall not" to mean "I will not." _____

10. In Japan, you <u>should not make</u> direct eye contact with people. _____

Present and Past Forms

For some modals, you must use a completely different word in the past tense. Review the differences between *can* and *could*, *will* and *would*.

Can and Could

Use *can* to indicate a present ability.

> Amir **can speak** Arabic.

Use *could* to indicate a past ability.

> When he was younger, he **could write** in Arabic, but he cannot do so now.

Also use *could* to show that something is possible.

> With globalization, some cultures **could disappear.**

Will and Would

Use *will* to discuss a future action from the present perspective.

> Michelle **will visit** Haiti next summer.

Use *would* to discuss a future action from a past perspective.

> Last month, I told her that I **would go** with her.

Also use *would* to indicate a desire.

> Michelle **would like** to visit her ancestral home.

 **Negative Forms of Modals**

Negative Forms
When you add *not* to modals, the full form consists of two words—for example, *could not* and *should not*. However, when you add *not* to the modal *can*, the result is one word.

cannot	should not	could not	would not	will not

Contracted Forms
You can contract the negative forms of modals. Note that *will* + *not* becomes *won't*.

can't	shouldn't	couldn't	wouldn't	won't

PRACTICE 2

Underline the correct modal forms.

EXAMPLE:

This year, the Carnival of Venice (<u>will</u>, would) occur during the last week of Lent.

1.   Grazia DeCesare lives in San Diego. Her family is originally from Italy, so Grazia (can, could) speak Italian. She (can, could) also speak Spanish. Next March, she (will, would) travel to Venice to visit her aunt. Grazia loves the Carnival of Venice, which is a unique and wonderful celebration.

2.   The Carnival of Venice occurs every spring. During the carnival, people wear elaborate disguises. If Grazia (can, could) afford it, she will buy a beautiful mask that she (will, would) wear during the carnival.

3.   The first carnival occurred in the twelfth century. At that time, the celebration (will, would) generally begin about December 26. Citizens (will, would) wear masks made of leather, papier-mâché, porcelain, or plaster. They (will, would) also wear brightly colored capes and elaborate three-cornered hats. Thus, in past centuries, people (can, could) dance in the streets, drink wine, and gamble in gaming houses without being recognized. Because the carnival lasted to the end of March, citizens (will, would) spend several months wearing disguises in public.

4.   During the Middle Ages, the Venetian authorities (will, would) sometimes try to stop the public debauchery, but the people of Venice loved their carnival and (can, could) not imagine giving it up. People from all over Europe (will, would) visit Venice because the city was known as an exciting place.

5.   In 1797, during the reign of Napoleon, Austria took control of Venice, and the city fell into decline. For over two hundred years, citizens (can, could) not celebrate the carnival. Then, in 1979, a group

of Venetians convinced the city authorities to reintroduce a one-week carnival. Nowadays, visitors (can, could) buy masks, and they (can, could) enjoy the special atmosphere in that beautiful city. The festival (will, would) definitely be fabulous next spring.

Past of *Should, Could,* and *Would*

To form the past tense of *should, could,* and *would*, add *have* + the past participle. Review the following examples.

> Before Anik and Richard went to Mexico, they **should have learned** a few words in Spanish. They **could have communicated** with the locals, and they **would have had** a better time.

 **Use Standard Past Forms**

Some people say *should of* or *shoulda*. These are nonstandard forms, and you should avoid using them, especially in written communication. When you write the past forms of *should, would,* and *could,* always include *have* + the past participle.

> *should have*
> Before Jeremy did business in Japan, he ~~shoulda~~ learned about Japanese business
> *have*
> etiquette. He would ~~of~~ offended fewer people.

PRACTICE 3

Correct eight errors with modal forms.

EXAMPLE:

> *should have*
> I ~~should of~~ learned about Geisha culture before I went to Japan.

1.   Mitsumi thinks she shoulda trained to become a Geisha. There were over 80,000 Geishas in Japan in the 1920s, but now there are only a couple of thousand. Many tourists believe that Geishas are prostitutes. But Geishas are traditional Japanese entertainers.

2.   Most girls start to learn how to become Geishas as teenagers. Mitsumi is now an accountant, but she woulda loved to be a Geisha. She would of acquired many skills in the art of entertainment. Her teacher woulda taught her music, dance, and conversational skills. She could also have learn how to prepare a Japanese tea ceremony. Mitsumi would have know how to wear a kimono and put on the complicated white face make-up.

3.   Last summer, my friend and I were in Kyoto in the Geisha district. I

shoulda brought my camera because I saw many young Geisha trainees.

These student Geishas are called *maiko*. I could of gone to a tea ceremony

with Geishas, but I could not afford it.

Nonstandard Forms: *gonna, gotta, wanna*

Some people commonly say *I'm gonna, I gotta,* or *I wanna.* These are nonstandard forms, and you should not use them in written communication.

Write *going to* instead of *gonna.*

>   *going to*
> My uncle is ~~gonna~~ help me learn Hungarian.

Write *have to* instead of *gotta.*

>   *have to*
> I ~~gotta~~ learn to speak with my grandparents.

Write *want to* instead of *wanna.*

>   *want to*
> Next year, I ~~wanna~~ go to Hungary.

 **Forming the Main Verb**

When you use modals, make sure to form your main verb correctly. Use the base form of the verb that directly follows a modal.

>   *visit*   *go*
> We <u>should</u> ~~visited~~ France. We <u>can</u> ~~going~~ in March.

PRACTICE 4

Correct ten errors with nonstandard verbs and modal forms.

EXAMPLE:

>   *are going to learn*
> You ~~are gonna learn~~ about gestures.

1.   If you take a trip to a foreign country, you should studied nonverbal

communication. According to experts, humans can expressing up to eighty

percent of their thoughts nonverbally.

2.   One gesture can had different meanings in various countries. For

example, in the United States, if you wanna indicate that you like

something, you can join your thumb and forefinger into an "okay" gesture.

However, you are gonna insult a waiter in France if you give the okay sign

because the gesture means "zero" or "worthless." In Russia, use the okay

sign only if you wanna insult someone.

3.   If you gotta go on a business trip to Brazil, do not use the thumbs-up

gesture because it is highly offensive. If you raise your forefinger and your

pinky in Italy, you are gonna make someone very angry because the sign

means that a man's wife is cheating on him. In Australia, if you wanna lose

friends, make the V for "victory" sign with your palm facing toward you.

It is Australia's most obscene gesture.

4.   Clearly, if you wanna get along with people from other cultures, it is a

good idea to learn about their gestures.

Conditional Forms

In a **conditional sentence,** there is a condition and a result. This type of sentence usually contains the word *if* and has two parts, or clauses. The main clause depends on the condition set in the *if* clause. There are three conditional forms.

First Conditional Form: Present or Possible Future

Use the "possible future" form when the condition is true or very possible.

If + present tense $\longrightarrow$ present or future tense

Condition (*if* clause)	**Result**
If he **needs** help,	he **can call** me.
If you **visit** Mexico,	you **will see** some amazing murals.

Second Conditional Form: Unlikely Present

Use the "unlikely present" form when the condition is not likely and probably will not happen.

If + past tense $\longrightarrow$ *would* (expresses a condition)
could (expresses a possibility)

Condition (*if* clause)	**Result**
If I **knew** how to speak Spanish,	I **would live** in Mexico for a year.
If she **were** taller,	she **could be** a runway model.

CHAPTER 12

 **If I Were . . .**

In informal English, you occasionally hear *was* in the *if* clause. However, in academic writing, when the condition is unlikely, always use *were* in the *if* clause.

If I **were** rich, I would buy a new car.

If my sister **were** rich, she would invest in the stock market.

Third Conditional Form: Impossible Past

Use the "impossible past" form when the condition cannot happen because the event is over.

If + past perfect tense ⟶ *would have* (+ past participle)

Condition (*if* clause)	**Result**
If you **had asked** me,	I **would have traveled** with you.
If Karl **had done** his homework,	he **would have passed** the course.

PRACTICE 5

In each case, identify the type of conditional sentence, and write *A*, *B*, or *C* in the blank.

A (possible future):   If you ask me, I will help.

B (unlikely present):   If you asked me, I would help.

C (impossible past):   If you had asked me, I would have helped.

EXAMPLE:

If I could, I would travel to Spain.   *B*

1. If Carmen Morales were younger, she would return to school.   _____

2. If she had known how difficult it is to make a career in dance, she would have found a different profession.   _____

3. If you want to learn the tango, she will teach it to you.   _____

4. According to Carmen, the tango is not difficult to master if you practice a lot.   _____

5. If she had taken better care of herself, she would not have required knee surgery.   _____

6. Today, if she takes it easy, she can teach three dance classes a week.   _____

7. She would teach more classes if her doctor permitted it.   _____

8. Perhaps if she had not danced with passion, she would have felt unfulfilled.   _____

Avoid Mixing Conditional Forms

Avoid mixing conditional forms. If you are discussing a past event, use the third conditional form. Do not mix the second and third forms.

       had been
If I ~~were~~ you, I would have done the assignment.

PRACTICE 6

Fill in the blanks with the correct forms of the verbs in parentheses.
EXAMPLE:

If you (plan) ___*plan*___ to do business abroad, you will benefit from diversity training courses.

1.   Eric Zorn went on a business trip to Japan, and, unfortunately, he made some cultural etiquette errors. While there, he made eye contact with his hosts, and he got down to business immediately. If he (take) _____ more time for small talk, his hosts would have felt more comfortable. Also, if he had avoided direct eye contact, he (appear) _____ less aggressive. Basically, if he (understand) _____ the cultural differences, he would not have insulted his hosts.

2.   Roger Axtell is an international business traveler. He has written a book called *Do's and Taboos of Humor Around the World*. If Axtell (travel, not) _____ extensively, he would have been unable to write about cultural differences.

3.   Axtell has had some interesting experiences. A few years ago, when he visited Saudi Arabia, he met with an important customer. One day, the customer grabbed his hand while they were walking. In Saudi Arabia, hand-holding is a sign of friendship and respect. If Axtell (pull) _____ away, he would have offended his host. If he (know) _____ in advance about the hand-holding, he (feel, not) _____ so uncomfortable.

4.   Axtell says that if he (be, not) _____ so busy, he would write more books about cultural diversity.

> **Problems with the Past Conditional**
>
> In "impossible past" sentences, the writer expresses regret about a past event or expresses the wish that a past event had worked out differently. Avoid the following errors.
>
> • Do not use *would have . . .* in the *if* clause. Instead, use the past perfect tense.
>
> > *had asked*
> > If you ~~would have asked~~ me, I would have traveled with you.
>
> • Do not write *woulda* or *would of*. These are nonstandard forms. When you use the past forms of *should*, *would*, and *could*, always include *have* + the past participle.
>
> > *had done*   *have*
> > If you ~~would have done~~ the work, you would ~~of~~ passed the course.

PRACTICE 7

Correct ten errors with conditional forms.

EXAMPLE:

> *would have*
> If Mawlid had stayed in Somalia, his life ~~woulda~~ been different.

1. In 1994, Mawlid and Myriam Abdul moved to San Diego from Somalia. If he would have had a choice, Mawlid would have stayed in his native country. He misses his mother and his extended family.

2. Mawlid is impressed by the respectful treatment of the elderly in Somalia: "My grandparents were treated with love and attention until their deaths. If my grandparents had moved to the United States, they would of been surprised by the treatment of old people. If they would have visited a typical nursing home, they woulda been shocked."

3. Mawlid's wife, Myriam, would not like to live in Somalia again, even if she was able to. She says, "In the United States, if I want to study or work, I can do it easily. However, if I would have stayed in Somalia, my brothers and aunts would have expected me to take care of them. When I was a child, my mother had to take care of my uncle's children because he wanted them to be educated in the city. He didn't ask my mother for permission.

If she had refused to care for her nephews, family members woulda been angry with her. If she would have had a choice, she would have preferred a quieter life."

4.   Mawlid says that he will return to his native country if he amassed enough money because he misses his close-knit family. If Mawlid and Myriam wanted to resolve their differences, they will have to compromise.

Gerunds and Infinitives

Sometimes a main verb is followed by another verb. The second verb can be a gerund or an infinitive. A **gerund** is a verb with an *-ing* ending. An **infinitive** consists of *to* and the base form of the verb.

> **Verb + gerund:**   We <u>finished</u> **reading** *Wild Swans*.
>
> **Verb + infinitive:**   I <u>want</u> **to write** about it.

Using Gerunds

Some verbs in English are always followed by a gerund. Do not confuse gerunds with progressive verb forms. Compare a progressive verb and a gerund.

> **Verb:**   Julie is studying now.   (*Studying* is in the present progressive form. Julie is in the process of doing something.)
>
> **Gerund:**   Julie <u>finished</u> **studying.** (*Studying* is a gerund that follows *finish*. After *finish,* you must use a gerund.)

Some Common Verbs and Expressions Followed by Gerunds

acknowledge	discuss	postpone
adore	dislike	practice
anticipate	enjoy	quit
appreciate	finish	recall
avoid	involve	recollect
can't help	justify	recommend
complete	keep	regret
consider	loathe	resent
delay	mention	resist
deny	mind	risk
detest	miss	tolerate

Using Prepositions Plus Gerunds

Many verbs have the structure **verb + preposition + object.** If the object is another verb, the second verb is a gerund.

> I dream <u>about</u> **traveling** to Greece.

Some Common Words Followed by Prepositions Plus Gerunds

accuse of	(be) excited about	(be) good at	prohibit from
apologize for	feel like	insist on	succeed in
discourage him from*	fond of	(be) interested in	think about
dream of	forbid him from*	look forward to	(be) tired of
(be) enthusiastic about	forgive me for*	prevent him from*	warn him about*

*Certain verbs must have a noun or pronoun before the preposition. Here, the pronouns are underlined.

Using Infinitives

Some verbs are followed by the infinitive (*to* + base form of verb).

> Helen wants **to travel** with me.
>
> (*To travel* is an infinitive that follows the verb *wants*.)

Some Common Verbs Followed by Infinitives

afford	decide	manage	refuse
agree	demand	mean	seem
appear	deserve	need	swear
arrange	expect	offer	threaten
ask	fail	plan	volunteer
claim	hesitate	prepare	want
complete	hope	pretend	wish
consent	learn	promise	would like

Using Gerunds or Infinitives

Some common verbs can be followed by gerunds or infinitives. Both forms have the same meaning.

begin	continue	hate	like
love	prefer	start	

> LaTasha <u>likes</u> **to live** alone.
> LaTasha <u>likes</u> **living** alone. } (Both sentences have exactly the same meaning.)

> **Hint**   **Used to . . .**
>
> You can follow *used to* with a gerund or an infinitive, but there is a difference in meaning.
>
> • *Used to* + infinitive expresses a past habit.
>
> > Rowan does not smoke now, but she <u>used to</u> **smoke.**
>
> • *Be used to* + gerund expresses something you are accustomed to.
>
> > Rowan has been on her own for years, so she <u>is used to</u> **living** alone.

PRACTICE 8

Correct any errors in the underlined gerund and infinitive forms. If the verb is correct, write C above it. (Be careful, you may have to change the preposition before the gerund.)

EXAMPLE:

on reforming
Social activist Bhimrao Ambedkar insisted to reform cultural norms.

1. The untouchables of India have been discriminated against for thousands

    of years. Bhimrao Ambedkar was born an untouchable in 1891, but he

    dreamt to change his circumstances.

2. His family was extremely poor, but Ambedkar enjoyed to study and wanted

    to pursue his education.

3. His father agreed sending him to college, and in 1907, Ambedkar became

    one of the first people from his caste to study at college.

4. Ambedkar disliked to see the way upper caste Hindus treated untouchables.

5. The young man became a leading political figure and succeeded to fight for

    civil rights of his caste.

6. When India received its independence in 1947, Indian politicians looked

    forward to work with Ambedkar.

7. He was one of the fathers of the Indian Constitution. It promises to provide

    civil liberties to all Indian citizens.

8. Today, many Indians are working to eradicate intolerance and deserve having

    recognition for their efforts.

FINAL REVIEW

Correct fifteen verb errors in the following text.

EXAMPLE:

could have
The government could of apologized many years ago.

1. Native residential schools started in the 1800s and closed in the 1970s. In

    June 2008, the Canadian government apologized to Native Canadians for

the treatment they had received at residential schools. When I was in school, I shoulda paid more attention in my history class. If I would have been more attentive, I would have known about this terrible policy.

2. Phil is an Ojibway from Manitoba. When he was a boy, he used to visiting his grandfather on the Sandy Bay Reserve. One evening, Phil's grandfather described his experiences in a residential school. Phil should of listened more closely. The government had hoped assimilating native children into white European society. Politicians thought the policy would help indigenous citizens.

3. In residential schools, children were forced to convert to Christianity. In addition, they were prohibited to communicate in their own language. If they risked to speak in their own language, they were beaten. Some students died because of inadequate medical care. The children shoulda run away from the school. If politicians would have been more respectful of indigenous culture, this situation would never have happen.

4. In Australia, Aboriginals were also removed from their homes and sent to residential schools. If officials would have valued Aboriginals, they would never of taken such action. Officials thought that the Aboriginals would becoming Christian if they were in residential schools. The Australian government apologized to the Aboriginals in February 2008.

5. I am interested in this historical event and wanna read more about it. I gotta do some research. I am gonna look for more information on the Internet.

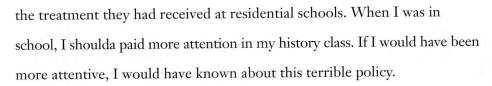

The Writer's Room

Write about one of the following topics. Make sure that you have formed any modals or conditionals correctly.

1. What can people learn when they interact with other cultures? List some things.

2. Think about someone you know who is from another culture. How are you and that person similar or different?

CHECKLIST: OTHER VERB FORMS

When you edit your writing, ask yourself these questions.

☐ Do I use the correct modal forms? Check for errors in the following:

–w*ill* vs. *would* and *can* vs. *could*
–past forms

       have
I should ~~of~~ packed an umbrella when I visited Ireland.

☐ Do I use the correct conditional forms? Check for errors in the following:

–possible future forms ("If I meet . . . , I will go . . .")
–unlikely present forms ("If I met . . . , I would go . . .")
–impossible past forms ("If I had met . . . , I would have gone . . .")

      had
If I ~~would have~~ more money, I would stay in good hotels.

☐ Do I use the correct gerund or infinitive form?

        traveling
I recommend ~~to travel~~ during the spring break.

The Writers' Circle   **Collaborative Activity**

Work with a group of about three students. You need one sheet of paper for this activity.

STEP 1   Write down as much as you know about the life of a famous entertainer (such as a musician, an artist, an athlete, or an actor). Do not mention the name of the entertainer. Write at least five sentences about the person.

    Example: He was born in Philadelphia, and he started rapping at age twelve. In 1990, he played a "prince" on a hit television show. Later, he had several hit movies. He is slender and tall. He has protruding ears. In 2006, he acted in a movie with his son.

STEP 2   Read your sentences aloud to another group of students. They must guess who your mystery person is. If they cannot guess, continue to give them more clues.

READING LINK

Entertainment and Culture
To read more about entertainment and culture, see the following essays:

"The New Addiction" by Josh Freed (page 412)
"What's Your Humor Style?" by Louise Dobson (page 418)
"A Cultural Minefield" by William Ecenbarger (page 420)
"The Cult of Emaciation" by Ben Barry (page 423)

PEARSON mywritinglab   To check your progress in meeting this chapter's objectives, log in to **www.mywritinglab.com**, go to the **Study Plan** tab, click on **The Editing Handbook—Section 2 Problems with Verbs** and choose **Other Verb Forms** from the list of subtopics. Read and view the resources in the **Review Materials** section, and then complete the **Recall, Apply,** and **Write** sets in the **Activities** section.

CHAPTER 13 Subject–Verb Agreement

Section Theme: **BELIEFS**

In this chapter, you will read about mysteries and urban legends.

Grammar Snapshot

Looking at Subject–Verb Agreement

David A. Locher is the author of *Collective Behavior*. In the following excerpt from his book, he describes an urban legend. The subjects are in bold print, and the verbs are underlined.

An **urban legend** gives specific details about an **event** that has supposedly occurred. For example, there is a **legend** about a **man** who wakes up in a bathtub full of ice. **He** finds a note left by the attractive woman **he** met at a party or bar the night before. **She** has purportedly stolen his kidney. This **urban legend** gives specific **details** that may change every time the **story** is told.

In this chapter, you will practice making subjects and verbs agree.

224

Basic Subject–Verb Agreement Rules

Subject–verb agreement simply means that a subject and a verb agree in number. A singular subject needs a singular verb, and a plural subject needs a plural verb.

                      S   V

Singular subject: **Jay** <u>believes</u> in urban legends.

                               S   V

Plural subject: The **stories** <u>have</u> strange endings.

Simple Present Tense

Writers use **simple present tense** to indicate that an action is habitual or factual. Review the rules for simple present tense agreement.

- Add *-s* or *-es* to the verb when the subject is *he, she, it,* or the equivalent (*Mike, Ella, Texas*). This is called the **third-person singular form.**

  Mr. Roy <u>believes</u> in ghosts.   (one person)

  The **museum** <u>displays</u> many exhibits.   (one place)

  Perhaps a **giant ape** <u>roams</u> the forests   (one thing)
  of the northwestern United States.

- When the subject is *I, you, we, they,* or the equivalent (*the Smiths, the books, Jay and I*), do not add an ending to the verb.

  The moment **we** <u>want</u> to believe something, **we** suddenly <u>see</u> all the arguments for it and <u>become</u> blind to the arguments against it.

  —George Bernard Shaw

To see how these rules work, review the forms of the verb *run*.

GRAMMAR LINK

For more information about present tense verbs, see Chapter 9.

Present Tense of *Run*

	Singular Forms	**Plural Forms**
First person:	I run	We run
Second person:	You run	You run
Third person:	He runs	They run
	She runs	
	It runs	

PRACTICE 1

In each sentence, underline the subject and circle the correct verb. Make sure that the verb agrees with the subject.

EXAMPLE:

    Some <u>stories</u> (seem)/ seems) fantastic.

1. Generally, <u>urban legends</u> (appear)/ appears) mysteriously.
2. The <u>stories</u> (spread)/ spreads) rapidly.
3. Usually, the <u>speaker</u> (say /says), "This happened to a friend of a friend."

4. Some <u>people</u> (spread)/ spreads) urban legends by e-mail.

5. In one message, a <u>man</u> (visit / visits) a tourist resort in Mexico.

6. A tiny <u>dog</u> (beg / begs) for food.

7. The young <u>man</u> (decide / decides) to keep the little Chihuahua.

8. Later, <u>he</u> (bring / brings) his new pet to a veterinarian.

9. The animal <u>doctor</u> (say / says), "Why are you keeping a sewer rat?"

10. Many <u>people</u> (believe / believes) such urban legends.

Troublesome Present-Tense Verbs: Be, Have, Do

Some present-tense verbs are formed in special ways. Review the verbs *be*, *have*, and *do*. Be particularly careful when writing these verbs.

	Be	**Have**	**Do**
Singular Forms			
First person:	I am	I have	I do
Second person:	You are	You have	You do
Third person:	He **is**	He **has**	He **does**
	She **is**	She **has**	She **does**
	It **is**	It **has**	It **does**
Plural Forms			
First person:	We are	We have	We do
Second person:	You are	You have	You do
Third person:	They are	They have	They do

PRACTICE 2

Fill in each blank with the correct form of *be*, *have*, or *do*.

EXAMPLE:

Some people _____*have*_____ irrational fears. Max _____*is*_____ afraid of cats.

1.   All people ____*have*____ fears. Some fears ____*are*____ universal and arise from our human history. They ____*are*____ a response to harmful situations. For example, spiders and snakes ____*have*____ the potential to harm us. Heights ____*are*____ also potentially dangerous, so a fear of heights is common. Basically, fear ____*is*____ a healthy response.

2. A phobia _____*is*_____ an irrational or excessive fear. For example, Shane _____*is*_____ extremely uncomfortable on a bridge or in a tunnel. Elaine Chen _____*has*_____ an extreme stress reaction in airplanes. She _____*does*_____ not enjoy flying, but she still _____*does*_____ it sometimes. She _____*is*_____ aware that flying is safer than driving a car. So, in airplanes, Elaine _____*does*_____ relaxation exercises to overcome her anxiety. According to the Anxiety Disorders Association of America, almost 20 million people _____*have*_____ specific phobias. Some therapists _____*do*_____ a good job of helping people overcome their phobias.

PRACTICE 3

In the following paragraphs, the verbs are underlined. Identify and correct ten subject–verb agreement errors. Write *C* above the correct verbs.

EXAMPLE:

> *has*
> Mario <u>have</u> strange opinions about urban legends.

1. *are* *C*
    Urban legends <u>is</u> not new. The "earwig" legend <u>is</u> over one thousand
    has *climbs*
    years old. In the story, an earwig <u>have</u> an unusual idea. It <u>climb</u> into the ear
    C *eat*
    of a woman to lay eggs. The eggs <u>hatch</u>, and tiny earwigs <u>eats</u> the brain of
    C *are*
    the woman. Perhaps people <u>repeat</u> this story because they <u>is</u> afraid of
    insects.

2. *C* *are*
    Urban legends <u>serve</u> a purpose. They <u>is</u> about ordinary people in
    warns
    frightening situations, and each legend <u>warn</u> us about a possible danger.
    has *speak*
    Sometimes, a story <u>have</u> a moral. Additionally, when people <u>speaks</u> about a
    C
    scary or traumatic event, they <u>release</u> their collective anxiety.

Agreement in Other Tenses
Simple Past Tense

Writers use the **simple past tense** to indicate that an action was completed at a past time. In the past tense, all verbs except *be* have one form.

Regular: I worked.   He worked.   We worked.   You worked.   They worked.
Irregular: I ate.   He ate.   We ate.   You ate.   They ate.

Exception: In the past tense, the only verb requiring subject–verb agreement is the verb *be*. It has two past forms: *was* and *were*.

Past Tense of *Be*	
Was	**Were**
I was	You were
He was	We were
She was	They were
It was	

Present Perfect Tense

The present perfect tense is formed with *have* or *has* before the past participle. If the subject is third-person singular, always use *has*.

She has <u>finished</u> a book about Native American legends. **I** <u>have</u> <u>read</u> it.

GRAMMAR LINK

For more information about using the present perfect tense, see Chapter 10.

Other Tenses

When writing in most other verb tenses and in modal forms (*can, could, would, may, might,* and so on), use the same form of the verb with every subject.

Future	Past Perfect	Modals
I <u>will</u> read.	I <u>had</u> finished.	I <u>can</u> go.
She <u>will</u> read.	She <u>had</u> finished.	She <u>should</u> go.
He <u>will</u> read.	He <u>had</u> finished.	He <u>might</u> go.
They <u>will</u> read.	They <u>had</u> finished.	They <u>could</u> go.

PRACTICE 4

In each sentence, underline the subject and circle the correct verb. Make sure that the subject and verb agree.

EXAMPLE:

   Some <u>mysteries</u> (have / has) been solved.

1. Most mysteries (is / are) not mysterious at all, according to author Benjamin Radford.

2. For example, perhaps giant apelike creatures (live / lives) in the mountainous region between British Columbia and California.

3. Radford (have / has) visited the sites where Bigfoot sightings were reported, but he (is / are) not convinced that the evidence is legitimate.

4. He (give / gives) interesting reasons for his opinion.

5. First, when a giant ape (die / dies), there should be a dead body, yet no bodies (have / has) been found.

6. Second, many people (claim / claims) that they have seen Bigfoot, but these eyewitness testimonies (is / are) probably unreliable.

7. Finally, believers (refer / refers) to sightings of giant footprints, but in 2000, a man named Ray Wallace admitted that he and his son had made fake footprints.

8. They (was / were) just having fun, and they (was / were) surprised when many people believed them.

9. Many people (continue / continues) to believe in Bigfoot.

10. Radford (admit / admits) that the legend will probably continue for centuries.

Verb Before the Subject

Usually the verb comes after the subject, but in some sentences, the verb comes *before* the subject. In such cases, you must still ensure that the subject and verb agree.

Sentences Beginning with *There* or *Here*

When a sentence begins with *there* or *here*, the subject always follows the verb. *There* and *here* are not subjects.

>   V   S   V   S
> Here is a new **book** about Atlantis. There are many new **theories** about it.

Questions

In most questions, the helping verb or the verb *be* appears before the subject. In the next examples, the main verb is *be*.

>   V   S   V   S
> Where is the mysterious **island?** Was Plato's **story** about Atlantis fictional or factual?

In questions in which the main verb is not *be*, the subject agrees with the helping verb.

>   H   S   V H   S   V
> Where does the sunken **city** rest? Do **scientists** have any answers?

PRACTICE 5

In each sentence, underline the subject and circle the correct verb.

EXAMPLE:

What (is / are) England's most well-known tourist <u>attraction</u>?

1. (Is / Are) there ancient ruins in the southern part of England?

2. What (do / does) people see when they visit Stonehenge?

3. When (do / does) the summer solstice occur?

4. Why (is / are) the giant stones arranged in a circular pattern?

5. What (do / does) the tour guide say about the stones?

6. How much (do / does) a ticket cost to visit Stonehenge?

7. (Is / Are) each stone larger than a house?

8. (Is / Are) religious groups attracted to Stonehenge?

9. (Have / has) many authors written about the mysterious ruins?

10. (Do / Does) tourists visit Stonehenge each year?

PRACTICE 6

Correct any subject–verb agreement errors. If a sentence is correct, write *C* in the blank.

EXAMPLE:

       is

There ~~are~~ a fascinating woman in my neighborhood.   _____

1. There is many stories about Anna Madeo.   _____

2. Do she see the future?   _____

3. There are five customers who want Anna to read their palms.   _____

4. Is her predictions often correct?   _____

5. There is some strange coincidences.   _____

6. Do that woman have a special gift?   _____

7. Do you know Anna Madeo?   _____

8. There is many possible reasons for her popularity.   _____

More Than One Subject

There are special agreement rules when there is more than one subject in a sentence.

- When two or more subjects are joined by *and*, use the plural form of the verb.

  And: **Florida, Bermuda,** and **Puerto Rico** <u>form</u> the Bermuda Triangle.

- When two or more subjects are joined by *or* or *nor*, the verb agrees with the subject that is the closest to it.

  plural
  Nor: Neither Clara Jackson nor her **children** <u>like</u> to fly in airplanes.

  singular
  Or: Either Diego or **Clara** <u>has</u> to sit by the window.

PRACTICE 7

In each sentence, underline the subject and circle the correct verb. Make sure the verb agrees with the subject.

EXAMPLE:

There (is)/ are) an interesting <u>legend</u> about a ship that disappeared.

1. In 1872, the *Mary Celeste* (was / were) launched from New York.

2. There (was / were) ten people on the ship when it left port.

3. Later, the ship (was / were) found floating in the sea, but no survivors (was / were) on board.

4. Neither the captain nor the crew members (was / were) ever found.

5. Today, there (is / are) many versions of the story.

6. Many theories (have / has) been put forward.

7. Maybe strong winds or a giant storm (was / were) responsible for the missing crew members.

8. Perhaps either one or several crew members (was / were) violent and murderous.

9. Maybe man-eating monsters (live / lives) in the sea.

10. (Do / Does) you (know / knows) the true story?

Special Subject Forms

Some subjects are not easy to identify as singular or plural. Two common types are indefinite pronouns and collective nouns.

Indefinite Pronouns

Indefinite pronouns refer to a general person, place, or thing. Carefully review the following list of indefinite pronouns.

Indefinite Pronouns				
Singular:	another	each	nobody	other
	anybody	everybody	no one	somebody
	anyone	everyone	nothing	someone
	anything	everything	one	something
Plural:	both	many	several	
	few	others		

Singular Indefinite Pronouns

In the following sentences, the subjects are singular, so they require third-person singular verb forms.

Almost **everyone** <u>has</u> theories about the Bermuda Triangle.

According to Norm Tyler, **nothing** <u>proves</u> that the Bermuda Triangle is dangerous.

Plural Indefinite Pronouns

Both, few, many, others, and *several* are all plural subjects. The verb is always plural.

The two survivors talked about their journey. **Both** <u>have</u> frequent nightmares.

Many <u>were</u> still on the boat when it mysteriously disappeared.

PRACTICE 8

Underline the subject and circle the correct verb in each sentence.

EXAMPLE:

<u>Everybody</u> (has / have) an opinion on the role of religion in schools.

1.   In 1859, Charles Darwin wrote *On the Origin of Species.* In Victorian England, Darwin's ideas (was / were) regarded as a threat to Christianity. Years later, the theory of evolution (was / were) still controversial.

2.   In 1925, John Scopes (was / were) accused of violating the Butler Act by teaching Tennessee biology students about evolution. If anybody (teach / teaches) a theory that denies the story of divine creation, that person is breaking the law. The Scopes Monkey Trial lasted for fifteen days, but nobody (was / were) prepared for defense lawyer Clarence

CHAPTER 13

Darrow's decision. He asked the jury to find his client guilty because he wanted to take the case to the Tennessee supreme court.

3. Today, there (is / are) debates about the teaching of religion and science in schools. In this country, one controversial issue (is / are) school prayer. Some (think / thinks) that students should pray every day under the direction of a teacher. Others (disagree / disagrees) and (argue / argues) that parents, not schools, should teach religion and morality.

4. If someone (say / says) that the United States is a multicultural society with a variety of religious beliefs, then someone else (reply / replies) that it was founded on Christian religious principles and that school prayer is necessary. Certainly, everyone (has / have) an opinion about this issue.

Collective Nouns as Subjects

Collective nouns refer to a group of people or things. The group acts as a unit. Here are some common collective nouns.

army	class	crowd	group	population
association	club	family	jury	public
audience	committee	gang	mob	society
band	company	government	organization	team

Generally, each group acts as a unit, so you must use the singular form of the verb.

The **public** <u>loves</u> to hear about urban myths.

GRAMMAR LINK

For more information about using collective nouns with pronouns, see page 133 in Chapter 7.

PRACTICE 9

Underline the subject of each sentence. Then, circle the correct form of the verb.

EXAMPLE:

In many communities throughout the world, <u>people</u> (believe / believes) in ghosts.

1. Scientists and other rational thinkers (is / are) likely to question the existence of a spirit world. However, even skeptics (admit / admits) that they may not know the whole truth.

2. In *The Power of Myth*, Joseph Campbell (state / states), "A fairy tale is the child's myth. There (is / are) proper myths for proper times of life. As you (grow / grows) older, you (need / needs) a sturdier mythology." Every society (invent / invents) stories to try to explain basic truths.

3.   Each nation (have / has) its own version of ghost stories. In the Chinese lunar tradition, the seventh month (is / are) "ghost month." During ghost month, a gate (open / opens), and spirits (enter / enters) the human world. Buddhist priests (pray / prays) to subdue the spirits. A band (play / plays) music to welcome the spirits, and the crowd (listen / listens) with reverence. In China, a typical family (welcome / welcomes) the ghosts during ghost month.

Interrupting Words and Phrases

Words that come between the subject and the verb may confuse you. In these cases, look for the subject and make sure that the verb agrees with the subject. To help you see the interrupting words in the following two examples, we have put parentheses around the words that come between the subject and the verb.

Some old **legends** (about vampires and spirits) <u>continue</u> to scare people.

A **student** (in my creative writing class) <u>writes</u> updated vampire stories.

 **Identify Interrupting Phrases**

To make it easier to find subject–verb agreement errors as you edit for subject–verb agreement, place parentheses around any words that separate the subject and the verb in the sentence. Then you can see whether the subjects and verbs agree.

   Many **directors**, *(including the late Stanley Kubrick),* <u>have made</u> horror films.

When interrupting phrases contain *of the,* the subject generally appears before the phrase.

   One *(of the neighbors)* <u>knows</u> everybody's secrets.

PRACTICE 10

Place parentheses around any words that come between each subject and verb. Then circle the correct form of the verb.

EXAMPLE:

   Anne Rice, *(a popular author,)* <u>write</u> / <u>writes</u> about vampires.

1. One of this era's most enduring legends <u>is / are</u> the Dracula legend.

2. Tales about vampires <u>was / were</u> common in Eastern Europe and India.

3. The story about the blood-drinking human <u>was / were</u> especially popular after Bram Stoker wrote the novel *Dracula* in 1897.

4. Current myths about vampires <u>emphasize / emphasizes</u> the creature's aversion to sunlight and garlic.

5. Some believers in Eastern Europe <u>surround / surrounds</u> their homes with garlic.

6. Many Internet sites, such as Vampires.com, <u>cater / caters</u> to people's interest in vampires.

7. Dracula, with his blood-covered fangs, <u>remain / remains</u> a popular fictional character.

8. Some legends, especially the Dracula legend, <u>last / lasts</u> a long time.

PRACTICE 11

Correct any subject–verb agreement errors. If the sentence is correct, write *C* in the blank.

EXAMPLE:

> *enjoy*
> Many of us, in the opinion of Dr. Raoul Figuera, ~~enjoys~~ horror
> stories.   _____

1. Villains and heroes in most gothic novels is very distinct.   _____

2. Evil characters, including Dracula, does not have a good side.   _____

3. One novel, *Dr. Jekyll and Mr. Hyde,* show us two sides of human

   nature.   _____

4. The hero of the story has a dark side.   _____

5. Sometimes Dr. Jekyll, away from the prying eyes of others,

   drink a powerful potion.   _____

6. His personality, usually very sweet and friendly, changes completely. _____

7. The doctor, with a lack of control, become the evil Mr. Hyde.   _____

8. Both characters, however, resides within the same man.   _____

9. In the novel, Robert Louis Stevenson shows us a shocking truth.   _____

10. Both good and evil exists within us.   _____

"THE FELLOW HAD A KEY"

Interrupting Words: *Who, Which,* and *That*

Some sentences include a relative clause beginning with the pronoun *who, which,* or *that*. In the relative clause, the verb must agree with the antecedent of *who, which,* or *that*.

In the first example below, the antecedent of *who* is *man*. In the second example, the antecedent of *that* is *books*. And in the third example, the anecedent of *which* is *book*.

There is a **man** in southern Mexico **who** <u>writes</u> about Aztec beliefs.

Here are some old **books that** <u>discuss</u> unsolved mysteries.

One **book, which** <u>contains</u> stories about crop circles, is very interesting.

PRACTICE 12

The next excerpt is originally from Chapter 13 of Bram Stoker's 1897 novel, *Dracula*. In the novel, the following story appears in *The Westminster Gazette*, the town's local newspaper. Read the excerpt. Underline each subject and circle the correct verb form.

EXAMPLE:

A mysterious <u>man</u> who (wear /(wears)) a dark cloak is in our town.

1.   During the past two or three days, several cases of young children straying from home (have / has) occurred. In all these cases, the children (was / were) too young to give properly **intelligible** accounts of events. Most of the children who (have / has) gone missing (say / says) that they (have / has) been with a "bloofer lady." It (have / has) always been late in the evening when they (have / has) been missed, and on two occasions the children (have / has) not been found until early the following morning.

2.   Some of the children, indeed all who (have / has) been missed at night, (have / has) been slightly torn or wounded in the throat. The wounds (seem / seems) such as might be made by a rat or a small dog. The animal that (inflict / inflicts) the wounds (have / has) a system or method of its own. The police officers of the division (have / has) been instructed to keep a sharp lookout for straying children, especially those who (is / are) very young.

intelligible:
understandable

FINAL REVIEW

Underline and correct fifteen errors in subject–verb agreement.

EXAMPLE:

                                     are

Legends about a magical stork ~~is~~ common.

1.   In every culture, parents tell their children special stories and pass on particular traditions. Each story have a purpose. For example, a worry doll, which is made of rags, have an important function for Guatemalan children. Before going to bed, the child tell the doll about a particular concern. Then the child carefully leave the doll under his or her pillow. During the night, the doll worries so that the child don't have to.

2.   Everybody, at the age of five or six, lose baby teeth. The loss of teeth are an important time in most cultures. The family celebrate the end of babyhood. In Costa Rica, children keep their first tooth after it fall out. Covered in gold, the tooth become an earring. In Japan, when somebody lose a baby tooth from the lower jaw, he or she throws the tooth straight up. The goal is to have straight permanent teeth. In Mexico, either the child or the parent place the tooth in a special box. El Raton, a magic mouse, exchanges the tooth for money. In parts of Europe and North America, stories about a magical tooth fairy is common.

3.   One of the most interesting legends are about leprechauns. The tiny fairy with the face of an old man play tricks on people. Such stories and traditions exist in all cultures.

 The Writer's Room

Write about one of the following topics. When you finish writing, underline each subject, and ensure that all of your subjects and verbs agree.

1. What are the causes of urban legends? Why do people pass along such stories?

2. Many adults tell children stories about magical or mythical people, creatures, or events. For example, they might tell a tale about the tooth fairy, Santa, elves, or a stork that brings babies. Children often believe the stories. Should parents tell such yarns to children? Why or why not?

✔ CHECKLIST: SUBJECT–VERB AGREEMENT

When you edit your writing, ask yourself these questions.

☐ Do my subjects and verbs agree? Check for errors with the following:
 –present tense verbs
 –*was* and *were*

                                were   **are**
Dr. Figuera and his associates ~~was~~ surprised; men ~~is~~ more superstitious than women.

☐ Do I use the correct verb form with indefinite pronouns? Check for errors with singular indefinite pronouns such as *everybody*, *nobody*, and *somebody*.

                    knows
Everybody ~~know~~ about urban legends.

☐ Do my subjects and verbs agree when there are interrupting phrases? Check for errors in these cases:

–when prepositional phrases separate the subject and the verb
–when sentences contain relative pronouns such as *who* or *that*

> *rents*
> One of our cousins often ~~rent~~ horror movies. She is a girl who
> *gets*
> never ~~get~~ scared.

☐ Do my subjects and verbs agree when the subject comes after the verb? Check for errors with the following:

–sentences containing *here* and *there*
–question forms

> *are*
> There ~~is~~ two horror movies on television tonight.

mywritinglab To check your progress in meeting this chapter's objectives, log in to **www.mywritinglab.com**, go to the **Study Plan** tab, click on **The Editing Handbook—Section 3 Verb Agreement and Consistency** and choose **Subject–Verb Agreement** from the list of subtopics. Read and view the resources in the **Review Materials** section, and then complete the **Recall, Apply,** and **Write** sets in the **Activities** section.

CHAPTER 13

CHAPTER 14

Tense Consistency

Section Theme: **BELIEFS**

In this chapter, you will read about religious beliefs, fortune tellers, and astrology.

Grammar Snapshot

Looking at Tense Consistency

In this excerpt from David A. Locher's *Collective Behavior*, the author describes what happened during the Y2K millennium panic. The verbs are underlined.

> Intense, credible media coverage <u>plays</u> a role in spreading false beliefs in many collective delusions. This <u>was</u> certainly true for the Y2K hysteria. Mainstream media sources <u>circulated</u> false rumors of "Y2K failures" that <u>had</u> supposedly already <u>occurred</u>. It <u>was</u> constantly <u>reported</u> that sewage systems, electrical systems, financial and school records, and a variety of other systems <u>had shut</u> down completely or wildly <u>malfunctioned</u> when <u>tested</u> for Y2K compliance.

In this chapter, you will identify and correct tense inconsistencies.

Consistent Verb Tense

2/14/2011

When you write, the verb tense you use tells the reader when the event occurred. A **tense shift** occurs when you shift from one tense to another for no logical reason. If you shift verb tenses unnecessarily, you risk confusing your audience. The next sentence begins in the past tense but then shifts to the present tense.

Tense shift: Nostradamus had a great memory and <u>becomes</u> a well-known doctor.

Consistent tense: Nostradamus had a great memory and <u>became</u> a well-known doctor.

Sometimes the time frame in a narrative really does change. In those circumstances, you would change the verb tense. The following example accurately shows two different time periods. Notice that certain key words (*In 1550*, *today*) indicate what tense the writer should use.

CHAPTER 14

In 1550, Nostradamus <u>wrote</u> a book of prophesies. Today, some
<small>past</small>

researchers <u>debate</u> his ideas.
<small>present</small>

PRACTICE 1

Underline the verbs in each sentence, and then correct each tense shift. If a sentence is correct, write *C* in the blank.

EXAMPLE:

In 2005, the ABC News program *Primetime* <u>presented</u> a story about a

family from Louisiana, and I <s>watch</s> the program with my brother. _____
watched

1. During World War II, a twenty-one-year-old Navy fighter pilot

   <u>was flying</u> over an island when Japanese artillery <u>shoots</u> at the
   shot

   plane. _____

2. The plane <u>went</u> down, and the pilot, James Huston, <u>died</u>. _____

3. Many years later, a child from Louisiana <u>had</u> vivid dreams *Past tense*

   about the pilot's death, and in 2005, the family <u>tells</u> their *Present tense*
   told

   story to ABC News. _____

4. When James Leininger <u>was</u> eighteen months old, he <u>becomes</u>
   became

   fascinated with airplanes. _____
   Past tense

5. At age two, James <u>began</u> to have severe nightmares, and his

   parents <u>don't</u> understand what <u>was happening</u>. _____
   didn't   *LV*

6. One night, James's father, Bruce, listened as his son ~~speaks~~ *spoke* about the fire in his airplane. _____

7. Over time, James revealed details about a specific plane crash and was able to describe the type of plane he ~~is~~ *was* flying. _____

8. James also said that he took off from a boat called the *Natoma*. *C.*

9. According to the Leiningers, their small child did not have access to any war documentaries, and they never discussed World War II with James. *C.*

10. As James's memories became more detailed, his father ~~decides~~ *decided* to do some research. _____

11. Bruce Leininger discovered that the details matched James Huston's plane crash, which ~~occurs~~ *occurred* at Iwo Jima, in Japan. _____

12. Today, James Huston's sister, Anna, believes that the boy is the reincarnation of her brother, and the Leiningers ~~agreed~~ *agree* with her. _____

Hint   **Would and Could**

When you tell a story about a past event, use *would* instead of *will*, and use *could* instead of *can*.

would
Nostradamus predicted that in the year 1999, a great terror ~~will~~ descend

could
from the skies, and nobody ~~can~~ stop the event.

PRACTICE 2

Correct the six tense inconsistencies in the following paragraphs.

EXAMPLE:

Fortune-tellers and psychics try to predict the future, and some psychics
believe
genuinely ~~believed~~ that they have a special gift.

1. A fifteenth-century British woman, Ursula Shipton, made many accurate predictions about the future. For example, she predicted that iron boats ~~will~~ *would* float on water, and she also said that thoughts ~~will~~ *would* fly around the world. She

spoke of human flight, modern ships, submarines, and wireless

communications. However, one of her most famous predictions ~~does~~ [did] not

come true. She predicted that the world ~~will~~ [would] end in 1881.

2.　　　In 1990, Gordon Stein wrote an article expressing his doubts about

Shipton. He said that her predictions were often vague and ~~can~~ [could] be

interpreted in many different ways. In addition, Charles Hindley, who

edited an 1862 version of Shipton's verses, ~~adds~~ [added] his own verses to make her

prophesies seem more accurate. Perhaps readers should be skeptical when

they read about ancient prophecies.

Telling a Story

When you narrate, or tell a story, you can describe events using the present, past, or future tense. The important thing is to be consistent. The next two paragraphs tell the same story using different tenses.

Past Tense
　　　Mark Twain **went** to see a magic show. At the show, a hypnotist **made** the audience members do ridiculous things. Twain **asked** to go onstage, and he **did** not fall under the hypnotist's spell. However, he **decided** to act out everything that the hypnotist **asked.**

Present Tense
　　　Mark Twain **goes** to see a magic show. At the show, a hypnotist **makes** the audience members do ridiculous things. Twain **asks** to go onstage, and he **does** not fall under the hypnotist's spell. However, he **decides** to act out everything that the hypnotist **asks.**

PRACTICE 3

The following paragraph shifts between the present and the past tenses. Edit the paragraph to make the tenses consistent. You might choose to tell the story using the present or past tense.

　　　According to Chinese astrology, one day Buddha invites all of the

animals in the kingdom to the Chinese New Year's celebration. The rat

received an invitation, and he was supposed to invite the cat. However,

the rat was jealous of the cat, and he did not pass along the information.

On the day of the celebration, only twelve animals can attend; the first to

arrive is the rat and the last to arrive is the pig. Buddha assigned each animal a year of its own, and people born in that year will have the characteristics of the animal. The next day, the cat heard about the celebration, and she sent word that she will soon arrive. Later, when the cat met Buddha, she asked to have a year named after her, but Buddha tells her that it is too late. Buddha decides that there will be no year of the cat.

FINAL REVIEW

Correct fifteen tense inconsistencies in the following paragraphs.

EXAMPLE:

Some people read horoscopes because they ~~wanted~~ *want* to know about the future.

1. Early humans used the stars to guide them and to help them choose when to hunt, fish, and migrate. Then, as soon as people can write, they looked to the stars and write of relationships between the sky and humans.

2. In the past, ancient Greeks, Aztecs, Babylonians, and Chinese all develop sophisticated astrological charts. For centuries, astrology's appeal has endured. There is a brief setback when, in 1594, Galileo proved that the earth was not the center of the universe. However, Sir Isaac Newton pointed out that astrology was about the relationships between the planets; therefore, it did not matter what the center of the universe was. Today, in this age of reason, people around the globe still consulted horoscopes.

3. Ella Brown, a college student, believes in horoscopes. In 2008, she read that she will have an accident, and that evening she broke her arm in a car crash. Then, last year, her horoscope said that she will find love, and it happened. However, most of Ella's peers are

dismissive of horoscopes, and they did not believe in astrology. Brian Bowman says that horoscopes are worthless, and anybody who believed in them is a little crazy.

4.   In the past, many astrologers focused on predictions. In 1960, Jeane Dixon predicted that the next president will be a Democrat and will be assassinated. When President John F. Kennedy was elected and subsequently killed, Dixon's fame skyrocketed. However, many of Dixon's predictions were inaccurate. For example, she predicted that World War III will begin in 1958, and she said that Russia can and will be the first nation to place a man on the moon. Of course, both predictions were wrong. Today, most astrologers avoided making predictions about future events. Instead, they concentrate on making links between astrological signs and personality traits.

 The Writer's Room

Write about one of the following topics. When you finish writing, ensure that your verb tenses are consistent.

1. Think of a typical fairy tale, myth, or legend, such as "The Three Little Pigs" or "Little Red Riding Hood." You could also think of a tale that is special in your culture. Retell the story using more modern names and places.

2. Were you superstitious when you were a child? For example, did you consult your horoscope, or did you have a lucky charm? Are your beliefs different today? Compare your past and current beliefs.

 CHECKLIST: TENSE CONSISTENCY

When you edit your writing, ask yourself the following question.

☐ Are my verb tenses consistent? Check for errors with the following:
–shifts from past to present or from present to past
–*can, could* and *will, would*

                                        would
    If a black cat crossed your path, ~~will~~ you have bad luck?

READING LINK

To learn more about beliefs, read the following essays:

"The Cult of Emaciation" by Ben Barry (page 423)

"Shopping for Religion" by Ellen Goodman (page 426)

CHAPTER 14

 *The Writers' Circle*   **Collaborative Activity**

Survey an equal number of males and females. Try to survey at least three people of each gender. Ask them if they believe, or do not believe, in the following. Write *M* (for "male") and *F* (for "female") in the spaces.

	Don't Believe	Believe
1. Dead people visit the earth as ghosts.		
2. It is possible to create a society in which everyone has equal wealth.		
3. Some people can contact the dead or predict future events.		
4. Horoscopes provide useful information about future events.		
5. Capital punishment helps lower the crime rate.		
6. Aliens have visited the earth and kidnapped some people.		
7. Human beings have walked on the moon.		
8. There is life on other planets.		
9. The universe is expanding.		
10. People are safer when they have guns in their homes.		

Next, ask people why they believe a certain thing. Did they read about it? Did someone tell them about it? Keep notes about their answers. Then work with your team members, and write a paragraph about one of the following topics. Ensure that your verb tenses are consistent.

1. Choose one person you asked about his or her beliefs, and write a paragraph about that person. What does he or she believe in? Why does he or she have those beliefs? (Because you are writing about one person, take extra care to ensure that your subjects and verbs agree.)

2. Write a paragraph about the results of the survey. You could discuss any differences between males and females regarding superstitions and beliefs.

mywritinglab   To check your progress in meeting this chapter's objectives, log in to **www.mywritinglab.com**, go to the **Study Plan** tab, click on **The Editing Handbook—Section 3 Verb Agreement and Consistency** and choose **Tense Consistency** from the list of subtopics. Read and view the resources in the **Review Materials** section, and then complete the **Recall, Apply,** and **Write** sets in the **Activities** section.

Compound Sentences

Section Theme: **TRADES AND TECHNOLOGY**

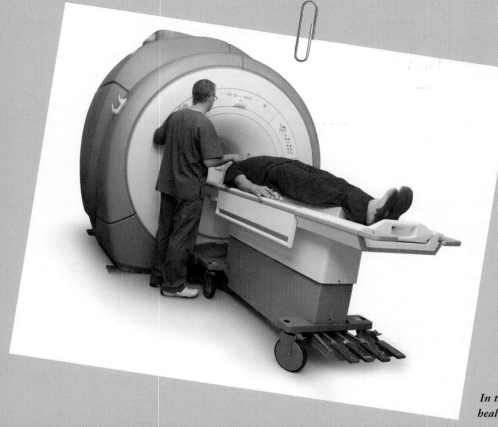

In this chapter, you will read about health care and technology.

Grammar Snapshot

Looking at Compound Sentences

In a recent newspaper article, Alexei Cunningham wrote about the health-care sector. This excerpt contains two compound sentences.

> The field of healthcare is one of the fastest growing professions in America; consequently, many students are taking advantage of this phenomenon. The medical field employs over four million people, and the number for the moment is increasing.

In this chapter, you will practice identifying and writing compound sentences.

Comparing Simple and Compound Sentences

When you write, you can use sentences of varying lengths to make your writing more appealing. One of the easiest ways to create variety is to combine simple sentences to form compound sentences.

A **simple sentence** expresses a complete idea. It has one or more subjects and verbs.

One subject, one verb:	**Josh** <u>drives</u> an ambulance.
Two subjects:	**Jobs** and **apprenticeships** <u>are</u> important for graduating students.
Two verbs:	The **nurse** <u>speaks</u> and <u>writes</u> about hospital procedures.

A **compound sentence** contains two or more simple sentences, and the two complete ideas can be joined in several ways.

	Josh is ambitious. + He hopes to find a job.
Add a coordinator:	Josh is ambitious, **and** he hopes to find a job.
Add a semicolon:	Josh is ambitious; he hopes to find a job.
Add a semicolon and conjunctive adverb	Josh is ambitious; **therefore,** he hopes to find a job.

Combining Sentences Using Coordinating Conjunctions

A **coordinating conjunction** joins two complete ideas and indicates the connection between them. When you combine two sentences with a coordinating conjunction, put a comma before the conjunction.

	, for	
	, and	
	, nor	
Complete idea	**, but**	complete idea.
	, or	
	, yet	
	, so	

The technician examined the X-ray, **and** he placed it in the file.

 **Recognizing Compound Sentences**

To be sure that a sentence is compound, place your finger over the coordinator, and then ask yourself whether the two clauses are complete sentences.

Simple:	Josh is ambitious and hopes to become a paramedic.
Compound:	Josh is ambitious, and he hopes to become paramedic.

PRACTICE 1

Indicate whether the following sentences are simple (S) or compound (C). Underline the coordinating conjunction in each compound sentence.

EXAMPLE:

During the Civil War, many males worked as nurses, <u>but</u> the most famous was the poet Walt Whitman.   *C*

1. Howard Garcia studies nursing and works part time as an orderly at the hospital.   *S*

2. He wants to specialize in pediatrics, but he is also interested in surgery.   *C*

3. During the Middle Ages, monks cared for and nursed the sick and the elderly.   *S.*

4. Since that time, nursing has become a female-dominated profession, so male nurses have sometimes encountered discrimination.   *C*

5. Jeremy Woodrow experienced some stereotyping in the workplace, for he was one of the first male nurses to be employed in a hospital.   *C*

6. Today, male nurses are earning respect and gaining acceptance in most workplaces.   *S*

7. Presently, about five percent of nurses in the United States are males, but this number is growing.   *7*

8. Nursing offers a variety of opportunities and provides flexibility for career development.   *S*

Meanings of Coordinating Conjunctions

Each coordinating conjunction has a specific meaning. Review the next table to see how each coordinator can be used.

Coordinating Conjunction	Function	Example
and	to join two ideas	Florence Nightingale was a nurse, **and** she was a writer.
but	to contrast two ideas	Nightingale was very rich, **but** she cared for the poor.
for	to indicate a reason	She studied nursing, **for** she felt it was a divine calling.
nor	to indicate a negative idea	She did not want to marry, **nor** did she want a family.
or	to offer an alternative	You can read her biography, **or** you can see a documentary.
so	to indicate a cause and effect relationship	Nightingale was wealthy, **so** she didn't need payment for her work.
yet	to introduce a surprising idea	She saw the horrors of war, **yet** she continued to help the sick.

PRACTICE 2

Read each sentence carefully and decide how the two parts of the sentence are related. Then add a comma and an appropriate coordinating conjunction.

EXAMPLE:

Medical illustrators may draw surgical procedures _____, or_____ they may produce 3D-animated films.

1. Soshanna Murphy wants to be a medical illustrator _____ she must take courses in anatomy and biology.

2. She is a good artist ___, but___ she needs to develop her computer skills.

3. Textbook medical illustrations are complex _____ they must be accurate.

4. Medical illustrators use the latest graphic design software _____ they illustrate many complicated medical concepts.

5. Soshanna could specialize in forensic reconstruction _____ she could work as a surgical illustrator.

6. Marco Greenwood does not want to work in forensics _____ does he want to specialize in surgical drawings.

7. He is a medical photographer _____ he creates digital videos of his work.

8. Soshanna's program is very demanding _____ she is determined to succeed.

PRACTICE 3

Create compound sentences by adding a coordinating conjunction and another complete sentence. Remember that the two ideas must be related. Try to use a variety of coordinating conjunctions.

EXAMPLE:

I just got a diploma in surgical nursing, _so now I am looking for a job._

_____

1. Vanessa wants to be a laboratory technician, _____.

2. She is a full-time college student, _____.

CHAPTER 15

3. Vanessa studies hard, _____

_____ .

4. Many students enroll in health science programs, _____

_____ .

5. Vanessa plays basketball well, _____

_____ .

PRACTICE 4

In the following paragraphs, join at least eight pairs of sentences using coordination conjunctions. You can keep some of the short sentences so that your paragraph has variety.

EXAMPLE:

, but he

Godfrey Jones is studying to be a paramedic. ~~He~~ also works part time driving an ambulance.

1.   Some professions have developed recently. Others have had a long history. During the Crusades, many Christian noblemen marched to Jerusalem. They wanted to fight against Muslim rule. Thousands of young men were injured during battle. Many died. The Knights of St. John fought in the battles. They also performed a more critical task. They gave medical help to those injured in the battlefields. They transported the injured to nearby tents for treatment. It was the first official ambulance service.

2.   The first motorized ambulance started in Chicago in 1899. The vehicle was very heavy. It traveled very slowly. During World War I, most ambulances were horse driven. The United States eventually joined the war. It donated Model T Fords. Today, there are different types of ambulance vehicles, such as vans, helicopters, airplanes, and boats.

3.   Modern ambulances are fitted with specialized equipment. For example, ambulances have computers. Paramedics can send a patient's medical information directly to the hospital. Ambulance services play a vital role in our society. They should be praised.

Combining Sentences Using Semicolons

A semicolon can join two complete sentences. The semicolon replaces a conjunction.

> Complete idea   ;   complete idea.

> The X-ray clinic is open all day; you don't need an appointment.

PRACTICE 5

Each sentence is missing a semicolon. Put a semicolon in the appropriate place.

EXAMPLE:

> An MRI gives high-quality imaging of soft tissue; it can be used to locate tumors in the body.

1. In 1977, some members of the medical community gasped in wonder; they had just witnessed an amazing event.

2. Dr. Damadian and his colleagues had worked on an invention for seven years; they had developed a magnetic resonance imaging (MRI) machine.

3. The initial MRI image took five hours to develop the images were unclear.

4. The first machine was named "Indomitable" by the inventors it is now exhibited at the Smithsonian Institution.

5. MRI machines have revolutionized modern medicine; they use a magnetic field and radio-waves to generate body images.

6. MRIs show images of the brain, spine, abdomen, and soft tissue; they can detect cancer and other diseases in these areas.

7. The images give an extremely clear view inside the body; the image can be in 2-D or 3-D maps.

8. Clearly, MRI technology has helped to advance health care; many patients will be diagnosed accurately and treated quickly for disease.

 **Use a Semicolon to Join Related Ideas**

Do not use a semicolon to join two unrelated sentences.

Incorrect: Clara Barton participated in the American Civil War; she loved to read.

Correct: Clara Barton participated in the American Civil War; she tended the wounded.

PRACTICE 6

Create compound sentences by adding a semicolon and another complete sentence to each simple sentence. Remember that the two ideas must be related.

EXAMPLE:

Last year, I worked as an intern at a company *; I gained a lot of experience.*

1. Apprenticeships help students to acquire on-the-job training _____
   _____.

2. An apprenticeship generally lasts around one or two years _____
   _____.

3. Many companies and institutions offer apprenticeships _____
   _____.

4. At my college, there is an annual job fair _____
   _____.

5. I will apply for an internship _____
   _____.

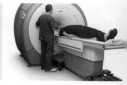

Combining Sentences Using Transitional Expressions

A **transitional expression** can join two complete ideas and show how they are related. The next table shows some common transitional expressions.

Transitional Expressions

Addition	Alternative	Contrast	Time	Example or Emphasis	Result or Consequence
additionally	in fact	however	eventually	for example	consequently
also	instead	nevertheless	finally	for instance	hence
besides	on the contrary	nonetheless	later	namely	therefore
furthermore	on the other hand	still	meanwhile	of course	thus
in addition	otherwise		subsequently	undoubtedly	
moreover					

If the second sentence begins with a transitional expression, put a semicolon before it and a comma after it.

> Complete idea   **;**   **transitional expression**   **,**   complete idea.

The first images were failures; **nevertheless,** Dr. Damadian did not lose hope.
                                ; still,
                                ; however,
                                ; nonetheless,

PRACTICE 7

Punctuate the following sentences by adding any necessary semicolons and commas.

EXAMPLE:

> Some heart patients must have pacemakers **;** however **,** they are able to participate in most activities.

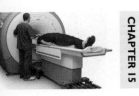

1. In 1889, a Scottish doctor made an interesting discovery in fact his find led to the development of the first artificial pacemaker.

2. Other scientists refined Dr. John A. McWilliam's experiments eventually researchers developed a sophisticated pacemaker.

3. In the 1950s, Else-Marie Larsson heard about pacemakers of course she convinced her sick husband Arne to have one implanted.

4. In 1958, Arne Larsson became the first person to have one however his pacemaker lasted just three hours.

5. Mr. Larsson received twenty-six pacemakers in total nevertheless he greatly advocated the technology.

6. Current pacemakers are very sophisticated for instance they can record and adjust a patient's heartbeat patterns.

7. Millions of people wear pacemakers undoubtedly their quality of life has improved.

PRACTICE 8

Create compound sentences using the following transitional expressions. Try to use a different expression in each sentence.

consequently   furthermore   however
in fact   nevertheless   ~~therefore~~

EXAMPLE:

Many students work part time *; therefore, they must be very organized with*

their time.

1. Roy works as a medical assistant _____

   _____.

2. He deals with patients _____

   _____.

3. On many days, he is extremely busy _____

   _____.

4. Eventually, Roy wants to study health-care management _____

   _____.

5. Roy also volunteers at a seniors residence _____

   _____.

PRACTICE 9

Add a transitional expression to join each pair of sentences. Choose an expression from the following list, and try to use a different expression in each sentence.

consequently	eventually	for example	~~for instance~~
however	nevertheless	thus	

EXAMPLE:

                              ; for instance, surgeons

Technology has changed the field of health care. ~~Surgeons~~ perform surgery using sophisticated cameras.

1. Telemedicine is a fast-growing health-care network. A nurse may send

   medical information about a patient to a doctor in another city.

2. Health-care workers can consult colleagues in far locations. The system

   works very well in remote areas.

3. Telenursing is spreading in the United States. Other long-distance medical

   systems like teleradiology are also expanding rapidly. *consequently.*
   thus.

4. In Sweden, nurses at call centers consult with patients at home. The

   scheme is cost efficient and timesaving. *; however.*

5. Telenursing uses highly trained professionals. The system has developed

   some ethical problems.

6. Telenursing may not provide patients with privacy or face-to-face

   support. Such issues will have to be dealt with.

FINAL REVIEW

Read the following paragraphs. Create compound sentences by adding semicolons, conjunctive adverbs (*however*, *therefore*, etc.) or coordinating conjunctions (*for*, *and*, *nor*, *but*, *or*, *yet*, *so*). Try to create at least ten compound sentences.

EXAMPLE:

; for example, computers

Many disabled people lead active lives due to technology. ~~Computers~~ help people with visual, auditory, or manual difficulties.

1.   Technology has permeated the field of health care. Computers, digital software, and new inventions have transformed medicine. There are both positive and negative effects of technology on health care.

2.   Indeed, new medical innovations help countless people. Michael Price has Parkinson's disease. His hands shake too much. In the past, he could not type reports at work. Modern technology now enables him to be self-sufficient. He dictates into a microphone attached to a computer. The software allows him to correct mistakes verbally. Some people use electric wheelchairs for mobility. Others with paralysis have battery-powered diaphragm pacers. Such devices allow the users to breathe normally. Charles Krauthammer, the columnist, uses a computerized van. He was paralyzed in a diving accident nineteen years ago.

3.   However, intricate medical technology presents some problems. Health-care workers are relying increasingly on machines to diagnose patients. Traditional doctor–patient relationships are changing. MRIs, CT scans, and video surgery help doctors to understand a problem. Machines cannot offer comfort and support to patients. New technology can prolong a person's life. This process can lead to an ethical dilemma. Furthermore, the costs to the public are enormous. In 1960, Americans spent about 5.9 percent of all government revenue on health care. Today, the cost has nearly doubled. In 2000, a birth of a baby was

CHAPTER 15

about $350.00 in hospital costs. Currently, the hospital costs for a noncomplicated birth are about $1,300.

4.   Clearly, Americans need to weigh the benefits of technology against the rising costs of health care. Technology can improve people's lives. The ethical questions and the costs have to be assessed.

The Writer's Room

Write about one of the following topics. First, write at least ten simple sentences. Then, combine some of your sentences to create compound sentences. When you have finished, edit your writing and ensure that your sentences are combined correctly.

1. What do you do to keep yourself healthy? Give some examples.
2. Have you ever been in a hospital? Describe your experience.

✔ CHECKLIST: COMPOUND SENTENCES

When you edit your writing, ask yourself these questions.

☐ Are my compound sentences correctly punctuated? Remember to do the following:

–place a comma before a coordinating conjunction.

Laboratory technicians may work in hospitals, **or** they may work in industry.

–use a semicolon between two complete ideas.

I want to work in emergency services; I need to make a résumé to apply for a job.

–use a semicolon before a transitional expression and a comma after it.

The college has a nursing program; **in addition,** it has a hospital management program.

mywritinglab To check your progress in meeting this chapter's objectives, log in to **www.mywritinglab.com**, go to the **Study Plan** tab, click on **The Editing Handbook—Section 4 Effective Sentences** and choose **Compound Sentences** from the list of subtopics. Read and view the resources in the **Review Materials** section, and then complete the **Recall, Apply,** and **Write** sets in the **Activities** section.

CHAPTER 15

CHAPTER 16

Complex Sentences

Section Theme: **TRADES AND TECHNOLOGY**

LEARNING OBJECTIVES

1 Understanding Complex Sentences (p. 259)
2 Using Subordinating Conjunctions (p. 259)
3 Using Relative Pronouns (p. 264)
4 Combining Questions (p. 266)

In this chapter, you will read about construction and computer industries.

Grammar Snapshot

Looking at Complex Sentences

The next except appears in *Architectural Drawing and Light Construction* by Grau, Muller, and Fausett. The complex sentences are underlined.

Baled straw is an inexpensive and environmentally sound material for building construction. The greatest danger to straw bale construction is moisture. <u>If bales become wet and are not permitted to dry out, they will rot.</u> <u>When construction begins, it is important to start with dry bales and to keep them dry.</u>

In this chapter, you will identify and write complex sentences.

Understanding Complex Sentences

A **complex sentence** contains one independent clause (complete idea) and one or more dependent clauses (incomplete ideas).

- An **independent clause** has a subject and a verb and can stand alone because it expresses one complete idea.

  The building has a concrete foundation.

- A **dependent clause** has a subject and a verb, but it cannot stand alone. It "depends" on another clause to be complete.

Incomplete:	Although the solar panel was expensive.
Complete:	Although the solar panel was expensive, <u>Jeremiah installed it on his roof.</u>

  dependent clause   independent clause

> **Hint**   **Compound-Complex Sentences**
>
> You can combine compound and complex sentences. The next example is a **compound-complex sentence**.
>
> complex
>
> After the concrete had hardened, the floor cracked, and water poured in.
>
> compound

Using Subordinating Conjunctions

When you add a **subordinating conjunction**—a word such as *after, because,* or *although*—to a clause, you make the clause dependent. *Subordinate* means "secondary," so subordinating conjunctions are words that introduce secondary ideas.

Main idea	**subordinating conjunction**	secondary idea.

The tower swayed **whenever** the wind blew.

Subordinating conjunction	secondary idea,	main idea.

Whenever the wind blew, the tower swayed.

Some Subordinating Conjunctions

after	because	since	until	whereas
although	before	so that	when	wherever
as	even if	that	whenever	whether
as if	even though	though	where	while
as though	if	unless		

Subordinating conjunctions create a relationship between the clauses in a sentence. Review the next table to see how you can use subordinating conjunctions.

Subordinating Conjunction	Usage	Example
as, because, since, so that	To indicate a reason, a cause, or an effect	Romans made concrete because it was a strong building material.
as long as, even if, if, so that, unless	To indicate a condition or result	They mixed milk and blood into cement so that it would bond.
although, even though, though, whereas	To contrast ideas	Although concrete is an old product, it is still useful.
where, wherever	To indicate a location	Wherever you travel, you will find concrete buildings.
after, before, since, until, when, whenever, while	To show a point in time	Visit the Colosseum when you go to Rome.

CHAPTER 16

PRACTICE I

Practice identifying dependent and independent clauses. Circle the subordinating conjunction and then underline the dependent clause in each sentence.

EXAMPLE:

The restaurant has the shape of a ship (because) it specializes in seafood.

1. When you travel around the United States, you will find some very odd buildings.

2. In 1920, the High Point Chamber of Commerce built a giant chest of drawers because it wanted a distinctive building.

3. After construction workers finished the exterior, they added giant socks to one of the drawers.

4. Designers added giant socks because the town has a hosiery industry.

5. Although the building looks unusual, it has useable office space.

6. If you visit North Carolina, enjoy the architectural marvels.

 **Punctuating Complex Sentences**

If you use a subordinator at the beginning of a sentence, put a comma after the dependent clause. Generally, if you use a subordinator in the middle of the sentence, you do not need to use a comma.

| Comma: | **Even though** the computer is expensive, she will buy it. |
| **No comma:** | She will buy the computer **even though** it is expensive. |

GRAMMAR LINK

See Chapter 26 for more information about comma usage.

PRACTICE 2

Underline each subordinating conjunction and add five missing commas.

EXAMPLE:

<u>After</u> we poured the cement , someone walked on it.

1.   <u>Although</u> most American homes have wood-frame construction , homes in other countries often have cement walls and floors. <u>After</u> an earthquake hit Morocco , international aid agencies rebuilt some homes using wooden frames. <u>Even though</u> the inhabitants appreciated their new homes , they were not used to the wood construction. Citizens poured water onto the wood floors <u>whenever</u> the floors were dirty. Because of the constant humidity the wood floors warped. After a disaster hits an area aid agencies should hire local builders.

PRACTICE 3

The following sentences are missing a subordinating conjunction. Put one of the following conjunctions in each space. Use a different conjunction each time.

~~before~~	because	so that
although	unless	whenever
after	~~until~~	when

EXAMPLE:

Before _____ she built the cabinet, Selma created a plan.

1.   Selma Sussman began building cabinets ___when___ she turned twelve years old. Later, ___Whenever___ a faucet leaked or a door handle jammed, Selma did the repairs. She would never ask a man to help her ___unless___ she needed help lifting very heavy objects.

2. _____*At*_____ women do a lot of home renovations, most tools are made for men. However, some enterprising women have entered the tool business. _____ Barbara Kavovit created a lightweight tool kit, most tools were too large and cumbersome for female hands. In 2000, Mary Tatum and Janet Rickstrew decided to sell small tool belts _____*So tha*_____ women could carry their tools easily. Their company, Tomboy Tools, is a great success.

3. In 2005, Marissa McTasney formed a company called Moxie Trades _____*so tha*_____ she wanted to sell pink work boots to women. _____*after*_____ those entrepreneurs developed some great products, home renovation outlets started to acknowledge their female customers. Today, many national hardware chains market to women.

CHAPTER 16

 **Hint** ▷ **Putting a Subject After the Subordinator**

When you combine sentences to form complex sentences, always remember to put a subject after the subordinator.

it
The house collapsed because ‸ was not well built.

PRACTICE 4

Add five missing subjects to this selection. Remember that a subject can be a noun or a pronoun.

EXAMPLE:

he
Mawlid Abdhul was born in Somalia although ‸ currently has an American passport.

Mawlid Abdhul wants a career in information technology because wants to earn a good living. He knows that could be a technician. However, many help-desk jobs are being outsourced. He believes the safest option is to become a specialist in anti-virus software. Stores, banks, hospitals, and government offices require secure computer systems. Viruses are dangerous because pose a threat to databases. For example, in February 2009, people realized a Houston courtroom was closed when came to pay their traffic tickets. A computer virus had shut down the court's 470 computers. Mawlid needs to finish a math course before will be accepted into the college computer program. However, he is very motivated. He wants to learn to outsmart hackers.

PRACTICE 5

Combine the sentences by adding a subordinating conjunction. Write each sentence twice: once with the dependent clause at the beginning of the sentence, and once with the dependent clause at the end of the sentence. From the following list, use each conjunction once.

~~even though~~   after   although   when   because

EXAMPLE:

The college was far away. Kate enrolled.

Even though the college was far away, Kate enrolled.

Kate enrolled even though the college was far away.

1. Kate loves to draw. She decided to study graphic design.

   _____

   _____

2. She entered a career college. She learned to design Web sites.

   _____

   _____

3. Design software is expensive. Kate had to buy it.

   _____

   _____

4. A company needs a logo. It hires a graphic artist.

   _____

   _____

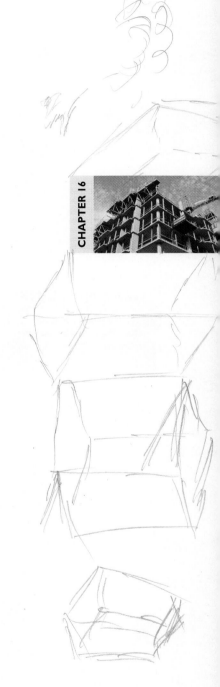

CHAPTER 16

Using Relative Pronouns

A **relative pronoun** describes a noun or pronoun. You can form complex sentences by using relative pronouns to introduce dependent clauses. Review the most common relative pronouns.

who	whomever	which
whom	whose	that

Use *who* (*whom, whomever, whose*) to add information about a person.

> John Aspdin, **who** was a stone mason, invented Portland cement.

Use *that* to add information about a thing.

> He made a product **that** would easily harden.

Use *which* to add information about a thing.

> Aspdin's cement, **which** contained lime and clay, was a popular building material.

GRAMMAR LINK

For more information about punctuating relative clauses, refer to Chapter 26, "Commas."

 **Hint**   **Punctuating Sentences with Relative Pronouns**

Which
Use commas to set off clauses that begin with *which*.

> The virus, **which was created by a young hacker**, infected many computers.

That
Do not use commas to set off clauses beginning with *that*.

> The computer **that I own** is very old.

Who
When a clause begins with *who*, you may or may not need a comma. If the clause contains nonessential information, put commas. If the clause is essential to the meaning of the sentence, then it does not require commas.

| **Essential:** | The woman **who repairs computers** is very friendly. |
| **Not essential:** | Eli Marcos, **who used to work as a banker**, will study in a technical program. |

PRACTICE 6

Underline ten relative clauses.

EXAMPLE:

> People <u>who repair computers</u> must continually update their knowledge.

An article that I recently read described ten hot jobs in the computer field. Someone who cares about the environment can become an environment simulations developer. He or she would create programs that predict the effects of global warming. Another job that sounds interesting is in video game development. Video games are not just for people who want to play. Health and education industries use video games to train employees. A woman whom I have recently met told me about the benefits of video games in therapy. The animation engages children who are having family problems. She described a boy who was acting violently. The child, who was very shy, would not speak to the therapist. Then the therapist watched the boy play. A video game that had special segments helped the therapist make a diagnosis.

PRACTICE 7

Combine each set of sentences by using the relative pronoun in parentheses. There may be more than one way to combine some sets of sentences.

EXAMPLE:

(who) Alvaro is very handy. He often works on night shifts.

Alvaro, who is very handy, often works on night shifts.

1. (which) Computers often break down. They can have complicated problems.

2. (that) Alvaro works with computers. The computers need rebuilding.

3. (who) People repair computers. They are taken for granted.

4. (who) His friend had a computer problem. She asked Alvaro to fix it.

5. (who) Alvaro spent his weekend working on the computer. He did not get paid.

PRACTICE 8

Add dependent clauses to each sentence. Begin each clause with a relative pronoun (*who*, *which*, or *that*). Add any necessary commas.

EXAMPLE:

People ___who work on towers_____ risk their lives.

1. Skyscrapers are buildings _____.

2. The people _____ are skilled workers.

3. Ironworkers _____ must overcome their fear of heights.

4. The building _____ sometimes sways slightly on windy days.

5. My friend _____ will become an electrician.

CHAPTER 16

Combining Questions

It is possible to combine a question with a statement or to combine two questions. An **embedded question** is a question that is set within a larger sentence.

Question:	How tall was the building?
Embedded question:	The tourists wondered <u>how tall the building was</u>.

In questions, there is generally a helping verb before the subject. However, when a question is embedded in a larger sentence, remove the helping verb or place it after the subject. As you read the following examples, pay attention to the word order in the embedded questions.

Combine two questions

Separate:	Why **do** humans build skyscrapers? Do you know? (In both questions, the helping verb is *do*.)
Combined:	Do you know <u>why humans build skyscrapers</u>? (The helping verb *do* is removed from the embedded question.)

Combine a question and a statement

Separate:	What **should** people do during a fire? I wonder about it. (In the question, the helping verb *should* appears before the subject.)
Combined:	I wonder <u>what people should do during a fire</u>. (In the embedded question, *should* is placed after the subject.)

> **Hint** **Use the Correct Word Order**
>
> When you edit your writing, ensure that you have formed your embedded questions properly.
>
>   *were*   *he solved*
>
> Otis wondered why ~~were~~ elevators unreliable. Do you know how ~~did he solve~~
> the problem?

PRACTICE 9

Make a new sentence from each question.

EXAMPLE:

     Why is the elevator stuck? I wonder *why the elevator is stuck* _____ .

1. Why is the alarm is ringing? Do you know _____
2. When will someone help us? I wonder _____
3. What can we do? Do you know _____
4. Where is the phone? Can you tell me _____
5. What did he say? Can you hear _____

PRACTICE 10

Identify and correct nine errors with embedded questions.

EXAMPLE:

                                elevators are
     The writer explains why ~~are elevators~~ safe.

1.   Before 1853, elevators were not reliable. Do you know why

     would people refuse to enter an elevator? The hemp rope could break and

     the elevator could fall. You can imagine why were people scared of

     elevators. Then in 1853, Elisha Otis had an insight. Do you know what

     was his idea? Otis created a safety device out of two hooks and a spring.

     When an elevator's rope became slack, the hooks would snap into a guide

     rail and stop the elevator from falling.

2.   Otis decided to enter the elevator business. At first, he wasn't

     successful. He wondered why did nobody buy his elevators. Then, at the

CHAPTER 16

CHAPTER 16

1853 World's Fair in New York, he had the chance to show off his invention. Every day, Otis rose to the top of a shaft on his elevator. Then he instructed his helper to cut the cable with an axe. You can imagine why did the spectators scream. Instead of falling, the elevator jolted to a stop. Citizens wondered how did Otis survive. Soon, orders for Otis's safety elevator poured in.

3.   Today, elevators are quite safe. In *The New Yorker*, Nick Paumgarten lists some elevator facts. First, do you wonder why does the close button rarely work? In fact, most elevators built since the 1990s have fake close door buttons. Their purpose is to give people the illusion that they can control the elevator. Also, if an elevator falls, most people wonder what should they do. According to Otis spokesman Rick Pulling, jumping just before impact is a bad idea. You cannot jump fast enough to counteract the speed of the descent. Instead, do you know what can you do? Lie flat on the floor to distribute your weight.

FINAL REVIEW

The following paragraphs contain simple sentences. To give the paragraphs more sentence variety, form at least ten complex sentences by combining pairs of sentences. You will have to add some words and delete others.

EXAMPLE:

When construction ~~Construction~~ workers build *high rises, they* ~~high rises. They~~ risk injury or death.

1.   People in many fields are responsible for the design and construction of buildings. Architects, engineers, plumbers, electricians, computer programmers, and drywall specialists are just some of the people. They help construct skyscrapers.

2.   Ironworkers have one of the most dangerous jobs. Many people like that job. In the past, high-rise builders had to be very careful. They had no

safety equipment. For example, workers built the Empire State

building. They had to walk on beams 102 stories high. The ironworkers

had no head protection or special boots. The risks were great. Today, all

workers wear hard hats and safety harnesses. Construction companies must

provide those items.

3.   People study engineering. They have to consider the integrity of

structures. Tall buildings must be carefully designed. They have to

withstand high winds. The foundations must be solid. They can shift during

earthquakes. Modern skyscrapers are made with steel frames. They must

bear the weight of hundreds of windows. Sometimes engineers design

buildings. They make mistakes. For instance, the John Hancock Tower in

Boston has mirrored glass. The glass is not secure during high winds. Huge

panels of glass weigh up to 500 pounds. They have fallen to the pavement.

Luckily, the glass has not hit pedestrians.

4.   These days, our city is planning to build a tower. It will have over eighty

floors. People in many fields will receive jobs.

The Writer's Room

Choose one of the following topics and write a paragraph. After you finish
writing, ensure that you have formed and punctuated the complex sentences
correctly.

1. Examine this photo. What are some terms that come to mind? Some ideas
   might be *blue collar*, *manual labor*, *American dream*, *dangerous work*, or
   idealism. Define a term or expression that relates to the photo.

2. What are the advantages of doing manual labor? Give examples to support your point.

CHECKLIST: COMPLEX SENTENCES

When you edit your writing, ask yourself the following:

☐ Are my complex sentences complete?

> *The basement flooded because*
>
> ~~Because~~ of the storm.

☐ Are my complex sentences correctly punctuated?

> The storm sewer overflowed/ after the heavy rains.
>
> The wallboards which have gotten wet need to be replaced.

☐ Do I have any embedded questions? Check for errors in these cases:
   –word order
   –unnecessary helping verbs

> *I will*
>
> I don't know what ~~will I~~ study. Do you know what ~~is~~ the
>
> *is*
>
> tuition rate?

mywritinglab To check your progress in meeting this chapter's objectives, log in to **www.mywritinglab.com**, go to the **Study Plan** tab, click on **The Editing Handbook—Section 4 Effective Sentences** and choose **Complex Sentences** from the list of subtopics. Read and view the resources in the **Review Materials** section, and then complete the **Recall, Apply,** and **Write** sets in the **Activities** section.

Sentence Variety

CHAPTER
17

Section Theme: **TRADES AND TECHNOLOGY**

LEARNING OBJECTIVES

1. Vary the Opening Words (p. 272)
2. Vary the Length of the Sentences (p. 274)

In this chapter, you will read about infrastructure and technical programs.

Grammar Snapshot

Looking at Sentence Variety

In his book *Building Construction*, Michael Smith discusses structural failures. Notice how the sentence lengths are varied.

> A critical error for both residential and commercial construction occurs when key support members are removed before the entire system is stabilized. This mistake often happens during remodeling or renovating. In the early 1970s, the Vendumme Hotel in Boston was being remodeled when a major fire broke out. The building collapsed, and nine firefighters lost their lives.

In this chapter, you will vary the length and structure of sentences in order to produce sentence variety.

Vary the Opening Words

Sentence variety means that your sentences have assorted patterns and lengths. One way to make your sentences more effective is to vary the opening words. Instead of beginning each sentence with the subject, you could try the following strategies.

Begin with an Adverb

An **adverb** is a word that modifies a verb, and it often ends in *-ly*. *Slowly, carefully, clearly,* and *suddenly* are adverbs. Non *-ly* adverbs include words such as *sometimes, often, always,* and *never*.

> <u>Eventually</u>, the road collapsed.
>
> <u>Obviously</u>, she should remain in technical college.
>
> <u>Sometimes</u>, jobs exist in unusual places.

PRACTICE 1

Read the following sentences. Identify and cross out the adverb, and then rewrite it in the blank at the beginning of the sentence.

EXAMPLE:

_____Clearly_____, America's rotting infrastructure is ~~clearly~~ a major problem.

1. _____, a Philadelphia overpass is gradually crumbling.

2. _____, the cost of repairing a highway is usually very high.

3. _____, hundred-year-old sewer pipes are generally made of clay.

4. _____, residents undoubtedly do not want to pay higher taxes.

5. _____, the government obviously needs to invest in the nation's highways, bridges, and water lines.

Begin with a Prepositional Phrase

A **prepositional phrase** consists of a preposition and its object. *After the storm, beside the river,* and *in my lifetime* are prepositional phrases.

> <u>In past decades</u>, cities have not invested in highways.
>
> <u>During the election campaign</u>, media coverage was intense.
>
> <u>With a loud bang</u>, the bridge collapsed.

PRACTICE 2

Read the following sentences. Identify and cross out the prepositional phrase, and rewrite it in the blank at the beginning of the sentence.

EXAMPLE:

_____In 2007_____, a surprising event occurred in midtown Manhattan ~~in 2007~~.

1. _____, a one-hundred-year old steam pipe burst in New York City in July.

2. _____, people heard a loud rumbling noise for ten minutes.

3. _____, thick plumes of ash shot up without any warning.

4. _____, a large crater appeared in the middle of the street.

5. _____, asbestos was detected in the air.

6. _____, people saw the smoke for miles around.

Punctuation tip

Hint   **Punctuation Tip**

When a sentence begins with an adverb or prepositional phrase, put a comma after the opening word or phrase.

Suddenly, the levee broke.

Without any warning, water gushed into the streets.

PRACTICE 3

To have a variety of sentence openings, place adverbs or prepositional phrases at the beginnings of appropriate sentences. Choose from the list of words and phrases below. Do not repeat your choices. The first one has been done for you.

additionally	eventually	of course	throughout the country
after much debate	~~in 2002~~	over a few years	unexpectedly

1. _In 2002,_
   Atlanta was losing 20 percent of its drinking water through leaking

   pipes. Altanta's mayor declared herself the "sewer mayor." Atlanta's

   engineers replaced 1,800 miles of pipes. Engineers built a massive

   underground tank to store rainwater. City officials decided to raise water

   taxes because the tank cost 4 billion dollars.

2. Mayor Shirley Franklin had supporters and detractors. Some citizens

   protested about the cost of the projects. However, other citizens wanted the

   city to do more. Atlanta is not alone. Storm sewers overflow and contribute

   to flooding. Many American cities will have to replace old water systems.

Vary the Length of Sentences

If a passage contains only simple sentences, it can be quite boring. You can vary the lengths of sentences by combining some short sentences to make compound and complex sentences.

No sentence variety

Potholes are a major problem in northern states. Cold weather conditions contribute to pothole formation. First, ice causes pavement to crack. Then water seeps in and expands. The water freezes and thaws. The cracks widen. Cars can hit potholes, of course. They can be damaged.

With sentence variety

In northern states, potholes are a major problem. Cold weather conditions contribute to pothole formation. First, ice causes the pavement to crack, and then water seeps in and expands. As the water freezes and thaws, the cracks widen. Of course, cars that hit potholes can be damaged.

CHAPTER 17

GRAMMAR LINK

For more information about comma usage, see Chapter 26, Commas.

 **Punctuation Tip**

Compound Sentences
When you join two complete sentences with a coordinating conjunction (*for, and, nor, but, or, yet, so*), put a comma before the conjunction.

The levee broke, **and** water gushed into the streets.

Complex Sentences
In complex sentences, place a comma after the dependent clause.

Comma:	Because water filled the streets, people evacuated.
No comma:	People evacuated because water filled the streets.

PRACTICE 4

Combine some sentences to provide sentence variety. You can keep some long and some short sentences. Also try to vary the opening words in sentences.

EXAMPLE:

Aisha will apply at a technical college. She may study computer drafting and design. She is not sure. She has many choices, of course. We are living in difficult economic times. She wants to make a practical choice.

Aisha will apply at a technical college. Although she may study computer drafting and design, she is not sure. Of course, she has many choices. We are living in difficult economic times, and she wants to make a practical choice.

1. Orange County is in California. Orange County is turning waste water into drinking water. The idea may seem distasteful. The system really works. Water

drains from sinks and toilets. The water is filtered three times. The water is truly safe to drink. It has no odor. It tastes ultimately like regular tap water.

_____

_____

_____

_____

_____

2. There are 100,000 miles of levees in the United States. Levees are amazing. They can hold back water from oceans, lakes, and rivers. Levees can settle over time. Levees can develop cracks. Tree roots can destroy levees. The roots push through the clay. Small animals occasionally build tunnels in levees.

_____

_____

_____

_____

_____

FINAL REVIEW

Combine some sentences to provide sentence variety. You should have some long and some short sentences. Also try to vary the opening words in sentences. Make at least five modifications to each paragraph.

1.   Napa is a town in California. It usually has a calm river. The river

unexpectedly overflowed in 2006. The city decided not to build more

levees. Planners worked with the river instead. The river has natural bends.

The city built a flood basin. Now, the basin acts as a sink. It can lower the

height of the river. Napa also connected two parts of the river. The river no

longer overflows, fortunately.

2.   Minneapolis construction workers built an eight-lane bridge

in 1967. The bridge spanned the Mississippi River. The bridge had a design

flaw. Steel sheets connected the support beams. The sheets were

undersized. Some experts issued warnings. Nothing was done.

The bridge collapsed on August 1, 2007. It fell during the evening rush

hour. Thirteen people lost their lives. It was a tragedy.

READING LINK

Trades and Technology

To read more about trades and technology, see the next paragraphs and essays.

"Safety in Welding" by Kelly Bruce (Chapter 4, page 63)

"The Allure of Apple" by Juan Rodriguez (page 440)

"The Rewards of Dirty Work" by Linda L. Lindsey and Stephen Beach (page 449)

CHAPTER 17

The Writer's Room

Choose one of the following topics and write a paragraph. Make sure that your paragraph has sentences of varying lengths. Also ensure that the sentences have varied opening words.

1. Describe a district, waterway, or park near you. Use language that appeals to the senses.

2. Is there a problem in your area with roads, bridges, or flooding? Does an area of your town or city need rebuilding? Argue that funds should be spent to improve a specific area. Explain what needs repairing.

✔ CHECKLIST: SENTENCE VARIETY

When you edit your writing, ask yourself the following question.

☐ Do my sentences have varied openings?

> *Beside the river, there*
>
> ~~There~~ are steep cliffs ~~beside the river~~. There are red-colored boulders by the water.

☐ Are my sentences varied in length and structure? Check for problems in these areas:

–too many short sentences.
–long sentences that are difficult to follow.

> *, and it*
>
> The road collapsed. A car drove into the hole. ~~The car~~ was destroyed.

The Writers' Circle   **Collaborative Activities**

Work with a group of three to five students. First, using the words below, create as many new words as possible by combining and moving letters. For example, you can create the word *car*. You can only use the letters given; you cannot add or double any letters.

technological discoveries

Then after you have a list of words, use your list to create sentences. You can add words to make your sentences complete. Make simple, compound, and complex sentences.

---

mywritinglab To check your progress in meeting this chapter's objectives, log in to **www.mywritinglab.com**, go to the **Study Plan** tab, click on **The Editing Handbook—Section 4 Effective Sentences** and choose **Sentence Variety** from the list of subtopics. Read and view the resources in the **Review Materials** section, and then complete the **Recall, Apply,** and **Write** sets in the **Activities** section.

Fragments

CHAPTER 18

Section Theme: **THE EARTH AND BEYOND**

In the next chapters, you will read about the world of chemistry and hazardous substances.

Grammar Snapshot

Looking at Fragments

Student writer Amin Baty Konde wrote a paragraph about working with chemicals. The underlined errors are called fragments.

Working with hazardous chemicals. It can have far-reaching consequences on a person's life. I have personal experience because for three years I worked for a pesticide company. I sprayed large expanses of lawn with commercial pesticides each day. I was not always careful about wearing a protective mask or gloves. After two years, I began to develop red rashes on my arms. Then, asthma. Although I cannot be certain that exposure to chemicals caused my problems, the timing of my illness has convinced me that it is possible.

In this chapter, you will identify and correct sentence fragments.

2/4/2011

Understanding Fragments

A **sentence** must have a subject and a verb, and it must express a complete thought. A **fragment** is an incomplete sentence. Either it lacks a subject or a verb, or it fails to express a complete idea. You may see fragments in newspaper headlines and advertisements ("Three-month trial offer"). However, in college writing, it is unacceptable to write fragments.

> **Sentence:**   Exposure to radium is very serious.
>
> **Fragment:**   Causes various illnesses.

The following sections explain common types of fragments.

Phrase Fragments

Phrase fragments are missing a subject or a verb. In the examples, the fragment is underlined.

> **No subject:**   My father did a dangerous job. <u>Worked with hazardous chemicals.</u>
>
> **No verb:**   <u>First, sulfuric acid.</u> It is very dangerous.

How to Correct Phrase Fragments

To correct phrase fragments, add the missing subject or verb, or join the fragment to another sentence.

> **Add a word(s):**   My father did a dangerous job. **He** worked with hazardous chemicals.
>
> **Join sentences:**   First, sulfuric acid is very dangerous.

Hint   **Incomplete Verbs**

If a sentence has an incomplete verb, it is a phrase fragment. The following example contains a subject and part of a verb. However, the helping verb is missing; therefore, the sentence is not complete.

> **Fragment:**   Many of the experiments with radium done by Marie Curie.

To make this sentence complete, you must add the helping verb.

> **Sentence:**   Many of the experiments with radium <u>were</u> done by Marie Curie.

PRACTICE 1

Underline and correct five phrase fragments.

EXAMPLE:

<u>First, Marie Curie.</u> ~~She~~ was a great scientist.

Marie Curie discovered radium. In 1898. After her discovery, there

across

was a radium craze. Across the United States. Companies added radium

CHAPTER 18

to different products. In some factories, the workers used paint with

radium in it. ~~To~~ ^{to} paint the faces of clocks and wristwatches. Sometimes

they licked their paintbrushes to make the ends pointed. ^{very} Very dangerous,

indeed. The factory owners knew the radium-laced paint was not safe.

They were more concerned with protecting their business interests than

with protecting the health of their workers. Unfortunately.

Explanatory Fragments

An **explanatory fragment** provides an explanation about a previous sentence and is missing a subject, a complete verb, or both. Such fragments are often written as an afterthought. Explanatory fragments begin with one of the following words.

also	especially	for example	including	particularly
as well as	except	for instance	like	such as

In these two examples, the fragment is underlined.

We did many new experiments. <u>For example, with mercury.</u>

Some new chemical compounds are useful. <u>Particularly in the production of fabrics.</u>

How to Correct Explanatory Fragments

To correct explanatory fragments, add the missing subject or verb, or join the explanation or example to the previous sentence.

Add words: We did many new experiments. For example, **we learned** about mercury.

Join sentences: Some new chemical compounds are useful, particularly in the production of fabrics.

PRACTICE 2

Underline and correct five explanatory fragments.

EXAMPLE:

The media reports high levels of blue algae. ^{, especially} ~~Especially~~ <u>in nearby lakes.</u>

In the 1970s, many new models of household appliances were

marketed. For instance washing machines. Cleaning products also

changed, ^{Especially} Especially laundry detergent. Phosphates were added to

washing detergent to make laundry very clean. However, phosphates

had a negative effect on the environment, ~~Particularly~~ particularly on water systems. When they reached lakes and rivers, phosphates harmed the water system. Harmful bacteria started growing in the water. Like blue algae. Blue algae causes a lot of problems. Such as reducing oxygen in lakes and rivers.

PRACTICE 3

Underline and correct five phrase and explanatory fragments.

EXAMPLE:

Water pollution made headlines. ~~Across~~ *across* the nation.

Phosphates are found in the soil, in food, and in chemical fertilizer. Legislators became concerned about phosphate pollution. ~~And~~ and decided to act. In 1972, the United States and Canada signed a treaty limiting the amount of phosphates in various products. ~~For~~ for example, laundry detergent. The law was successful because it reduced the amount of phosphates entering lakes and rivers. By fifty percent. Presently, however, there is a recurrence of blue algae. In some areas of the country. Experts blame the current outbreak on common products. Like dishwashing detergent and fertilizers.

Dependent-Clause Fragments

A **dependent clause** has a subject and a verb, but it cannot stand alone. It "depends" on another clause to be a complete sentence. Dependent clauses may begin with subordinating conjunctions or relative pronouns. This chart contains some of the most common words that introduce dependent clauses.

Common Subordinating Conjunctions				Relative Pronouns
after	before	though	whenever	that
although	even though	unless	where	which
as	so that	until	whereas	who(m)
because	that	what	whether	whose

In each example, the fragment is underlined.

> Marie Curie had a successful professional life. <u>Although her personal life was plagued with scandal.</u>

> <u>Marie Curie, who won the Nobel Prize for chemistry.</u> She was born in Poland.

How to Correct Dependent-Clause Fragments

To correct dependent-clause fragments, join the fragment to a complete sentence, remove words, or add the necessary words to make it a complete idea.

Join sentences:	Marie Curie had a successful professional life, although her personal life was plagued with scandal.
Join sentences and remove words:	Marie Curie, who won the Nobel Prize for chemistry, was born in Poland.

Another way to correct dependent-clause fragments is to delete the subordinating conjunction or relative pronoun that makes the sentence incomplete.

Delete *although*:	Her personal life was filled with scandal.
Delete comma and *who*:	Marie Curie won the Nobel Prize for chemistry.

PRACTICE 4

Underline and correct five dependent-clause fragments.

EXAMPLE:

The ancient Greeks liked working with ~~asbestos. Because~~ <u>*asbestos because*</u> they could weave <u>the fibers into beautiful tablecloths.</u>

Asbestos is a common mineral. That has been used in many household products for approximately 4,000 years. Since the Industrial Revolution, asbestos has been used in cement, wall board, putty, paints, hair dryers, vinyl floor tiles, and so on. However, in the 1980s, legislators implemented regulations limiting the use of asbestos. Because of potential health risks to the public. If people breathe in asbestos fibers, they may contract illnesses such as cancer. Some people may not know that they are exposed to asbestos. Unless *undless* they have the material in their homes tested. Homeowners and contractors should be extremely careful. Whenever they are doing home renovations. Older *older* homes may have been built with materials containing asbestos. When removing insulation, replacing vinyl asbestos floor tiles, or sanding plaster that contains asbestos, they should be careful. They should wear masks and goggles, ~~So~~ so that they are protected.

PRACTICE 5 REVIEW

Write *C* next to correct sentences and *F* next to fragments.

EXAMPLE:

Industrial accidents harm people's health. ___C___ As well as the environment. ___F___

CHAPTER 18

1. In 1984, a terrible chemical accident happened. ___C___ In Bhopal, India. ___F___ Union Carbide was one of the largest chemical companies in the United States. ___C___ It built a plant in downtown Bhopal in 1969. ___C___ In 1984, a holding tank leaked toxic gas. ___C___ Which killed thousands of people. ___F___ Other victims suffered from health problems. ___C___ Such as blindness and respiratory diseases. ___F___ The company refused to take any responsibility for the accident. ___C___ Even though the Indian government accused it of negligence. ___F___ The government sued the firm for monetary compensation. ___C___ For the victims. ___F___ It wanted billions of dollars. ___C___ However, the victims' families only received about two thousand dollars. ___C___

2. In 1986, another human and environmental tragedy occurred. ___C___ The Chernobyl nuclear power plant. ___F___ It was built in Ukraine. ___F___ The reactor exploded and released radioactivity into the atmosphere. ___C___ It was the largest radioactive fallout in history. ___C___ For example, greater than the atom bombing of Hiroshima. ___F___ The accident was such a terrible catastrophe. ___C___ That people in the vicinity had to be evacuated. ___F___ The radioactive particles affected people's health. ___C___ The accident also harmed the environment. ___F/C___ In particular,

contaminated ground water, soil, rivers, and lakes. _____ Presently, the

damaged reactor is covered. _____ In concrete. _____

PRACTICE 6   REVIEW

The next paragraphs contain various types of fragments. Underline and correct ten
fragment errors.

EXAMPLE:

reduced by

Environmental waste can be greatly ~~reduced. By~~ recycling and using
biodegradable products.

1.   Nowadays, the public has become very aware of environmental

pollution, Because of education, urban regulations, and media attention.

Many citizens recycle household items. Such as plastic containers,

newspapers, and tin cans. People also try to use biodegradable products;

However, this term is often misunderstood and misused.

2.   The term *biodegradable* means that a product has the ability to break

down into raw materials. A product can be decomposed. By biological

organisms. Such products break up into soil. Or water. A flower is a

good example of a biodegradable product. First, it grows and matures.

Then, falls to the ground. Finally, it decomposes and fertilizes the soil.

3.   There is a difference between products that are biodegradable and

recyclable. Many common products are biodegradable. For instance,

soap and oil. However, crude oil spills are an environmental

hazard. Because the oil spill is usually large, and there are not enough

microorganisms to break the oil down. Ecologists worry about the 2010 BP

oil spill in the Gulf of Mexico. Because toxins from the spill continue to

affect wildlife in the region. The term *recyclable* refers to items that can be

turned into other products. For example, glass bottles. They can be melted

into new glass bottles.

4.   Concerned citizens recycle and use biodegradable products. So that

environmental damage is minimized. For instance, if a glass bottle is not

recycled and reused, it will take approximately one million years to

biodegrade. As science advances, people will develop improved ways

to cut waste.

FINAL REVIEW

Identify and correct fifteen fragment errors.

EXAMPLE:

First, lead poison. It causes people serious harm.

1.   Not all scientists develop products beneficial to human beings. For

example, Thomas Midgely. He has an interesting reputation. He is

known as an inventor. Who caused great damage to the earth's

atmosphere.

2.   Midgley was born in 1889. In Pennsylvania. He trained as an

engineer. Interested in chemistry. In 1921, he developed a compound

called tetraethyl lead. While he was working for General Motors.

Lead reduced engine knock when added to gasoline.

3.   In 1923, General Motors and Standard Oil built a factory to produce

lead. Company workers became sick. From lead poisoning. They

experienced poor health. Especially confusion and hallucinations.

By the 1950s, lead had become a serious problem. Because

people's blood-lead levels had significantly increased.

4.   At that time, little was known about the effects on people's health

from lead in the atmosphere. Until a man named Clair Patterson

began to look into the problem. Patterson published his findings.

That lead accumulates in the human body. He also showed that there

had been no lead in the atmosphere. Before 1923. Patterson began a campaign. Against the lead industry. By 1986, the United States had stopped selling leaded gasoline.

5.   Thomas Midgely continued experimenting after his success. With leaded gasoline. The next dangerous product he invented was CFC gas. It was used in many products. Including, refrigerators, deodorant sprays, and air conditioners. Eventually, scientists realized that CFCs were destroying the ozone layer. Midgley never knew that his two inventions were possibly the worst discoveries of the twentieth century. He died in 1944. When he accidentally strangled himself.

 The Writer's Room

Write about one of the following topics. After you finish writing, underline the sentences. Make sure you do not have any sentence fragments.

1. Have modern scientific discoveries made our lives easier? Compare contemporary life with life in a previous era.

2. In your opinion, what is the world's greatest invention? Explain why that invention is so important.

✔ **CHECKLIST: SENTENCE FRAGMENTS**

When you edit your writing, ask yourself the next questions.

☐ Are my sentences complete? Check for different types of fragments.

–phrase fragments
–explanatory fragments
–dependent clause fragments

He also
First, Joseph Priestly. He discovered eight gases. ~~Also~~ drank soda
, which
water. ~~Which~~ he invented in 1772.

mywritinglab To check your progress in meeting this chapter's objectives, log in to **www.mywritinglab.com**, go to the **Study Plan** tab, click on **The Editing Handbook—Section 5 Common Sentence Errors** and choose **Fragments** from the list of subtopics. Read and view the resources in the **Review Materials** section, and then complete the **Recall, Apply,** and **Write** sets in the **Activities** section.

CHAPTER 19 Run-Ons

Section Theme: **THE EARTH AND BEYOND**

LEARNING OBJECTIVE

1 Understanding Run-Ons (p. 287)

In this chapter, you will read about geology and the diamond trade.

Grammar Snapshot

Looking at Run-Ons

College student Marnie Harris wrote a definition paragraph about volcanoes. The error in bold print is called a run-on sentence.

> A volcano is a fissure in the earth's crust that allows hot magma to rise up. There are many active volcanoes in the world. One of the most famous is Mount Etna, located in Sicily, Italy. The first recorded eruption was in 475 B.C., and since then it has erupted about 250 times. **The last time it erupted was in 1979 it displaced many people who lived around the mountain.** People should be aware of the destructive force of volcanoes.

In this chapter, you will identify and correct run-on sentences.

286

Understanding Run-Ons

Sometimes two or more complete sentences are joined together without correct connecting words or punctuation. In other words, a **run-on sentence** "runs on" without stopping. There are two types of run-on sentences.

- A **fused sentence** is a run-on sentence that has no punctuation to mark the break between ideas.

Fused sentence:	Geologists learn about the origins of the earth they study rocks.
Correct sentence:	Geologists learn about the origins of the earth through their study of rocks.

- A **comma splice** is a run-on sentence that uses a comma to connect two complete ideas. In other words, the comma "splices" or "splits" the sentence.

Comma splice:	Mount St. Helens is an active volcano, it violently erupted on May 18, 1980.
Correct sentence:	Mount St. Helens is an active volcano. It violently erupted on May 18, 1980.

 **Identifying Run-Ons**

To identify run-on sentences in your writing, look for sentences that are too long. Such sentences may either lack punctuation or have incorrect comma placement.

CHAPTER 19

PRACTICE I

Write *C* beside correct sentences and *RO* beside run-ons.

EXAMPLE:

Scientists refused to accept the idea that continents drift they laughed at the premise until recently.   *RO*

1. In 1908, an amateur geologist, Frank Taylor, examined a map of the Earth, Africa and South America seemed to fit together like pieces of a puzzle.   _____

2. A German meteorologist, Alfred Wegener, heard about Taylor's theories he tried to prove them by studying rocks and plants of these regions.   _____

3. Wegener developed a new hypothesis all the continents had once formed a single mass.   _____

4. Because Wegener was not an expert in geology, geologists dismissed his theory.   _____

5. In 1944, a geologist, Arthur Holmes, proposed another theory at some point in the past, continents had drifted apart.   _____

6. Radioactivity caused currents under the earth's crust, forcing continents to move.   _____

7. Scientists had difficulty accepting his theory, even Einstein was doubtful. _____

8. By the 1970s, scientists had accepted the idea of moving continents, today geologists refer to this movement as plate tectonics. _____

How to Correct Run-Ons

You can correct run-on sentences in a variety of ways.

> **Run-On:** Some volcanoes erupt violently others erupt very slowly.

1. **Make two separate sentences by adding end punctuation, such as a period.**

   Some volcanoes erupt violently. **Others** erupt very slowly.

2. **Add a subordinator** (*after, although, as, because, before, since, when, while, whereas*).

   Some volcanoes erupt violently, **whereas** others erupt very slowly.

3. **Add a coordinator** (*for, and, nor, but, or, yet, so*).

   Some volcanoes erupt violently, **but** others erupt very slowly.

4. **Add a semicolon.**

   Some volcanoes erupt violently; others erupt very slowly.

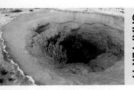

CHAPTER 19

PRACTICE 2

A. Correct each run-on by writing two complete sentences.

EXAMPLE:

. There

Yellow Stone National Park has a sensitive ecosystem ~~there~~ are thousands of species of flora and fauna in the park.

1. Yellowstone National Park has unique geological features, it sits on the

   largest active volcano in the world.

2. The park is often called a supervolcano its vents go down 125 miles to the

   Earth's mantel.

B. Correct the run-ons by joining the two sentences with a semicolon.

EXAMPLE:

;

Yellowstone National Park is located on a high plateau its altitude is 8,000 feet above sea level.

3. The supervolcano last erupted around 640,000 years ago its ash covered

   half of the United States.

4. The ashfall caused the extinction of thousands of species, it also changed

   weather patterns.

C. Correct the run-on by joining the two sentences with a coordinator (*for, and, nor, but, or, yet, so*)

EXAMPLE:

> *, and*
> Geologists monitor the volcanic activity at Yellowstone ^ they share information.

5. The volcano holes release heat from the Earth's mantel the heat is the

   source of the park's geysers and hot springs.

6. Old Faithful blows at regular intervals. it is the most popular site in the park.

D. Correct the run-ons by joining the two sentences with a subordinator such as *after, although,* or *when.*

EXAMPLE:

> *so that*
> Scientists study the geothermal features of the park ^ they can gather important geological information.

7. The first men to discover the geyser used it to do their laundry the boiling

   water washed the clothes thoroughly.

8. The U.S. Congress created Yellowstone National Park in 1872 scientists

   realized that it was home to many different ecosystems.

CHAPTER 19

PRACTICE 3 REVIEW

Correct eight run-on errors using a variety of correction methods.

EXAMPLE:

> *Because the*   *luck, many*
> ~~The~~ Hope Diamond had a reputation of bad ~~luck many~~ people refused to buy it.

1. The world's largest diamond is called the Star of Africa, in 1905,

    Frederick Wells, the superintendent of the Premier Mine in South Africa,

    discovered it. He saw something shining on the mine wall, it was a crystal.

    Tests showed that the crystal was a diamond, and it weighed about 1⅓

    pounds. In 1907, the Transvaal government of South Africa gave the stone

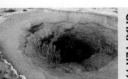

CHAPTER 19

to King Edward VII it was a gift to mark his sixty-sixth birthday. This diamond remains a part of the British crown jewels.

2. De Beers has been in the diamond business since diamonds were first discovered in South Africa. The company was started by Cecil Rhodes in 1888 it is the largest diamond firm in the world. In the 1940s, in response to competition, De Beers wanted to increase its sales of diamonds, the corporation launched a successful marketing campaign by promoting diamonds as engagement rings. The company endorsed the diamond as a symbol of love and marriage, the sales of diamond rings increased. De Beers also had another marketing strategy. The slogan "A diamond is forever" was used to reduce the secondhand diamond market. The idea behind the catchphrase was to discourage people from buying used diamonds. Both campaigns were extremely successful, they influenced the shopping habits of consumers in many different cultures. Now the diamond ring represents the idea of love and marriage around the world, De Beers' profits have swelled.

FINAL REVIEW

Correct ten run-on sentence errors. Use a variety of correction methods.

1. Diamonds have been a symbol of love and glamour they have also become a symbol of violence and exploitation. In many countries, diamonds are linked to severe human rights abuses. In those countries, diamonds are used to perpetuate wars, they are also used to finance the activities of terrorist groups.

2. Sierra Leone had a ten-year civil war, it ended in 2001. The cause of the conflict was greed. Sierra Leone has many diamond deposits, antigovernment groups waged military warfare to gain control of the

diamonds. Rebel groups in Angola and Liberia have also financed wars, they used money obtained from the diamond trade to do so.

3.   Terrorist groups also benefit from the illegal diamond trade they use diamonds to buy arms and pay informants. *Washington Post* reporter Douglas Farah brought attention to this problem he spoke at a congressional hearing in 2003. Diamonds are small, they are easy to move from one country to another. Therefore, officials find them harder to trace than other contraband items.

4.   Trade in diamonds has come under international scrutiny, to decrease the illicit trade, many countries have agreed to abide by the Kimberley Process. This agreement requires that all international diamonds have a certificate of origin such regulations will curb violence created by the illegal diamond trade.

CHAPTER 19

The Writer's Room

Write about one of the following topics. After you finish writing, ensure that you do not have any run-on sentences.

1. Describe your jewelry. What is your favorite type of jewelry? If you do not like to wear jewelry, explain why not.

2. Examine this photo and think of a term that you could define. Some ideas might be *bling bling*, *costume jewelry*, or *ostentatious*. Write a definition paragraph about any topic related to the photo.

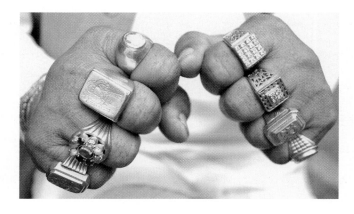

CHECKLIST: RUN-ONS

When you edit your writing, ask yourself the next questions.

☐ Are my sentences joined together without punctuation or with incorrect punctuation? Check for fused sentences and comma splices.

volcano, and it

Mauna Loa is the world's largest ~~volcano it~~ is located in Hawaii.

volcano. It

Kilauea is the world's most active ~~volcano, it~~ has been erupting continuously since 1983.

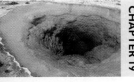

mywritinglab   To check your progress in meeting this chapter's objectives, log in to **www.mywritinglab.com**, go to the **Study Plan** tab, click on **The Editing Handbook—Section 5 Common Sentence Errors** and choose **Run-Ons** from the list of subtopics. Read and view the resources in the **Review Materials** section, and then complete the **Recall, Apply,** and **Write** sets in the **Activities** section.

Faulty Parallel Structure

Section Theme: **THE EARTH AND BEYOND**

In this chapter, you will read about astronomy and space exploration.

Grammar Snapshot

Looking at Parallel Structure

President John F. Kennedy's 1962 speech at Rice University was about the U.S. space program. Review the underlined ideas to see how they are parallel.

> There is <u>no strife</u>, <u>no prejudice</u>, and <u>no national conflict</u> in outer space as yet. <u>Its hazards</u> are hostile to us all. <u>Its conquest</u> deserves the best of all mankind, and <u>its opportunity</u> for peaceful cooperation may never come again.

In this chapter, you will identify and correct faulty parallel structure.

Identifying Parallel Structure

Parallel structure occurs when pairs or groups of items in a sentence are balanced. By using parallel grammatical structure for words, phrases, or clauses, you will make your sentences clearer and your writing smoother.

In the following sentences, the underlined phrases contain repetitions of grammatical structure, but not repetitions of ideas. Each sentence has parallel structure.

> The <u>United States</u>, <u>Russia</u>, and <u>Japan</u> have spent funds on the space station.
> (The nouns are parallel.)

> The astronomer went <u>through the doors</u>, <u>up the stairs</u>, and <u>into the observatory</u>.
> (The prepositional phrases are parallel.)

> She <u>observes</u>, <u>records</u>, and <u>predicts</u> planet cycles.
> (The present tenses are parallel.)

> I am <u>awed</u>, <u>excited</u>, and <u>terrified</u> at the prospect of space flight.
> (The adjectives are parallel.)

> Copernicus was a scientist <u>who took risks</u>, <u>who made acute observations</u>, and <u>who developed new theories</u>.
> (The "who" clauses are parallel.)

CHAPTER 20

PRACTICE I

All of the following sentences contain parallel structures. Underline the parallel items.

EXAMPLE:

> The space race was a <u>hazardous</u>, <u>exciting</u>, and <u>innovative</u> adventure.
>

1. In 1957, the space race began when Soviet scientists developed, built, and launched the space satellite *Sputnik*.

2. Soviet engineers, scientists, and politicians worked together.

3. American government officials felt shock, anxiety, and then determination.

4. The officials wanted to build their own satellite, to launch it quickly, and to surpass Soviet achievements.

5. With an injection of funds, with some planning, and with the support of many scientists, the United States launched a satellite called *Explorer* in 1958.

6. The National Aeronautics and Space Administration (NASA) began operations on October 1, at noon, in Florida.

7. U.S. scientists who used available resources, who took risks, and who believed in their vision were able to create an automated moon probe.

8. President John F. Kennedy said that humans choose to go to the moon and do other difficult things "not because they are easy, but because they are hard."

Correcting Faulty Parallel Structure

Faulty parallel structure occurs when you present equivalent ideas with different grammatical structures. The result is a sentence with ideas that are not balanced. To avoid imbalances, use parallel structure.

A Series of Words or Phrases

Use parallel structure when words or phrases are joined in a series.

> **Not parallel:** I like to read articles, watch documentaries, and listening to seminars.
>
> **Parallel:** I like <u>to read</u> articles, <u>to watch</u> documentaries, and <u>to listen</u> to seminars.
> (The infinitives are parallel.)
>
> **Not parallel:** The expanding universe, black holes, and scientists studying matter are all problems relating to the study of cosmology.
>
> **Parallel:** The <u>expanding universe</u>, <u>black holes</u>, and <u>matter</u> are all problems relating to the study of cosmology.
> (The nouns are parallel.)

Paired Clauses

Use parallel structure when independent clauses are joined by *and*, *but*, or *or*.

> **Not parallel:** The space station is costing a lot of money, but it provides essential data.
>
> **Parallel:** The space station <u>costs</u> a lot of money, but it <u>provides</u> essential data.
> (The present tense verbs are parallel.)
>
> **Not parallel:** Copernicus observed the stars carefully, and he recorded his findings with accuracy.
>
> **Parallel:** Copernicus observed the stars <u>carefully</u>, and he recorded his findings <u>accurately</u>.
> (The adverbs are parallel.)

 **Correcting Faulty Parallel Structure**

When you identify faulty parallel structure, correct it by looking carefully at repeated grammatical units and then rewriting the unit that is not parallel.

sends
The satellite collects data, stores it, and ~~is sending~~ images.

PRACTICE 2

Correct the faulty parallel structure in each sentence.

EXAMPLE:

Today, amateur astronomers are looking for satellites, watching the

observing

constellations, and ~~to observe~~ shooting stars.

CHAPTER 20

1. Scientists are doing research on the expanding universe, on the Big Bang theory, and black and white holes.

2. To observe the universe, astrophysicists not only use powerful telescopes, but they are also relying on modern satellite images.

3. In ancient times, the Babylonians, the Greeks, and people from Egypt observed and predicted the position of planets and stars.

4. Copernicus worked quietly and at a slow pace on his observations.

5. When Copernicus announced that the sun was the center of the universe, the public reacted angrily, passionately, and with force.

6. Galileo Galilei invented the telescope to look at the night sky and recording his observations.

7. Galileo discussed his theories, experiments, and what he observed.

8. Large telescopes and cameras that are powerful have helped scientists observe poorly lit celestial bodies.

9. Early photographers attempted to take pictures of the moon, the stars, and photograph solar eclipses.

10. The general public can learn about the universe by going to planetariums, to observatories, and science museums.

Comparisons

Use parallel structure in comparisons containing *than* or *as*.

> **Not parallel:**   I wanted a better explanation rather than to remain confused.
>
> **Parallel:**   I wanted <u>to receive</u> a better explanation rather than <u>to remain</u> confused.
>
> (The infinitive forms are parallel.)

Not parallel: His raw intelligence was as important as working hard.

Parallel: <u>His raw intelligence</u> was as important as <u>his hard work</u>.
(The nouns are parallel.)

Two-Part Constructions

Use parallel structure when comparing or contrasting ideas using these constructions: *either . . . or; not . . . but, both . . . and,* or *neither . . . nor.*

Not parallel: My experience was both exciting and a challenge.

Parallel: My experience was both <u>exciting</u> and <u>challenging</u>.
(The adjectives are parallel.)

Not parallel: She decided either to publish her research or burning it.

Parallel: She decided either <u>to publish</u> her research or <u>to burn</u> it.
(The infinitives are parallel.)

PRACTICE 3

Correct any errors in parallel construction. If the sentence is correct, write *C* in the blank.

EXAMPLE:

Albert Einstein influenced not only how physicists looked at natural
$\qquad$ *how the general public viewed science.*
laws but also ~~the view of science on the general public~~ _____

1. When Albert Einstein wrote his famous article on the special

   theory of relativity, he was neither a research scientist nor

   teaching at a university. _____

2. He worked both as a bureaucrat and evaluating patents. _____

3. Although he did his job patiently, thoroughly, and with care,

   he was more interested in physics and mathematics. _____

4. While working at the patent office, he had an idea that was unique

   and full of significance. _____

5. In 1905, he could either send his calculations to a scientific journal,

   or he could publish them independently. _____

6. Einstein's papers caused both surprise and a sense of awe in

   the physics community. _____

7. When they read his theories, some physicists realized that
   Einstein was not only insightful but also had intuition. _____

8. Einstein's contribution to scientific knowledge was more
   important than his work at the patent office. _____

9. In 1921, Einstein accepted the Nobel Prize happily and
   with pride. _____

PRACTICE 4

A. Fill in the blanks with parallel and logical words, phrases, or clauses.

EXAMPLE:

> We studied _____*after class*_____ and _____*on weekends*_____.

1. At college, I am studying both _____ and
   _____.

2. To get to the college library, you must go _____,
   _____, and _____.

3. My friend is _____, _____, and
   _____.

4. As a child, I _____, _____, and
   _____.

PRACTICE 5 REVIEW

Correct eight errors in parallel construction.

EXAMPLE:

> Living in outer space is both a possibility and ~~challenging~~ *a challenge*.

1.   Can humans live on other
   planets? Novelists, movie producers,
   and people who write for television
   have explored the topic. It is based
   on the human desire to discover and
   conquer new territories. For
   example, NASA researchers want to

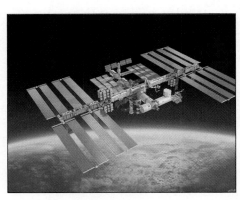

International Space Station

explore space not only for scientific research, but also they want to investigate

for possible human habitation on distant planets.

2.   Presently, the International Space Station (ISS) is the only permanent

residence for humans in outer space. The construction of the Space Station

started in 1998. Astronauts from different countries work at the station.

For example, crew members are Russian, American, Canadian, and

they also come from Europe.

3.   The ISS is a research laboratory. Scientists conduct both short-term

experiments and experiments that last a long period of time. Researchers

carry out trials in astronomy, meteorology, and in biological sciences.

In addition, scientists investigate the effects of the space environment on

bone density, on muscle deterioration, and body fluids. The results help

them to evaluate the feasibility of humans living in space.

4.   There are many variables that need to be in place before humans can

colonize outer space. For example, engineers must consider how to

transport people, how to communicate with them, and keeping them alive.

Also, governments will have to determine how much such a project will

cost, the colony's size, and how the community will be organized. The

possibility of human habitation in outer space is fascinating.

FINAL REVIEW
Correct twelve parallel structure errors.

EXAMPLE:

People are either enthusiastic or ~~full of doubt~~ *doubtful* about finding life on
other planets.

1.   Is there life on other planets? Humans have debated this question

sincerely, intellectually, and with passion. Since ancient times, the poor, the middle class, and people who are rich have believed in extraterrestrial life. Today, scientists are searching for extraterrestrial life by trying to locate exoplanets.

2.   Exoplanets exist in different solar systems from our own. In 1995, Swiss physicists were happy, proud, and full of excitement. They had discovered a planet orbiting a star like our sun. Their discovery was among the first exoplanets to be reported. Since then, around three hundred such planets have been located. Scientists attribute the findings to better instruments, more sensitive electronic sensors, and computer software has become more sophisticated.

3.   Presently, scientists are searching for signs of life, as we know it to be. The exoplanets already discovered have either a mass that is too large or a too short orbit. Thus, these exoplanets are unlike the Earth and probably cannot sustain life. On Earth, life requires carbon, oxygen, nitrogen, and life needs hydrogen.

4.   Astrophysicists want to locate, to research, and are mapping exoplanets. On March 6, 2009, NASA engineers marched through the lobby, down the corridor, and then they went into the control room to launch the Kepler Mission. The rocket will spend three and a half years surveying, photographing, and record data from the Cygnus-Lyra region of our Milky Way galaxy. Kepler's camera is both technologically advanced and has a lot of power. From its location, the camera can detect a porch light on Earth being turned off. Kepler will look for planets like Earth. If such planets are found, scientists, philosophers, and people in politics will debate the consequences of the discovery.

5.   We have always wanted to know if other worlds exist, there are other life forms, or if we are alone. The possibility of life on other planets will continue to intrigue scientists.

The Writer's Room

Write about one of the following topics. After you finish writing, make sure that you have no faulty parallel structure.

1. How are space explorers comparable to other types of explorers? Compare space explorers with other explorers.
2. Explain why you would or would not travel to outer space.

READING LINK

The Earth and Beyond
To read more about space travel, see the following essay:
"What It Feels Like to Walk on the Moon" by Buzz Aldrin (page 429)
"The Fire Below" by Bill Bryson (page 432)

✔ **CHECKLIST: PARALLEL STRUCTURE**

When you edit your writing, ask yourself the next questions.

☐ Are my grammatical structures balanced? Check for errors in these cases:

–when words or phrases are joined in a series
–when independent clauses are joined by *and*, *but*, or *or*
–in comparisons or contrasts

the harshest weather
Mars has the largest volcano, the deepest valley, and ~~its weather is very harsh~~ of any planet in our solar system.

 The Writers' Circle **Collaborative Activity**

Form a team with two other students. Imagine that your team has won first-class seats on a space cruise. Each one of you can bring only five small items on the flight. Work together to create a paragraph explaining what items you would bring. You can share the items, so consider what items would be most useful for all of you.

When you finish writing, verify that your paragraph contains no fragments or run-ons. Also, make sure that your sentences have parallel structure.

mywritinglab To check your progress in meeting this chapter's objectives, log in to **www.mywritinglab.com**, go to the **Study Plan** tab, click on **The Editing Handbook—Section 5 Common Sentence Errors** and choose **Faulty Parallel Structure** from the list of subtopics. Read and view the resources in the **Review Materials** section, and then complete the **Recall, Apply,** and **Write** sets in the **Activities** section.

CHAPTER 20

Adjectives and Adverbs

CHAPTER 21

Section Theme: **RELATIONSHIPS**

**LEARNING
OBJECTIVES**

1. Adjectives (p. 303)
2. Adverbs (p. 307)
3. Comparative and Superlative Forms (p. 310)

In this chapter, you will read about famous couples in history and in literature. You will also read about relationship issues.

Grammar Snapshot

Looking at Adjectives and Adverbs

Comedian Bill Cosby describes a high school romance. Review the underlined adjectives and adverbs.

> During my last year of high school, I fell in love so hard with a girl that it made my love for Sarah McKinney seem like a stupid infatuation with a teacher. Charlene Gibson was the real thing, and she would be Mrs. Charlene Cosby, serving me hot dogs, watching me drive to the hoop, and giving me the full-court press for the rest of my life.

In this chapter, you will identify and use adjectives and adverbs.

Adjectives

Adjectives describe nouns (people, places, or things) and pronouns (words that replace nouns). In other words, adjectives add more information and detail to the words they are modifying. They add information explaining how many, what kind, or which one. They also describe how things look, smell, feel, taste, and sound.

The **proud** <u>parents</u> paid for the **expensive** <u>wedding</u>.

The bride had **four** <u>bridesmaids</u>.

The <u>groom</u> is **nervous** and **excited**.

PRACTICE I

Underline all of the adjectives and adverbs in these sentences.

EXAMPLE:

Marilyn Monroe was a <u>gorgeous</u> and <u>troubled</u> woman.

1. The stunning blond woman, Marilyn Monroe, transformed herself from plain actress to American sex icon.

2. Americans adored her striking face, sexy body, and charming personality.

3. The aggressive paparazzi loved her public romances, and photographed her with famous actors and powerful politicians.

4. The media portrayed her as a tragic dumb blond, and as a sad, lonely, and insecure woman.

5. The unhappy and vulnerable celebrity had three volatile marriages.

Placement of Adjectives

You can place adjectives either before a noun or after a linking verb such as *be, look, appear,* or *become.*

Before the noun: The **young** <u>Frida Kahlo</u> fell in love with a much older painter.

After a linking verb: Their <u>relationship</u> was **passionate** and **volatile**.

 **Hint** **Problems with Adjective Placement**

In some languages, adjectives can appear directly after nouns. However, in English, never place an adjective directly after the noun that it is describing.

                                    very elegant lady.
Martha Dandridge Washington was a ~~lady very elegant.~~

                                    forty and a half years.
She was married to George Washington for ~~forty years and half.~~

PRACTICE 2

Some of the following sentences have errors in adjective placement. Underline and correct each error. If a sentence is correct, write *C* in the blank.

EXAMPLE:

The young lovers lived in a ~~palace magnificent.~~ *magnificent palace.*   _____

1. Cleopatra, the last queen of Egypt, and Marc Antony, the man

   she loved, planned to conquer the powerful city of Rome.   _____

2. After the fierce battle, Marc Antony heard a rumor false that

   the vivacious Cleopatra was dead.   _____

3. The handsome and shrewd general Marc Antony became

   depressed and killed himself.   _____

4. Cleopatra heard the horrible news about Marc Antony, and she

   committed suicide by allowing a snake poisonous to bite her.   _____

5. With the death of Cleopatra, the rule of the pharaohs ended,

   and Egypt became a province Roman.   _____

Order of Adjectives

When using two or more adjectives together, place them in this order: number, quality, size, age, color, origin, and type. The following chart indicates the order of adjectives.

Determiner (number, etc.)	Quality	Size or Shape	Age	Color	Origin	Type	Noun
We bought two	beautiful		old	red		Persian	rugs.
Santa Fe is a	lovely	large			New Mexico	desert	town.

> ## *Hint*   Punctuating Adjectives
>
> Place commas between adjectives of equal weight. In other words, if two adjectives describe a quality, place a comma between them.
>
> **Comma:**   Shah Jahan presented the <u>lovely, rare</u> sculpture to the princess.
>
> Do not place commas between adjectives of unequal weight. For example, if one adjective describes a quality and another describes a place of origin or color, do not put a comma between them.
>
> **No comma:**   Shah Jahan presented the <u>rare Greek</u> sculpture to the princess.

PRACTICE 3

Complete these sentences by writing the adjectives in parentheses in the correct order.

EXAMPLE:

The (young / handsome) ___*handsome young*___ Shah Jahan became the
Mughal emperor of seventeenth-century India.

1. A (Indian / 15-year-old / shy) _____ princess
   named Mumtaz married Shah Jahan in 1612 and became his favorite wife.
   They shared a (long / passionate) _____ love that
   lasted until she died in 1629.

2. Shah Jahan constructed the (white / beautiful)
   _____ Taj Mahal as a symbol of their
   love. Around (skilled / 20,000) _____
   workers and (Indian / gray / 1,000)
   _____ elephants took nearly twenty
   years to complete the Taj Mahal.

3. The mausoleum is made of (white / smooth)
   _____ marble and sits on a sandstone
   platform. The interior contains (intricate / Islamic)
   _____ designs made of semiprecious stones. Shah
   Jahan planned to build a (marble / black / stunning)
   _____ mausoleum for himself, but the project was
   never started. When he died, he was buried beside his (beloved / young)
   _____ queen in the Taj Mahal.

Problems with Adjectives

You can recognize many adjectives by their endings. Be particularly careful when
you use the following adjective forms.

Adjectives Ending in *-ful* or *-less*

Some adjectives end in *-ful* or *-less*. Remember that *-ful* ends in one *l* and *-less* ends
in two *s*'s.

> Diego Rivera, a **skillful** artist, created many **beautiful** paintings and murals.
> His work appeared **effortless** because he was so prolific.

Adjectives Ending in *-ed* and *-ing*

Some adjectives look like verbs because they end in *-ing* or *-ed*.

■ When the adjective ends in *-ed*, it describes someone's expression or feeling.

> The **pleased** and **well-regarded** artist presented his mural to the public.

- When the adjective ends in *-ing*, it describes the quality of the person or thing.

  His **exciting, surprising** images are displayed on public buildings in Mexico.

Hint ▸ Keep Adjectives in the Singular Form

When a noun describes another noun, always make it singular, even if the noun following it is plural.

year
Juliet was a thirteen-~~years~~-old girl when she met Romeo.

dollar
We bought several ten-~~dollars~~ tickets to see the play *Romeo and Juliet*.

PRACTICE 4

Correct nine adjective errors in the paragraphs. The adjectives may have the wrong form, or they may be misspelled.

EXAMPLE:

interesting
Men and women can have ~~interested~~ platonic friendships.

1.   Can men and women be friends? The thirty-*year*-~~years~~-old film *When Harry Met Sally* suggests that it is impossible. In the movie, and in most television shows, male–female friendships end in romance. But some well-*regarded*~~regarding~~ psychologists now argue that such friendships are both possible and beneficial.

2.   Don O'Meara published a *surprising* ~~surprised~~ study in the journal *Sex Roles*. He began the study because his best friend is a *wonderful* ~~wonderfull~~ woman. They have a very *rewarding* ~~rewarded~~ friendship. According to O'Meara, men and women can have pleasants friendships. However, cross-gender friendships are not *effortless.* ~~effortles~~. Participants must be carefull when they deal with mutual attraction, with the balance of power, and with doubters. Friends and family may be skeptical, asking, "Are you really just friends?" But such friendships are valuable. In fact, 62 percent of men report that they are more truthfull with their female friends than they are with their male friends.

Adverbs

Adverbs add information to adjectives, verbs, or other adverbs. They give more specific information about how, when, where, and to what extent an action or event occurred.

verb   adverb

Brad Pitt <u>fell</u> in love with Angelina Jolie **quickly**.

adverb verb
of time

Paparazzi **often** <u>take</u> photos of celebrities.

verb   adverb adverb

Brad and Angelina's family <u>expanded</u> quite **rapidly**.

adverb   adjective

People are **extremely** <u>curious</u> about famous couples.

Adverb Forms

Adverbs often end in *-ly*. In fact, you can change many adjectives into adverbs by adding *-ly* endings.

Adjective: honest   **Adverb:** honestly

- If you add *-ly* to a word that ends in *l*, then your new word will have a double *l*.

joyful + -ly

Eros watched **joyfully** as Psyche walked toward him.

- If you add *-ly* to a word that ends in *e*, keep the *e*. Exceptions to this rule are *true-truly* and *due-duly*.

passionate + -ly

In Greek mythology, Eros, the god of love, fell **passionately** in love with Psyche.

CHAPTER 21

 Some Adverbs and Adjectives Have the Same Form

Some adverbs look exactly like adjectives. The only way to distinguish them is to see what they are modifying or describing.

Examples:	early	fast	high	often	right
	far	hard	late	past	soon

Adjective: In the **early** morning, Eros pierced the heart of a mortal.

Adverb: Psyche arrived **early** at the wedding.

PRACTICE 5

Change each adjective into an adverb. Make sure that you spell the adverb correctly.

EXAMPLE:

pure   *purely*_____

1. beautiful _____
2. often _____
3. virtual _____
4. soon _____
5. real _____

6. extreme _____
7. delightful _____
8. heavy _____
9. wonderful _____
10. entire _____

Placement of Frequency Adverbs

Frequency adverbs are words that indicate how often someone performs an action or when an event occurs. They are words such as *always, often, sometimes, usually,* and *ever.*

- Place frequency adverbs before regular present and past tense verbs.

  Zeus **usually** <u>lived</u> on Mount Olympus.

- Place frequency adverbs after the verb *be.*

  The bridegroom <u>is</u> **usually** very dependable.

- Place frequency adverbs after helping verbs.

  Michael <u>has</u> **never** <u>been married</u> before.

PRACTICE 6

Underline and correct six errors with word order or adjective and adverb forms.

EXAMPLE:

often contain
Magazines <u>contain often</u> articles about the President.

1.   In 1964, Michelle Robinson was born in Chicago. Her father was a pump operator, and he worked tireless to support his family. He suffered from multiple sclerosis, and he often was in pain. He encouraged his son and daughter to work hard. Nobody in the family ever had been to university. However, Michelle, a very brightly woman, was accepted at Princeton. She graduated with honors.

2.   In 1989, Barack Obama had a job as a summer associate in a Chicago

law firm. Michelle Robinson was assigned to be his advisor. Obama asked

sometimes his beautiful advisor for a date. The first few times, she rejected

him. Eventualy, she agreed, and three years later, the couple married.

Problems with Adverbs

Sometimes people use an adjective instead of an adverb after a verb. Ensure that you always modify your verbs using an adverb.

>   *really quietly*
> Samson waited ~~real quiet~~ for the celebrations to begin.

PRACTICE 7   REVIEW

Each sentence has one error with adverb or adjective forms or placement. Correct the errors.

EXAMPLE:

>   *sincerely*
> Some people ~~sincerelly~~ believe in arranged marriages.

1. Arranged marriages are commonly in many parts of the world.

2. Parents find often a mate for their son or daughter based on criteria such as level of education, job prospects, and family background.

3. Advocates of arranged marriages believe real strongly that love can come later in the relationship.

4. Love marriages happen regular in many countries.

5. In love marriages, people sometimes fall in love quick.

6. In some Western societies, common-law unions have gradualy become popular.

7. The Netherlands officialy recognizes common-law unions.

8. In your opinion, should common-law couples have the same legally rights as married couples?

CHAPTER 21

Good and *Well, Bad* and *Badly*

Good is an adjective, and *well* is an adverb.

Adjective:	The pastry chef made a **good** wedding cake.
Adverb:	The pastry chef cooks **well.**

Exception: Use *well* to describe a person's health.

Adverb:	I do not feel **well**.

Bad is an adjective, and *badly* is an adverb.

Adjective:	I am a **bad** singer.
Adverb:	I sang **badly** at the wedding.

PRACTICE 8

Underline the correct adjectives or adverbs.

EXAMPLE:

Generally, couples who communicate (good, <u>well</u>) have successful relationships.

1. Varied wedding traditions exist in the world. In Fiji, it is considered a (good, well) practice to give a whale tooth symbolizing wealth to the bride's father.

2. At Greek weddings, guests throw dishes on the floor for (good, well) luck.

3. In North American Christian weddings, it is (bad, badly) luck for the groom to see the bride's dress before the wedding. There is usually a big wedding feast, and sometimes the food is cooked (bad, badly).

4. At traditional Jewish weddings, an Israeli dance called the hora is performed. Some people dance (good, well) while others dance (bad, badly).

5. Many people consider a community center to be a (good, well) place to hold a wedding reception.

CHAPTER 21

Comparative and Superlative Forms

Use the **comparative form** to compare two items.

Adjectives:	Michelle is <u>younger</u> than Barack.
	Michelle became <u>more famous</u> than her best friend.
Adverb:	Barack used the Internet <u>more effectively</u> than his opponent.

Use the **superlative form** to compare three or more items.

Adjectives:	Michelle Obama became one of the <u>youngest</u> First Ladies.
	Michelle was the <u>most famous</u> of her high school friends.
Adverb:	Barack used the Internet the <u>most effectively</u> of all the presidential candidates.

How to Write Comparative and Superlative Forms

You can write comparative and superlative forms by remembering a few simple guidelines.

Using -er and -est Endings

Add *-er* and *-est* endings to one-syllable adjectives and adverbs.

	Comparative	**Superlative**
short	shorter than	the shortest
fast	faster than	the fastest
quick	quicker than	the quickest

Double the last letter when the adjective ends in one vowel + one consonant.

	Comparative	**Superlative**
hot	hotter than	the hottest

Using *More* and *The Most*

Generally add *more* and *the most* to adjectives and adverbs of two or more syllables.

	Comparative	**Superlative**
modern	more modern than	the most modern
clearly	more clearly than	the most clearly
worried	more worried than	the most worried

When a two-syllable adjective ends in *y*, change the *y* to *i* before you add the *-er* or *-est*.

	Comparative	**Superlative**
happy	happ**ier** than	the happ**iest**

Using Irregular Comparative and Superlative Forms

Some adjectives and adverbs have unique comparative and superlative forms. Study this list to remember how to form some of the most common ones.

	Comparative	**Superlative**
good, well	better than	the best
bad, badly	worse than	the worst
some, much, many	more than	the most
little (a small amount)	less than	the least
far	farther, further	the farthest, the furthest

 **Farther Versus Further**

• *Farther* indicates a physical distance.

> The wedding reception was **farther** from my home than it was from my fiancé's home.

• *Further* means "additional."

> I need **further** information before I can make a decision.

PRACTICE 9

Write the comparative and superlative forms of each adjective and adverb.

	Comparative	**Superlative**
EXAMPLE:		
famous	*more famous*	*most famous*
1. easy	_____	_____
2. easily	_____	_____
3. good	_____	_____
4. bad	_____	_____
5. happy	_____	_____
6. quickly	_____	_____
7. careful	_____	_____
8. fast	_____	_____
9. thin	_____	_____
10. lazy	_____	_____
11. red	_____	_____
12. decent	_____	_____

CHAPTER 21

PRACTICE 10

Underline the correct comparative or superlative form of each adjective or adverb.

EXAMPLE:

In my opinion, William Shakespeare's tragedy *Romeo and Juliet* is his (better / <u>best</u>) play.

1. William Shakespeare is considered to be the (greater / greatest) playwright in English literature.

2. During the Renaissance, Shakespeare was (better / best) known than his contemporaries.

3. Queen Elizabeth I regarded him as the (more / most) talented author in her kingdom.

4. His (better / best)-known play is *Romeo and Juliet*.

5. In the play, Romeo thinks that Juliette is the (more / most) beautiful girl in the city.

6. Romeo wants (farther / further) information about Juliet, so he interrogates his cousin.

7. One of the (worse / worst) days of Romeo's life occurs when he realizes that his family is feuding with Juliet's family.

8. The (bigger / biggest) mistake Romeo makes is when he believes that Juliet has died.

9. *Romeo and Juliet* is a (sadder / saddest) play than some of Shakespeare's other tragedies.

10. Critics claim that Shakespeare's plays have been the (more / most) studied works in English literature.

PRACTICE 11

Complete the sentences in this paragraph by writing either the comparative or superlative form of the adjective or adverb in parentheses.

EXAMPLE:

Is Valentine's Day the (commercial) _____*most commercial*_____ holiday of the year?

1.   For chocolate stores, Valentine's Day is one of the (busy)

_____ days of the year. According to a retail survey,

males are (generous) _____ than females on

February 14. Perhaps women are (angry) _____

than men are if they do not receive a gift. Chocolate and flowers are the

(popular) _____ presents.

2.   In Japan, Valentine's Day is (important) _____

for men than for women. On that day, women buy "giri" chocolate for

their male co-workers and bosses, but women do not receive gifts. For

instance, Kaori Kato buys the (good) _____ giri

chocolate she can find for the men in her office. Then she buys "Honmei"

chocolate for her boyfriend. Such chocolate is usually even (tasty)

_____ and (expensive) _____

than giri chocolate. In some stores, green tea chocolate balls sell (quickly)

_____ than regular chocolate balls.

CHAPTER 21

3.   In Japan, March 14 is White Day. The holiday began in 1965 when a marshmallow company launched an advertising campaign. The company urged men to repay their Valentine's Day gifts by giving women the (soft) _____ marshmallow candies they could find. Nowadays, white chocolate is (popular) _____ than marshmallows. According to a survey by a Tokyo department store, flowers are the (good) _____ gift of all for women.

Problems with Comparative and Superlative Forms

In the comparative form, never use *more* and *-er* to modify the same word. In the superlative form, never use *most* and *-est* to modify the same word.

> *better*
> His date with Jan was ~~more better~~ than his date with Catherine.

> *best*
> It was the ~~most best~~ date of his life.

 **Using "the" in the Comparative Form**

Although you would usually use *the* in superlative forms, you can use it in some two-part comparatives. In these expressions, the second part is the result of the first part.

      action   result
<u>The more</u> you work at a relationship, <u>the better</u> it will be.

PRACTICE 12

Correct ten adjective and adverb errors.

EXAMPLE:

> *most*
> One of the ~~more~~ famous relationships in the twentieth century was between Charles Lindbergh and Anne Morrow.

1.   Charles Lindberg was an all-American hero because, in 1927, he was the first person to fly safe across the Atlantic Ocean. Charles fell in love with Anne Morrow, who was real beautiful. They lived happy for a while. She wrote a memoir of their relationship that led to more greater celebrity status for the pair. The more Anne wrote, the happiest she became.

2. In some respects, the couple had a perfect relationship. Anne worked tireless beside her husband, helping him navigate during his flights. In an era when most women did not work outside the home, Anne was more happier pursuing her writing and flying careers than being a housewife.

3. However, the relationship between Charles and Anne was not perfect. They both had affairs, and at one point, Anne fell in love with one of the most best writers of the era, Antoine de Saint-Exupéry. Charles and Anne also lived through the more tragic event of their lives. In 1932, their first child was kidnapped and murdered. About four years later, Bruno Richard Hauptmann was executed for the crime.

4. The more Charles and Anne suffered, the strongest their relationship became. They went on to have more children, and they were together until the death of Charles in 1974.

FINAL REVIEW

Correct twenty adjective or adverb errors.

EXAMPLE:

surprising
Reporters write ~~surprised~~ articles about same-sex marriage.

1. Possibly the more controversial issue in contemporary American politics is same-sex marriage. Same-sex marriage refers to a legally union between people of the same sex. People have strong held opinions about this topic.

2. In the United States, individual states have jurisdiction over marriage. Therefore, the laws are not consistently across the nation. Massachusetts recognized gay marriage more quicker than other states. California accepted gay marriage and then *rapidly* ~~rapid~~ reversed the decision. Most states bar gay marriage, arguing that it is worst for society than heterosexual marriage.

3.   The more this issue remains unsolved, the most divisive it becomes. Jim and Paul have been together for five years. Paul writes good and runs a magazine for the gay community. They both work tireless to lobby their state government to change laws about marriage. They argue that same-sex marriage is a civil right. Therefore, as citizens, gay couples should have the same rights as heterosexual couples. The worse mistake a government can make is to discriminate against a minority group. On the other hand, Edward and Christabel are opposed to same-sex marriages. They have been married for ten years and have a seven-years-old daughter. They believe that procreation can only happen naturaly between a man and a woman. Families are the most greatest cornerstones of civilization.

4.   Religious groups have also opinions about the issue. Some conservative Christians believe that same-sex marriage is real terrible. Other religious groups support same-sex marriage. They believe that two consented adults should have the right to form a loving and committed union.

5.   Differents groups voice various opinions. This issue will eventualy be resolved, but in the meantime, the interested debate continues.

CHAPTER 21

The Writer's Room

Write about one of the following topics. After you finish writing, underline any adjectives and adverbs. Decide whether your paragraph has enough descriptive words and phrases.

1. Describe your ideal partner. What characteristics should he or she have?
2. Narrate what happened on a funny, boring, or romantic date that you have had.

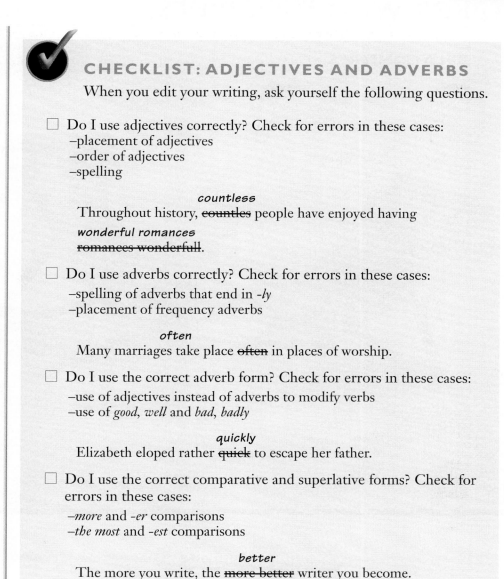

CHECKLIST: ADJECTIVES AND ADVERBS

When you edit your writing, ask yourself the following questions.

☐ Do I use adjectives correctly? Check for errors in these cases:
  –placement of adjectives
  –order of adjectives
  –spelling

countless
Throughout history, ~~countles~~ people have enjoyed having
wonderful romances
~~romances wonderfull~~.

☐ Do I use adverbs correctly? Check for errors in these cases:
  –spelling of adverbs that end in *-ly*
  –placement of frequency adverbs

often
Many marriages take place ~~often~~ in places of worship.

☐ Do I use the correct adverb form? Check for errors in these cases:
  –use of adjectives instead of adverbs to modify verbs
  –use of *good, well* and *bad, badly*

quickly
Elizabeth eloped rather ~~quick~~ to escape her father.

☐ Do I use the correct comparative and superlative forms? Check for errors in these cases:
  –*more* and *-er* comparisons
  –*the most* and *-est* comparisons

better
The more you write, the ~~more better~~ writer you become.

CHAPTER 21

mywritinglab To check your progress in meeting this chapter's objectives,
log in to **www.mywritinglab.com**, go to the **Study Plan**
tab, click on **The Editing Handbook—Section 6 Modifiers** and choose **Adjectives
and Adverbs** from the list of subtopics. Read and view the resources in the **Review
Materials** section, and then complete the **Recall, Apply,** and **Write** sets in the
Activities section.

Mistakes with Modifiers

Section Theme: **RELATIONSHIPS**

In this chapter, you will read about relationship issues such as Internet dating and workplace romances.

Grammar Snapshot

Looking at Modifiers

In an essay titled "Marriage Is an Outdated Institution," college student Winston Murray writes about the decline of marriage. In the following excerpt, some of the modifiers are underlined.

> Weddings are expensive and extravagant affairs <u>that indebt families for years to come</u>. Parents of the bride and groom <u>often</u> take out second mortgages to give their children the ideal wedding. <u>After paying for the wedding dress</u>, they must pay for the reception hall, flowers, music, catering, and limousines to have a one-night party.

In this chapter, you will identify and correct misplaced and dangling modifiers.

Misplaced Modifiers

A **modifier** is a word, phrase, or clause that describes or modifies nouns or verbs in a sentence. To use a modifier correctly, place it next to the word(s) that you want to modify.

<u>modifier</u>   modified noun
<u>Holding her hand</u>, **Charles** proposed.

A **misplaced modifier** is a word, phrase, or clause that is not placed next to the word that it modifies. When a modifier is too far from the word that it is describing, the meaning of the sentence can become confusing or unintentionally funny.

Confusing: I saw the Golden Gate Bridge riding my bike.
(How could a bridge ride a bike?)

Clear: **Riding my bike,** I saw the Golden Gate Bridge.

Confusing: Boring and silly, Amanda closed the fashion magazine.
(What is boring and silly? Amanda or the magazine?)

Clear: Amanda closed the **boring and silly** fashion magazine.

Commonly Misplaced Modifiers

Some writers have trouble placing certain types of modifiers close to the words they modify. As you read the sample sentences for each type, notice how they change meaning depending on where a writer places the modifiers. In the examples, the modifiers are underlined.

Prepositional Phrase Modifiers

A prepositional phrase is made of a preposition and its object.

Confusing: Sheila talked to the man in the bar <u>with dirty hands.</u>
(Can a bar have dirty hands?)

Clear: When Sheila was in the bar, she talked to the man <u>with dirty hands.</u>

CHAPTER 22

PRACTICE 1

In each sentence, underline the prepositional phrase modifier. Then draw an arrow from the modifier to the word that it modifies.

EXAMPLE:

<u>With anticipation</u>, Arianne contacted the dating service.

1. Arianne found Cupid Dating Service on a Web site.

2. On the table, a glossy pamphlet contained additional information.

3. Arianne, in a red dress, entered the dating service office.

4. With a kind expression, the interviewer asked Arianne personal questions.

5. Arianne, with direct eye contact, discussed her preferences.

Present Participle Modifiers

A present participle modifier is a phrase that begins with an -*ing* verb.

Confusing:	The young man proposed to his girlfriend <u>holding a diamond ring</u>. (Who is holding the diamond ring?)
Clear:	While <u>holding a diamond ring</u>, the young man proposed to his girlfriend.

PRACTICE 2

In each sentence, underline the present participle modifier. Then draw an arrow from the modifier to the word that it modifies.

EXAMPLE:

<u>Swallowing nervously</u>, Arianne explained her dating history.

1. <u>Hoping to find a soul mate</u>, Arianne described what she wanted.

2. Matching people with similar tastes, Cupid Dating Service is very successful.

3. Some customers using the service express satisfaction.

4. Feeling disappointed, customer Stephen Rooney has never met a suitable companion.

5. However, the owner of Cupid Dating, citing statistics, says that most clients are very satisfied.

Past Participle Modifiers

A past participle modifier is a phrase that begins with a past participle (*walked, gone, known*, and so on).

Confusing:	<u>Covered with dust</u>, my girlfriend wiped the windshield of her new car. (What was covered with dust? The girlfriend or the car?)
Clear:	My girlfriend wiped the windshield of the car that was <u>covered with dust</u>.

PRACTICE 3

In each sentence, underline the past participle modifier. Then draw an arrow from the modifier to the word that it modifies.

EXAMPLE:

<u>Shocked</u>, Arianne met her first blind date.

1. <u>Covered in paint</u>, Stephen sat at Arianne's table.

2. Torn between staying and leaving, Arianne smiled at Stephen.

3. Bored with life, Stephen talked for hours.

4. Trapped in a horrible date, Arianne longed to escape.

5. Stephen, surprised by her actions, watched Arianne stand up and leave.

Other Dependent-Clause Modifiers

Other dependent-clause modifiers can begin with a subordinator or a relative pronoun such as *who, whom, which,* or *that.*

> **Confusing:** I presented Jeremy to my mother who is my boyfriend.
> (How could "my mother" be "my boyfriend?")
>
> **Clear:** I presented Jeremy, who is my boyfriend, to my mother.

PRACTICE 4

In each sentence, underline the relative clause modifier. Then draw an arrow from the modifier to the word that it modifies.

EXAMPLE:

Arianne complained about the date that had gone horribly wrong.

1. She discussed the date with her friend, Maggie, who was sympathetic.

2. Maggie knew about a place that had many single people.

3. The women went to a club where they met a new friend, Mel.

4. Maggie told Mel, who was also single, about her dating problems.

5. But Mel, whom Maggie really liked, asked Arianne out on a date instead.

PRACTICE 5

Read each pair of sentences on the next page. Circle the letter of the correct sentence. Then, in the incorrect sentence, underline the misplaced modifier.

EXAMPLE:

a. We read about the love lives of celebrities with curiosity.

(b.) With curiosity, we read about the love lives of celebrities.

1. a. Today, many journalists publish stories about celebrities on the front page.

(b.) Today, many journalists publish stories on the front page about celebrities.

2. a. Followed by paparazzi, celebrities such as Rhianna have no privacy.

    b. Celebrities such as Rhianna have no privacy followed by paparazzi.

3. a. In 2003, Kobe Bryant spoke to a female reporter with his wife.

    b. In 2003, with his wife, Kobe Bryant spoke to a female reporter.

4. a. I read an article saying that some celebrities are angry in the newspaper.

    b. I read an article in the newspaper saying that some celebrities are angry.

5. a. Celebrities should not complain about the curiosity of the public appearing on thousands of movie screens daily.

    b. Appearing on thousands of movie screens daily, celebrities should not complain about the curiosity of the public.

 **Correcting Misplaced Modifiers**

To correct misplaced modifiers, do the following:

1. Identify the modifier.
    Ricardo and Alicia found a wedding ring shopping in Dallas.

2. Identify the word or words that are being modified.
    Ricardo and Alicia

3. Move the modifier next to the word(s) that are being modified.
    Shopping in Dallas, **Ricardo and Alicia** found a wedding ring.

CHAPTER 22

PRACTICE 6

Correct the misplaced modifiers in the following sentences.

EXAMPLE

    Sitting in my car,
    I listened to the radio ~~sitting in my car.~~

1. The law professor spoke on the radio about marriage laws from Indiana.

2. Mixed-race couples were prohibited from marrying by legislators lacking their basic human rights.

3. Mixed-race couples felt angry who were prohibited from marrying legally.

4. In 1967, allowing interracial couples to marry, a decision was made by the U.S. Supreme Court.

5. The professor explained why these laws were morally wrong last week.

6. My sister married a man of another race who is my twin.

7. The wedding was in a beautiful garden photographed by a professional.

8. My parents welcomed the groom with champagne who supported my sister's choice.

Dangling Modifiers

A **dangling modifier** opens a sentence but does not modify any words in the sentence. It "dangles," or hangs loosely, because it is not connected to any other part of the sentence. To avoid having a dangling modifier, make sure the modifier and the first noun that follows it have a logical connection.

Confusing: Phoning the company, a limousine was booked in advance.
                 (Can a limousine book itself?)

Clear: Phoning the company, **the groom** booked the limousine in advance.

Confusing: Walking down the aisle, many flower petals were on the ground.
                 (Can flowers walk down an aisle?)

Clear: Walking down the aisle, **the bride** noticed that many flower petals were on the ground.

PRACTICE 7

Read each pair of sentences. Circle the letter of each correct sentence, and underline the dangling modifiers.

EXAMPLE:

   a. Enjoying the single life, it is not necessary to look for your soul mate.

   (b.) Enjoying the single life, DePaulo has stopped looking for her soul mate.

1. (a.) Feeling stigmatized as a single woman, Bella DePaulo decided to start a singles movement.

   b. Feeling stigmatized as a single woman, a singles movement would be started.

2. a. To learn more, some research was completed.

   (b.) To learn more, DePaulo completed some research.

3. a. To her immense surprise, DePaulo discovered a thirty-year-old singles movement.

   (b.) To her immense surprise, a thirty-year-old singles movement was discovered.

4. a. Published in 1974, *The Challenge of Being Single* was a popular manifesto.

   b. Published in 1974, people love the popular manifesto, *The Challenge of Being Single*.

5. a. Living as a single woman, loneliness was not a problem.

   b. Living as a single woman, Marie Edwards was not lonely.

6. a. Loved by friends and family, it is possible to have a content life.

   b. Loved by friends and family, Edwards had a content life.

 **Correcting Dangling Modifiers**

To correct dangling modifiers, follow these steps.

1. Identify the modifier.

   <u>Walking down the aisle,</u> many flower petals were on the ground.

2. Decide who or what should be modified.

   the bride

3. Add the missing subject (and in some cases, also add or remove words) so that the sentence makes sense.

   Walking down the aisle, the bride noticed that many flower petals were on the ground.

PRACTICE 8

Correct the dangling modifiers in the following sentences. Begin by underlining each dangling modifier. Then rewrite the sentence. You may have to add or remove words to give the sentence a logical meaning.

EXAMPLE:

<u>Always having to remain beautiful,</u> bodies are changed.

Always having to remain beautiful, movie stars change their bodies.

1. Reading through old magazines, ideas about beauty have changed over time.

   _____

   _____

2. In the past, seeing curvy movie stars, dieting was not very common.

   _____

   _____

3. Today, making their clients thinner, the bodies of famous people are altered.

   _____

   _____

4. Watching Angelina Jolie, her natural beauty is envied.

_____

_____

5. Looking at pictures of Lady Gaga, her costumes are really wild.

_____

_____

PRACTICE 9   REVIEW

Underline each dangling or misplaced modifier, and correct the mistakes. Remember that you may have to add or remove words to give some sentences a logical meaning. If a sentence does not have modifier errors, simply write *C* to indicate it is correct.

EXAMPLE:

whom I like
I met a man at my workplace ~~whom I like~~.   _____

1. Some personnel department employees are debating the

   subject of workplace relationships in their meetings.   _____

2. Two employees can have a lot of problems with their   *who fell in love*

   superiors ~~who fall in love~~.   _____

3. Some people believe that companies should develop

   policies prohibiting workplace romance.   _____

4. Debating sexual harassment, discussions have been

   heated.   _____

5. Couples can develop antagonistic feelings who work

   together.   _____

6. Policies can cause problems in people's lives that prohibit

   workplace romance.   _____

7. Workplace romance in the future is a topic that will be

   debated.   *C*

8. Dealing with the issue, humane policies should be implemented.   _____

FINAL REVIEW

Correct ten errors with dangling or misplaced modifiers.

EXAMPLE:

Divorcing her husband, ~~her lawyer earned a lot of money~~.
she paid her lawyer a lot of money

1.   Living in difficult economic times, weddings are becoming more modest. Nonetheless, there are still many people who indebt themselves with expensive weddings. Karla Gowan admits that she was a "bridezilla" during her 2010 wedding. Her parents gave her a fancy and impressive wedding who paid the expenses.

2.   Karla Gowan made many unreasonable demands. She asked her parents to pay for crystal champagne glasses in a huff. She asked guests to avoid wearing blue or black because the colors would clash with the tablecloths in the invitations. The bridesmaids had to buy identical dresses made of pink Chinese silk who could not afford them. Getting more and more stressed, feelings were hurt. Taking out a loan, an antique Aston Martin was rented for the wedding day.

3.   The wedding occurred on July 31. Then three months later, Gowan's father lost his job. Feeling very guilty, apologies have been made to her family. Gowan has offered to repay her parents in tears. The money spent on the wedding could have gone to much better use. Making the relationship a priority, huge debts can be avoided.

The Writer's Room

Write about one of the following topics. Take care to avoid writing misplaced or dangling modifiers.

1. How are romance movies unrealistic? List examples of some movies or scenes that are not realistic.

2. Can men and women be friends? Give some steps to have a successful friendship with someone of the opposite gender.

3. What causes people to search for love on the Internet? Explain why people visit online dating sites.

CHECKLIST: MODIFIERS

When you edit your writing, ask yourself the following questions.

☐ Are my modifiers in the correct position? Check for errors with the following:
  –prepositional phrase modifiers
  –present participle modifiers
  –past participle modifiers
  –*who, whom, which,* or *that* modifiers

  Eating chocolate, the
  ~~The~~ young couple looked at the sportswear ~~eating chocolate~~.

☐ Do my modifiers modify something in the sentence? Check for dangling modifiers.

  my girlfriend created
  Reading love poetry, a romantic atmosphere ~~was created~~.

READING LINK

Relationships
To read more about relationships, see the following essays:
"Fish Cheeks" by Amy Tan
    (page 408)
"Birth" by Maya Angelou (page 410)
"Fat Chance" by Dorothy Nixon
    (page 414)

 The Writers' Circle   **Collaborative Activity**

Work with a group of students on the following activity.

STEP 1   Choose one of the following topics. Brainstorm and come up with adjectives, adverbs, and phrases that describe each item in the pair.
  a. A good date and a bad date
  b. A great relationship and an unhappy relationship
  c. A good romance movie and a bad romance movie

EXAMPLE: A good friend and a bad friend.

  A good friend: smart, makes me laugh, good talker

  A bad friend: ignores my calls, insults me, rude

STEP 2   For each item in the pair, rank the qualities from most important to least important.

STEP 3   As a team, write a paragraph about your topic. Compare the good with the bad.

STEP 4   When you finish writing, edit your paragraph. Ensure that you have written all adjectives and adverbs correctly. Also, ensure that you have no dangling or misplaced modifiers.

CHAPTER 22

mywritinglab   To check your progress in meeting this chapter's objectives, log in to **www.mywritinglab.com**, go to the **Study Plan** tab, click on **The Editing Handbook—Section 6 Modifiers** and choose **Mistakes with Modifiers** from the list of subtopics. Read and view the resources in the **Review Materials** section, and then complete the **Recall, Apply,** and **Write** sets in the **Activities** section.

Exact Language

Section Theme: **CREATURES LARGE AND SMALL**

In this chapter, you will read about animal behavior and careers with animals.

Grammar Snapshot

In his book *Animal Watching,* Desmond Morris describes the action of a skunk. The descriptive language is underlined.

Before actually firing its spray, the skunk must revert to a position in which all four feet are on the ground, the tail is raised, and the back is <u>fully arched</u>. Then, looking back over its shoulder at the enemy behind it, it aims and shoots. As it does so, it <u>swings its body slightly from side to side, like a machine-gunner raking the enemy ranks</u>. This gives its <u>nauseating, pungent</u> spray a wider range—an arc of about 45 degrees—and greatly increases the defender's chances of covering its target.

In this chapter, you will identify and correct clichés and slang.

Using a Dictionary and Thesaurus

Dictionary

A dictionary provides more than just a word's meaning. It also provides information about the part of speech, pronunciation, and even the word's history. Review the following tips for proper dictionary usage.

- Look at the preface and notes in your dictionary. The preface contains explanations about the various symbols and abbreviations. Find out what your dictionary has to offer.

- If the difficult word has a prefix such as *un-* or *mis-*, you may have to look up the root word.

- When you write a word in your text, ensure that you use the correct part of speech!

Incorrect: I hope to become a veterinary.

           (*Veterinary* is an adjective.)

Correct: I hope to become a **veterinarian**.

           (*Veterinarian* is a noun.)

For example, the word *sensible* has the following definitions.

Word-Break Divisions
Your dictionary may use heavy black dots to indicate places for dividing words.

Stress Symbol (') and Pronunciation
Some dictionaries provide the phonetic pronunciation of words. The stress symbol (') lets you know which syllable is stressed.

Parts of Speech
This means that *sensible* is an adjective. If you don't understand the "parts of speech" symbol, look in the front or the back of your dictionary for a list of symbols and their meanings.

sen•si•ble /(sen′sə-bəl)/ *adj* 1. reasonable. 2. aware; cognizant. 3. perceptible through the senses. 4. capable of sensation.

From *The New American Webster Handy College Dictionary,*
New York: Signet, 2000 (606)

CHAPTER 23

 Cognates

Cognates are English words that may look and sound like words in another language. For example, the English word *graduation* is similar to the Spanish word *graduacion*, but it is spelled differently.

    If English is not your first language, and you see an English word that looks similar to a word in your language, check how the word is being used in context. It may or may not mean the same thing in English that it means in your language. For example, in English, *deception* means "to deliberately mislead someone." In Spanish, *decepcion* means "disappointment." Both English and German have the word *fast*, but in German it means "almost." If you are not sure of a word's meaning, you can always consult a dictionary.

PRACTICE I

Part A: Look at the front of your dictionary to find the abbreviations key. Then write down the abbreviations that your dictionary uses for the following parts of speech.

EXAMPLE:

verb   _____*v*_____

1. adjective   _____   3. preposition   _____

2. adverb   _____   4. pronoun   _____

Part B: Using a dictionary, write two brief definitions beside each word. (Note that some words have multiple definitions. Just choose two.) Beside each definition, indicate the part of speech in parentheses.

EXAMPLE:

ticket *(n): a printed document indicating a price or fare* _____

(v): to give a summons for a traffic or parking violation _____

1. fine _____

    _____

2. ruler _____

    _____

3. suit _____

    _____

4. stake _____

    _____

 **Hint**   **Online Dictionaries and Thesauruses**

Many dictionaries are available online. Some Web sites may provide definitions from multiple sources, and they may indicate stress marks differently from regular dictionaries. For instance, on *dictionary.reference.com*, the stressed syllable is indicated in bold, and by clicking on the loudspeaker, you can hear the word being pronounced. (Note that *dictionary.reference.com* also has a "Thesaurus" tab.)

co·op·er·a·tion   ◁))   [koh-op-*uh*-**rey**-sh*uh*n]

From dictionary.reference.com

PRACTICE 2

Use your dictionary to determine which syllable is accented in each word. Underline the accented syllable.

EXAMPLE:

r e <u>c e</u> p t i o n i s t

1. l a b o r a t o r y
2. s e c r e t a r y
3. e q u i t a b l e
4. i n v e n t
5. i n v e n t o r y

6. p s y c h i a t r i s t
7. c o o p e r a t e
8. f i l t r a t i o n
9. m o t i v a t e
10. m o t i v a t i o n

Thesaurus

To avoid repeating the same word over and over in a text, use a thesaurus. A thesaurus provides you with a list of synonyms, which are words that have the same meaning as the word you looked up. However, be careful to pick a word that means what you intended. Sometimes synonyms are similar but not exactly the same in meaning. For example, look at the various synonyms for the word *serious*. Some of the words have particular nuances, or shades of meaning.

> Serious, adj. austere, contemplative, downbeat, grim, humorless, poker-faced, sincere, somber, thoughtful, unsmiling, weighty

PRACTICE 3

Using a thesaurus, find a minimum of five synonyms for each word. Choose words that are familiar to you.

1. shy_____
2. interesting _____
3. sad _____
4. terrible _____
5. hot _____

Using Specific Vocabulary

When you revise your writing, ensure that your words are exact. Replace any vague words with more specific ones. For example, the following words are vague.

good   bad   nice   interesting   great   boring

Look at the following example. The second sentence creates a very clear image.

Vague: The bird is beautiful.

More precise: The bird has a brilliant turquoise head and red breast, with black and white stripes on its wings.

How to Create Vivid Language

When you choose the precise word, you convey your meaning exactly. To create more vivid and detailed vocabulary, try these strategies:

Modify your nouns. If the noun is vague, make it more specific by adding one or more adjectives. You could also rename the noun with a more specific term.

> **Vague:**   the woman
>
> **Vivid:**   the agreeable trainer   the nervous marine biologist

Modify your verbs. Use more vivid, precise verbs. You could also use adverbs.

> **Vague:**   said
>
> **Vivid:**   whispered   commanded   yelled   spoke sharply

Include more details. Add more information to make the sentence more complete.

> **Vague:**   She yelled at the bad dog.
>
> **Precise:**   The obedience trainer spoke firmly to the aggressive black Doberman.

PRACTICE 4

Read the excerpt from George Orwell's story "Shooting an Elephant." In the story, a police officer must shoot an elephant that had killed someone. Underline words or phrases that help you imagine the scene. Look for vivid language that describes the sights and sounds. The first sentence has been done for you.

CHAPTER 23

When I pulled the trigger, I heard the <u>devilish roar of glee</u> that went up from the crowd. In that instant, a mysterious, terrible change had come over the elephant. He looked suddenly stricken, shrunken, immensely old, as though the frightful impact of the bullet had paralysed him without knocking him down. At last, after what seemed a long time, he sagged flabbily to his knees. His mouth slobbered. An enormous senility seemed to have settled upon him. One could have imagined him thousands of years old. I fired again into the same spot. At the second shot he did not collapse but climbed with desperate slowness to his feet and stood weakly upright, with legs sagging and head drooping. I fired a third time. You could see the agony of it jolt his whole body. But in falling he seemed for a moment to rise, for as his hind legs collapsed beneath him, he seemed to tower upward like a huge rock toppling, his trunk reaching skyward like a tree. He trumpeted, for the first and only time. And then down he came, his belly toward me, with a crash that seemed to shake the ground.

PRACTICE 5

In each of the following sentences, replace the words in parentheses with more precise words or add more vivid details.

EXAMPLE:

The weather is (bad) ____windy and cool_____.

1. Frogs (look funny) _____.

2. The tiny creatures live near (water) _____

   and eat (bugs) _____.

3. Frogs are disappearing (for many reasons) _____.

4. The situation is (bad) _____.

5. (Someone) _____ should focus

   on the problem and (do something) _____.

Avoiding Clichés

Clichés are overused expressions. Because they are overused, they lose their power and become boring. You should avoid using clichés in your writing. In each example, the underlined cliché has been replaced with a more direct word.

clichés	direct words
The dog trainer was as cool as a cucumber.	relaxed
It was raining cats and dogs.	pouring

Some Clichés and Their Substitutions

Cliché	Possible Substitution	Cliché	Possible Substitution
a dime a dozen	common	as luck would have it	fortunately
apple of my eye	my favorite	axe to grind	a problem with
as big as a house	very big	under the weather	sick
in the blink of an eye	quickly	rude awakening	shock
bear the burden	take responsibility	slowly but surely	eventually
break the ice	start the conversation	top dog	boss
busy as a bee	very busy	tried and true	experienced
finer things in life	luxuries	true blue	trustworthy

PRACTICE 6

Underline each clichéd expression and replace it with words that are more direct.

EXAMPLE:

huge
The Great Dane was as big as a house.

1. Langston was stuck in a rut, and he wanted to find a new job.

2. He wanted a career with animals, but changing fields was

   easier said than done.

3. Online, he found information about veterinarians, wildlife biologists, and

   animal control officers, and in the blink of an eye he came to a conclusion.

4. It dawned on him that he should start by working in an animal shelter.

5. He was hired, and on his second day, he saw something that

   made his blood boil.

6. A group of dogs from a puppy mill had been brought to the shelter, and

   some of the puppies really pulled at the heartstrings.

7. Throwing caution to the wind, Langston adopted four of the dogs.

8. Langston probably bit off more than he can chew because the dogs have

   destroyed his furniture.

CHAPTER 23

Slang Versus Standard American English

Most of your instructors will want you to write using Standard American English. The word "standard" does not imply better. Standard American English is the common language generally used and expected in schools, businesses, and government institutions in the United States.

Slang is nonstandard language. It is used in informal situations to communicate common cultural knowledge. In any academic or professional context, do not use slang. Read the following examples.

Slang

Alex is a marine mammal trainer. She <u>hangs</u> with killer whales and dolphins. One particular dolphin was <u>miffed</u> when another trainer tried working with it. The dolphin <u>freaked</u> <u>cuz</u> it was scared. It refused to obey anyone but Alex.

Standard English

Alex is a marine mammal trainer. She works extensively with killer whales and dolphins. One particular dolphin was upset when another trainer tried working with it. The dolphin panicked because it was scared. It refused to obey anyone but Alex.

PRACTICE 7

In the sentences that follow, the slang expressions are underlined. Substitute the slang with the best possible choice of Standard American English. You may have to rewrite part of each sentence.

EXAMPLE:

                                     easy

Finding a good job is not a cakewalk.

1. On YouTube, some animal videos go viral.

2. A lame video called "Funny Animal Clips" has been viewed more than 20 million times.

3. In one segment, a lady is chilling when her dog knocks her over.

4. In another clip, a dog is lying on a couch when it gets all riled up and attacks its own foot.

5. In a popular video that really creeped me out, an eagle grabs the legs of a baby mountain goat and throws the goat to its death.

6. There is also a touchy-feely video called "Christian the Lion."

7. In the video, John Rendall and Anthony Bourke raise a baby lion, but then it trashes their apartment.

8. A year later, Bourke and Rendall ditch Christian at a Kenyan animal reserve.

9. You will be blown away when you see the owners reunite with their fully-grown lion.

10. When Christian sees his former owners, the lion looks really stoked as he runs to embrace the humans.

CHAPTER 23

FINAL REVIEW

Edit the following paragraphs. Change fifteen clichés and slang expressions into direct English words.

EXAMPLE:

caused some controversy

Masson's book really ~~opened a can of worms~~.

1.   Do animals have feelings? Some zoologists and wildlife specialists freak out when others attribute human emotions to animals. Nonetheless, Jeffry Masson decided to knuckle down and learn about feelings in the animal kingdom. Masson's book *When Elephants Weep* is filled with way cool stories about wildlife.

2.   Masson provides examples of animals showing compassion. The book has some stuff about apparent friendships across animal species. For example, some racehorses get all mopey and refuse to run when they are separated from their goat friends. A captive chimpanzee named Lucy got all mushy and gently kissed and groomed a pet kitten. In another example, a young female elephant had a badly broken leg. Other elephants in the herd refused to ditch their wounded companion. Instead, they showed the patience of a saint as they traveled slowly and waited for the injured friend to catch up.

3.   Masson also raps about possible altruism in animals. In one example, researcher Geza Teleki was playing it cool and observing some Gombe chimps. The chimps were stuffing their faces with fruit. When Teleki realized that he had forgotten his own lunch, he stood under a tree and tried to knock down some fruit with a stick. After ten minutes of unsuccessful efforts, he gave up. In the blink of an eye, an adolescent male chimpanzee collected some fruit, climbed down a tree, and handed the fruit to Teleki. Feeling extremely grateful, Teleki chowed down on the food.

4.   Many in the scientific community accuse Masson of
"anthropomorphism," which means "attributing human traits to
nonhumans." Basically, Masson can argue until he's blue in the face. He
will still get dissed by other scientists.

The Writer's Room

Choose one of the following topics and write a paragraph. Make sure that your
paragraph has sentences of varying lengths. Also ensure that the sentences have
varied opening words.

1. Tell a story describing how you or someone you know acquired an animal.
2. Argue that animals do, or do not, display emotions. Use examples to support
   your point of view.

✔ CHECKLIST: EXACT LANGUAGE

When you edit your writing, ask yourself the following questions.

☐ Do I use clear and specific vocabulary? Check for problems with
   these elements:

   –vague words
   –clichés
   –slang

   unhappy   *screamed*
   The child was ~~bummed~~ when he couldn't have a pet, and he ~~kicked up a
   stink~~.

CHAPTER 23

mywritinglab To check your progress in meeting this chapter's objectives,
log in to **www.mywritinglab.com**, go to the **Study Plan**
tab, click on **The Editing Handbook—Section 7 Word Use and Spelling** and
choose **Exact Language** from the list of subtopics. Read and view the resources in the
Review Materials section, and then complete the **Recall, Apply,** and **Write** sets
in the **Activities** section.

Spelling

Section Theme: **CREATURES LARGE AND SMALL**

In this chapter, you will read about zoos and the conservation of endangered species.

Grammar Snapshot

Looking at Spelling

In this excerpt from the novel *The Life of Pi*, writer Yann Martel discusses the characteristics of zoos. The underlined words are sometimes difficult to spell.

A house is a <u>compressed</u> territory where our basic needs can be <u>fulfilled</u> close by and safely. Such an enclosure is <u>subjectively</u> neither better nor worse for an animal than its condition in the wild; so long as it <u>fulfills</u> the animal's needs, a territory, natural or constructed, simply *is*, without <u>judgment</u>, a given, like the spots on a leopard.

In this chapter, you will identify and correct misspelled words.

Improving Your Spelling

It is important to spell correctly. Spelling mistakes can detract from good ideas in your work. You can become a better speller if you always proofread your written work and if you check a dictionary for the meaning and spelling of words about which you are unsure.

 **Reminders About Vowels and Consonants**

When you review spelling rules, it is important to know the difference between a vowel and a consonant. The vowels are *a, e, i, o, u,* and sometimes *y.* The consonants are all of the other letters of the alphabet.

The letter *y* may be either a consonant or a vowel, depending on its pronunciation. In the word *happy,* the *y* is a vowel because it is pronounced as an *ee* sound. In the word *youth,* the *y* has a consonant sound.

PRACTICE I

Answer the following questions.

1. Write three words that begin with three consonants.

   EXAMPLE: strong   _____ _____ _____

2. Write three words that begin with *y* and contain at least two vowels.

   EXAMPLE: yellow   _____ _____ _____

3. Write three words that have double vowels.

   EXAMPLE: moon   _____ _____ _____

4. Write three words that end with three consonants.

   EXAMPLE: birth   _____ _____ _____

Writing *ie* or *ei*

Words that contain *ie* or *ei* can be tricky. Remember to write *i* before *e* except after *c* or when *ei* is pronounced *ay,* as in *neighbor* and *weigh.*

i **before e:**	chief	patient	priest
ei **after c:**	conceit	perceive	deceive
ei **pronounced as *ay*:**	weigh	neighbor	freight
Exceptions:	ancient	height	society
	efficient	leisure	species
	either	neither	their
	foreigner	science	weird

CHAPTER 24

PRACTICE 2

Underline the correct spelling of each word.

EXAMPLE:

ceiling   cieling

1. conceive   concieve
2. field   feild
3. receipt   reciept
4. hieght   height
5. vien   vein
6. science   sceince

7. efficient   efficeint
8. weird   wierd
9. deciet   deceit
10. acheive   achieve
11. weight   wieght
12. decieve   deceive

PRACTICE 3

Correct the spelling error with *ie* or *ei* in each sentence. If the sentence is correct, write *C* in the blank.

EXAMPLE:

Efficient
~~Efficeint~~ management of natural habitats is necessary for the
preservation of many animals.   _____

CHAPTER 24

1. The giant panda is one of the most endangered speceis in the

   world.   _____

2. The giant panda is revered in Chinese soceity, but there are fewer

   than two thousand of these animals left in the wild.   _____

3. The pandas inhabit the Yangtze River basin, an area that has been

   heavily populated since anceint times.   _____

4. A loss of habitat and poaching are the cheif reasons that the

   population of the giant pandas is diminishing.   _____

5. Pateintly conserving the natural biodiversity of the area will help

   the pandas.   _____

6. For example, well-conceived tourism management will boost the

   economy of the area.   _____

7. In the last ten years, the Chinese government has acheived

    significant success in creating panda nature reserves.   _____

8. In addition, most foriegn zoos have a partnership with China

    to help conserve the giant panda.   _____

Adding Prefixes and Suffixes

A **prefix** is added to the beginning of a word, and it changes the word's meaning.

<u>re</u>organize   <u>pre</u>mature   <u>un</u>fair   <u>mis</u>understand

A **suffix** is added to the ending of a word, and it changes the word's tense or meaning.

amuse<u>ment</u>   sure<u>ly</u>   offer<u>ing</u>   watch<u>ed</u>

When you add a prefix to a word, keep the last letter of the prefix and the first letter of the main word.

u**n** + **n**erve = u**nn**erve   di**s** + **s**imilar = di**ss**imilar

When you add the suffix -*ly* to a word that ends in *l*, keep the *l* of the root word. The new word will have two *l*'s.

beautiful + **ly** = beautiful**ly**   real + **ly** = real**ly**

 **Hint**   **Words Ending in -*ful***

Although the word *full* ends in two *l*'s, when -*full* is added to another word as a suffix, it ends in one *l*.

wonder**ful**   peace**ful**

Notice the unusual spelling when *full* and *fill* are combined: *fulfill*.

PRACTICE 4

Underline the correct spelling of each word.

EXAMPLE:

<u>awful</u>   awfull

1. unecessary   unnecessary   3. personally   personaly

2. dissolve   disolve   4. irational   irrational

CHAPTER 24

5. immature	imature	10. usually	usualy
6. mispell	misspell	11. disrespectfull	disrespectful
7. plentiful	plentifull	12. joyfuly	joyfully
8. universaly	universally	13. useful	usefull
9. fullfilled	fulfilled	14. ilogical	illogical

Adding *-s* or *-es* Suffixes

Generally, add *-s* to nouns and to present tense verbs that are third-person singular. However, add *-es* to words in the following situations.

- When a word ends in *s*, *sh*, *ss*, *ch*, or *x*, add *-es*.

  Noun: porch–porch**es**   **Verb:** mix–mix**es**

- When a word ends in the consonant *y*, change the *y* to *i* and add *-es*.

  Noun: lady–lad**ies**   **Verb:** carry–carr**ies**

- Generally, when a word ends in *o*, add *-es*.

  Noun: tomato–tomato**es**   **Verb:** go–go**es**

  Exceptions: piano–piano**s**, radio–radio**s**

- When a word ends in *f* or *fe*, change the *f* to a *v* and add *-es*.

  Nouns: calf–cal**ves**   wife–wi**ves**

  Exceptions: roof–roof**s**, belief–belief**s**

PRACTICE 5

Add an *-s* or *-es* ending to each word.

EXAMPLE:

reach *reaches* _____

1. piano _____
2. watch _____
3. fax _____
4. leaf _____
5. box _____
6. berry _____

7. volcano _____
8. potato _____
9. kiss _____
10. belief _____
11. vanish _____
12. baby _____

Adding Suffixes to Words Ending in -e

When you add a suffix to a word ending in *e*, make sure that you follow the next rules.

- If the suffix begins with a vowel, drop the *e* on the main word. Some common suffixes beginning with vowels are *-ed*, *-er*, *-est*, *-ing*, *-able*, *-ent*, and *-ist*.

   creat**e**–creating   move**e**–movable

   Exceptions: For some words that end in the letters *ge*, keep the *e* and add the suffix.

   courag**e**–courag**e**ous   chang**e**–chang**e**able

- If the suffix begins with a consonant, keep the *e*. Some common suffixes beginning with consonants are *-ly*, *-ment*, *-less*, and *-ful*.

   definit**e**–definit**e**ly   improv**e**–improv**e**ment

   Exceptions: Some words lose the final *e* when you add a suffix that begins with a consonant.

   argu**e**–argument   tru**e**–truly   judg**e**–judgment

PRACTICE 6

Rewrite each word by adding the suggested ending.

EXAMPLE:

   use + ed   *used*

1. advertise + ment _____   6. produce + er   _____

2. convince + ing _____   7. believe + ing   _____

3. complete + ly _____   8. move + ing   _____

4. give + ing _____   9. use + able   _____

5. cure + able _____   10. late + er   _____

PRACTICE 7

Correct the spelling mistakes in the underlined words.

EXAMPLE:

                                        truly

The story of the gray wolf in Yellowstone is <u>truely</u> amazing.

1.   Before the arrival of Europeans, gray <u>wolfs</u> were found in all parts of

North America. By the 1920s, these animals had been almost <u>completly</u>

destroyed in the United States. Early settlers <u>unecessarily</u> shot large

numbers of the animals. Biologists from the Fisheries and Wildlife

CHAPTER 24

Department decided to try <u>reintroduceing</u> the gray wolf into the wild in

Yellowstone National Park. In 1995, fifteen animals were transferred from

Alberta, Canada, to Yellowstone.

2. The wolf reintroduction program has <u>definitly</u> been a success. The

animals have multiplied and the secondary effects have <u>actualy</u> been very

positive. For example, the elk population has been reduced. As a result,

trees around the banks of lakes are <u>thriveing</u>. The numbers of <u>foxs</u> have

increased in the area because they eat the carcasses of the elks.

3. Today, there are many wolf packs in the park, and it is <u>ilegal</u> to hunt

them. Each wolf pack <u>flourishs</u> in Yellowstone National Park.

Adding Suffixes by Doubling the Final Consonant

Sometimes when you add a suffix to a word, you must double the final consonant.
Remember these tips when spelling words of one or more syllables.

One-Syllable Words

- Double the final consonant of one-syllable words ending in a consonant–
  vowel–consonant pattern.

      stop–sto**pp**ing   drag–dra**gg**ed

Exception: If the word ends in *w* or *x*, do not double the last letter.

      snow–snowing   fix–fixed

- Do not double the final consonant if the word ends in a vowel and two
  consonants or if it ends with two vowels and a consonant.

      look–looking   list–listed

Words of Two or More Syllables

- Double the final consonant of words ending in a stressed consonant-vowel-
  consonant pattern.

      confer–confe**rr**ing   omit–omi**tt**ed

- If the word ends in a syllable that is not stressed, then do not double the last
  letter of the word.

      open–opening   focus–focused

PRACTICE 8

Rewrite each word with the suggested ending.

Add -*ed*		Add -*ing*	
EXAMPLE:		**EXAMPLE:**	
park	*parked*	open	*opening*
1. answer	_____	6. happen	_____
2. clean	_____	7. run	_____
3. prod	_____	8. drag	_____
4. mention	_____	9. refer	_____
5. prefer	_____	10. question	_____

Adding Suffixes to Words Ending in -y

When you add a suffix to a word ending in *y*, follow the next rules.

- If a word has a consonant before the final *y*, change the *y* to an *i* before adding the suffix.

     heavy–heavily   angry–angrily   easy–easily

- If a word has a vowel before the final *y*, if it is a proper name, or if the suffix is *-ing*, do not change the *y* to an *i*.

     play–played   fry–frying   Kennedy–Kennedys

Exceptions: Some words do not follow the previous rule.

     day–daily   lay–laid   say–said   pay–paid

PRACTICE 9

Rewrite each word by adding the suggested ending.

EXAMPLES:

say + ing =   *saying*

1. justify + able	_____	6. lively + hood	_____
2. fly + ing	_____	7. day + ly	_____
3. enjoy + ed	_____	8. mercy + less	_____
4. Binchy + s	_____	9. duty + ful	_____
5. beauty + ful	_____	10. pretty + est	_____

PRACTICE 10

Underline and correct eight spelling mistakes in the next selection.

EXAMPLE:

mentioned

Some environmentalists <u>mentionned</u> that sharks are an endangered species.

1.   Sharks have a bad reputation. Many people display their negative opinion of sharks by refering to them as man-eating predators. The movie *Jaws* emphasized the menacing nature of sharks. It draged their image down to an all-time low. In the past, nobody questionned shark hunters. But sharks must be protected from extinction because they help keep the marine environment in balance.

2.   Sharks are being overfished dayly. Millions of sharks are killed each year by commercial fishers who depend on shark products for their livelyhood. The mercyless overfishing of sharks has led to dramatic consequences for the environment and the economy. Sharks eat other predators like stingrays. Smaller predators eat seafood such as shrimps and scallops, and that is begining to hurt the commercial fishing industry. Therefore, ecologists are developing new ways to save the shark population.

Writing Two-Part Words

The following indefinite pronouns sound as if they should be two separate words, but each is a single word.

Words with *any*:   anything, anyone, anybody, anywhere

Words with *some*:   something, someone, somebody, somewhere

Words with *every*:   everything, everyone, everybody, everywhere

 **Writing *Another* and *A lot***

• *Another* is always one word.

    <u>Another</u> gorilla has escaped from the zoo.

• *A lot* is always two words.

    <u>A lot</u> of people are looking for the animal.

PRACTICE 11

Underline and correct twelve spelling errors in the next paragraph.

EXAMPLE:

Everyone
Every one should be concerned about the destruction of animal species.

In the last century, some amazeing animals have become extinct. Some times animals are overhunted. Other times they lose their habitat. In China, the beautifull white dolphin has disappearred from the Yangtze Delta. An other animal that no longer exists is the golden toad. The last time any one saw the toad was in 1989. Alot of bird species have also vanished. You will not find Hawaiian crows any where in the wild. The only remaining birds are in zoos. Additionaly, the Brazilian Macaw has not been seen since 2000. Like many other species, macaws have been ilegally captured. According to *Scientific American* magazine, many more species will disappear in the next ten years. Every body knows the problem is serious. But maybe no thing can stop the extinctions.

120 Commonly Misspelled Words

The next list contains some of the most commonly misspelled words in English. Learn how to spell these words. You might try different strategies, such as writing down the word a few times or using flash cards to help you to memorize the spelling of each word.

absence	argument	cemetery	desperate
absorption	athlete	clientele	developed
accommodate	bargain	committee	dilemma
acquaintance	beginning	comparison	disappoint
address	behavior	competent	embarrass
aggressive	believable	conscience	encouragement
already	business	conscientious	environment
aluminum	calendar	convenient	especially
analyze	campaign	curriculum	exaggerate
appointment	careful	definite	exercise
approximate	ceiling	definitely	extraordinarily

familiar	medicine	privilege	technique
February	millennium	probably	thorough
finally	mischievous	professor	tomato
foreign	mortgage	psychology	tomatoes
government	necessary	questionnaire	tomorrow
grammar	ninety	receive	truly
harassment	noticeable	recommend	Tuesday
height	occasion	reference	until
immediately	occurrence	responsible	usually
independent	opposite	rhythm	vacuum
jewelry	outrageous	schedule	Wednesday
judgment	parallel	scientific	weird
laboratory	performance	separate	woman
ledge	perseverance	sincerely	women
legendary	personality	spaghetti	wreckage
license	physically	strength	writer
loneliness	possess	success	writing
maintenance	precious	surprise	written
mathematics	prejudice	sympathy	zealous

Hint   **Using a Spelling Checker**

Most word processing programs have spelling and grammar tools that will alert you to some common errors. They will also suggest ways to correct them. Be careful, however, because these tools are not 100 percent accurate. For example, a spelling checker cannot differentiate between *your* and *you're*.

PRACTICE 12

Underline the correctly spelled words in parentheses.

EXAMPLE:

Many interest groups (campaine / <u>campaign</u>) to raise public awareness.

CHAPTER 24

1.   Ever since the (legendary / ledgendary) French actress Brigitte Bardot photographed herself with a baby harp seal in 1977, the Canadian seal hunt has been (aggresively / aggressively) debated. The sight of celebrities on ice floes protecting baby seals from being killed has become a (familar / familiar) scene. It has raised public (sympathie / sympathy) for the seals. Yet there are two (oposite / opposite) views in this debate.

2.   Animal rights activists claim that the seal hunt is cruel to animals and must be stopped (immediately / imediately). The seal hunt is (unnecesary / unnecessary) for the economy. People who rely on the (business / buisness)

can make their money elsewhere. For instance, activists are (encourageing / encouraging) the Canadian (goverment / government) to develop the northern region for ecotourism. Animal rights groups also (recommand / recommend) that (foriegn / foreign) countries ban seal product imports.

3.   According to the pro-sealing movement, animal welfare activists have greatly (exaggerated / exagerrated) the claim that sealing is inhumane. Moreover, sealers have a (responsibility / responsability) to support their families in a region where jobs are scarce. In addition, sealers also point out that it is (convenient / convienient) to accuse hunters of cruelty to animals simply because baby harp seals are cute.

4.   Clearly, each group will continue to influence the other's (jugement / judgment) about the seal hunt, and the seal hunt issue will remain a (dilemma / dillema).

 **Becoming a Better Speller**

These are some useful strategies to improve your spelling.

• In your spelling log, which could be in a journal, binder, or computer file, keep a record of words that you commonly misspell. (See Appendix 5 for more on spelling logs.)
• Use memory cards or flash cards to help you memorize difficult words.
• Write down the spelling of difficult words at least ten times to help you remember how to spell them.
• Always check a dictionary to verify the spelling of difficult words.

FINAL REVIEW

Underline and correct twenty spelling errors in the following selection.

EXAMPLE:

their
Historically, zoos have displayed <u>thier</u> collections of wild animals for public entertainment and profit.

1.   Since the begining of civilization, human beings have always enjoyed viewing animals. Originaly, wild animals were captured and displayed for the pleasure of the upper classes. By the early twentieth century, zoos were openned to the general public. Today, the role of zoos is a hotly debated subject in our soceity.

2.   Supporters of zoos argue that in the past two decades, zoos have tried to acheive different goals and objectives. Zoos in the Western world have spent millions of dollars creating truely natural enviroments for the animals. Furthermore, zoos are neccesary and educational. Zoo breeding programs have helped bring about a noticable increase in the population of alot of threatened species.

3.   Zoo opponents from countrys around the world beleive that zoos are imoral prisons for wild animals. A zoo's only function is to entertain the public and run a profitable buisness. Displaying animals in cages is cruel, unatural, and unethical. Furthermore, zoo opponents have questionned the validity of breeding statistics released by zoos. Animal Aid, an animal rights group in the United Kingdom, argues that only 2 percent of endangered animals are bred in zoos.

4.   Conservationist Gerald Durrell, who started the Jersey Zoological Park, has stated that a zoo is successfull if it can contribute to the conservation of forests and feilds. However, others think that zoos should be banned. Everyone should consider whether zoos are helpfull or harmfull.

The Writer's Room

Write about one of the following topics. After you finish writing, circle any words that you may have misspelled.

1. If you could live in a natural environment, what type of environment would you prefer: a forest, a seashore, a mountain, a desert, a lakefront, or a prairie? Explain your answer.

2. Examine this photo. What are some terms that come to mind? Some ideas might be *zoo*, *captivity*, or *conservation*. Define a term or expression that relates to this photo.

GRAMMAR LINK

Keep a list of words that you commonly misspell. See Appendix 5 for more about spelling logs.

✓ CHECKLIST: SPELLING RULES

When you edit your writing, ask yourself the next questions.

☐ Do I have any spelling errors? Check for errors in words that contain these elements:
   – an *ie* or *ei* combination
   – prefixes
   – suffixes

       species   *disappearing*
   Many ~~speices~~ of animals and plants are ~~dissappearing~~ from our planet.

☐ Do I repeat spelling errors that I have made in previous assignments? (Each time you write, check previous assignments for errors or consult your spelling log.)

CHAPTER 24

---

mywritinglab To check your progress in meeting this chapter's objectives, log in to **www.mywritinglab.com**, go to the **Study Plan** tab, click on **The Editing Handbook—Section 7 Word Use and Spelling** and choose **Spelling** from the list of subtopics. Read and view the resources in the **Review Materials** section, and then complete the **Recall, Apply,** and **Write** sets in the **Activities** section.

CHAPTER 25 Commonly Confused Words

Section Theme: **CREATURES LARGE AND SMALL**

LEARNING OBJECTIVE

I Commonly Confused Words (p. 353)

In this chapter, you will read about pet ownership and exotic animals.

(**Grammar Snapsh•t**)

Looking at Commonly Confused Words

In his book *Animal Wonderland*, Frank W. Lane examines experiments with animals. In this excerpt, commonly confused words are underlined.

> A feeding apparatus was installed in a cage whereby a pellet of food fell <u>through</u> a slot when a lever was pressed. Lever and slot <u>were</u> side by side. Three rats were placed one at a time in the cage, and soon each learned <u>to</u> use the lever. <u>Then</u> Mowrer put the lever on the side of the cage opposite the food slot, thus making it necessary for a rat to run from one end of the cage to the other for every <u>piece</u> of food. Again the rats learned, separately, how to obtain <u>their</u> food.

In this chapter, you will identify and use words that sound the same but have different spellings and meanings.

Commonly Confused Words

Some English words can sound the same but are spelled differently and have different meanings. For example, two commonly confused words are *for*, which is a preposition that means "in exchange," and *four*, which is the number. Dictionaries will give you the exact meaning of unfamiliar words.

Here is a list of some commonly confused words.

Commonly Confused Words

	Meaning	Examples
accept	to receive; to admit	Presently, the public <u>accepts</u> the need for wildlife preservation.
except	excluding; other than	Everyone in my family <u>except</u> my sister wants a pet.
affect	to influence	Pollution <u>affects</u> our environment in many ways.
effect	the result of something	Deforestation has bad <u>effects</u> on global climate.
aloud	spoken audibly; out loud	Please read the story <u>aloud</u> so others can hear you.
allowed	permitted	Tenants are not <u>allowed</u> to keep snakes.
been	past participle of the verb *be*	Joy Adamson has <u>been</u> a role model for conservationists.
being	present progressive form (the *-ing* form) of the verb *be*.	She was <u>being</u> very nice when she agreed to give a speech.
by	next to; on; before	Gerald Durell sat <u>by</u> the rocks to film the iguana. He hoped to finish filming <u>by</u> next year.
buy	to purchase	Many people <u>buy</u> exotic animals for pets.
complement	to add to; to complete	The book will <u>complement</u> the library's zoology collection.
compliment	to say something nice about someone or something	Ann Struthers receives many <u>compliments</u> for her book on snakes.

PRACTICE 1

Underline the appropriate word in each set of parentheses.

EXAMPLE:

Owners of exotic pets must (<u>accept</u> / except) responsibility for the behavior of these creatures.

1.   Many people (buy / by) exotic animals for pets. Stop (buy / by) some pet stores, and you will see monkeys, snakes, and wild cats. For example, a capuchin monkey is (been / being) displayed at our local pet shop. The monkey has (being / been) on display for three weeks. Evan, a good friend

of mine, wants to buy the monkey to (complement / compliment) his menagerie of exotic pets. Everyone, (accept / except) me, supports Evan's plan. I don't think that Evan would make a good monkey owner.

2.   Capuchin monkeys are tiny and appealing creatures, but they are difficult to care (for / four). Owners must (accept / except) a change in lifestyle because the monkeys require a great deal of attention. Capuchins bond with their owners and are badly (affected, effected) (buy, by) change. They can suffer negative (effects, affects) if the original owner decides to sell the animal.

3.   Certainly, people (compliment / complement) monkeys because the creatures are so cute and human-like. However, monkeys are expensive to house and feed. Those wanting to own monkeys must (accept / except) that they are making a serious long-term commitment. Perhaps people should not be (aloud / allowed) to own such animals.

Commonly Confused Words

CHAPTER 25

	Meaning	Examples
conscience	a personal sense of right or wrong	Poachers have no <u>conscience</u>.
conscious	to be aware; to be awake	The poacher was <u>conscious</u> of his crime.
considered	thought about; kept in mind; judged	Dian Fossey was <u>considered</u> a leader in her field. She never <u>considered</u> leaving Africa.
considerate	thoughtful; understanding; selfless	She was very <u>considerate</u> and patient with the gorillas.
die	to stop living or functioning	I wonder what will happen after I <u>die</u>.
dye	to color; a coloring compound	Those women <u>dye</u> their hair.
everyday	ordinary; common	Poaching is an <u>everyday</u> occurrence.
every day	during a single day; each day	Government officials search <u>every day</u> for poachers.
find	to locate	Biologists are trying to <u>find</u> the nesting grounds of parrots.
fine	of good quality; a penalty of money for a crime	A robin prepares a <u>fine</u> nest. Poachers must pay a <u>fine</u> when caught.
its	possessive case of the pronoun *it*	The baby elephant was separated from <u>its</u> herd.
it's	contraction for *it is*	<u>It's</u> known that elephants are very intelligent.
knew	past tense of *know*	We <u>knew</u> that the lioness had three cubs.
new	recent; unused	We used a <u>new</u> camera to film the cubs.
know	to have knowledge of	Photographers <u>know</u> that the public loves pictures of animals.
no	a negative	I have <u>no</u> photos of Bengal tigers.

PRACTICE 2

Underline the appropriate word in each set of parentheses.

EXAMPLE:

(<u>Every day</u> / Everyday), people do extreme things to their pets.

1.   Many people love their pets, but some spoil their animals. New York
pet owners can (fine / find) designer jackets for their dogs. With no
(conscience / conscious), some citizens walk past the unemployed to go buy
Louis Vuitton carriers for their Chihuahuas. Did you (no / know) that in
Naples, Florida, dog owners can take their pooches to a therapist? At Elite
Pet Haven in New Jersey, a dog can engage in (fine / find) dining and then
have (its / it's) back massaged. And of course, when pets (die / dye), they
can be buried in private pet cemeteries.

2.   In dog salons, (new / knew) grooming trends are an (everyday / every
day) occurrence. In some dog competitions, (it's / its) (considerate /
considered) normal for dogs to have colored fur. However, in the town of
Boulder, Colorado, pet owners are not (aloud / allowed) to color their pets.
Salon owner Joy Douglas paid a $1,000 (fine / find) for using beet juice to
(die / dye) her poodle pink. Officials want pet owners to be (conscious /
conscience) of the risks that (dye / die) poses to animals.

3.   Basically, people should be gentle and (considered / considerate) pet
owners. But they should also remember that (no / know) animal needs
luxuries.

CHAPTER 25

Commonly Confused Words

	Meaning	**Examples**
lose	to misplace or forfeit something	If we <u>lose</u> a species to extinction, we will <u>lose</u> a part of our heritage.
loose	too big or too baggy; not fixed	They wear <u>loose</u> clothing at work.
loss	a decrease in an amount; a serious blow	The <u>loss</u> of forests is a serious problem.
past	previous time	In the <u>past</u>, people shot big game for fun.
passed	accepted or sanctioned; past tense of *to pass*	Recently, governments have <u>passed</u> laws forbidding the killing of endangered species.

	Meaning	**Examples**
peace	calmness; an end to violence	I feel a sense of <u>peace</u> in the wilderness.
piece	a part of something else	I found a <u>piece</u> of deer antler in the woods.
personal	private	My professor showed us her <u>personal</u> collection of snake photographs.
personnel	employees; staff	The World Wildlife Fund hires a lot of <u>personnel</u>.
principal	main; director of a school	The <u>principal</u> researcher on snakes is Dr. Alain Leduc.
principle	rule; standard	I am studying the <u>principles</u> of ethical research techniques.
		Stealing is against my <u>principles</u>.

PRACTICE 3

Commonly confused words are underlined. Correct twelve word errors. If the word is correct, write C above it.

EXAMPLE:

$$\text{piece}$$
Sometimes, a snake can regrow its tail if a <u>peace</u> of it breaks off.

1.   In the <u>past</u>, marine parks bought dolphins that had been captured in the wild. Since 1993, many laws have been <u>past</u> to protect dolphins. Today, American parks rely on captive breeding to replenish their stocks. They cannot <u>except</u> wild dolphins. But overseas, there is a booming "swimming with the dolphins" industry, and the rules are much <u>loser</u>.

2.   Christopher Porter, a former dolphin trainer, owns a <u>peace</u> of property in the Solomon Islands. The dolphin trade is his <u>principle</u> source of income. He captures wild dolphins and then sells them to resorts. Porter says that he has strong <u>principals</u> and would never hurt the mammals. However, he may <u>loose</u> a percentage of his stock. Animals can <u>dye</u> from stress during transportation. Also, Porter can suffer a <u>lost</u> if the dolphins become ill.

3.   Many tourists do not <u>know</u> or care about the controversy. For example, Kaya Wilson had a <u>personnel</u> experience with dolphins. In 2008, she swam with dolphins in Mexico. The resort <u>personnel</u> encouraged her to gently touch the mammals. She went into the water wearing a <u>lose</u> top over her bathing suit, and a dolphin pulled at her shirt. Kaya says that she felt happy and at <u>piece</u> with the dolphins.

Commonly Confused Words

	Meaning	Example
quiet	silent	It was quiet in the woods.
quite	very	The herd was moving quite fast.
quit	stop	The zoo director quit after receiving a bad report.
sit	to seat oneself	I will sit on this rock to watch the birds.
set	to put or place down	He set his book about birds on the grass.
taught	past tense of *to teach*	Dr. Zavitz taught a class on sharks.
thought	past tense of *to think*	His students thought that he was a good teacher.
than	word used in comparisons	Whales are larger than dolphins.
then	at a particular time; after a specific time	The grizzly entered the river, and then it caught some salmon.
that	word used to introduce a clause	Some people do not realize that grizzlies are extremely dangerous.
their	possessive form of *they*	Anita and Ram went to see their favorite documentary on bird migration.
there	a place; something that exists	There are many birds in the park. The students went there by bus.
they're	contraction of *they are*	They're both very interested in falcons.

PRACTICE 4

Underline the appropriate word in each set of parentheses.

EXAMPLE:

(There / Their) are many types of exotic birds.

1. One hundred years ago, parrots were (quiet / quite) common in tropical
    countries. Today, (there / their / they're) are about 350 different types of
    parrots, each with a distinct size and appearance. With (there / their /
    they're) beautiful colors, parrots have become one of the most sought-after
    exotic animals.

2. Some people think (than / then / that) parrots are easy to maintain. In
    fact, parrots are more difficult to care for (than / then / that) many other
    bird species. For one thing, some types of parrots love to vocalize, so
    (there / their / they're) not ideal for owners who want peace and (quite /
    quiet). Parrots are social creatures (than / then / that) mate for life, and
    they become very attached to (there / their) owners. They do not like to
    (sit / set) in one place for long periods of time. Instead, (there / their /

they're) happiest when being caressed or permitted to fly around a room. When owners ignore parrots, the birds can develop (quiet / quite) strange behavior. For instance, a neglected parrot might pull out (its / it's) own feathers.

3.   In the (past / passed), people (taught / thought) that parrots simply mimicked human sounds. In fact, recent research has shown (than / then / that) parrots are capable of complex thinking. Irene Pepperberg began studying African gray parrots thirty years ago. (Than / Then / That), after many experiments, she published articles about them. She (taught / thought) a parrot named Alex to recognize about one hundred objects. Nowadays, gray parrots are (considered, considerate) the most intelligent bird species.

Commonly Confused Words

	Meaning	Examples
through	in one side and out the other; finished	The monkeys climbed through the trees. Although they were still active, we were through for the day.
threw	past tense of *throw*	The monkeys threw fruit down from the tree.
thorough	complete	The biologist did a thorough investigation of monkey behavior.
to	indicates direction or movement; part of an infinitive	I want to go to Africa.
too	*very* or *also*	Kenya is too hot in the summer. It is hot in Somalia, too.
two	the number after one	Africa and the Amazon are two places that intrigue me.
write	to draw symbols that represent words	I write about conservation issues for the newspaper.
right	correct; the opposite of *left*	Is this the right way to go to the village? The right turn signal of the jeep does not work.
where	question word indicating location	Where did the zoo keep the gorillas?
were	past tense of *be*	The gorillas were in the enclosure.
we're	contraction of *we are*	We're going to see a film about gorillas.
who's	contraction of *who is*	Makiko, who's a friend of mine, is doing research on lemurs.
whose	pronoun showing ownership	Animals whose habitat is disappearing need to be protected.
you're	contraction of *you are*	You're going on the field trip, aren't you?
your	possessive adjective	Your sister went to the pet store.

PRACTICE 5

In the next sentences, write one of the words in parentheses in each blank.

EXAMPLE:

(We're / Were) __*We're*__ going to watch a presentation about primates.

1.   (we're / were / where) _____ learning a lot about chimpanzee
     intelligence. In Illinois, research scientists work with Bonono chimps. Ten
     years ago, the animals _____ put into a room _____ there
     were several computers. The chimps _____ able to use the machines
     to talk to humans.

2.   (to, two, too) In a 1960 experiment, _____ scientists wanted
     _____ communicate with chimps. Allen and Beatrice Gardner knew
     that chimps would not be able _____ speak because their vocal
     cords are _____ high and _____ short. They decided
     _____ teach a chimp American Sign Language.

3.   (threw, through, thorough) We sat outside a lab and watched spider
     monkeys _____ a window. The zoologist _____ some food
     behind a door. The monkeys smelled the food and did a _____
     search of their cage. Then one monkey noticed the door and reached
     _____ it to pick up the food. When the experiment was
     _____, the zoologist rewarded the monkeys with more
     food.

4.   (right / write) We plan to _____ an article about the monkey
     experiment. At the _____ time, we will present our paper to our
     instructor.

5.   (who's / whose) A zoologist _____ profession involves close
     contact with various species studies animal habitats. A friend of
     ours, _____ an excellent zoologist, will receive government
     funding.

6.   (your / you're) _____ welcome to come with us to a presentation.
     You can bring _____ friend with you. If _____ late, the
     presentation will start without you.

FINAL REVIEW

Underline and correct fifteen errors in word choice.

EXAMPLE:

through
The parrot escaped <u>thorough</u> the window.

1.   Some states ban the ownership of exotic pets. In other states,
      people are aloud to buy lions, monkeys, and other exotic creatures.
      Ownership of exotic animals has become a passionately debated
      subject.

2.   Animal activists argue than it is cruel to capture and cage exotic
      animals. Furthermore, such animals can have diseases that are
      considerate dangerous for humans. Additionally, exotic animals are
      often released into the wild when there owners become tired of them.
      For example, Thomas Sawland, whose a fisherman, found the Chinese
      snakehead fish thriving in some lakes and killing native fish species.
      Unfortunately, many owners of exotic pets do not really no how to take
      care of their animals because they have never been thought. For
      example, 90 percent of pet snakes dye within the first year of captivity
      because they have been mistreated.

3.   Owners of exotic pets state that its perfectly reasonable to keep such
      animals. Proponents say that accept for the occasional case, most exotic
      pet owners are very responsible and have strong principals. Owners with
      a strong conscious would never neglect their pets. Moreover, many
      business owners would loose their income if the sale of exotic pets were
      prohibited. Also, everyday some people abuse dogs and cats, but few
      people pressure the government to ban the ownership of such pets.

4.   More states may past laws that limit the exotic animal market. Some
      people will support the legislation, and others will oppose it.

The Writer's Room

Write about one of the following topics. After you finish writing, proofread your paragraph for spelling or word-choice errors.

1. What are some reasons that people own pets? How can pet ownership affect a person's life? Write about the causes or effects of owning pets.

2. Would you ever own an exotic pet such as a snake, an alligator, or a tiger? Explain why or why not.

 CHECKLIST: COMMONLY CONFUSED WORDS

When you edit your writing, ask yourself whether you have used the correct words. Check for errors with commonly confused words.

My friend Patricia, ~~whose~~ *who's* a veterinarian, believes ~~than~~ *that* pet owners

should take courses on how to take care of ~~they're~~ *their* pets.

READING LINK

Creatures Large and Small
To read more about zoology, see the following essay:

"The Zoo Life" by Yann Martel
    (page 434)
"Is it Love or a Trick?" by Jon Katz
    (page 436)

The Writers' Circle   **Collaborative Activity**

Work with a partner. You will have two minutes to come up with as many homonyms as possible. A homonym is a word that sounds exactly like another word, but the spelling and meaning differ. Write your homonyms beside each word.

EXAMPLE: write   *right*

hair	_____	pale	_____	flower	_____
cents	_____	nose	_____	missed	_____
wait	_____	medal	_____	patience	_____
ate	_____	whale	_____	whether	_____
bare	_____	foul	_____	cite	_____
disgust	_____	cruise	_____	waste	_____
gorilla	_____	pear	_____	witch	_____

CHAPTER 25

PEARSON **mywritinglab** To check your progress in meeting this chapter's objectives, log in to **www.mywritinglab.com**, go to the **Study Plan** tab, click on **The Editing Handbook—Section 7 Word Use and Spelling** and choose **Commonly Confused Words** from the list of subtopics. Read and view the resources in the **Review Materials** section, and then complete the **Recall, Apply,** and **Write** sets in the **Activities** section.

CHAPTER 26 Commas

Section Theme: **THE BUSINESS WORLD**

In this chapter, you will read about business-related topics, including job searching and unusual jobs.

Grammar Snapshot

Looking at Commas

Jeff Kemp is a former NFL quarterback. In his article "Sports and Life: Lessons to Be Learned," Kemp narrates his experiences as a professional athlete. Notice the use of commas in this excerpt from his article.

> In 1988, I was playing for the Seattle Seahawks against my old team, the 49ers, when I learned firsthand that there are two competing value systems. I wasn't bitter that my old team had traded me, but I wanted to beat them all the same. Quarterback Dave Krieg had been injured, and I was to start.

In this chapter, you will learn how to use commas correctly.

3/14/2011

Understanding Commas

A **comma (,)** is a punctuation mark that helps keep distinct ideas separate. Commas are especially important in series, after introductory words and phrases, around interrupting words and phrases, and in compound and complex sentences.

Some jobs, especially those in the service industry, pay minimum wage.

Commas in a Series

Use a comma to separate items in a series of three or more items. Remember to put a comma before the final *and* or *or.*

item 1	,	item 2	,	and or	item 3

Series of nouns: The conference will be in Dallas, Houston, Galveston, or Austin.

Series of verbs: During the conference, guests will eat, drink, and network.

Series of phrases: She dressed well, kept her head up, and maintained eye contact.

comma, comma, and

Hint **Punctuating a Series**

In a series of three or more items, do not place a comma after the last item in the series (unless the series is part of an interrupting phrase).

His mother, father, and sister were at the ceremony.

Do not use commas to separate items if each item is joined by *and* or *or.*

✱ The audience clapped <u>and</u> cheered <u>and</u> stood up after the speech. *example* ✱

PRACTICE I

Each sentence contains a series of items. Add the missing commas.

EXAMPLE:

John L. Holland, a psychology professor from Johns Hopkins University, has taught students, done research, and published books.

1. According to John L. Holland, the six basic types of jobs include realistic jobs, conventional jobs, investigative jobs, artistic jobs, social jobs, and leadership jobs.

2. When trying to choose a career, you should try a variety of jobs, work in different places, and volunteer for various tasks.

3. Realistic jobs involve working with tools large machines or other types of equipment.

4. People who work with tools or machines are usually strong competitive and physically healthy.

5. Bank tellers secretaries office managers and accountants have conventional jobs.

6. People who describe themselves as outgoing cooperative helpful and responsible have social jobs.

7. Eric Townsend wants to be a teacher nurse or social worker.

8. Investigative workers often do market surveys develop military strategies or tackle economic problems.

9. Adela Sanchez is energetic self-confident and ambitious.

10. Sanchez hopes to get a leadership job in sales politics or business.

Commas After Introductory Words and Phrases

Place a comma after an **introductory word**. The word could be an interjection such as *yes* or *no*, an adverb such as *usually*, or a transitional word such as *therefore*.

| Introductory word(s) | , | sentence | . |

Yes, I will help you finish the project.   *NO,*

Honestly, you should reconsider your promise.

However, the job includes a lot of overtime.

Introductory phrases of two or more words should be set off with a comma. The phrase could be a transitional expression such as *of course* or a prepositional phrase such as *in the morning*.

As a matter of fact, the manager explained the new policy.

In the middle of the meeting, Nancy decided to leave.

After his speech, the employees asked questions.

CHAPTER 26

PRACTICE 2

Underline the introductory word or phrase in each sentence. Add fifteen missing commas.

EXAMPLE:

Honestly, interviews can be very stressful.

1. Before, a job interview, you should do certain tasks. After, contacting the company, take some time to prepare for the interview. First, of all, do some research about the company. As soon as possible, you could go on the Internet and find out about the company's performance. Certainly, you can impress the hiring committee if you appear knowledgeable about the business.

2. Undoubtedly, talking to new people adds to the stress of a job interview. Nonetheless, you can do well if you are confident. In fact, try to make direct eye contact with the interviewer. After a difficult question, take the time you need to think about it. Of course, it is important to answer questions honestly. However, try to find a positive spin. For example, the interviewer may ask why you left a previous job. At that moment, do not criticize your former boss or complain about your former job. Instead, simply say that you needed new challenges. Clearly, it is important to be positive.

Commas Around Interrupting Words and Phrases

Interrupting words or phrases appear in the middle of sentences. Such interrupters are often asides that break the sentence's flow but do not really affect the meaning.

Noun	,	interrupting word(s)	,	rest of sentence.

My co-worker, for example, has never taken a sick day.
Kyle, frankly, should never drink during business lunches.
The company, in the middle of an economic boom, went bankrupt!

Using Commas with Appositives

An appositive comes before or after a noun or pronoun and adds further information about the noun or pronoun. The appositive can appear at the beginning, in the middle, or at the end of the sentence. Set off appositives with commas.

beginning
An ambitious man, Donald has done well in real estate.

middle
Cancun, a coastal city, depends on tourism.

end
The hotel is next to Alicia's, a local restaurant.

CHAPTER 26

PRACTICE 3

Underline any interrupting phrases and add commas where needed to the following sentences.

EXAMPLE:

Some young entrepreneurs, <u>for instance</u>, are very successful. _____

1. Young entrepreneurs, showing ingenuity, continue to develop interesting products. _____

2. Mark Zuckerberg, for example, was a young college student when he and his friends developed Facebook. _____

3. Facebook, a social Internet site, was first aimed at Harvard undergraduates. _____

4. Evan Williams, another young entrepreneur, created one of the first Web applications for blogs. _____

5. Google bought Williams's Web site, Blogger.com, in 2003. _____

6. YouTube, one of the fastest growing Web sites, was bought by Google in 2006. _____

7. Three young friends, former PayPal employees, created this popular site. _____

8. Risk takers, with insight and skill, are finding creative ways to profit from the Internet. _____

PRACTICE 4 REVIEW

Add ten missing commas to the following passages.

EXAMPLE:

Life coaches, funeral directors, and square dance callers are people who have out-of-the-ordinary careers.

1. Many people have interesting, fulfilling and unique jobs. Newton Proust is a freelance greeting card writer. He writes verses for birthday cards graduation cards, and sympathy cards. He feels that the sentiments expressed in a greeting card bring people together. To express accurate emotions Mr. Proust studies the latest cultural trends. In fact he constantly reads magazines, comic strips and pulp fiction to acquire knowledge of what people are thinking and feeling.

2.   Angelica Pedersen a master coffee taster, travels to coffee-producing regions around the world. She works for Blue Coffee a small business. However the company is a supplier to some of the biggest coffee retailers in North America. Ms. Pedersen, an experienced professional must develop the perfect blend of coffee for her clients. She smells and tastes about three hundred cups of coffee per day. Clearly she loves her job and would not consider doing anything else.

Commas in Compound Sentences

A **compound sentence** contains two or more complete sentences joined by a coordinating conjunction (*for, and, nor, but, or, yet, so*).

Sentence	, and	sentence.

The job is interesting, **and** the pay is decent.

The job requires fluency in Spanish, **so** maybe I will be hired.

Michael works as a bank teller, **but** he is looking for a better position.

 **Hint**   **Commas and Coordinators**

You do not always have to put a comma before coordinating conjunctions such as *and, but,* or *or*. To ensure that a sentence is truly compound, cover the conjunction with your finger and read the two parts of the sentence.

• If each part of the sentence contains a complete idea, then you need to add a comma.

   Comma: Anna does marketing surveys**,** and she sells products.

• If one part is incomplete, then no comma is necessary.

   No Comma: Anna does marketing surveys and sells products.

PRACTICE 5

Add the missing commas to the next compound sentences.

EXAMPLE:

I like to travel, so I am applying for a job on a cruise ship.

1. My brother likes nature, so he always looks for outdoor jobs.

2. He is very good at sports, and he will be working as a group leader at a wilderness camp.

3. A group leader does not need experience, but he or she has to have some wilderness survival skills.

4. I have also worked in adventure camps, for I like challenging jobs.

CHAPTER 26

PRACTICE 6 REVIEW

Add six missing commas to the following letter.

EXAMPLE:

I like to travel ,^ so I volunteer overseas.

Hi Leeann,

I know I haven't written in a long time but I have been busy getting used to my daily life here. As you know, I volunteer with the Human Connections Foundation. Last week I arrived in Honduras. I was met by Fredo my supervisor. We traveled to the village together. After a couple of days of training, I started work on the project. The volunteers build houses, install water pumps and repair roads. My job actually, is to dig holes for the pumps. I start work very early so I usually take a siesta in the afternoon. I will send you some photos and videos in a couple of days.

Cheers,
Antonio

Commas in Complex Sentences

A **complex sentence** contains one or more dependent clauses (or incomplete ideas). When a **subordinating conjunction**—a word such as *because*, *although*, or *unless*—is added to a clause, it makes the clause dependent.

        dependent clause   independent clause
When opportunity knocks ,^ you should embrace it.

Use a Comma After a Dependent Clause

If a sentence begins with a dependent clause, place a comma after the clause. Remember that a dependent clause has a subject and a verb, but it cannot stand alone. When the subordinating conjunction comes in the middle of the sentence, it is not necessary to use a comma.

Dependent clause	**,**	main clause.

Comma: Because she loves helping people ,^ she is studying nursing.

Main clause	**dependent clause.**

No comma: She is studying nursing because she loves helping people.

PRACTICE 7

Edit the following sentences by adding or deleting commas. If a sentence is correct, write *C* in the blank.

EXAMPLE:

Before she went to the interview, Ellen removed her eyebrow ring. _____

1. Because first impressions count, it is important to dress well for an interview. *C*

2. Before you leave the house, review your wardrobe. _____

3. Although your current boss may accept casual clothing, your future boss may object. *C*

4. Monica Zacharias wants to work as a restaurant manager, because she is ambitious. _____

5. Although she loves her tattoos, she will cover them with clothing during the interview. _____

6. After she gets the job, Zacharias will dress to show her personality. _____

7. When Clayton Townsend wore a T-shirt and baggy pants to the interview, he was not hired. _____

8. Because Townsend wanted to be hired, he should have tried to make a better impression. *C*

9. After she left her job as a personnel director, Amy Rowen started an employment consulting business. _____

10. According to Rowen, unless job applicants want to work in an artistic milieu, they should wear conservative clothing to interviews. _____

Use Commas with Nonrestrictive Clauses

Clauses beginning with *who*, *that*, and *which* can be restrictive or nonrestrictive. A **restrictive clause** contains essential information about the subject. Do not place commas around restrictive clauses.

No commas: The woman <u>who invented the windshield wiper</u> never became wealthy.

(The clause is essential to understand the sentence.)

A **nonrestrictive clause** gives nonessential information. In such sentences, the clause gives additional information about the noun, but it does not restrict or define the noun. Place commas around nonrestrictive clauses.

Commas: The restaurant, which is on Labelle Boulevard, has excellent seafood.

(The clause contains extra information. If you removed it, the sentence would still have a clear meaning.)

 **Hint** **Using *Which, That,* and *Who***

which
Use commas to set off clauses that begin with *which*.

Apple Computer, **which** started in 1976, was co-founded by Steve Wozniak and Steve Jobs.

that
Do not use commas to set off clauses that begin with *that*.

One product **that** changed the world was the personal computer.

who
When a clause begins with *who*, you may or may not need a comma. If the clause contains nonessential information, put commas around it. If the clause is essential to the meaning of the sentence, then it does not require commas.

Essential: The man **who** employs me uses Apple computers.

Not Essential: Steve Jobs, **who** has four children, is a billionaire.

PRACTICE 8

Underline the clause in each sentence that begins with *who, which,* or *that*. Add commas if necessary.

EXAMPLE:

The sea captain who was hijacked by pirates appeared in the news.

1. Jobs that are interesting are often the subject of news articles.

2. Ranvir Shah, who likes to travel, is the captain of a merchant ship.

3. His ship which is named *Prospector*, is a medium-sized cargo vessel.

4. The ship, which carries dry goods, often sails near the Horn of Africa.

5. The vessel that Shah sails has been a target of pirates.

6. In 2008, over sixty ships that were near the Somali coast were hijacked.

7. Pirates who plunder the waters off the Horn of Africa are considered to be the most dangerous in the world.

8. Last year, an experience that Shah had was memorable.

9. Somali pirates who were in small boats tried to capture Shah's vessel.

10. Only the crew members who had weapons fought with the pirates.

Commas in Business Letters

When you write or type formal correspondence, ensure that you use commas correctly in all parts of the letter.

Addresses

In the address at the top of a business letter, put a comma between these elements.

- The street and apartment number
- The city and state or country

Do not put a comma before the zip code.

> Anita Buchinsky
>
> XYZ Company
>
> 11 Maple Lane, Suite 450
>
> Brownfield, Texas 79316

If you include an address inside a complete sentence, use commas to separate the street address from the city as well as the city from the state or country. If you include only the street address, do not put a comma after it.

Commas: The building at 1600 Pennsylvania Avenue, Washington, D.C., is called the White House.

No comma: The building at 1600 Pennsylvania Avenue is called the White House.

Dates

In the date at the top of the letter, put a comma between the full date and the year. If you write just the month and the year, then no comma is necessary.

> January 28, 2011   January 2011

If you include a date inside a complete sentence, separate the elements of the date with commas.

> We flew to Dallas on Friday, March 14, 2010.

 **Writing Numbers**

In business letters, do not write ordinals, which are numbers such as *first* (1st), *second* (2nd), *third* (3rd), and *fourth* (4th). Instead, write just the number *1, 2, 3, 4,* and so on.

> May 13, 2009   September 25, 1961

Salutations

Salutations are formal letter greetings. The form "To Whom It May Concern" is no longer used regularly. The best way to address someone is to use the recipient's name followed by a comma.

Dear Ms. Cheng,   Dear Mrs. Kulkarni,   Dear Sir or Madam,

Dear Miss Kim,   Dear Mr. Copely,   Dear Claims Department,

Complimentary Closings

Capitalize the first word of a complimentary closing, and place a comma after the closing. Here are some formal complimentary closings.

Respectfully,   Sincerely,   Yours truly,

Respectfully yours,   Yours sincerely,   Many thanks,

PRACTICE 9

Add eight missing commas to the following business letter.

Amanda Sitlali
33 Green Avenue
Las Vegas, NV 89101

September 4, 2010

Elwood River Rafting
1771 Center Street
Redwood Falls, MN 56283

Dear Mr. Elwood,

On Tuesday August 2, 2010, I went on a river rafting expedition with your company. When I returned home, I realized that I had lost a bracelet. It may have dropped inside the raft. The bracelet is made of gold, and it has great sentimental value.

If you have found it, please contact my parents. They live at 34 Reed Avenue, Redwood Falls. Their phone number is 309-555-3933.

Yours truly,

Amanda Sitlali

Amanda Sitlali

FINAL REVIEW

Edit the following essay by adding or removing commas. There are twelve missing commas and three unnecessary commas.

EXAMPLE:

Many actors, musicians, and artists hire personal coaches.

1.   Last month Hanna Brandon hired a life coach. She wanted to make changes in her life. After graduating from college Hanna worked as a social worker but she quit her job last year. Since then Hanna has been working with Bram Connor her life coach, to help her realize her aims.

2.   Connor, who has been a life coach since April 1 2006, works for a company called Ready, Set, Go. His firm, which is a respected organization has many clients. The company has offices in Houston, Boston and Fort Lauderdale. Connor works with clients to set personal, business or career objectives. According to Connor clients want help to clarify goals, to make a plan to achieve those goals, and to overcome any obstacles in their way. People, who have hired Connor claim to be very satisfied with his advice.

3.   A life coach initially assesses the client through a series of tests. The tests, that Connor uses help him to understand his client's personality. Each week, Connor gives Hanna homework. The assignment, for example may require Hanna to compare her future goals to her present reality. Indeed Hanna is getting closer to her target, because the homework aids her to take practical steps toward her objectives.

The Writer's Room

Write about one of the following topics. After you finish writing, make sure that you have used commas correctly.

1. Have you, or someone you know, ever had an interesting or unusual job? Describe the job.

2. What are some types of Facebook users?

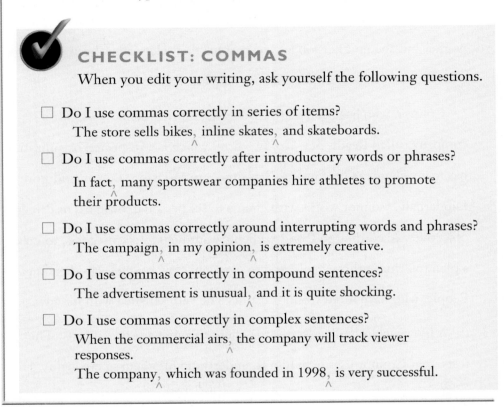

✔ CHECKLIST: COMMAS

When you edit your writing, ask yourself the following questions.

☐ Do I use commas correctly in series of items?
The store sells bikes, inline skates, and skateboards.

☐ Do I use commas correctly after introductory words or phrases?
In fact, many sportswear companies hire athletes to promote their products.

☐ Do I use commas correctly around interrupting words and phrases?
The campaign, in my opinion, is extremely creative.

☐ Do I use commas correctly in compound sentences?
The advertisement is unusual, and it is quite shocking.

☐ Do I use commas correctly in complex sentences?
When the commercial airs, the company will track viewer responses.
The company, which was founded in 1998, is very successful.

mywritinglab To check your progress in meeting this chapter's objectives, log in to **www.mywritinglab.com**, go to the **Study Plan** tab, click on **The Editing Handbook—Section 8 Punctuation and Mechanics** and choose **Comma Usage** from the list of subtopics. Read and view the resources in the **Review Materials** section, and then complete the **Recall, Apply,** and **Write** sets in the **Activities** section.

The Apostrophe

CHAPTER 27

Section Theme: **THE BUSINESS WORLD**

LEARNING OBJECTIVES

1 Understanding Apostrophes (p. 376)
2 Using Apostrophes in Contractions (p. 376)
3 Using Apostrophes to Show Ownership (p. 379)
4 Using Apostrophes in Expressions of Time (p. 381)

In this chapter, you will read about controversies in the business world.

Grammar Snapshot

Looking at Apostrophes

This excerpt is taken from the article "How to Handle Conflict" by P. Gregory Smith. Review the underlined words.

> "I <u>don't</u> mind doing my fair share of the dirty jobs around here," Ramon continued, "but I feel like <u>I'm</u> getting a lot more mop time than anyone else." By using a statement that began with "I," Ramon was able to state his feelings honestly, without accusing Mr. Jefferson. "I" statements usually <u>can't</u> be considered false or cause an argument because <u>they're</u> a simple statement of feelings.

In this chapter, you will learn to use apostrophes correctly.

3/4/11 (handwritten in margin)

Understanding Apostrophes

An **apostrophe** (') is a punctuation mark. It shows that two words have been contracted into one word, or it shows ownership.

> **Richard's** business is new, but **it's** growing.

Using Apostrophes in Contractions

A **contraction** is two words joined into one. When you contract two words, the apostrophe generally indicates the location of the omitted letter(s).

> is + not = isn't   I + am = I'm

Hint   **Formal Writing**

Do not use contractions when you write a formal academic paper. For example, in a literary analysis, you would not use contractions.

Common Contractions

There are two types of common contractions. You can join a verb with *not;* you can also join a subject and a verb.

(handwritten in margin) Dallas' teams — shows possession

(handwritten in margin) Joneses' grandfather

Verb + *not*

When a verb joins with *not*, the apostrophe replaces the letter *o* in *not*.

Common Contractions

is + not = isn't	did + not = didn't
are + not = aren't	has + not = hasn't
was + not = wasn't	have + not = haven't
were + not = weren't	must not = mustn't
could + not = couldn't	should + not = shouldn't
do + not = don't	can + not = can't
does + not = doesn't	would + not = wouldn't

Exceptions: am + not cannot be contracted. The contraction for *I am not* is *I'm not;* will + not = won't

PRACTICE I

Write contractions for the underlined words in the next sentences.

EXAMPLE:

don't

Many American companies <u>do not</u> think twice about outsourcing to other countries.

(handwritten in margin) virtual library
user: student
PW: cleveland

CHAPTER 27

1. If you plan to get information about a credit card, chances are great that you <u>will not</u> speak to an American customer service representative.

2. It <u>is not</u> unusual to speak with a person from another part of the world.

3. You <u>would not</u> even know that he or she <u>is not</u> an American.

4. He or she <u>does not</u> have an accent when speaking English.

5. Also, you <u>should not</u> be surprised that the person at the call center is very familiar with American culture.

6. Companies outsource because they <u>do not</u> have to pay high salaries to workers in other nations.

Subject + Verb

When you join a subject and a verb, you must remove one or more letters to form the contraction.

Contractions with *be*
I + am = I'm
he + is = he's
it + is = it's
she + is = she's
they + are = they're
we + are = we're
you + are = you're
who + is = who's

Contractions with *will*
I + will = I'll
he + will = he'll
it + will = it'll
she + will = she'll
they + will = they'll
we + will = we'll
you + will = you'll
who + will = who'll

Contractions with *have*
I + have = I've
he + has = he's
it + has = it's
she + has = she's
they + have = they've
we + have = we've
you + have = you've
who + has = who's

Contractions with *had or would*
I + had *or* would = I'd
he + had *or* would = he'd
it + had *or* would = it'd
she + had *or* would = she'd
they + had *or* would = they'd
we + had *or* would = we'd
you + had *or* would = you'd
who + had *or* would = who'd

Exception: Do not contract a subject with the past tense of *be*. For example, do not contract *he + was* or *they + were*.

                                                    she was
When you asked her about the product, ~~she's~~ not helpful.

                                            They were
The sales staff were in a meeting. ~~They're~~ discussing new products.

Hint   **Contractions with Proper Nouns**

You can contract a proper noun with the verb *be* or *have*.

Shania is   *Deiter has*
Shania's late for work. **Deiter's** been waiting for her since 9:00 a.m.

PRACTICE 2

Add the missing apostrophes to the underlined words in this selection.

EXAMPLE:

I've
Ive been reading about the Swiss banking scandal.

1.   Mark Schyler's great grandparents perished in the Holocaust. These days, <u>Mark</u> tracing their financial records in Switzerland. When he uncovers enough information, <u>hell</u> forward it to the authorities. <u>Hed</u> like to see the property of his great grandparents restored to his family.

2.   In the 1930s, the Nazis started to persecute German Jews, so they deposited their money in Swiss banks. Jews <u>whod</u> try to escape to Switzerland were turned away. After the war, Jewish survivors knew about family deposits in Swiss banks. Swiss bankers were secretive and required death certificates. The victims, however, had died in concentration camps. <u>Theyd</u> left no death or bank records.

3.   The U.S. government pressured Swiss banks for information. The Swiss government agreed to help resolve the issue. <u>Its</u> already released some bank details. Many people have found documents concerning family property. <u>Theyve</u> already received some money. Mark Schyler is one person <u>whos</u> working hard to uncover facts about his family so that he can reclaim his great grandparents' legacy.

CHAPTER 27

 **Hint**   **Contractions with Two Meanings**

Sometimes one contraction can have two different meanings.

> **I'd** = I had *or* I would   **he's** = he is *or* he has

When you read, you can usually figure out the meaning of the contraction by looking at the words in context.

> *He is*   *He has*
> **He's** starting up a new company. **He's** had three successful businesses.

PRACTICE 3

Look at each underlined contraction, and then write out the complete word.

EXAMPLE:

He'd like to hire more people.   *He would* _____

1. Hanif's a chocolatier.   _____

2. He's been working at his present job for three years.   _____

3. His company's been providing chocolate fountains
    to catering services.   _____

4. He'd like to expand the business.   _____

5. When we met last year, I was impressed because
    I'd never seen such a hardworking person before.   _____

Using Apostrophes to Show Ownership

Possession means that someone or something owns something else. Nouns and indefinite pronouns such as *anyone* and *everyone* use an apostrophe to show ownership.

> the office of the businessman = the businessman's office

Singular Nouns: To show possession of singular nouns, add -'s to the end of the singular noun.

> **Sheila's** mother works as a dispatcher.

> **Everyone's** computer was upgraded.

Even if the noun ends in *s*, you must still add -'s.

> **Dennis's** dad helped him find a job.

> My **boss's** assistant arranges her schedule.

Plural Nouns: To show possession when a plural noun ends in *s*, add just an apostrophe.

> Many **employees'** savings are in pension plans.

> **Taxi drivers'** licenses are regulated.

Add -'s to irregular plural nouns to indicate ownership.

> That **men's** magazine is very successful.

> The **children's** toy department is on the main floor.

Compound Nouns: When two people have joint ownership, add the apostrophe to the second name only.

> joint ownership
> Mason and **Muhammad's** restaurant is successful.
> (They share ownership of a restaurant.)

When two people have separate ownership, add apostrophes to both names.

> separate ownership
> **Mason's** and **Muhammad's** cars are parked in the garage.
> (They each own a car.)

PRACTICE 4

Write the possessive forms using apostrophes.

EXAMPLE:

the office of Nicolas   *Nicolas's office*

1. the business partner of Charles   _____
2. the committee of the ladies   _____
3. the company of Matt and Harrison   _____
4. the promotion of the manager   _____
5. the desks of Marcia and Lewis   _____
6. the building of the company   _____
7. the club of the women   _____
8. the accounting book of Dolores   _____
9. the workforce of China   _____
10. the lawyers of the Smiths   _____

PRACTICE 5

Correct nine errors in possessive forms.

EXAMPLE:

    company's
The ~~companys~~ profits are very high this year.

1.   Nike has become synonymous with Americas corporate success.

   Nikes' beginnings are very interesting. The business started from the

   back of Phil Knights car in the early 1960s. In 1963, Knight went to

Japan. By chance, he met with Japanese businessmen who manufactured running shoes. At the businessmens' meeting, Knight asked to import Japanese running shoes to America.

2.   Back in the United States, Knight taught an accounting class at Portland State University. In the departments hallway, he saw several design student's work. He commissioned student Carolyn Davidson to come up with a design. Davidsons swoosh symbol became Nikes logo. At the time, she was paid only $35 for her design. However, several years later, Knight presented her with an envelope containing some of the companys stock. Davidson says that she has been adequately compensated for her design.

Using Apostrophes in Expressions of Time

If an expression of time (year, week, month, or day) appears to possess something, you can add an apostrophe plus -s.

My mother won a **month's** supply of groceries.

Eve Sinclair gave **three weeks'** notice before she left her job.

When you write out a year in numerals, you can use an apostrophe to replace the missing numbers.

The graduates of the class of '**04** often networked with each other.

However, if you are writing the numeral of a decade or century, do not put an apostrophe before the final *s*.

In the **1800s,** many farmers took factory jobs in nearby towns.

Many investors lost money in the **1990s.**

 **Hint**   **Common Apostrophe Errors**

• Do not use apostrophes before the final *s* of a verb.

   wants
   Zaid ~~want's~~ to start a new business.

• Do not confuse contractions with possessive pronouns that have a similar sound. For example, the contraction *you're* sounds like the pronoun *your.* Remember that possessive pronouns never have apostrophes.

   Its
   The corner store is new. ~~It's~~ owner is very nice.

   theirs
   That is our account. It is not ~~their's~~.

PRACTICE 6

Correct the apostrophe mistakes in each sentence.

EXAMPLE:

       your

I saw ~~you're~~ friend at the meeting.

1. Its well known that many clothing manufacturers receive criticism for poor working conditions of employees in Third World countries.

2. Theres documented evidence that these workers are usually underpaid.

3. For example, Nikes directors have admitted that there was a problem in Indonesia in the late 1990's.

4. In 2001, Nike realized that its' Indonesian plant managers were abusing workers.

5. Kathie Lee Giffords clothing line for Wal-Mart was manufactured in Honduras.

6. In 1995, reports revealed that the plants employees were working under terrible conditions.

7. Gifford publicly acknowledged that working condition's had to be improved.

8. Mitsumi work's as a buyer for an internationally known clothing company.

9. Her companys official policy is to buy clothing from manufacturers who pay fair wages.

10. As a consumer, Ill always try to be well informed about the things that I buy.

FINAL REVIEW

Correct fifteen apostrophe errors. Apostrophes may be used incorrectly, or there may be errors with possessive nouns.

EXAMPLE:

       should've

The government ~~shouldve~~ known about the bonuses.

1.   In 2009, American Insurance Group (AIG) became the most hated business in the United States. AIG is one of the worlds largest insurance companies. During the 08 world economic crisis, AIG lost a lot of money. It's credit rating was downgraded. The companys coffers emptied. To

prevent AIGs collapse, the United States government offered to loan it more than $100 billion.

2.   Soon after receiving the governments money, AIG executives were accused of spending over $400,000 from the bailout at a California spa. Apparently, the trip was a reward for managers whod been promised it before the bailout. The firm had also paid over $165 million in bonuses to senior executives. Theyd received the money because the company wanted to retain top managers. The public was outraged.

3.   These days, theres a growing demand by Americans to regulate business. The public want's the government to develop policies so that the situation wont happen again. Executives whove accepted government money shouldnt have the right to keep the bonuses. Managers mustnt feel entitled to rewards if their businesses fail. Certainly, many companies business practices need to be reexamined.

The Writer's Room

Write about one of the following topics. After you finish writing, underline any words with apostrophes, and verify that you have correctly used the apostrophes.

1. Think about at least three types of jobs. Divide your topic into categories and find a classification principle. For example, you could write about jobs that are high stress, medium stress, and low stress.

2. Define a term or expression that relates to the photo. Examples are *plugged in*, *drone*, or *workaholic*.

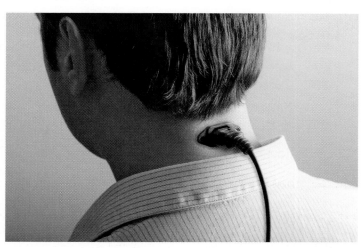

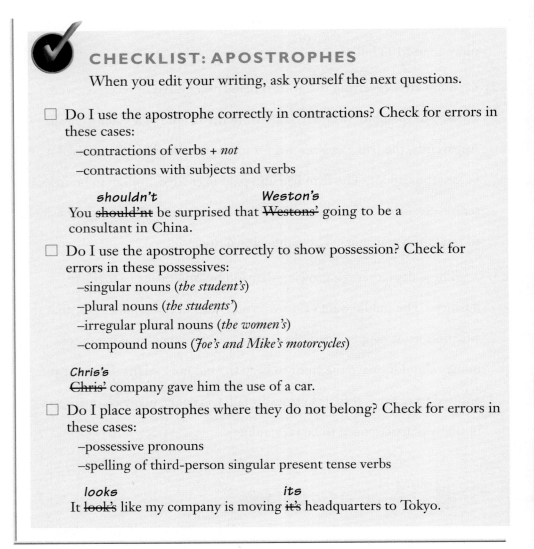

✓ CHECKLIST: APOSTROPHES

When you edit your writing, ask yourself the next questions.

☐ Do I use the apostrophe correctly in contractions? Check for errors in these cases:

–contractions of verbs + *not*

–contractions with subjects and verbs

      shouldn't   *Weston's*

You ~~should'nt~~ be surprised that ~~Westons'~~ going to be a consultant in China.

☐ Do I use the apostrophe correctly to show possession? Check for errors in these possessives:

–singular nouns (*the student's*)

–plural nouns (*the students'*)

–irregular plural nouns (*the women's*)

–compound nouns (*Joe's and Mike's motorcycles*)

  Chris's

~~Chris'~~ company gave him the use of a car.

☐ Do I place apostrophes where they do not belong? Check for errors in these cases:

–possessive pronouns

–spelling of third-person singular present tense verbs

    looks   *its*

It ~~look's~~ like my company is moving ~~it's~~ headquarters to Tokyo.

mywriting**lab**   To check your progress in meeting this chapter's objectives, log in to **www.mywritinglab.com**, go to the **Study Plan** tab, click on **The Editing Handbook—Section 8 Punctuation and Mechanics** and choose **The Apostrophe** from the list of subtopics. Read and view the resources in the **Review Materials** section, and then complete the **Recall, Apply,** and **Write** sets in the **Activities** section.

CHAPTER 27

Quotation Marks and Capitalization

CHAPTER 28

Section Theme: **THE BUSINESS WORLD**

In this chapter, you will read about business success stories.

Grammar Snapshot

Looking at Quotation Marks

This excerpt is taken from Ben Carson's autobiography, *Gifted Hands*. The quotation marks and associated capital letters are underlined.

> One of the counselors at our high school, Alma Whittley, knew my predicament and was very understanding. One day I poured out my story, and she listened with obvious concern. "I've got a few connections with the Ford Motor Company," she said. While I sat next to her desk, she phoned their world headquarters. I particularly remember her saying, "Look, we have this young fellow here named Ben Carson. He's very bright and already has a scholarship to go to Yale in September. Right now the boy needs a job to save money for this fall." She paused to listen, and I heard her add, "You have to give him a job."

In this chapter, you will learn how to use direct quotations correctly. You will also learn about capitalization and punctuation of titles.

385

Direct and Indirect Quotations

A **direct quotation** reproduces the exact words of a speaker or writer. An **indirect quotation,** however, simply summarizes someone's words. Indirect quotations often begin with *that*.

    Direct quotation: Mrs. Delaware said, "I'm moving to a new office."

    Indirect quotation: Mrs. Delaware said **that** she was moving to a new office.

The next sections discuss proper capitalization and punctuation of direct quotations.

Quotation Marks

Use **quotation marks** (" ") to set off the exact words of a speaker or writer. If the quotation is a complete sentence, there are some standard ways that it should be punctuated.

- Capitalize the first word of the quotation.
- Place quotation marks around the complete quotation.
- Place the end punctuation inside the closing quotation marks.

Generally, attach the name of the speaker or writer to the quotation in some way.

     . . . said,   **"Complete sentence."**

    Mrs. Delaware said, "You are hired."

Using Quotation Marks with an Introductory Phrase

When the quotation is introduced by a phrase, place a comma after the introductory phrase.

     . . . says,   "_____."

    Miguel Lanthier says, "You should feel passionate about your work."

PRACTICE I

Place quotation marks around the direct quotations in the following sentences. Add capitals and other punctuation where necessary.

EXAMPLE:

Beverly Sills stated , "You may be disappointed if you fail, but you are doomed if you don't try."

1. According to businessman J. C. Penney, " every business is built on friendship."

2. Mahatma Gandhi once said, " you must be the change you wish to see in the world."

3. Booker T. Washington, a political pundit, stated success is to be measured not so much by the position that one has reached in life as by the obstacles one has overcome.

4. Senator Dianne Feinstein said toughness doesn't have to come in a pinstripe suit.

5. General Norman Schwarzkopf declared when placed in command, take charge.

Using Quotation Marks with an Interrupting Phrase

When the quotation is interrupted, do the following:

- Place a comma after the first part of the quotation.
- Place a comma after the interrupting phrase.

"_____," . . . **says,** "_____."

"To cultivate kindness," said essayist Samuel Johnson, "is a valuable part of business life."

PRACTICE 2

Place quotation marks around the direct quotations in the following sentences. Add capital letters and other punctuation marks where necessary.

EXAMPLE:

"One chance," said Jessie Owens, "is all you need."

1. Hard work without talent is a shame said entrepreneur Robert Half but talent without hard work is a tragedy.

2. I like Mr. Gorbachev remarked former British Prime Minister Margaret Thatcher so we can do business together.

3. Whether you think you can said famous automaker Henry Ford or whether you think you can't, you're right!

4. When you're riding declared jockey Bill Shoemaker only the race in which you're riding is important.

CHAPTER 28

5. Singleness of purpose is one of the chief essentials for success in life said millionaire John D. Rockefeller no matter what may be one's aim.

Using Quotation Marks with an End Phrase

When you place a phrase at the end of a quotation, end the quotation with a comma instead of a period.

"_____," **says . . . .**

"There's no business like show business," said Irving Berlin.

If your quotation ends with another punctuation mark, put it inside the ending quotation mark.

"_____?" **says . . . .**

"Don't do that!" he yelled.

"Why did you hire her?" she asked.

PRACTICE 3

Place quotation marks around the direct quotations in the following sentences. Add capital letters and other punctuation marks where necessary.

EXAMPLE:

"
You're never beaten until you admit it, said General George S. Patton.

1. To succeed in business or to reach the top, an individual must know all it is possible to know about that business stated businessman John Paul Getty.

2. The first one gets the oyster and the second one gets the shell! said steel magnate Andrew Carnegie.

3. We fall forward to succeed declared Mary Kay Ash, the founder of Mary Kay Cosmetics.

4. Power is the ability to do good things for others said philanthropist Brooke Astor.

5. What I do best is share my enthusiasm stated Bill Gates, the founder of Microsoft.

CHAPTER 28

Using Quotation Marks with an Introductory Sentence

You can introduce a quotation with a complete sentence. Place a colon (:) after the introductory sentence.

> **He explains his views: "_____."**

Writer William Feather explains his views on parenthood: "Setting a good example for children takes all the fun out of middle age." ^

PRACTICE 4

Place quotation marks around the direct quotations in the following sentences. Add capital letters and other punctuation marks where necessary.

EXAMPLE:

The philosopher Friedrich Nietzsche explained perseverance ~~what~~ : "What doesn't kill us makes us stronger. "

1. Entrepreneur P. D. Armour expressed his views anybody can cut prices, but it takes a brain to produce a better article.

2. Malcolm Forbes, a magazine publisher, discusses how to succeed try hard enough.

3. Spanish writer Miguel Cervantes referred to his success to be prepared is half the victory.

4. We discussed the words of Norman Vincent Peale it's always too soon to quit.

5. Philanthropist Thomas Dewar discusses human minds they only function when open.

 **Integrating Partial Quotations**

Sometimes, you may want to use only a small part of a quotation in your own sentence because the full quotation is unnecessary. Add quotation marks only around the words that you are using.

Example:

Direct Quotation:	Bill Cosby says, "In order to succeed, your desire for success should be greater than your fear of failure."
Partial Quotation:	Comedian Bill Cosby states that "your desire for success should be greater than your fear of failure."

CHAPTER 28

PRACTICE 5

Place quotation marks around the direct quotations in bold print. Add capital letters and punctuation marks to the direct quotations.

EXAMPLE:

Coco Chanel often said , "A **a fashion that does not reach the streets is**
"
not fashion.

1.   Coco Chanel was a risk taker. People often heard her say **I have never done anything by halves**. Chanel was born in 1883 into an extremely impoverished family in Samur, France. Her mother died when Coco was young, so her father sent her to a convent school where the nuns taught her to sew. After graduating from school, Chanel worked as a seamstress in a tailor's shop. During that period, she began designing hats. By 1913, she had opened her first fashion store in Paris. She wanted women to look elegant. **fashion fades, but style remains** she once stated.

2.   Chanel was one of the first women designers to introduce fashionable wear for women. She designed clothes by following her values **a girl should be two things: classy and fabulous**. Many celebrities began to wear her clothes. For example, the Chanel jacket has been worn by generations of women. She often declared **luxury must be comfortable; otherwise it is not luxury**. In an interview, the designer expressed her philosophy **one cannot be forever innovating. I want to create classics**. Her clothes were known for their timeless simplicity.

3.   Chanel's designs liberated women from the earlier corset and lace fashions. **In fashion, you know you have succeeded** she stressed **when there is an element of upset**. She claimed that she was **not a feminist,** but she brought out the femininity in women. She was ahead of her time because she became a successful businesswoman when women were mostly housewives.

Capitalization

Remember to always capitalize the following:

- The pronoun *I*
- The first word of every sentence

    My coworkers and **I** share an office.

There are many other instances in which you must use capital letters. Always capitalize the following:

- **Days of the week, months, and holidays**

    Wednesday   **J**anuary 1   **N**ew **Y**ear's **E**ve

    Do not capitalize the seasons: summer, fall, winter, spring.

- **Titles of specific institutions, departments, companies, and schools**

    IBM   **U.S. D**epartment   **P**inewood **E**lementary **S**chool
                    of **D**efense

    Do not capitalize general references.

    the company   the department   the school

- **Names of specific places, such as buildings, streets, parks, cities, states, countries, and bodies of water**

    Dale **S**treet   **T**imes **S**quare   **L**os **A**ngeles, **C**alifornia
    Central **P**ark   **M**ississippi   **L**ake **E**rie

    Do not capitalize general references.

    the street   the state   the lake

- **Names of specific languages, nationalities, tribes, races, and religions**

    Portuguese   **N**avaho   **B**uddhist   an **I**talian restaurant

- **Titles of specific individuals**

    General **E**isenhower   **P**resident **K**ennedy   **D**r. **M**arcos
    Professor **W**ong   **P**rime **M**inister **B**lair   **M**rs. **E**leanor **R**oosevelt

    If you are referring to the profession in general, or if the title follows the name, do not use capital letters.

    a senator   my professor   the doctors

- **Titles of specific courses and programs**

    Mathematics 201   **C**ivil **E**ngineering 100   **B**eginner's **S**panish

    If you refer to a course but do not mention the course title, then it is not necessary to use capitals.

    He is in economics.   I study hard for my civil engineering class.

- **The major words in titles of literary or artistic works**

    The Lord of the Rings   *The Bourne Identity*   *War and Peace*

- **Names of historical events, eras, and movements**

    the **K**orean **W**ar   **I**mpressionism   the **I**ndustrial **R**evolution

> ## _Hint_   **Capitalizing Computer Terms**
>
> Always capitalize the following computer terms.
>
> Internet   World Wide Web
>
> Capitalize software titles as you would any other published work.
>
> Netscape   Microsoft Office

PRACTICE 6

Add any necessary capital letters to the following sentences.

EXAMPLE:

W

The creation of the World Wide web has allowed many new entrepreneurs to become successful.

1. In 1996, Larry Page and Sergei Brin started out as graduate students at Stanford university but ended up founding google inc.

2. They created an internet search engine, which is one of the most used products in america.

3. The company headquarters are located in googleplex, 1600 amphitheatre Parkway, Mountain view, california.

4. The search engine is so popular that the verb "to google" can be found in the _Merriam webster collegiate dictionary_.

5. Another successful product is Google earth, which allows users to see aerial maps through satellite imaging.

6. In december 2006, Google bought youTube, an online video site.

7. For the past few years, i have mainly used Google to research many subjects.

8. In my political science 201 class, my instructor, professor Warner, asked us to find out about criticism directed against the company.

9. Google has been criticized for infringing copyright laws, violating privacy laws, and complying with censorship rules in china.

10. In march 2010, Google shut down its service in beijing to protest internet censorship in China.

CHAPTER 28

Titles

Punctuating Titles

Place the title of a short work in quotation marks. Italicize the title of a longer work. If you are handwriting your text, underline the title.

Short Works		Long Works	
Short story:	"The Bear"	**Novel:**	*The Da Vinci Code*
Chapter:	"Abbreviations"	**Book:**	*MLA Handbook for Writers of Research Papers*
Newspaper article:	"Missing in Action"	**Newspaper:**	*New York Times*
Magazine article:	"History's Fools"	**Magazine:**	*Newsweek*
Web article:	"Music Artists Lose Out"	**Web site:**	*Blackbeat.com*
Essay:	"Neighborhoods of the Globe"	**Textbook:**	*Essentials of Sociology*
TV episode:	"Fixed"	**TV series:**	*The Good Wife*
Song:	"Naughty Girl"	**CD:**	*Dangerously in Love*
Poem:	"The List of Famous Hats"	**Collection:**	*Reckoner*

Capitalizing Titles

When you write a title, capitalize the first letter of the first word and all the major words. Do not capitalize the letters *.com* in a Web address.

> *This Side of Paradise*   *Monster.com*   "Lucy in the Sky with Diamonds"

Also, do not capitalize the following words, except as the first or last word in a title.

Articles:	a, an, the
Coordinators:	but, and, or, nor, for, so, yet
Short prepositions:	of, to, in, off, out, up, by

PRACTICE 7

Add ten capital letters to the next paragraph. Also, add quotation marks or underlining to six titles. If you were typing this essay, you would put titles of long works in italics.

EXAMPLE:

       A

Ayn Rand's book ~~a~~nthem begins with strong words: "It was a sin to write this."

Ayn Rand, a writer and philosopher, was born in 1905 in st.

petersburg, Russia. Her most famous novel, The fountainhead, was

published in 1943. Her next novel was Atlas shrugged. Rand

proposed that self-interest should guide people, and her views have been widely debated. Michael Shermer criticized Rand in a magazine called skeptics. He compares her followers to sheep in the article The Unlikeliest cult in history. Rand also has numerous supporters, and her philosophy, objectivism, has been analyzed by many distinguished thinkers. Peter St. Andre, for example, wrote the essay Why I Am a libertarian, which appeared in the magazine full context. Rand's books continue to sell millions of copies, and her supporters have created numerous Web sites to promote her work and philosophy.

FINAL REVIEW

A. Add three missing capital letters, and properly punctuate the two quotations in bold print.

EXAMPLE:

After graduating from college, Jeff Bezos worked on Wall street.
(S above "street")

1. Since the creation of the world Wide Web, many businesses have been selling products to customers online. One of the largest internet companies in the world is Jeff Bezos's book-selling business. In 1994, Bezos founded his firm in his garage. **I am going to do a crazy thing** he recalls saying **by selling books online**. Bezos, unlike other businesspeople, did not expect to make a profit for a few years. **What we wanted to be was something completely new** Bezos reminisced. His business plan proved to be excellent, and the company has slowly grown. When the dot-com bubble burst, and many online companies failed, amazon.com posted profits.

B. Add seven missing capital letters and properly punctuate three titles. If you were typing the essay, the titles of long works would be in italics.

EXAMPLE:

There are many articles in the *New York times* about Jeff Bezos's company.
(T above "times")

CHAPTER 29

2. The first book sold by Amazon.com was titled Fluid Concepts and Creative analogies: Computer Models of the Fundamental Mechanisms of thought. Soon after, Bezos's company became very successful, and, in 1999, he was named Person of the year by *Time*.

3. Nowadays, Amazon.com does not sell just books. It sells electronics, food, toys, and other products. While its headquarters is in seattle, Washington, the company has also expanded its business in China, the United Kingdom, canada, and other countries. In 2008, in an article called America's best Leaders, the magazine US News and world Report included Bezos for his innovative approach to business.

 ## The Writer's Room

Write about one of the following topics. After you finish writing, check that you have capitalized words and placed quotation marks correctly in your text.

1. What are some things that you should do to get your dream job? List at least five steps that you should take.

2. Do you prefer to shop online or do you like traditional methods of shopping? Explain the similarities or differences of shopping online and traditional shopping.

✔ CHECKLIST: QUOTATION MARKS AND CAPITALIZATION

When you edit your writing, ask yourself the next questions.

☐ Are there any direct quotations in my writing? Check for errors with these elements:

  –punctuation before or after quotations
  –capital letters
  –placement of quotation marks

  "   ,"
  You're fired said Donald Trump to his latest apprentice.

READING LINK

The Business World

To read more about the business world, see the next essays:

"The Allure of Apple" by Juan Rodriquez (page 440)

"How to Remember Names" by Roger Seip (page 444)

☐ Do my sentences have all the necessary capital letters?

                   I   *War*

About two years ago, ~~i~~ saw a movie about World ~~war~~ II.

☐ Are the titles of artistic works properly punctuated?

                                                     Saving

Steven Spielberg directed the award-winning movie ~~Saving~~

Private Ryan

~~private ryan~~.

 The Writers' Circle   **Collaborative Activity**

Work with a partner. Take turns reading a dialogue from an essay at the back of this book. Write down everything that your partner says. When you are both finished, exchange papers, compare them with the original essays, and mark any misspelled words or incorrectly placed punctuation or quotations marks. Here are some suggested readings.

"Birth" (page 410), paragraphs 3 to 8 (stop at the word *condemnation*)

"The New Addiction" by Josh Freed (page 412), paragraphs 4 to 6 (stop at the end of paragraph 6)

In a dialogue, begin a new paragraph every time the speaker changes.

PEARSON **mywritinglab**   To check your progress in meeting this chapter's objectives, log in to **www.mywritinglab.com**, go to the **Study Plan** tab, click on **The Editing Handbook—Section 8 Punctuation and Mechanics** and choose **Quotation Marks and Capitalization** from the list of subtopics. Read and view the resources in the **Review Materials** section, and then complete the **Recall, Apply,** and **Write** sets in the **Activities** section.

CHAPTER 28

Editing Practice

In this chapter, you will practice editing different types of writing, including a memo and a letter.

After you finish writing the first draft of a paragraph or essay, it is important to edit your work. When you edit, carefully review your writing to verify that your grammar, punctuation, sentence structure, and capitalization are correct. In this chapter, you can practice editing written pieces that you see every day, including e-mail, paragraphs, essays, and business correspondence.

PRACTICE I

Correct fifteen underlined errors. An editing symbol appears above each error. To understand the meaning of each symbol, refer to the revising and editing symbols on the inside front cover of this book.

Television undoubtedly has a negative influence on people.

First, the lives of a normal children have changed a lot.

                     wc   RO

Nobody spends <u>no</u> time playing<u>,</u> such inactivity contributes

to childhood obesity. Additionally, children watch too

    wc   pl   agr

<u>much</u> violent images on TV. <u>Theses</u> images <u>affects</u> the way that

                                         vt

children see the world. In a psychological study <u>did</u> at the University of

                                      vt

Pennsylvania, fifty preschool children were <u>expose</u> to violent images

                                   vt

and fifty were not. The children who <u>seen</u> violent programs were

          ad

more <u>likelier</u> to show aggressive behavior. Also, the average American

    agr

<u>waste</u> too much time staring at the television. All that time could

    vt

be <u>use</u> for other activities such as reading, doing sports, and simply

        //

<u>to communicate</u> with others. On a weekday evening, visit a typical

American home. Family members are probably <u>gonna</u> be sitting in

                             m

front of their television sets <u>who are lazy</u>.

PRACTICE 2

There are no editing symbols in the next paragraph. Proofread it as you would your own writing, and correct ten errors.

    People often wonder what do motivational speakers do. In fact, they

inspire audience members to achieve particular goals. Many companies

hire motivational speakers to encourage its employees and to give keynote speeches at conferences. Companies look for speakers who has a positive message and who are engaging. Much people who have achieved success have become motivational speakers, including General Norman Schwarzkopf and former New York City mayor Rudolph Giuliani. Actors, former presidents, and sports heroes also inspires audiences. Some times, a motivational speaker can earn more than fifty-thousands for an appearance. The best motivational speakers encourages the audience members to analyze their own beliefs, and goals.

PRACTICE 3

In the next memo, there are no editing symbols. Identify and correct ten errors.

Memo: Summer Party

This year, Winston and me are in charge of organizing the company party that is gonna take place on July 12. The summer partys theme is baseball. Please dress appropriate. Any body who plays baseball really good or who just wants to play is invited. Everyone is welcome to bring their friends. There is baseball equipments in the supply room. Let's make this party, the most best event of the year.

Uma Kamarchung, Party Organizer

PRACTICE 4

Identify and correct fifteen errors in the next letter.

Dear Maya,

I have being at the police training center for two weeks. It is real hard. Every day, we have to get up at 5:30 and go for a ten-mile run in the dark. It is very likely than I will get into great shape by the end of my training.

Each morning, we receive our schedule. For the rest of the day. We don't have no time to relax. Their is no time for leisure activities. The older students have said that there used to the long hours.

Last week, we visited a police department and learned some investigative techniques. In one workshop, we pretended to arrest thiefs. I prefered target shooting to any other activity on our visit. I am more better at shooting than the other students in my class.

I imagine that your busy this summer. Did you go to Puerto Rico last april? Did your mother go to? I hear that your brother and his friend are local heroes, they rescued a boy. Who was drowning.

I have to go, but I will write again soon.

Your friend,

Christine

PRACTICE 5

Identify and correct twelve errors.

There is several things you should do to avoid credit card fraud. First, make sure that you sign your credit card as soon as it arrive. Keep a record of your card number, the expiration date, and the phone number, of the credit card company. When you give your credit card to a cashier, watch the transaction, then get your card back immediatly. Keep your receipt untill you get your credit card bill. Check each months bill carefully, and report any suspicious transactions. Do not throw away receipts who contain your credit card information. Criminals go often through recycling bins and garbage cans to find old receipts. It is adviseable to burn receipts or tear it into very small peaces.

PRACTICE 6

Identify and correct fifteen errors.

To have a healthy diet, ensure that you make the good choices. First, avoid to eat red meat. It is preferable having lean meat such as pork or chicken. Also, proteins can be found in fish, wich has less calories than meat and contains omega-3 fatty acids. Moreover, you should have five to ten portion of fruits and vegetables per day. Try to eat a variety of vegetables. Such as carrots, spinach, broccoli, and peppers. Cut the amount of sugar you eat because it can leads to belly fat. Which is bad for blood pressure. For example, instead eating cake, choose fruit salad. Also, sugar. Do you know what is the recommended amount of sugar? You should just have four to six spoons per day. Finally, remember that too much salt it can cause high blood pressure in some adults. According to HealthCastle.com, you should "reduce the amount of salt called for in recipes". Always remember that eating good is important.

PRACTICE 7

Identify and correct twenty editing errors in this student essay.

1.   Many people and events have influenced my life and changed my way of thinking. For exemple, sports were important to me when I was a child. At the age of seventeen, I had problems with my back, so my doctor recomended that I start weight lifting. Weight lifting has changed my life in a profound way. In fact, if I would have known the benefits of exercise, I would have started weight lifting sooner.

2.   Before becoming a weight lifter, I did not like how I looked physicaly. When I started lifting weights, I learned to like my appearance and to respect my body. I realized that I only have one body, so I gotta take care of it. Now that I am more conscience of my health, I make an effort to eat good. As a result, I am more stronger and more energetic. I am finally treating my body with the respect he deserves.

3.   Furthermore, weight lifting has taught me to persevere, to work hard, and having confidence. At the beginning of my fitness program, I consulted my cousin who showed me how to do the exercises correctly, the more I trained, the better the effects were. I could lift heavy weights more easy than before. Now I no longer wonder how can I do something. I make goals and stay with them.

4.   Moreover, weight lifting it has also changed my personallity and helped me be more confident. I am able to accept each success and failures with grace. I am also more focused, and I do not loose my temper as easily as I used to.

5.   Fitness training, wich has both physical and psychological benefits, has improved my body, my health, and my self-esteem. I have been practicing this sport since ten years, and I will continue to do so. People should choose activities. That motivate them.

mywritinglab   To check your progress in meeting this chapter's objectives, log in to **www.mywritinglab.com**, go to the **Study Plan** tab, click on **The Editing Handbook—Section 9 Editing** and choose **Editing Practice** from the list of subtopics. Read and view the resources in the **Review Materials** section, and then complete the **Recall, Apply,** and **Write** sets in the **Activities** section.

CHAPTER 29

Reading Strategies and Selections

Reading Strategies and Selections

CHAPTER 30

LEARNING OBJECTIVES

1 Reading Strategies (p. 405)
2 Reading Selections (p. 408)

Aspiring sculptors study historical and contemporary works to learn about composition, technique, and material. In the same way, by reading different types of writing, you can observe how other writers develop their essays.

Reading Strategies

Reading helps you develop your writing skills. Each time you read, you accomplish these goals.

- Expand your vocabulary.
- Learn how other writers develop topics.
- Learn to recognize and use different writing patterns.
- Find ideas for your own paragraphs and essays.

The strategies discussed in this chapter can help you become a more successful reader and writer.

Previewing

When you **preview** a passage, you quickly look at key points. You can get a general sense of a passage's topic and main ideas by checking visual clues.

- Read the title and the main headings.
- Look at the first and last sentence of the introduction.
- Look at the first sentence of each paragraph.

- Look at the concluding sentences in the essay.
- Review any photos, graphs, or charts, and read the captions that accompany them.

Previewing helps you prepare for the next step, which is reading the essay.

Taking Notes

To help you remember and quickly find the important points in a text, you can highlight key ideas and make annotations. An **annotation** is a comment, question, or reaction that you write in the margin of a passage.

Highlighting and Making Annotations

Each time you read a passage, do the following:

- Look at the introductory and concluding paragraphs, and underline sentences that sum up the main idea.
- Using your own words, write the main idea in the margin.
- Underline or highlight supporting ideas. You might even want to number the arguments or ideas. This will allow you to understand the essay's development.
- Circle words that you do not understand.
- Write questions in the margin if you do not understand the author's meaning.
- Write notes beside passages that are interesting or that relate to your own experiences.
- Jot down possible writing topics.

If you are reading a library book, or if you have borrowed a book from somebody else, use sticky notes to make annotations. Do not write in the book!

An Annotated Passage

Why? I don't get it. ➤

main point? offended his hosts? ➤

What is naan? ➤

   In Sydney, Australia, I simply hailed a taxi, opened the door, and jumped in the back seat. The driver narrowed his eyes. "Where to, mate?" he asked in a voice that could chill a refrigerator. In Marrakech, Morocco, I crossed my legs during an interview with a government official. Immediately, a hush fell over the room. In a restaurant in Mumbai, India, all I did was reach for the naan. A diner at the next table shot me a look that stuck two inches out my back.

Understanding Unfamiliar Words

When you read, you will sometimes come across an unfamiliar word. You can try to guess the word's meaning, or you can circle it and look it up later.

Use Context Clues

Context clues are hints in the text that help define a word. To find a word's meaning, try the next steps.

1. **Determine the word's function.** For example, is it a noun, a verb, or an adjective? Sometimes you can understand a word if you know how it functions in the sentence.

2. **Look at surrounding words.** Try to find a relation between the difficult word and the words that surround it. Maybe there is a **synonym** (a word that means the same thing) or an **antonym** (a word that means the opposite). Maybe other words in the sentence help define the word.

3. **Look at surrounding sentences.** Look at the sentences, paragraphs, and punctuation surrounding the word. If you use logic, you may understand what the word means.

PRACTICE I

Can you define the word *heed?*   ____ Yes   ____ No

Can you define *yearn?*   ____ Yes   ____ No

If you do not understand the meaning of those two words, then read the words in context in the next example. You will notice that it is much easier to guess their meanings in context.

> Travel makes it impossible to pay no **heed** to the suffering of others, simply because they are far away. It erases distance, and makes you a more sensitive citizen of the world, **yearning** for peace everywhere.
>
> —Arthur Frommer, "How Travel Changed My Life"

Now write your own definitions of the words.

1. heed: _____

2. yearn: _____

 **Hint**   **Using a Dictionary**

Some words have many definitions. When you look up a word in a dictionary, do not stop after you read the first meaning. Keep reading, and look for the meaning that best fits the context of your sentence. To learn more about dictionary usage, see Chapter 23, Exact Language.

Writing About the Reading

After you finish reading a text, you may have to answer questions about it or write about it. There are several steps you can take to help you better understand a reading passage.

- **Summarize** the reading. When you summarize, you use your own words to write a condensed version of the reading. You leave out all information except for the main points.

- **Outline** the reading. An outline is a visual plan of the reading. First, write the main idea of the essay, and then write the most important idea from each paragraph. Under each idea, you can include a detail or an example.

Respond to the Reading

Before you make a written response to the reading, ask yourself the next questions.

- What is the writer's main point?
- What is the writer's purpose: to entertain, to persuade, or to inform?

- Who is the intended reader? Is the writer directing the message at someone like me?
- What is my opinion of the reading?
- What aspects of the topic can I relate to?

Reading Selections

Theme: **Lifestyles and Relationships**

READING 1

Fish Cheeks

Amy Tan

> Amy Tan, the author of the best-selling novel *The Joy Luck Club*, wrote this essay for an issue of *Seventeen* magazine. Using vivid detail, Tan describes a family dinner. As you read, notice how the author uses mainly description but also elements of narration and illustration.

1   I fell in love with the minister's son the winter I turned fourteen. He was not Chinese but as white as Mary in the manger. For Christmas, I prayed for this blond-haired boy, Robert, and a slim new American nose.

2   When I found out that my parents had invited the minister's family over for Christmas Eve dinner, I cried. What would Robert think of our shabby Chinese Christmas? What would he think of our noisy Chinese relatives who lacked proper American manners? What terrible disappointment would he feel upon seeing not a roasted turkey and sweet potatoes but Chinese food?

3   On Christmas Eve, I saw that my mother had outdone herself in creating a strange menu. She was pulling black veins out of the backs of fleshy prawns. The kitchen was littered with appalling mounds of raw food: a slimy rock cod with bulging eyes that pleaded not to be thrown into a pan of hot oil; tofu, which looked like stacked wedges of rubbery white sponges; a bowl soaking dried fungus back to life; and a plate of squid, their backs crisscrossed with knife markings so they resembled bicycle tires.

4   And then they arrived—the minister's family and all my relatives in a clamor of doorbells and rumpled Christmas packages. Robert grunted hello, and I pretended he was not worthy of existence.

5   Dinner threw me deeper into despair. My relatives licked the ends of their chopsticks and reached across the table, dipping them into the dozen or so plates of food. Robert and his family waited patiently for platters to be passed to them. My relatives murmured with pleasure when my mother brought out the whole steamed fish. Robert grimaced. Then my father poked his chopsticks just below the fish eye and plucked out the soft meat. "Amy, your favorite," he said, offering me the tender fish cheek. I wanted to disappear.

6   At the end of the meal, my father leaned back and belched loudly, thanking my mother for her fine cooking. "It's a polite Chinese custom to show you are satisfied," explained my father to our astonished guests. Robert was looking down at his plate with a reddened face. The minister managed to muster up a quiet burp. I was stunned into silence for the rest of the night.

7   After everyone had gone, my mother said to me, "You want to be the same as American girls on the outside." She handed me an early gift. It was a miniskirt in beige tweed. "But inside you must always be Chinese. You must be proud you are different. Your only shame is to have shame."

8   And even though I didn't agree with her then, I knew that she understood how much I had suffered during the evening's dinner. It wasn't until many years later—long after I had gotten over my crush on Robert—that I was able to fully appreciate her lesson and the true purpose behind our particular menu. For Christmas Eve that year, she had chosen all my favorite foods.

VOCABULARY AND COMPREHENSION

1.   What is the meaning of *muster* in paragraph 6?
     a.   To summon up or create
     b.   To gather
     c.   A yellow sauce

2.   What three reasons does Tan give for her embarrassment when Robert comes for dinner? Use your own words.

     _____

     _____

     _____

3.   What lesson was the writer's mother trying to teach her?

     Sher: Mother trying to tell that Be yourself and
     Respect your Nationality.

4.   On the surface, Tan's purpose is to entertain, but what is her deeper purpose?

     _____

     _____

5.   Tan uses descriptive imagery. Imagery includes active verbs, adjectives, and other words that appeal to the senses (sight, smell, touch, sound, taste). Highlight at least five examples of imagery.

GRAMMAR LINK

6.   Underline six adjectives in paragraph 3. Then circle the nouns that the adjectives modify. Discuss how the adjectives make the writing more vivid.
7.   In the essay, identify six irregular past tense verbs not including the verb *be*. Write the present- and past-tense forms of each verb on the lines provided.

     _____   _____

     _____   _____

     _____   _____

DISCUSSION AND WRITING

8.   Think about a time when you felt different from others. Explain what happened. Try to use some descriptive vocabulary.
9.   What are the possible causes for a person to give up his or her own cultural traditions (language, dress, food, ceremonies, etc.)? What are the effects when people lose their cultural distinctiveness? Discuss the causes or effects of losing cultural traditions.

READING 2

Birth

Maya Angelou

Maya Angelou is an award-winning author. In this selection from her best-known autobiographical work, *I Know Why the Caged Bird Sings*, Angelou writes about the birth of her son. As you read, notice how the author uses mainly narration but also elements of description and cause and effect writing.

1   Two days after V-Day, I stood with the San Francisco Summer School class at Mission High School and received my diploma. That evening, in the bosom of the now-dear family home, I uncoiled my fearful secret, and in a brave gesture left a note on Daddy Clidell's bed. It read, "Dear Parents, I am sorry to bring this disgrace upon the family, but I am pregnant. Marguerite."

2   The confusion that ensued when I explained to my stepfather that I expected to deliver the baby in three weeks, more or less, was **reminiscent** of a **Molière** comedy. Daddy Clidell told Mother that I was "three weeks gone." Mother, regarding me as a woman for the first time, said indignantly, "She's more than any three weeks." They both accepted the fact that I was further along than they had first been told but found it nearly impossible to believe that I had carried a baby, eight months and one week, without their being any the wiser.

3   Mother asked, "Who is the boy?" I told her. She recalled him, faintly.

4   "Do you want to marry him?"

5   "No."

6   "Does he want to marry you?" The father had stopped speaking to me during my fourth month.

7   "No."

8   "Well, that's that. No use ruining three lives." There was no **overt** or subtle **condemnation.**

9   Daddy Clidell assured me that I had nothing to worry about. He sent one of his waitresses to I. Magnin's to buy maternity dresses for me. For the next two weeks, I whirled around the city going to doctors, taking vitamin shots and pills, buying clothes for the baby, and except for the rare moments alone, enjoying the imminent blessed event.

10   After a short labor, and without too much pain (I decided that the pain of delivery was overrated), my son was born. Just as gratefulness was confused in my mind with love, so possession became mixed up with motherhood. I had a baby. He was beautiful and mine. No one had bought him for me. No one had helped me endure the sickly gray months. I had had help in the child's conception, but no one could deny that I had had an **immaculate** pregnancy.

11   I was afraid to touch him. Home from the hospital, I sat for hours by his bassinet and absorbed his mysterious perfection. His extremities were so dainty they appeared unfinished. Mother handled him easily with the casual confidence of a baby nurse, but I dreaded being forced to change his diapers. Wasn't I famous for awkwardness? Suppose I let him slip, or put my fingers on that throbbing pulse on the top of his head?

12   Mother came to my bed one night bringing my three-week-old baby. She pulled the cover back and told me to get up and hold him while she put rubber sheets on my bed. She explained that he was going to sleep with me.

13   I begged in vain. I was sure to roll over and crush out his life or break those fragile bones. She wouldn't hear of it, and within minutes the pretty golden baby was lying on his back in the center of my bed, laughing at me.

reminiscent:
similar to

Molière:
a French playwright
(1622–1673)

overt:
evident, open

condemnation:
criticism; disapproval

immaculate:
untainted by other people's knowledge and actions
(in the biblical sense of Immaculate Conception)

14   I lay on the edge of the bed, stiff with fear, and vowed not to sleep all night long. But the eat-sleep routine I had begun in the hospital, and kept up under Mother's dictatorial command, got the better of me. I dropped off.

15   My shoulder was shaken gently. Mother whispered, "Maya, wake up. But don't move."

16   I knew immediately that the awakening had to do with the baby. I tensed. "I'm awake."

17   She turned the light on and said, "Look at the baby." My fears were so powerful I couldn't move to look at the center of the bed. She said again, "Look at the baby." I didn't hear sadness in her voice, and that helped me to break the bonds of terror. The baby was no longer in the center of the bed. At first I thought he had moved. But after closer investigation, I found that I was lying on my stomach with my arm bent at a right angle. Under the tent of blanket, which was poled by my elbow and forearm, the baby slept touching my side.

18   Mother whispered, "See, you don't have to think about doing the right thing. If you're for the right thing, then you do it without thinking."

19   She turned out the light, and I patted my son's body lightly and went back to sleep.

VOCABULARY AND COMPREHENSION

1. Find a word in paragraph 9 that means "soon to arrive; forthcoming."

   _____ IMMINENT _____

2. How does Angelou's family react to the pregnancy?

   _____ CONFUSE AND SHOCK _____

3. In paragraph 11, the author says that she was afraid to touch her own baby. Why did she feel this way? HIS EXTREMITIES WERE SO DAINTY THEY APPEARED UNFINISHED
   CONFUS AND SHOCK BABY IS SO FRAGILE

4. Were her fears well-founded? Why or why not?

   _____

5. What does the reading suggest about becoming a parent?

   BE PREPARED TO BE A MOTHER

GRAMMAR LINK

6. The author uses quotations in her narration. How do the quotations enhance the story?

   _____

   _____

7. Angelou uses the following vivid verbs. Look at the verbs in the paragraphs. Then write two or three synonyms next to each verb.

   whirled (paragraph 9) _____

   handled (paragraph 11) _____

dreaded (paragraph 11) _____

begged (paragraph 13) _____

DISCUSSION AND WRITING

8. In paragraph 18, the author's mother says, "See, you don't have to think about doing the right thing." Do you agree that people instinctively know how to become parents? Explain your answer and provide examples.

9. The author acted impulsively when she was an adolescent. Write about an impulsive act that you did when you were an adolescent. What happened, and what were the consequences? Try to use some descriptive language in your writing.

READING 3
The New Addiction
Josh Freed

Josh Freed is an award-winning columnist for the *Montreal Gazette*. Freed has published many books, including *Fear of Frying and Other Fax of Life*. In the essay, Freed compares and contrasts two items. As you read, notice how the author also uses definition writing.

scourge:
affliction; serious problem

1   Is the cell phone the cigarette of our times? That is what I have been asking myself lately as the **scourge** of smokers slowly disappears from city life, and a scourge of cell-phone users takes their place. Everywhere I look, people hold cell phones up to their mouths instead of cigarettes, and non-users react as intolerantly as nonsmokers ever did. How does the cell phone resemble the cigarette? Let me count the ways.

2   It is an oral habit. For many users, the cell phone is an obvious substitute for smoking. It is a nervous habit that gives them something to do with their hands—whether they are dialing, checking their messages, texting, or just fondling the buttons. Just like cigarettes, the phone sits in a person's breast pocket or on a restaurant table, ready to bring quickly to his or her mouth. Often, it is in a fliptop case that pops open as easily as a cigarette pack.

3   It pollutes. Instead of filling the air with smoke, cell-phone users fill it with words. For those nearby, the cell is just as annoying as the cigarette because instead of secondhand smoke, they get secondhand conversation. It is voice pollution. One phone can pollute a room more quickly than a cigarette, especially on a bus, or in a checkout line, when others hear someone hollering about his or her cousin's prostate operation or planning the night's dinner menu.

4   "Honey! The veal chops were expensive so I got lamb chops instead. Whaddya think we should serve with them? Do we need potatoes?"

5   Many people feel they must yell to be heard, and there is usually only one way to shut them up. Join into their conversation and say, "You know, I don't really feel like lamb chops tonight—how about turkey and wild rice?"

6   Cell-phone users do not blow smoke rings from the next restaurant table, like smokers. But cell-phone rings can be just as annoying, whether they play the "William Tell Overture" or yodeling sounds or Christmas tunes like "Sleigh Bells Ringing." Phone users are even more oblivious to their own noise than smokers are to their wisps of smoke.

7   Furthermore, there is an anti-cell lobby. Cell-phone users are the target of a growing intolerance that is almost as zealous as the anti-smoking movement's. Go to a movie, play, or concert and no one bothers to tell you not to smoke anymore. They know your seatmates will take care of that. Instead, movie ads and other warnings are all about shutting off your cell, the new public enemy No. 1. Anti-cell rage is so extreme that if you forget to shut off your phone in a movie, there is only one safe strategy to avoid a lynching when your phone goes off. Look around for the culprit accusingly, like everyone else in the place, and bluff your way out until your phone stops ringing.

8   Lately, "No Cell Phone" signs are getting even bigger than "No Smoking" signs. I was in San Francisco recently, where half the shops were plastered with warnings like "Don't even think about it. Cell-phone users will be escorted out and made to feel extremely embarrassed." On the train from Washington to New York, there is now a special "quiet" car where cell phones are banned. How long before the whole train is divided into cell and noncell sections, in a new version of smoking **apartheid?** If they ever find the slightest link between cell phones and any illness, you can expect to see hotel rooms, cell-free rest rooms, and a growing number of cell-free cities.

apartheid:
former political system in South Africa that separated the privileged whites from people of other races

9   Cell phones may be addictive. Just like cigarettes, the cell phone spreads by targeting the young. The Big Phone companies keep offering teenagers dirt-cheap plans, trying to hook them for life. The cell is a cool teen status symbol, as powerful as the cigarette, though less lethal. How long before we see class actions against the big phone companies for deliberately addicting our kids to the nicotine of words? How long will it be before the first cell-phone pollution settlement?

10   I suspect cell-phone makers will eventually be forced to come up with special filters, like cigarettes. All phones will be sold with a soundproof helmet or at least a mask-and-muffler to protect others from the noise. Get ready for the cell-phone snorkel.

VOCABULARY AND COMPREHENSION

1.   What is the meaning of *zealous* in paragraph 7? Guess the meaning using context clues.

_____

2.   What is Freed's main point?

_____

_____

3. List five examples the author uses to support his main point.

    _____

    _____

    _____

    _____

    _____

4. What is the author's tone (his attitude toward the subject)?
    a. Serious   c. Lighthearted
    b. Cynical   d. Detached

GRAMMAR LINK

5. In paragraph 4, the author writes "Whaddya." What does this word mean? Why does the author include an invented word in his text?

    _____

    _____

6. Why does the author use dialogue in paragraphs 4 and 5?

    _____

    _____

DISCUSSION AND WRITING

7. Choose two addictive items and compare them, just as Freed did in this essay. Do not compare cell phones and cigarettes.
8. Should cell phones be banned or restricted? Explain your answer. If you think cell phones should be restricted, what types of restrictions should be placed on them?

READING 4

Fat Chance
Dorothy Nixon

> Dorothy Nixon, a freelance writer, has written for *Salon.com*, *Chatelaine*, and *Today's Parent* magazine. In this text, she ponders about parental responsibility. As you read this cause and effect essay, also look for elements of argument and definition.

1   Being a parent, these days, can make me feel like a fish. I feel like a splish-splashing salmon, to be specific, forced to gamely swim upstream against the currents of society to guarantee the safe propagation of the species. Lately, there have been a spate of studies, widely reported in the press, telling us how North American kids are getting fatter and fatter—and claiming it's mostly up to parents to do something about it. This kind of news puts more stress on my cardiovascular system than a daily dose of cheeseburger and fries. What can I do, I wonder. I'm only one person. I didn't invent the car or the computer—or those delicious double-chunk-chocolate-chip cookies.

2   True, the researchers behind the most recently published studies don't directly blame parents for this so called "epidemic of childhood obesity." They point fingers at our sedentary modern lifestyle. But they do say that it is up to parents to get kids moving again, one family at a time. I must admit, these social scientists serve up some convincing reasons for reversing the trend. Overweight kids suffer from poor self-esteem. Overweight kids become overweight adults, predisposed to heart disease and diabetes. However, the solution isn't a simple matter of slapping a padlock on the fridge door, as my mother always threatened to do. Kids aren't eating more, anyway. They are just exercising less, much less. And dieting has never been the answer, as experts have shown.

3   Obesity, (I simply hate that word—what exactly is "obese," compared to kinder, gentler cousins like chunky or chubby?) is a side effect of a technological society. We've moved indoors, en masse, and pulled up a soft, comfy chair in the process. Most of us would rather watch just about any sport, even one-armed alpine unicycle racing on cable, than participate in it. Even would-be jocks like my sons can't help but be sidetracked—or, dare I say, seduced—by the siren call of TV, video games, and online chat rooms.

4   Besides, it's costly to counteract this slothful societal trend: I've spent hundreds of dollars outfitting my boys for tennis and skiing. Do you know that credit card commercial? Tennis shoes: 100 dollars. Tennis whites: 80 dollars. Tennis racquet and lessons: 300 dollars. The look on your face when your son says he doesn't want to go to tennis anymore: PRICELESS.

5   I can lead my sons to the courts, but I can't make them serve. And neither can I make society rewind to a time where free play and arduous physical activity were woven into the cloth of everyday life, a time before remote controls, microwaves, indoor plumbing, and the Internet. I can't even go back to the sixties, when girls skipped and boys rode bikes with no brakes.

6   I shouldn't have to put my sons through this kind of humiliation. They are average children, genetically wired to move, jump, and play, play, play 'til they drop. But nobody plays outside most of the time—and when the neighborhood kids do have some down time, they spend ten minutes outside skateboarding and three hours inside playing "Final Fantasy."

7   I read somewhere that male brains are designed to "hit the target," which is why some boys can spend hours taking slap shots at a garbage can or tossing basketballs into a hoop. But for about a decade now, they've had video games to gratify this primal urge. Modern boys don't have to budge a muscle to get a testosterone buzz.

8   The experts have a point when they say it's up to parents to act as role models in this regard. It sure wouldn't hurt us oldsters to get off our duffs, too. I have noticed, over the years, that the active couples I know have active kids. But then I ask my son, "Why don't you come exercise to Sweatin to the Oldies with me?" He just stares at me in horror.

9   If childhood obesity is as big a problem in North America as these researchers say, it's likely we have to do something more to help our kids and to help society. We should lobby school boards and governments. We need to

demand more gym classes and more money for subsidized sports programs in communities. We need to do one more thing, as well. Let our kids engage in more free play—unstructured, inexpensive, creative play beyond the toddler years, even if it entails some misguided bravura, a steep hill, and a bike with no brakes.

VOCABULARY AND COMPREHENSION

1. Find a word in paragraph 1 that means "large number of."

   _____

2. Why is the writer anxious?

   _____

   _____

3. What is causing the childhood obesity epidemic?

   _____

   _____

4. According to the writer, what are some negative aspects of being overweight?

   _____

   _____

5. Why do parents fail to make their children more active?

   _____

   _____

   _____

6. What suggestions does the writer give to get children to exercise more?

   _____

   _____

   _____

GRAMMAR LINK

7. The first sentence in paragraph 5 contains a comma. Why is there a comma before *but*?

   _____

   _____

8. In paragraph 6, underline the verb that follows *nobody*. Why does the verb end in *s*?

   _____

   _____

DISCUSSION AND WRITING

9. What advice would you give to the government to combat obesity?
10. Parents should be blamed for their children's obesity. Argue for or against this statement.

The Writer's Room **Images of Lifestyles and Relationships**

Writing Activity 1: Photo Writing

1. Would you prefer to have a large or small family? Give your reasons.

2. Compare and contrast a large family and a small family.

3. Why do most people decide to have small families? List some reasons and give examples to support your points.

Writing Activity 2: Film Writing

1. Find a movie about obsession. For instance, you can watch *Julia and Julia*, *The Hurt Locker*, *Inside Man*, or another film of your choice. Define a particular obsession and give examples of how it is portrayed in the film.

2. Find a movie about a family. You can watch one of Tyler Perry's Madea films such as *Madea's Big Happy Family*. You can also watch a film such as *The Blind Side* or *Precious*. Compare and contrast two characters in the film.

Theme: **Entertainment, Culture, and Beliefs**

READING 5

What's Your Humor Style?

Louise Dobson

> Louise Dobson has written for *Psychology Today*. As you read this text, look
> for patterns of classification and illustration.

1   In today's personality stakes, nothing is more highly valued than a sense
of humor. We seek it out in others and are proud to claim it in ourselves,
perhaps even more than good looks or intelligence. If someone has a great
sense of humor, we reason, it means that he or she is happy, socially confident,
and has a healthy perspective on life.

2   This attitude would have surprised the ancient Greeks, who believed
humor to be essentially aggressive. And in fact, our admiration for the
comedically gifted is relatively new, and not very well founded, says Rod
Martin, a psychologist at the University of Western Ontario who studies the
way people use humor. Being funny isn't necessarily an indicator of good
social skills and well-being, his research has shown; it may just as likely be a
sign of personality flaws.

3   He has found that humor is a double-edged sword. It can forge better
relationships and help us cope with life, or it can be corrosive, eating away at
self-esteem and antagonizing others. "It's a form of communication, like
speech, and we all use it differently," says Martin. We use bonding humor
to enhance our social connections—but we also may wield it as a way of
excluding or rejecting an outsider. Likewise, put-down humor can at times be
an adaptive, healthy response: Employees suffering under a vindictive boss
will often make the office more bearable by secretly ridiculing their tyrant.

4   Though humor is essentially social, how people use it says a lot about
their sense of self. Those who use self-defeating humor, making fun of
themselves for the enjoyment of others, tend to maintain that hostility toward
themselves even when alone. Similarly, those who are able to view the world
with amused tolerance are often equally forgiving of their own shortcomings.

Put-down Humor

5   This aggressive type of humor is used to criticize and manipulate others
through teasing, sarcasm, and ridicule. When it's aimed against politicians,
it's hilarious and mostly harmless. But in the real world, it has a sharper
impact. Put-down humor, such as telling friends an embarrassing story about
another friend, is a socially acceptable way to deploy aggression and make
others look bad so the storyteller looks good.

6   When challenged on their teasing, put-down jokers often turn to the "just
kidding" defense, allowing the aggressors to avoid responsibility even as the
barb bites. Martin has found no evidence that those who rely on this type of
humor are any less well adjusted. But it does take a toll on personal
relationships.

Bonding Humor

banter:
exchange of light teasing
remarks

7   People who use bonding humor are fun to have around; they say amusing
things, tell jokes, engage in witty **banter,** and generally lighten the mood.

These are the people who give humor a good name. They're perceived as warm, down-to-earth, and kind, good at reducing the tension in uncomfortable situations, and able to laugh at their own faults.

8   Talk show host and comedian Ellen DeGeneres embraces her audience by sharing good-natured, relatable humor. Her basic message is that we're alike, we find the same things funny, and we're all in this together.

9   Nonetheless, bonding humor can have a dark side. After all, a feeling of inclusion can be made sweeter by knowing that someone else is on the outs. J.F.K. and his brothers would often invite a hated acquaintance to vacation with them; they'd be polite to his face, but behind his back, the brothers would unite in deriding the hapless guest.

Hate-me Humor

10   In this style of humor, the funny person is the butt of the joke for the amusement of others. Often **deployed** by people eager to ingratiate themselves, it's the familiar clown or "fat guy" playfulness that we loved in John Belushi and Chris Farley—both of whom suffered for their success. A small dose of it is charming, but a little goes a long way: Routinely offering oneself up to be humiliated erodes self-respect, fostering depression and anxiety. It also can backfire by making other people feel uncomfortable, finds Nicholas Kuiper of the University of Western Ontario. He proposes that it may remind others of their own tendency toward self-criticism.

deployed:
used strategically

11   Farley, who died at age thirty-three from an overdose, had a streak of self-loathing. "Chris chose the immediate pleasure he got in pleasing others over the long-term cost to himself," his brother wrote after his death. The bottom line: Excelling at this style of humor may lead to party invitations but can ultimately exact a high price.

Laughing at Life Humor

12   When we admire someone who "doesn't take himself too seriously," this is the temperament we're talking about. More than just a way of relating to other people, it's a prism that colors the world in rosier shades. Someone with this outlook deploys humor to cope with challenges, taking a step back and laughing at the absurdities of everyday life. *The Onion* is a repository of this benign good humor. The columnist Dave Barry has perfected it with quips like this: "Fishing is boring, unless you catch an actual fish, and then it is disgusting."

The Onion:
a satirical online newspaper

13   Studies that link a sense of humor to good health are probably measuring this phenomenon; when people have a wry perspective, it's hard to remain anxious or hostile for long. Martin calls it "self-enhancing humor," because they don't need other people to entertain them—if something peculiar or annoying happens, they're perfectly capable of laughing at it on their own.

VOCABULARY AND COMPREHENSION

1.   In paragraph 10, what is the meaning of *erodes*?
    a.   improves
    b.   adds to
    c.   slowly destroys

2. In your own words, state the writer's main point.

    _____

    _____

3. What is the difference between put-down humor and hate-me humor?

    _____

    _____

    _____

4. Which type of humor is the most positive? Support your answer with evidence from the text.

    _____

    _____

    _____

5. How has contemporary society's attitude toward humor changed from ancient times?

    _____

    _____

6. The author uses different types of support to develop her ideas. For each type of support listed, find an example from the text.

    expert opinion: _____

    example: _____

GRAMMAR LINK

7. There is a sentence in paragraph 2 that uses a semi-colon. Explain why the writer uses a semi-colon in this sentence.

    _____

8. The last sentence in paragraph 12 contains a quotation. Why is a colon instead of a comma before the quotation marks?

    _____

    _____

DISCUSSION AND WRITING

9. Think of another emotion such as pride, boredom, anger, or happiness. Then divide that emotion into categories, and list types of that emotion. Give examples to support each type.

10. What type of humor do you have? Describe your sense of humor.

READING 6

A Cultural Minefield
William Ecenbarger

> William Ecenbarger is an award-winning journalist. He has written numerous articles for magazines such as *Reader's Digest*. In the next essay, Ecenbarger gives many examples of international business etiquette. As you read this illustration essay, also look for elements of narration, cause and effect, and comparison and contrast.

1   In Sydney, Australia, I simply hailed a taxi, opened the door, and jumped in the back seat. The driver narrowed his eyes. "Where to, mate?" he asked in a voice that could chill a refrigerator. In Marrakech, Morocco, I crossed my legs during an interview with a government official. Immediately, a hush fell over the room. In a restaurant in Mumbai, India, all I did was reach for the naan. A diner at the next table shot me a look that stuck two inches out my back.

2   It took years before I realized what I'd done. It turns out that in each case I had, unwittingly, committed a **faux pas**. To varying degrees, I had offended my hosts. My only comfort is my ignorance. I take solace in Oscar Wilde's observation that a gentleman is someone who never gives offense— unintentionally. And after nearly twenty-five years of travel on six continents, I have learned the hard way that getting through customs is a lot more difficult than just filling out a declaration form. It means navigating a series of cultural booby traps. It means understanding that although people everywhere are the same biologically, they can be worlds apart in their habits and traditions.

faux pas:
a socially embarrassing act

3   Here's my advice for anyone visiting another country: Eat, drink—and be wary. My Australian taxi driver was offended because I sat in the back seat rather than up front next to him. His attitude is not uncommon, according to *Kiss, Bow or Shake Hands*, a book on business behavior. It stems from Australians' disdain of class distinctions. My interview with the Moroccan bureaucrat was cut short because in crossing my legs I had showed him the sole of one of my shoes, a grave affront to Muslims who see the foot as unclean. I reached for the bread in Mumbai. There's nothing wrong with this **per se**, but I did it with my left hand. Indians eat with their hands, in particular their right; their left hands are reserved for other matters, including after-toilet cleansing, and are therefore unacceptable for use at the dining table.

per se:
by itself

4   When I curled my thumb and index finger into a circle and pointed the other three fingers upward, my intention was to tell the Brazilian hotel clerk that everything had been "OK." That would have worked fine at home in the U.S., but in Brazil it's considered vulgar. The OK sign is not OK in many other places too, including most of the rest of Latin America, plus Germany, Malta, Tunisia, Greece, Turkey, Russia, and the Middle East.

5   There are many hand gestures that don't travel well. The "V" for victory sign was immortalized by Winston Churchill in the early, dark days of World War II, and the proper form is with the palm facing outward. A simple twist of the wrist puts you in dangerous cultural waters. Throughout much of Her Majesty's realm, the palm-in V sign is the equivalent of the more infamous middle-digit salute. During the Middle Ages, it was thought that French soldiers would permanently disarm English bowmen by cutting off their middle and index fingers, the ones they used to draw the bowstring. Consequently, the English were said to celebrate battlefield victories and taunt the French by displaying these two digits intact.

6   Even though the "thumbs up" (meaning everything is fine) has worldwide acceptance among many pilots, it can get you in big trouble outside the cockpit. If you're hitchhiking in Nigeria, for example, your upraised thumb may be interpreted as a take-this-and-shove-it insult to passing motorists. The rule of thumb there is, don't do it.

7   Sometimes I think the solution is to tie my hands behind my back, but there are countless other ways to offend while traveling. The entire area of food and drink is a cultural minefield. In Asia, for example, you would never

leave your chopsticks upright in your food. As Chin-ning Chu, author of *The Asian Mind Game*, advises, "In the ceremony to honor the dead, many Asians offer food to their deceased ancestors by placing incense in the bowl and burning it as a way to carry the food to the other world. It is a common Asian superstition that to place your chopsticks in such a way is bad luck and means that this meal is for the dead rather than the living." Furthermore, if you show up with flowers at Asian homes, you'll probably be welcomed warmly, unless, of course, you take white chrysanthemums (they're used only for funerals) or you offer an odd number (considered unlucky in some cultures).

8   When drinking with others in Prague, Czech Republic, before the first sip, the Czechs deem it important to look their companions in the eye and lightly clink glasses. But less than 300 miles away in Budapest, Hungary, that identical gesture can get you deep in goulash. The clink is considered unpatriotic because it was once the signal for a coup.

9   Travel won't broaden you unless your mind is broad to begin with. After all, a foreign country isn't designed to make the traveler comfortable; it's designed to make its own people comfortable.

VOCABULARY AND COMPREHENSION

1.   In paragraph 8, what is the meaning of *deem*?

_____

2.   In paragraph 2, what are "cultural booby traps"?

_____

_____

3.   In your own words, what is the main thesis of this essay?

_____

_____

4.   The author gives examples of what he did wrong in different countries. What was the author's mistake, and why was it a mistake?

Australia: _____

_____

Morocco: _____

_____

India: _____

_____

5.   Which North American hand gestures may possibly offend people of other cultures? Give three examples.

_____

_____

6.   In some Asian countries, why should a person never place chopsticks sticking up in a bowl?

_____

_____

7.   What is the difference in custom when drinking a beer in Prague and drinking a beer in Budapest?

_____

_____

8. How did the author acquire his information on cultural mistakes?

_____

_____

GRAMMAR LINK

9. *Kiss, Bow or Shake Hands* (paragraph 3) and *The Asian Mind Games* (paragraph 7) are in italics. Why are they italicized?

_____

10. The author uses contractions in his essay. Write out the long form for the following contractions.

paragraph 2: I'd = _____ paragraph 7: they're = _____

paragraph 3: there's = _____ paragraph 9: won't = _____

paragraph 6: don't = _____ paragraph 9: it's = _____

DISCUSSION AND WRITING

11. Think of some social and professional situations. Then give examples of good and bad manners particular to that situation. Explain why the manners are considered good or bad.
12. What kinds of skills does travel give a person? Give some examples of those skills and explain why they are important to have.

READING 7
The Cult of Emaciation
Ben Barry

Ben Barry is CEO of Ben Barry Agency, a model consultancy in Toronto. A graduate of Cambridge University, Barry is the author of *Fashioning Reality*. As you read this argument essay, notice how the author also uses cause and effect, illustration, narration, and description.

1   On this final day of L'Oreal Fashion Week, Canada's top models are strutting their stuff in Toronto. For some, this will have been their first chance to walk the runway. Others will be veterans of the global catwalk circuit. But they will all have one thing in common: extreme, some would say freakish, thinness.

2   Models are the stars of every fashion week. Sure, designers create the outfits, but the models bring those clothes to life. Their faces and bodies saturate our televisions, newspapers, and computer screens. Models are the ones with glamour on tap, the kind of glamour we all supposedly want to taste.

3   For the past nine years, since I was fifteen years old, I have attended countless fashion shows. I was initially an up-and-coming modeling agent sneaking into the shows through back doors. I eventually became established, and I was officially invited to sit among the fashion elite. "Ben, you're so lucky," my friends bemoan, "going to fashion shows and meeting the models. It must all be so glamorous." That sad truth is that I have always found fashion modeling to be a tragic and demeaning experience.

4   In the days before a fashion week begins, models rush to meet with designers for castings. The designers flip through models' portfolios, ask them to walk the length of the room, have them try on articles of clothing, and of course, take their pictures. The models are in and out without saying anything

more than "yes" and "thank you." When asked what they remember about the models, designers respond, "her size." Physical attributes constitute the only job requirement.

5   Things start going wrong for many models right away. At one casting, "Ashley," nineteen years old, size zero, 5'10", is asked to try on a pair of trousers. After a couple of minutes of struggling to close the top button, the designer marches over. "Your hips are too big, you need to make them smaller," he says in front of all the other models before shooing her out the door. Ashley leaves, humiliated and confused, wondering how she is supposed to alter the size of her hips.

6   The girls who do get booked for shows aren't allowed to leave their body stress behind them. Backstage is where things get really frightening. At London Fashion Week in 2007, I took it all in. One model, "Jennifer," was trying to close a zipper on her designer jacket. The designer stood before her, shaking his head. "You've gotten fat," he said to the eighteen-year-old, size zero model. "I'll need to let this jacket out. It will ruin the cut. They're not made for big girls like you." Jennifer turned red. She managed to hold back her tears as the designer made his adjustments, and everyone stopped to gawk.

7   On another occasion, I witnessed an equally thin model get even worse treatment when she couldn't fit into her size zero dress. The designer pointed to another model and proclaimed, "She'll wear the dress instead. Your stomach has gotten too big. Dismissed!" The girl tried to hide between the racks of clothing while she peeled off the tiny dress. She was later escorted out as everyone stared.

8   The situation is worse for mature models; we are talking about anyone older than twenty. Most begin their careers at a time when their body shape is still pre-pubescent. They get older, they develop curves, and bye-bye sample sizes. I met Rena, twenty-two years old, size two, backstage at London Fashion Week. She told me that this had to be her last season. "I can't handle it any more. Every time I do a show now, I get so anxious. There are so many teenage girls. I'm on Slim-Fast, but there's no way I can compete any longer." I offered her an apple. "No, thanks," she replied. "My agent said fruit causes bloating." I assured her that there is no fat in fruit, but she didn't care.

9   Megan, sixteen years old, put it this way: "No matter how skinny you are, you always think you can be skinnier, and there are other girls that are going to be skinnier than you." If the very women representing the beauty ideal feel excluded from it, how can anyone feel included?

10   Agents are always there to make sure a model's weight remains first and foremost in her mind. Rebecca, eighteen years old, dropped by her agency before a casting to surprise her hard-working booker with a latte. Her kindness was repaid by her being unexpectedly weighed and measured in front of everyone who happened to be there.

11   Constant public humiliation—whether at the casting, the fashion show, or the agency—is the norm in the so-called glamorous life of a model. Everyone in the fashion world, from the agents to the designers to the make-up artists, feels he or she has a God-given right to comment on a model's appearance. And everyone is prepared to tell painfully thin models that they need to be thinner. Such comments would amount to harassment in any other profession.

12   It is no wonder that many models develop eating disorders. No one values their thoughts, personalities, or feelings. Everyone values them for their bodies alone. In time, models internalize the dangerous idea that they

are worth what they look like. I have met many models who had a passion for politics or writing or basketball when they first started. Two or three years later, any other interests are squelched to make way for a deep and abiding obsession with weight and appearance. The sad irony is the qualities that make supermodels—the ones who rise to the very top of the industry exude energy, attitude, and character with every strut and pose—are progressively stripped away by the casting process when it comes to most girls.

13   Fashion industry insiders claim that they are not to blame for any deaths by malnutrition. Those are isolated incidents. The ways models are treated and valued supposedly has nothing to do with the tragedies. I beg to differ. Just You Tube any episode of *Top Model* and watch how girls are transformed in front of your eyes from multi-faceted, confident young women to weight-obsessed, insecure wrecks. The heartrending incidents are the result of working within an industry that objectifies women, which, in turn, teaches them to objectify themselves.

14   This must sound very hypocritical coming from a modeling agent. But I do things differently. My models span all ages, sizes, colors, and abilities. They are accepted, promoted, and hired based on their natural physical attributes. I don't represent any models full-time. They go to school, work as doctors and sales clerks, and run their own businesses. Modeling is something they do on the side for a few days every month—a performance to which they bring their varied experiences to bear.

15   I don't expect our entire "glamorous" modeling industry to follow my example overnight. What can we do to protect the wellbeing of models in the short term? L'Oreal Fashion Week needs to follow the lead of event organizers in Madrid and Milan by mandating medical tests for each model to ensure they are of healthy weight. Let them feel like they can get away with eating an apple now and then.

16   Any major fashion house choosing such a strategy would receive international attention. For those worried about the bottom line, diversity would allow consumers to relate to the models, relate to the brand, and demonstrate that positive relationship through spending power. Most significantly, women reading magazines and watching fashion television who say, "I could never look like that," will be free to rediscover themselves. Then, and only then, will modeling truly be a glamorous life.

VOCABULARY AND COMPREHENSION

1. Using context clues, define *bemoan* as it is used in paragraph 3.

    _____

2. Underline the thesis statement of the essay. Remember that it may not be in the first paragraph of the text.

3. How does the writer support his point that modeling is demeaning?

    _____

    _____

4. How does life in the modeling industry affect the models?

    _____

    _____

    _____

5.   What is the main problem that Ben Barry identifies in the fashion industry?

_____

_____

6.   What solution does Barry suggest to help solve the problem?

_____

_____

GRAMMAR LINK

7.   In the first sentence of paragraph 3, the author writes *have attended*, using the present perfect form of the verb. Why does he use the present perfect instead of the simple past (*attended*)?

_____

_____

8.   In the second sentence in paragraph 4, why does the word *models'* have an apostrophe after the final *s* rather than before the final *s*?

_____

_____

DISCUSSION AND WRITING

9.   Barry suggests that the modeling industry has contributed to the rise in eating disorders. What other factors cause people to develop eating disorders?

10.   What can the fashion industry and the media do to provide viewers with more positive body images? Give examples to support your point.

READING 8

Shopping for Religion
Ellen Goodman

Ellen Goodman is a columnist for the *Boston Globe*. She has also authored many books. In 1980, she received a Pulitzer Prize for distinguished commentary. As you read this argument essay, also look for elements of comparison and contrast.

1   Just below the text there was a Google ad inviting me to take a quiz. "Christian? Jewish? Muslim? Atheist? See Which Religion is Right for You." Aside from the eccentricity of listing atheism as a religion, I couldn't help wondering what my grandparents would make of this religious matching service. For that matter, what would they make of the idea that they could choose their religion at all? To them, religion was part of their identity, if not their DNA. They were born into it, grew up in it, and died with its prayers.

2   I noticed this ad because it was attached to the story of a new report on religion in America released by the Pew Forum on Religion and Public Life. The researchers interviewed 35,000 Americans. Their figures show that Protestants now comprise a bare majority—51 percent—of the population, and that the fastest-growing group is the 16 percent now self-described as "unaffiliated." But what is most fascinating is that 44 percent of Americans

have left the religious traditions in which they grew up. They left the religion of their parents with the frequency that they left their old neighborhood.

3   In my grandparents' day, Americans were divided between the big three religions, sort of like TV networks: Catholic, Protestant, and Jew. Now they have fragmented across a spectrum more like cable TV with satellite radio thrown in. The researchers describe a "vibrant marketplace where individuals pick and choose religions that meet their needs." They surf their options. "We are shopping for everything else, why wouldn't we shop for religion?" asks religion professor Donald Miller of the University of Southern California. Pew's John Green adds, "It's not surprising that we have a marketplace in religious or spiritual ideas." What's qualitatively different these days, he says, is that we have much more religious diversity.

4   I realize that for many Americans the idea of shopping for eternal truths is still jarring, even contradictory. The movement from one "tradition" to another may even suggest a kind of promiscuity—a faithless pursuit of faith. Yet the idea of religion as a personal choice seems thoroughly American—as American as religious tolerance. And increasingly these two ideas may be related.

5   America has long been regarded as the most religious of Western nations. Six in ten Americans say that religion plays a very important role in our lives. Polls show that Americans are more willing to vote for a woman, a black, or a Jew, than an atheist. **Secular** Europeans who look at those figures regard Americans as unthinking believers—conservatives following orders delivered from the pulpit.

secular:
not connected with religion

6   At home the culture wars are often polarized between the religious right and the secular left. Leaders of both sides often characterize—perhaps **caricature**—religious members as people rooted in old ways and immutable ideas. But a huge number of Americans are mobile in pursuit of the immutable. "We are, as a country, people who want to choose their own identity in a lot of areas of life, and religion is one more part of it," says Alan Wolfe of Boston College. There's a difference between an identity that's achieved rather than **ascribed**. Those who leave their childhood religions largely regard themselves as making their own individual choice. In this cultural context, even staying becomes an active decision.

caricature:
a portrait that exaggerates certain characteristics

ascribed:
given to someone

7   When religion was cast in stone, we were more likely to cast stones. It may be the new pluralism and the framing of religion as a choice that make us more accepting. "You are the artist of your own life when it comes to religion," says Miller. "This enables people to be more thoughtful about what they perceive to be true and right rather than inheriting what passes down to them."

8   Indeed, if we've left our childhood traditions, if our children may leave ours, there is good reason to nurture what Wolfe calls "intolerance insurance." The Pew study also shows that 40 percent of all marriages are of mixed religious traditions—including "none of the above." We take coexistence pretty literally.

9   I don't think Americans are just shopping for their beliefs in a trivial sense, trying on creeds like this year's **vestment**, searching for the latest spiritual fashion. But we are a people on the move. About 40 million of us move to another home every year. So too, we drop in and out of church, U-Hauling our beliefs off in search of a better fit. Today, we may shop in a spiritual mall but with the good fortune to find the mall paved over the old religious battlefields.

vestment:
clothing

VOCABULARY AND COMPREHENSION

1. Find a word in paragraph 6 that means *unchanging*.

    _____

2. Which sentence best expresses the main idea of this essay?
    a. In the past, Americans were divided between the big three religions.
    b. People shop for religion as casually as they shop for socks; they do not consider the consequences.
    c. In America, many people now choose their religion, leading to more religious diversity than in the past.
    d. There are many religious options available for people, but most are undecided and do not know what religion to follow.

3. According to the author, what is the difference between the present generation and past generations in terms of practicing a religion?

    _____

    _____

4. According to a report on religion in America, what percentage of people claim to have changed religious views?

    _____

5. Does the author support the notion of shopping for religion? Explain your answer and provide examples from the text.

    _____

    _____

    _____

    _____

GRAMMAR LINK

6. In paragraph 3, why are Catholic, Protestant, and Jew capitalized?

    _____

    _____

7. In paragraph 3, the author writes, "my grandparents' day" and in paragraph 9, she writes "this year's vestment" Why does she place the apostrophe after the *s* in the first example, and before the *s* in the second example? Explain the rule about possession.

    _____

    _____

DISCUSSION AND WRITING

8. Have you ever rejected your own religion or tried "shopping for religion"? Narrate some of your experiences.
9. Should high schools teach courses about comparative religion? Would it help to promote religious tolerance? Explain your views.
10. In 2007, Governor Sonny Perdue of Georgia led a public prayer for rain. In many states, politicians publicly oppose abortion on religious grounds. Should there be a more strict separation of church and state? Explain why or why not?

The Writer's Room — Images of Entertainment, Culture, and Beliefs

Writing Activity 1: Photo Writing

1. Describe a music concert or performance that you have seen. Use imagery that appeals to the senses.

2. Do you think music lessons should be compulsory in school? Explain why or why not.

3. Does a song bring back specific memories for you? Describe the song and the memories that it evokes.

Writing Activity 2: Film Writing

1. Watch *The Soloist*, *Dreamgirls*, or *Crazy Heart*. Choose one of the characters, and describe the process the character goes through to achieve his or her goals.

2. View a film biography about a real-life person. For example, watch *Milk*, *Invictus*, *The Informant*, *Ray*, or *Walk the Line*. Write about the causes or effects of the character's actions.

3. Watch a film clip from a silent movie, and then invent dialogue for the film.

Theme: The Earth and Its Creatures

READING 9

What It Feels Like to Walk on the Moon
Buzz Aldrin

On July 20, 1969, *Apollo 11* landed on the moon. Astronauts Neil Armstrong, Michael Collins, and Edwin E. Aldrin, Jr. (also known as Buzz Aldrin) spent two and a half hours walking on the moon's surface. In the next essay, Aldrin describes that experience. As you read this descriptive essay, notice how the writer also uses elements of process writing.

1   The surface of the moon is like fine talcum powder. It is very loose at the top. At a deeper level, a half inch or so, it becomes much more compact, almost

as if it were cemented together. It seems that way because there are no air molecules between the molecules of dust.

2   When I put my foot down in the powder, the boot print preserved itself exquisitely. When I would take a step, a little semicircle of dust would spray out before me. It was odd because the dust did not behave at all the way it behaves here on Earth. On Earth, dust is sometimes puffy or sandy. On the moon, the powdery dust travels through no air at all, so the dust is kicked up, and then it all falls at the same time in a perfect semicircle.

3   I am trying the best I can to put it into words, but being on the moon is just different—different from anything I have ever seen. To use the word *alien* would mislead people. *Surreal* is probably as good a word as I have. When I looked out the window of the lunar lander as we touched down, the sun was out, the sky was velvety black, the engine was shut down, and everything was silent. That was surreal.

contrivance:
deceitful invention

4   When I was on the moon, there was very little audio around, only the sounds of my suit—the hum of pumps circulating fluid. But I didn't hear any amplified breathing inside my mask; that is a Hollywood **contrivance.** The name of the game on the moon was staying cool and not exerting too much so that I would never be out of breath.

5   If you remember the television images we sent back, you know that I was attempting to demonstrate different walking motions, going back and forth in front of the camera. I tried what you might call a kangaroo hop, and then I demonstrated how I needed a few steps to change direction because of the

inertia:
inability to move with ease; sluggish movement

inertia that was up there. I found that the best way to move around at a fairly good clip was not by using a jogging motion—one foot, then the other—but rather by moving more the way a horse gallops: one-two, one-two, two steps in rapid succession, followed by a lope, followed by two more rapid steps.

6   And then there is the picture where I was standing next to the flag. I was leaning forward a good bit because of the center of gravity of the backpack that I was wearing. On the moon, it was sometimes hard to tell when I might be on the verge of losing my balance. As I leaned a little bit to one side or the other, I came in danger of falling. But it was easy to right myself by pushing down on the surface with my feet. The lunar surface is so easy, so natural, and so readily adapted to by any human being. The low gravity makes it very convenient to get around. It is really a very nice environment.

metaphysically:
refers to abstract, philosophical thinking

wafted:
floated

7   While we were on the moon, there was no time to savor the moment. It seemed as though what we were doing was so significant that to pause for a moment and reflect **metaphysically** was really contrary to our mission. We were not trained to smell the roses. We were not hired to utter philosophical truisms on the spur of the moment. We had a job to do.

8   I do remember that one realization **wafted** through my mind when I was up there. I noted that here were two guys farther away from anything than two guys had ever been before. That is what I thought about. And yet, at the same time, I was very conscious that everything was being closely scrutinized a quarter of a million miles away.

9   Everything and anything we did would be recorded, remembered, and studied for ages. It felt a little like being the young kid in the third or fourth grade who is all of a sudden asked to go up on stage in front of the whole school and recite the Gettysburg Address. And as he tries to remember the words, he has got gun-barrel vision. He does not see what is going on around him; he is focused on that particular task, conscious only of his performance. It

was like that but even more so. The eyes of the world were on us, and if we made a mistake, we would regret it for quite a while.

10   I guess, if I look back on things, there was one little moment of **levity,** a bit of unusual **extemporaneousness.** When the countdown came to lift off from the moon, when it got to twenty seconds, Houston said, "Tranquility Base, you're cleared for liftoff." And I said in response, "Roger, we're number one on the runway." Now comedy is the absurd put into a natural position. There was no runway up there. And there certainly wasn't anyone else waiting in line to lift off. I was conscious of that, being first.

levity:
lightness; humor
extemporaneousness:
improvised or unplanned
action

VOCABULARY AND COMPREHENSION

1. Find a word in paragraph 7 that means "to say."

    _____

2. In the introduction, Aldrin uses an analogy, or comparison of two things, to make the reader understand the situation. What is this analogy, and how effective is it?

    _____

    _____

3. In paragraph 3, Adrin describes the moonscape as *surreal*. What does he mean? You might try dividing *surreal* into the prefix and the main word.

    _____

    _____

4. What is the main point of paragraphs 5 and 6?

    _____

    _____

5. What does Aldrin mean when he writes in paragraph 7 that astronauts "were not trained to smell the roses"?

    _____

    _____

    _____

6. What did Aldrin hear when he was on the moon?

    _____

7. Underline five descriptive phrases that best describe what it feels like to walk on the moon.

GRAMMAR LINK

8. In the first sentence of paragraph 9, underline four main verbs and circle two helping verbs. Then explain which verbs in the sentence are active and which are passive.

    _____

9. Why does the author use a semicolon in the second sentence of paragraph 4?

    _____

    _____

DISCUSSION AND WRITING

10.   Go for a walk in a new place. Use your senses and give details about what you see, hear, smell, and touch.

11.   In the future, it may be possible for ordinary citizens to travel to outer space. Would you like to go on a space flight? Why or why not?

12.   Buzz Aldrin does not introduce his topic. Instead, he immediately describes his sensations when he walked on the moon. Write an introduction for this essay.

READING 10

The Fire Below

Bill Bryson

Bill Bryson is the author of many best-selling books including *Neither Here nor There* and *The Lost Continent*. The following excerpt, from *A Short History of Nearly Everything*, describes what happened when a volcano erupted in the state of Washington. In this narrative essay, also look for elements of cause and effect and comparison and contrast.

salutary:
beneficial

1   Perhaps nothing better demonstrates our inadequate grasp of the dynamics of the Earth's interior than how badly we are caught out when it acts up, and it would be hard to come up with a more **salutary** reminder of the limitations of our understanding than the eruption of Mount St. Helens in Washington in 1980. At that time, the lower forty-eight United States had not seen a volcanic eruption for over sixty-five years. Therefore, the government volcanologists called in to monitor and forecast St Helens' behavior primarily had seen only Hawaiian volcanoes in action, and they, it turned out, were not the same thing at all.

albeit:
although

2   St. Helens started its ominous rumblings on March 20. Within a week, it was erupting magma, **albeit** in modest amounts, up to a hundred times a day, and being constantly shaken with earthquakes. People were evacuated to what was assumed to be a safe distance of eight miles. As the mountain's rumblings grew, St. Helens became a tourist attraction for the world. Newspapers gave daily reports on the best places to get a view. Television crews repeatedly flew in helicopters to the summit, and people were even seen climbing over the mountain. On one day, more than seventy copters and light aircraft circled the summit. But as the days passed and the rumblings failed to develop into anything dramatic, people grew restless, and the view became general that the volcano wasn't going to blow after all.

3   On April 19, the northern flank of the mountain began to bulge conspicuously. Remarkably, no one in a position of responsibility saw that this strongly signaled a lateral blast. The seismologists resolutely based their conclusions on the behavior of Hawaiian volcanoes, which don't blow out sideways. Almost the only person who believed that something really bad might happen was Jack Hyde, a geology professor at a community college in Tacoma. He pointed out that St. Helens didn't have an open vent, as Hawaiian volcanoes have, so any pressure building up inside was bound to be released dramatically and probably catastrophically. However, Hyde was not part of the official team, and his observations attracted little notice.

4   We all know what happened next. At 8:32 A.M. on a Sunday morning, May 18, the north side of the volcano collapsed, sending an enormous avalanche of dirt and rock rushing down the mountain slope at 150 miles an hour. It was the biggest landslide in human history and carried enough material to bury the

whole of Manhattan to a depth of 400 feet. A minute later, its flank severely weakened, St. Helens exploded with the force of five hundred Hiroshima-sized atomic bombs, shooting out a murderous hot cloud at up to 650 miles an hour— much too fast, clearly, for anyone nearby to outrace. Many people who were thought to be in safe areas, often far out of sight of the volcano, were overtaken. Fifty-seven people were killed. Twenty-three of the bodies were never found. The toll would have been much higher except that it was a Sunday. Had it been a weekday, many lumber workers would have been working within the death zone. As it was, people were killed eighteen miles away.

5   The luckiest person on that day was a graduate student named Harry Glicken. He had been manning an observation post 5.7 miles from the mountain, but he had a college placement interview on May 18 in California, and so he had left the site the day before the eruption. His place was taken by David Johnston. Johnston was the first to report the volcano exploding; moments later he was dead. His body was never found. Glicken's luck, alas, was temporary. Eleven years later, he was one of forty-three scientists and journalists fatally caught up in a lethal outpouring of superheated ash, gases, and molten rock—what is known as a pyroclastic flow—at Mount Unzen in Japan when yet another volcano was catastrophically misread.

VOCABULARY AND COMPREHENSION

1.   In paragraph 3, what is the meaning of flank? Choose the best answer.
     a. line   c. side
     b. to defend or guard   d. occupy

2.   Underline a sentence that expresses the main idea of this essay.

3.   What mistakes did officials make regarding Mount St. Helens? Think of at least three mistakes.

     _____

     _____

     _____

     _____

4.   Why were the observations of Jack Hyde, a community college professor, ignored?

     _____

5.   In paragraph 4, Bryson describes the volcanic explosion. Which analogies, or comparisons, help readers understand the extent of the explosion?

     _____

     _____

6.   Why was the death toll so low?

     _____

GRAMMAR LINK

7.   In the last paragraph, Bryson writes that Glicken "had been manning an observation post 5.7 miles from the mountain." Why is the past perfect progressive verb tense—*had been manning*—used instead of *was manning*?

     _____

     _____

8. In paragraph 5, a passive verb form is used in the phrase "His place was taken." (For information about passive verbs, see page 191.) Identify another passive verb in paragraph 5 and write it here.

DISCUSSION AND WRITING

9. In the essay, Bryson says that humans have an "inadequate grasp" of the Earth's dynamics. Write an essay about another event that caught people off guard. What happened? What mistakes did experts make?
10. Write about a shocking or extreme weather event that occurred in your region. What happened? How did people react?

READING 11

The Zoo Life
Yann Martel

Yann Martel, the son of diplomats, was born in Spain but has lived in various countries throughout the world. In 2002, he won the prestigious Man Booker Prize for his novel *The Life of Pi*, from which this excerpt is taken. As you read the selection, notice how the author mainly uses comparison and contrast writing as well as elements of argument.

1   If you went to a home, kicked down the front door, chased the people who lived there out into the street, and said, "Go! You are free! Free as a bird! Go! Go!"—do you think they would shout and dance for joy? They wouldn't. The people you've just evicted would sputter, "With what right do you throw us out? This is our home. We own it. We have lived here for years. We're calling the police, you scoundrel."

2   Don't we say, "There's no place like home"? That's certainly what animals feel. Animals are territorial. That is the key to their minds. Only a familiar territory will allow them to fulfill the two relentless imperatives of the wild: the avoidance of enemies and the getting of food and water. A biologically sound zoo enclosure—whether cage, pit, moated island, corral, terrarium, **aviary,** or aquarium—is just another territory, peculiar only in its size and in its proximity to human territory. That it is so much smaller than what it would be in nature stands to reason.

aviary:
enclosure for birds

3   Territories in the wild are large not as a matter of taste but of necessity. In a zoo, we do for animals what we have done for ourselves with houses: We bring together in a small space what in the wild is spread out. Whereas before for us the cave was here, the river over there, the hunting grounds a mile that way, the lookout next to it, the berries somewhere else—all of them **infested** with lions, snakes, ants, leeches, and poison ivy—now the river flows through taps at hand's reach, and we can wash next to where we sleep, we can eat where we have cooked, and we can surround the whole with a protective wall and keep it clean and warm.

infested:
invaded by

4   A house is a compressed territory where our basic needs can be fulfilled close by and safely. A sound zoo enclosure is the equivalent for an animal (with the noteworthy absence of a fireplace or the like, present in every human habitation). Finding within it all the places it needs—a lookout, a place for resting, for eating and drinking, for bathing, for grooming, etc. and finding that there is no need to go hunting, food appearing seven days a week, an animal

will take possession of its zoo space in the same way it would lay claim to a new space in the wild, exploring it and marking it out in the normal ways of its species, with sprays of urine perhaps. Once this moving-in ritual is done and the animal has settled, it will not feel like a nervous tenant, and even less like a prisoner, but rather like a landholder, and it will behave in the same way within its enclosure as it would in its territory in the wild, including defending it tooth and nail should it be invaded.

5   Such an enclosure is neither better nor worse for an animal than its condition in the wild; so long as it fulfills the animal's needs, a territory, natural or constructed, simply *is*, without judgment, a given, like the spots on a leopard. One might even argue that if an animal could choose with intelligence, it would opt for living in a zoo, since the major difference between a zoo and the wild is the absence of parasites and enemies and the abundance of food in the first, and their respective abundance and scarcity in the second. Think about it yourself. Would you rather be put up at the Ritz with free room service and unlimited access to a doctor or be homeless without a soul to care for you? But animals are incapable of such **discernment**. Within the limits of their nature, they make do with what they have.

discernment:
judgment

6   A good zoo is a place of carefully worked-out coincidence: exactly where an animal says to us, "Stay out!" with its urine or other secretion, we say to it, "Stay in!" with our barriers. Under such conditions of diplomatic peace, all animals are content, and we can relax and have a look at each other.

VOCABULARY AND COMPREHENSION

1. In paragraph 5, what is the meaning of *scarcity*?
    a. shortage
    b. insufficient
    c. large amount

2. Martel compares a house and an animal's enclosure. What are the similarities?

    _____

    _____

    _____

3. Brainstorm the major difference(s) between a zoo enclosure and a person's house.

    _____

    _____

4. In your opinion, is Martel's comparison fair? Provide your reasons.

    _____

    _____

    _____

5. In paragraph 5, the writer asks, "Would you rather be put up at the Ritz with free room service and unlimited access to a doctor or be homeless without a soul to care for you?" How would you answer the question? Explain why.

    _____

    _____

    _____

GRAMMAR LINK

6. The next-to-last sentence in paragraph 2, beginning with "A biologically sound," has many commas. What rule could you write about the use of commas with a series of items?

   _____

   _____

7. The first sentence in paragraph 6 contains the word *carefully*. Why do you have to spell *carefully* with two *l*'s?

   _____

   _____

DISCUSSION AND WRITING

8. The author mentions that animals mark their territories in some way, perhaps with a spray of urine. What are ways that humans mark or identify their territory?

9. Compare and contrast a zoo enclosure and life in the wild. What are some similarities and differences?

10. Develop arguments that oppose Martel's main points.

READING 12

Is It Love or a Trick?

Jon Katz

> Jon Katz is the author of *A Good Dog: The Story of Orson, Who Changed My Life*. As you read this abridged cause and effect essay, also look for elements of argument.

1   My friend and fellow dog lover Edie, an occupational therapist in Massachusetts, has been looking for a mate for nearly ten years. She finally thought she'd found one in Jeff, a nice guy who teaches high school. They dated for several months, and just as there was talk about a future, it occurred to Edie that Jeff hadn't really bonded with her yellow Lab, Sophie. In fact, as she thought more about it, she wasn't sure Jeff was a dog guy at all.

2   She confronted him about this issue at dinner one night, and he confessed, in some anguish, that he didn't love Sophie, didn't love dogs in general, and never had. They broke up the next week. More accurately, she dumped him. "What can I say?" Edie told me, somewhat defensively. "Sophie has been there for me, day in and day out, for years. I can't say the same of men. She's my girl, my baby. Sooner or later, it would have ended."

3   Having just spent two months on a book tour talking to dog lovers, I can testify that this story isn't unusual. The lesson Edie gleaned, she says, was that she should have asked about Sophie first, not last. In North America, we love our dogs a lot. We love them so much that we rarely wonder why anymore.

4   This feeling, perhaps, is why God created academics. John Archer, a psychologist at the University of Central Lancashire, has been puzzling for some time over why people love their pets. In evolutionary terms, love for dogs and other pets "poses a problem," he writes. Being attached to animals is not, strictly speaking, necessary for human health and welfare. Studies show that people with pets live a bit longer and have better blood pressure than **benighted** non-owners, but in the literal sense, they don't really need all those dogs and cats to survive.

benighted:
unenlightened

5   Archer has a theory: "Consider the possibility that pets are, in evolutionary terms, manipulating human responses. Consider that they are the equivalent of social parasites." Social parasites inject themselves into the social systems of other species and thrive there.

6   Dogs are masters at that strategy. They show a range of emotions—love, anxiety, curiosity—and thus trick us into thinking they possess the full range of human feelings. They dance with joy when we come home, put their heads on our knees, and stare longingly into our eyes. Ah, we think, at last, the love and loyalty we so richly deserve and so rarely receive. Over thousands of years of living with humans, dogs have become wily and transfixing sidekicks with the particularly appealing characteristic of being unable to speak. We are therefore free to fill in the blanks with what we need to hear. What the dog may really be telling us, much of the time, is, "Feed me."

7   It's a good deal for the pets, too, since we respond by spending lavishly on organic treats and high-quality health-care. Psychologist Brian Hare of Harvard has also studied the human-animal bond and reports that dogs are astonishingly skilled at reading humans' patterns of social behavior, especially behaviors related to food and care. They figure out our moods, what makes us happy, and what moves us. Then they act accordingly, and we tell ourselves that they're crazy about us. "It appears that dogs have evolved specialized skills for reading human social and communicative behavior," Hare concludes, which is why dogs live so much better than moles.

8   These are interesting theories. Raccoons and squirrels don't show recognizable human emotions, nor do they trigger our nurturing "She's my baby" impulses. So, they usually don't move into our houses, get their photos taken with Santa or even get names. Thousands of rescue workers aren't standing by to move them lovingly from one home to another.

9   If the dog's love is just an evolutionary trick, is it diminished? I don't think so. Dogs have figured out how to **insinuate** themselves into human society in ways that benefit us both. We get affection and attention. They get the same, plus food, shelter, and protection. To grasp this exchange doesn't trivialize our love; it explains it.

insinuate:
to integrate slyly

10   I'm enveloped by dog love, myself. Izzy, a border collie who spent the first four years of his life running along a small square of fencing on a nearby farm, is lying under my desk at the moment, his head resting on my boot. Rose, my working dog, is curled into a tight ball in the crate to my left. Emma, the newcomer who spent six years inside the same fence as Izzy, prefers the newly re-upholstered antique chair. Plagued with health problems, she likes to be near the wood stove in the winter.

11   When I stir to make tea, answer the door, or stretch my legs, all three dogs move with me. I see them peering out from behind the kitchen table or pantry door, awaiting instructions, as border collies do. If I return to the computer, they resume their previous positions, with stealth and agility. If I analyzed it coldly, I would admit that they're probably alert to see if an outdoor romp is in the offing, or some sheepherding, or some beef jerky. But I'd rather think they can't bear to let me out of their sight.

VOCABULARY AND COMPREHENSION

1.   What is the meaning of *gleaned* in paragraph 3?
     a. removed   b. added   c. discovered

2. Which sentence best expresses the main idea of the essay?

    a. Our pets, and dogs in particular, have learned to manipulate humans to the benefit of both species.

    b. People love their pets too much and spend extravagantly, paying for items such as their pets' organic food and health care.

    c. Most animals, including raccoons and squirrels, do not trigger our nurturing response.

    d. Dogs trick humans into loving them, which is beneficial for the dogs but not for their human owners.

3. Explain how dogs are *social parasites.*

_____

_____

4. How do dogs manipulate their owners? List at least three actions.

_____

_____

_____

5. According to the writer, what is the real reason that dogs trick humans?

_____

_____

6. How is the behavior of dogs different from wild animals?

_____

_____

7. How do human beings benefit from their pets?

_____

_____

GRAMMAR LINK

8. Adverbs modify verbs, adjectives, and other adverbs. In paragraph 6, underline three adverbs and circle the words they modify.

9. In paragraph 11, what is the difference in meaning of the words *they're* and *their*?

_____

_____

DISCUSSION AND WRITING

10. In America, many people enter their pets in pet shows. They spend a lot of time and money grooming their pets and training them for the competitions. Why do people do that? What are the effects on the pets? Give the causes and/or effects of pet shows.

11. Define pet obsession. Give examples of people who are obsessed with their pets.

12. Sometimes pets turn on their owners or harm other people. Should certain types of pets such as Pitt Bulls or snakes be banned?

The Writer's Room

Images of the Earth and Its Creatures

Writing Activity 1: Photo Writing

1. What animal scares you the most? Explain why.

2. How do animals contribute to humans' lives? Think about products or services that animals provide for humans. List specific examples.

3. What can humans learn by watching animals? List specific examples.

Writing Activity 2: Film Writing

1. Watch a science fiction film about the future or about a fantasy world. For example, view *Inception*, *Avatar*, *Repo Men*, or any of the *Iron Man* or *Star Wars* movies. Describe the time and place. Include descriptions that appeal to the senses.

2. Watch a classic film about a fear of animals. For example, watch Spielberg's *Jaws*, Hitchcock's *The Birds*, or Cronenberg's *The Fly*. Classify the types of animal fears that people have. You might also choose one of the movies and describe the most frightening scene. Include details that appeal to the sentences.

3. View the film *Into the Wild*. Why does the main character want to retreat from civilization? What are the effects of his choices? Write about causes or effects of the character's actions.

Theme: **Trades, Technology, and the Business World**

READING 13

The Allure of Apple

Juan Rodriquez

> Juan Rodriguez writes about popular culture and music for various publications in Canada and the U.S. He writes a weekly column and feature essays for *The Montreal Gazette*. As you read this definition essay, also look for elements of comparison and contrast.

1   Born to shop, and looking for nirvana in an iMac or iPod or iPhone or iPad, I enter an ultra-sleek Apple Store anticipating a quasi-spiritual experience. It is a place of glass and mirrors and wood and stainless steel that acts as a shrine to the cult of Apple Computer, and more specifically of Steve Jobs, the corporation's co-founder, fearless leader, and inscrutable guru. The store is his gleaming interdenominational church (he is a Buddhist), offering a Grand Design for Living that he calls the "digital lifestyle." The buzz around Apple products—products Steve famously dubbed "insanely great"—is intense, but the **furtive** murmur inside the store is pure postmodern prayer. No doubt, the cult of Apple is a transformative experience. I've been hooked for twenty years without knowing the first thing about the science behind the computer revolution.

2   Part of the "Apple ecosystem," encompassing 275 outlets in nine countries, the Apple store is très chic. The ceiling appears higher than it is—the sky's the limit! You don't merely browse the goods in this sacred space. It's more like star-gazing: hardware as **objets d'art**. A pale sea green glass staircase (patented by Jobs) leads up to where accessories are sold. Apple personnel wear T-shirts over a simple cotton jersey to go with their open no-pressure faces.

3   Whenever I watch those cute PC versus Mac ads on the tube, I'm reminded of my first encounter with the cult of Apple. My journey in life had taken me on a whim to Berkeley, California to hook up with a teenage flame whom I hadn't seen in twenty-three years. One of the first things that she advised me to do was dump my PC and get a Macintosh Classic, the beginner computer that even an idiot—or an East Coaster—could operate hassle-free. She took me to BMUG (Berkeley Macintosh Users Group) meetings, on the University of California campus, that she attended religiously. The large auditorium in the round science building on a hill—the Mac cult's church of nerds—was populated by geeks speaking in exotic codes and futuristic tongues.

4   From the get-go, she set up the contrasts: The PC (then typified by IBM) was old, stuffy and hierarchical, sooo East Coast. Apple was the West, embodying the American frontier spirit—the digital frontier! Then there was the name itself: IBM refers to International Business Machines, the anonymous and crass anything-at-all-costs business. Apple and Macintosh, on the other hand, is a whole earth digital food inviting you to take a creative bite, like so many artists and designers did. Besides, Steve Jobs was way cooler than Bill Gates, head geek of the Evil Empire. It mattered little that Gates was the same age as Jobs (both were born in 1955), talked the same future-shock lingo and, like Steve, wore a modified Beatles hairdo.

5   Gates went ballistic over Apple's great campaign, PC versus Mac, in which the pompous portly PC's attempt to prove the superiority of his product

---

furtive:
quiet and stealthy to attract no notice

objets d'art:
art object

is frustrated every time while unassuming, polite, boy-next-door Mac looks on, trying not to be **smug**. Gates told tech reporter Steven Levy, "I don't know why they're acting superior. I don't even get it. I mean, do you get it? What are they trying to say? There's not even the slightest shred of truth to it!"

smug:
self satisfied

6   Steve Jobs is the Svengali-like digital shaman, and we're hooked on his aura. One columnist joked that Americans more keenly anticipated Steve's announcement of the brand-new iPad than they did Barack Obama's State of the Union the night before. Magician David Blaine described Jobs as "the ultimate showman who keeps the audience excited the whole way leading up to the reveal." His **iconic** introductions of new products are a kind of "news theater" that generates hundreds of millions of dollars in free advertising. "Our secret marketing program for the iPhone (prior to the launch) was none. We didn't do anything," Steve told his employees, who Kahney described as "captives who have fallen in love with their captor." He does not believe in focus groups, telling *Business Week*, "A lot of times, people don't know what they want until you show it to them." Spoken like a true cult leader.

iconic:
formulaic, memorable style

7   Talk about a brilliant iconic cult life—Steve even cheats death! In 2009, the biggest event at Apple was the Return of Steve Jobs after a kidney transplant. His health problems since his cancer surgery in the mid-2000s caused shareholder concern—would there be life without Steve, and who could take over? Then the wizard returned, Moses-like, with an iPad that promised to be a kind of digital scrapbook.

8   Call me a spiritualist or a sucker, but I'm possessed by a tingling feeling that my iLife is about to change again. Another visit to the Apple Store is as sure as Steve Jobs's quest for immortality.

VOCABULARY AND COMPREHENSION

1.   Find a word in paragraph 5 that means "irrationally angry."

_____

2.   What is Rodriquez defining in this essay?

_____

3.   What are some examples he uses to support his definition? List at least three examples.

_____

_____

_____

4.   What is the introductory style of the essay?
    a.   historical background
    b.   contrasting position
    c.   anecdote

5.   Rodriquez compares and contrasts PCs and Macs. What are the major differences?

PC   Mac

_____   _____

_____   _____

_____   _____

6.   Why does Rodriquez mention Obama's State of the Union address?

_____

_____

_____

_____

7.   How is Steve Jobs like a cult leader?

_____

_____

GRAMMAR LINK

8.   Paragraph 6 contains the following sentence: "His iconic introductions of new products are a kind of 'news theater' that generates hundreds of millions of dollars in free advertising." Why does *generates* end in *s*?

_____

_____

9.   Identify and underline a simple, compound, and complex sentence. Why does the writer use different types of sentences?

_____

_____

DISCUSSION AND WRITING

10.   Define *news theater*. Explain how an Apple announcement, or any other advertisement, becomes news theater. Give examples to support your definition.

11.   Some people identify strongly with brands such as Harley Davidson or Apple. Are you loyal to certain brands, or do you have no brand loyalty? Explain your answer.

12.   What is your approach to new technologies? Do you plunge in and learn the new systems? Are you more cautious? Does a new gadget scare you? Write about your relationship to technology.

READING 14

How to Handle Conflict
P. Gregory Smith

> P. Gregory Smith writes for *Career World*. In the next essay, he describes some steps a person can take to avoid conflict. As you read this process essay, notice how the author also uses elements of argument writing.

1   "Hey, college boy," Mr. Jefferson smirked as Ramon walked into the supermarket, "a lady just dropped a bottle of grape juice in aisle six. Do you think you could lower yourself enough to mop it up?" Ramon was seething inside as he grabbed the mop and headed off to clean up the spill. Ever since he told some of his co-workers that he had applied to the state university, Mr. Jefferson, the night manager, had teased and taunted him. As Ramon returned to the front of the store, he remembered the presentation his guidance counselor, Mrs. Chang, had given last week on something called assertiveness. It is a way of standing up for one's rights without creating conflict. As Ramon walked toward Mr. Jefferson, the main points of the presentation started to come back to him.

2   Find the right time and place. Mr. Jefferson was talking with a customer when Ramon reached the front of the supermarket. Ramon waited until Mr. Jefferson was finished and then asked, "Can I talk with you in your office when you have a moment?" By waiting for the right time, Ramon was likely to have Mr. Jefferson's attention. Also, by asking to speak with him in private, Ramon reduced the chances that Mr. Jefferson would feel that he had to impress others, protect his reputation, or save face.

3   Maintain good posture, eye contact, and a relaxed **stance.** Before Ramon said the first word, he reminded himself of a few important things. If he wanted to stand up for himself, he would need to stand up straight! He knew that it was important to make eye contact. Ramon also knew the importance of relaxing his hands and keeping a comfortable distance from Mr. Jefferson. He did not want to appear hostile or threatening. Even though he was angry, Ramon reminded himself that he must speak calmly, clearly, and slowly in order to get his point across. If he let his anger creep in, he would probably get an angry or defensive response from Mr. Jefferson. Even worse, if he hid his feelings behind a quiet tone or rapid speech, then Mr. Jefferson would probably doubt his seriousness.

stance:
manner; position

4   Use *I* statements. Mr. Jefferson closed the office door, folded his arms, and looked at Ramon questioningly. Ramon took a deep breath and began, "Mr. Jefferson, I really feel embarrassed when you call me 'college boy.' I like it a lot better when people call me Ramon. I don't mind doing my fair share of the dirty jobs around here," Ramon continued, "but I feel like I'm getting a lot more mop time than anyone else." By using a statement that began with *I*, Ramon was able to state his feelings honestly, without accusing Mr. Jefferson. *I* statements usually can't be considered false or cause an argument because they're simple statements of feelings.

5   Then introduce cooperative statements. Ramon said, "We used to get along fine until everybody started talking about me going to college next year. I haven't changed, and I'd like to go back to the way things were." Cooperative statements—or statements that connect you with the other person—create common ground for further discussion. They also serve as a subtle reminder that you share experiences and values with the other person.

6   "Remember that standing up for your personal rights, or being assertive, is very important," explains Betty Kelman of the Seattle University School of Nursing. "Standing up for your rights involves self-respect—respect for your rights and the other person's rights. Respecting yourself is the ability to make your own decisions involving relationships, how you spend your time, and whom you spend it with." Kelman also explains what assertiveness is not. "Standing up for yourself does not mean that you express yourself in an aggressive, angry, or mean way." She sums it up this way: "Think of standing up for yourself as being in a win-win situation. You win, and they win."

VOCABULARY AND COMPREHENSION

1.   What are *cooperative statements* (paragraph 5)?

_____

_____

2.   What introduction style does the essay have?
     a. Anecdote   c. Historical
     b. General   d. Contrasting position

3. What is Smith's main point?

_____

_____

4. List the steps in the process that Smith describes.

_____

_____

_____

_____

5. How does the quotation from Betty Kelman (paragraph 6) support the author's point of view?

_____

_____

_____

GRAMMAR LINK

6. Underline the verbs in the first sentences of paragraphs 2 through 5. Who or what is the subject in each sentence?

_____

7. In paragraph 5, the author says, "I haven't changed, and I'd like to go back to the way things were." Write out the long form of each contraction.

_____

DISCUSSION AND WRITING

8. Can you think of a time when you should have been more assertive? Describe what happened.
9. Explain the steps that you take when you are faced with a major problem. What do you usually do?

READING 15

How to Remember Names
Roger Seip

Roger Seip is the President of Freedom Speakers and Trainers, a company that specializes in memory training. In this process essay, he describes how to remember people's names. As you read, notice how the author uses elements of argument and cause and effect writing.

1   If you live in fear of forgetting people's names, sometimes within mere seconds of being introduced to them, you are not alone. Surveys show that 83 percent of the population worries about an inability to recall names. While common, this frustrating phenomenon can be relatively easy to overcome. The most important key to really effective learning of any kind is to understand that there are three learning styles: visual, auditory, and kinesthetic (physically interactive). The more you can apply all three of these styles to a task, the more quickly and solidly you will learn anything. Practice each of the following steps to improve your name recollection in every sales and social situation.

2   When you are first introduced to someone, look closely at his or her face and try to find something unique about it. Whether you find a distinctive quality or not is irrelevant; by really looking for a memorable characteristic in a new face, you are incorporating the visual learning style. And a word of advice: If you do find something that really stands out about someone's face, don't say anything!

3   The next step utilizes both auditory and kinesthetic learning styles. When you meet someone, slow down for five seconds, and concentrate on listening to him or her. Focus on the person, and repeat his or her name back in a conversational manner, such as "Susan. Nice to meet you, Susan." Also make sure to give a good firm handshake, which establishes a physical connection.

4   Creating a mental picture of someone's name incorporates the visual sense again. Many people have names that already are pictures: consider Robin, Jay, Matt, or Dawn, to name just a few. Some names will require you to play with them a bit to create a picture. Ken, for example, may not bring an immediate image to your mind, but a "can" is very close. Or you might envision a Ken doll. The point is not to create the best, most creative mental image ever, so don't get caught up in your head during this step of the process, thinking, "Oh, that's not a very good picture. What is a better one?" The worst thing you can do when learning is to stress yourself out and overthink the process. If an image does not come to you right away, skip it and do it later. You will undo all of your good efforts if you are staring dumbly at the person, insisting, "Hey. Hold still for a minute while I try to turn your name into a picture!"

5   Once you have identified a mental image that you associate with a person's name, the next step is to "glue" that image to the person's face or upper body. This bridges that gap many people experience between being able to recall faces but not the names that belong to those faces. If you met a new prospect named Rosalind, for example, you might have broken her name down into the memorable image of "rose on land." Now you must create a mental picture that will stick with you as long as you need it and pop into your head every time you meet her; this should be something fun, even a little odd, that will bring "rose on land" to mind when you see her face. You might imagine her buried up to her neck in earth, with roses scattered around her, for example. Because you created the image, it will come up next time you see her and enable you to recall her name.

6   At the end of the conversation, integrate auditory learning by repeating the prospect's name one more time, but don't ever overuse someone's name in an effort to place it more firmly in your mind. For example, in formal situations, use the person's name only at the beginning of the conversation, and then again at the end. If you feel that you can do so naturally, you might insert someone's name once or twice in a natural fashion during the course of the conversation, too.

7   Writing is a form of kinesthetic learning—you are getting a part of your body involved in the learning process—so if you are really serious about wanting to remember people's names for the long term, keep a name journal or a log of important people you meet, and review it periodically.

8   People can't remember names for one main reason: they are just not paying attention. This process forces you to think. If, for example, you struggle with the step of creating a mental picture, the other steps—looking at the person closely, shaking his or her hand confidently, and repeating the name a few times—are easy to do, will solidify the name in your memory, and will ultimately convey a positive image of you to others.

VOCABULARY AND COMPREHENSION

1. In the first paragraph, the writer mentions three learning styles. Using your own words, define each style:

   a. visual _____

   b. auditory _____

   c. kinesthetic _____

2. Why does the writer mention learning styles?

   _____

3. Who is the audience for this essay?

   _____

4. Underline the thesis statement.

5. Underline the topic sentences in paragraphs 2–6.

GRAMMAR LINK

6. In paragraph 1, highlight the first five commas. Then write three rules about comma usage.

   _____

   _____

   _____

7. The second sentence in paragraph 3 contains *him or her*. What is the antecedent for those pronouns? In other words, whom do the pronouns refer to?

   _____

DISCUSSION AND WRITING

8. Describe a process that people can follow to remember details such as birthdays, exam deadlines, appointments, telephone numbers, or computer passwords.

9. Think about a time when you forgot a person's name. What strategy did you use to deal with the situation?

10. Describe the first time you met your best friend, spouse, or colleague. Why did you decide to keep that person in your life?

READING 16

Meet the Zippies
Thomas L. Friedman

Thomas Friedman is a Pulitzer Prize-winning journalist for *The New York Times*. His most recent book is *The World Is Flat: A Brief History of the Twenty-First Century*, in which he analyzes the great changes in the world economy due to China's and India's rising economic clout. As you read, notice how the writer uses elements of definition, cause and effect, and argument.

1   We grew up with the hippies in the 1960s. Thanks to the high-tech revolution, many of us became yuppies in the 1980s. And now, fasten your seat belt because you may soon lose your job to a "zippie" in the 2000s.

2   "The Zippies Are Here," declared the Indian weekly magazine *Outlook*. Zippies are this huge cohort of Indian youth who are the first to come of age since India shifted away from socialism and dived headfirst into global trade, embraced the information revolution, and turned itself into the world's service center. *Outlook* calls India's zippies "Liberalization's Children," and defines a zippie as "a young city or suburban resident, between fifteen and twenty-five years of age, with a zip in the stride. Belongs to generation Z. Can be male or female, studying or working. Oozes attitude, ambition, and aspiration. Cool, confident, and creative. Seeks challenges, loves risks, and shuns fears." Indian zippies carry no guilt about making money or spending it. They are, says one Indian analyst quoted by *Outlook*, destination driven, not destiny driven; outward, not inward, looking; upwardly mobile, not stuck-in-their-station-in-life.

3   With 54 percent of India under the age of twenty-five—that's 555 million people—six out of ten Indian households have at least one zippie, *Outlook* says. And a growing slice of them (most Indians are still poor village-dwellers) will be able to do your white-collar job as well as you for a fraction of the pay.

4   I just arrived here in Bangalore, India's Silicon Valley, to meet the zippies on the receiving end of U.S. jobs. Judging from the construction going on every block here, the multiple applicants for every new tech job, the crowded pub scene, and the families of four you see zipping around on a single motor scooter, Bangalore is one hot town.

5   Taking all this in, two things strike me about this outsourcing issue. First, economists are surely right: The biggest factor in eliminating old jobs and churning out new ones is technological change—the phone mail system that eliminated many secretaries. Second, when the zippies soak up certain U.S. or European jobs, they will become consumers, the global pie will grow, and ultimately we will all be better off. As long as America maintains its ability to do cutting-edge innovation, the long run should be fine. Saving money by outsourcing basic jobs to zippies so Americans can invest in more high-end innovation makes sense.

6   But here's what I also feel: This particular short run could be politically explosive. The potential speed and scale of this outsourcing phenomenon make its potential impact enormous and unpredictable. As we enter a world where the price of digitizing information—converting it into little packets of ones and zeros and then transmitting it over high-speed data networks—falls to near zero, it means the vaunted "death of distance" is really here. And it means that many jobs you can now do from your house—whether data processing, reading an X-ray, or basic accounting or lawyering—can now also be done from a zippie's house in India or China.

7   And as education levels in these overseas homes rise to U.S. levels, the barriers to shipping white-collar jobs abroad fall, and the incentives for businesses to outsource rise. At a minimum, some very educated Americans used to high salaries—people who vote and know how to write op-ed pieces—will either lose their jobs or have to accept lower pay or become part-timers without health insurance.

8   "The fundamental question we have to ask as a society is, what do we do about it?" notes Robert Reich, the former labor secretary and now Brandeis University professor. "For starters, we're going to have to get serious about some of the things we just gab about—job training, life-long learning, and wage insurance. And perhaps we need to welcome more unionization in the personal services area—retail, hotel, restaurant, and hospital jobs that cannot be moved overseas—in order to stabilize wages and health care benefits."

Maybe, as a transition measure, adds Mr. Reich, companies shouldn't be allowed to deduct the full cost of outsourcing, creating a small tax that could be used to help people adjust.

9   Either way, managing this phenomenon will require a public policy response—something more serious than the Bush mantra of let the market sort it out, or the demagoguery of the Democratic candidates, who seem to want to make outsourcing equal to treason and punishable by hanging. It's time to get real.

VOCABULARY AND COMPREHENSION

1. In your own words, describe the zippies.

    _____

    _____

    _____

2. Friedman uses the expression "death of distance" in paragraph 6. Explain what he means by this phrase.

    _____

    _____

    _____

3. Why has outsourcing become an important political issue for Americans?

    _____

    _____

4. According to Friedman, what are some immediate consequences of outsourcing?

    _____

    _____

5. Why does Friedman think that outsourcing will have a positive effect on the American economy in the long term? See paragraph 5.

    _____

    _____

    _____

6. What is the writer's main point in paragraphs 6 and 7?

    _____

    _____

    _____

7. What can the American government do to offset some of the harsh consequences of outsourcing?

    _____

    _____

    _____

GRAMMAR LINK

8.   Circle four contractions in the text. Then write out the long form of each contraction.

_____

_____

9.   In paragraph 2, why is *Outlook* italicized?

_____

DISCUSSION AND WRITING

10.   Define one of the following terms: *office politics, glass ceiling, the corner office, wheeler-dealer, officespeak, watercooler discussions*, or *mouse potato*. Give examples to support your definition.

11.   Poll five students. Ask them why they have chosen to go to college. Write about your poll results, and mention the names and approximate ages of the people you have polled.

READING 17

The Rewards of Dirty Work
Linda L. Lindsey and Stephen Beach

Linda L. Lindsey teaches sociology at Maryville University of St. Louis, and Stephen Beach teaches at Kentucky Wesleyan College. In the next essay, they list some surprising rewards of dirty work. As you read, notice how the authors mainly use the illustration writing pattern but also use elements of description and argument.

1   As sociologist Everett Hughes once pointed out, in order for some members of society to be clean and pure, someone else must take care of unclean, often taboo work, such as handling dead bodies and filth. In India and Japan, such jobs were, and to some extent still are, relegated to the Dalits (or Untouchables) and the Eta, respectively. Both groups were regarded as ritually impure. Our society does not have formal taboos against dirty work, but some jobs are rated near the bottom of the scale of occupational prestige and are viewed as not quite respectable and certainly not something to brag about. Garbage collection is a good example. Why would anyone choose to become a garbage collector? Stewart Perry asked this question to sanitation workers for the Sunset Scavenger Business in San Francisco. For a job that requires little training or education, the pay is relatively good. But pay was not what drew men to the job.

2   One attraction of becoming a garbage collector was variety. The job involves many different activities. Collecting garbage also means being outdoors and moving around. On another level, variety means the unexpected. For the sanitation workers, every day brought something different: witnessing a robbery, calling in a fire alarm and getting residents out of the building before the fire truck arrived, and responding to FBI requests to save all the rubbish from a house under surveillance.

3   Also, the garbage itself was full of surprises. Almost every day the men found something of interest, whether a good book, a child's toy, or a fixable radio. Almost inevitably, garbage men became collectors. In the course of his research, Perry himself acquired a rare seventeenth-century book of sermons and a sheepskin rug.

4   Garbage men got to know intimately the neighborhoods in which they worked. Watching children grow up, couples marry or separate, or one house or block deteriorating while another was being renovated had the appeal of an ongoing story, not unlike a soap opera on TV. They witnessed not just public performances, but also what Erving Goffman called the "backstage" of life. The respectable facades in affluent neighborhoods cannot hide the alcoholism a garbage man detects from cans full of empty liquor bottles or the sexual longings symbolized by bundles of pornographic magazines.

5   Another attraction of garbage collection was a sense of camaraderie among workers. The friendships people make on the job are a major source of satisfaction in any occupation. Many Sunset workers came from the same ethnic background (Italian) and in some cases from the same neighborhood. All of the men hoped that their own sons would go to college and make something better of themselves. But at least thirty were following in their fathers' footsteps. These intergenerational family ties and friendships made the company a familiar and welcome place and a stronghold of tradition for members of ethnic communities that were beginning to break apart.

6   The garbage collectors liked working at their own pace, scheduling their own breaks, deciding when to do their paperwork—in short, being their own bosses. Collecting garbage may be "dirty work" in many peoples' eyes, but these men were proud of what they did for a living.

VOCABULARY AND COMPREHENSION

1.   What is a *taboo?* See paragraph 1 for clues.

   _____

2.   How is Western society different from other societies regarding garbage collecting or other dirty work?

   _____

   _____

   _____

3.   How do Western societies judge the profession of garbage collecting?

   _____

   _____

   _____

4.   The writers give a positive spin on garbage collecting. List the main points.

   _____

   _____

   _____

   _____

   _____

   _____

5.   How do garbage collectors see the "backstage" of life?

   _____

   _____

   _____

GRAMMAR LINK

6.   Underline five irregular past tense verbs in paragraphs 3 and 4. Then write the present and past forms of each verb.

   _____

   _____

7.   In paragraph 5, who does the word *themselves* refer to?

   _____

DISCUSSION AND WRITING

8.   List some jobs that might be considered dirty. What do the jobs have in common?
9.   What are some stereotypes that we have about other professions? These professions could be prestigious or nonprestigious. Give some examples.
10.   Think of another job that lacks prestige. Explain why that job has value and is rewarding.

The Writer's Room   **Images of Trades, Technology, and the Business World**

Writing Activity 1: Photo Writing

1.   Define videogame addiction, or explain the causes or effects of a videogame addiction.
2.   Classify computer dangers into three categories. For instance, there are dangers with hackers, online gambling, viruses, cyberstalkers, cyber bullying, and so on. Give examples to support the categories.
3.   Explain some ways that your life has changed because of technology.

Writing Activity 2: Film Writing

1. View a film about the business world such *Wall Street* or *Wall Street: Money Never Sleeps*. Explain the causes or effects of the main character's greed.

2. Watch *Shutter Island*, *500 Days of Summer*, *Brothers*, or a film of your choice. Then focus on a central character and explain the process he or she goes through to overcome a crisis.

3. Watch *Up in the Air* or another movie of your choice. Compare and contrast two characters in the film.

mywritinglab To check your progress in meeting this chapter's objectives, log in to **www.mywritinglab.com**, go to the **Study Plan** tab, click on **Reading Strategies and Selections** and choose **Reading Strategies and Selections** from the list of subtopics. Read and view the resources in the **Review Materials** section, and then complete the **Recall, Apply,** and **Write** sets in the **Activities** section.

Appendix 1
Grammar Glossary

Term	Meaning	Examples
Active voice	• Form of the verb when the subject does the action	Maria will mail the letter.
Adjective	• Adds information about the noun	quiet, clear, decent
Adverb	• Adds information about the verb; expresses time, place, or frequency	quietly, clearly, decently, easily; sometimes, often, usually, never
Base form of verb	• The main form of a verb that is found in a dictionary	eat, go, feel, listen, whisper
Clause	• An independent clause has a subject and verb and expresses a complete idea.	The athlete was thrilled.
	• A dependent clause has a subject and verb but cannot stand alone. It "depends" on another clause to be complete.	because she won a gold medal
Conditional sentence	• Explains possible, imaginary, or impossible situations; each type of conditional sentence has a condition clause and a result clause.	Possible future: If I win, I will fly to Morocco. Unlikely present: If I won, I would fly to Morocco. Impossible past: If I had won, I would have flown to Morocco.
Conjunctive adverb	• Shows a relationship between two ideas	also, consequently, finally, however, furthermore, moreover, therefore, thus
Conjunction	• Coordinating conjunction: connects two ideas of equal importance	but, or, yet, so, for, and, nor
	• Subordinating conjunction: connects two ideas when one idea is subordinate (or inferior) to the other idea	after, although, because, before, unless, until, when
Determiner	• Identifies or determines whether a noun is specific or general	a, an, the; this, that, these, those; any, all, each, every, some, one, two
Indirect speech	• Reports what someone said without using the person's exact words	Mr. Simpson said that he would never find a better job.
Infinitive	• *To* plus the base form of the verb	He wants to think about it.
Interjection	• A word expressing an emotion; interjections usually appear in quotations	ouch, yikes, wow, yeah, oh
Irregular verb	• A verb that does not have an *-ed* ending in at least one of its past forms	ate, broke, swam, went
Linking verb	• A verb that describes a state of being; joins the subject with a descriptive word	is, am, are, was, were, act, appear, look, seem
Modal	• A type of helping verb that indicates willingness, possibility, advice, and so on	may help, can go, should deliver
Noun	• A person, place, or thing	Singular: man, dog, person Plural: men, dogs, people
Passive voice	• Form of the verb when the subject does not perform the action (formed with *be* + the past participle)	The letter will be mailed shortly.
Preposition	• Shows a relationship between words (source, direction, location, etc.)	at, to, for, from, behind, above
Pronoun	• Replaces one or more nouns	he, she, it, us, ours, themselves

Term	Meaning	Examples
Regular verb	• A verb that has a standard -d or -ed ending in the past tense	walked, looked, checked, carried, moved
Sentence types	• A simple sentence has one independent clause that expresses a complete idea.	Some food is unhealthy.
	• A compound sentence has two or more independent clauses joined together.	Some restaurants serve junk food, and others serve healthy meals.
	• A complex sentence has at least one dependent and one independent clause joined together.	Although the food is not healthy, it is very tasty.
	• A compound-complex sentence has at least two independent clauses joined with at least one dependent clause.	Although the food is not healthy, it is very tasty, and I enjoy eating it.
Transitional word or expression	• Linking words or phrases that show the reader the connections between ideas	in addition, however, furthermore, in fact, moreover, for example
Verb	• Expresses an action or state of being	go, run, have, wear, believe

PRACTICE 1

Label each word with one of the following terms.

adjective	conjunction	noun	pronoun
adverb	interjection	preposition	verb

EXAMPLE:

carried _____verb_____

1. but _____   9. student _____

2. them _____   10. pretty _____

3. below _____   11. yikes _____

4. believe _____   12. behind _____

5. famous _____   13. laugh _____

6. slowly _____   14. we _____

7. although _____   15. never _____

8. ouch _____   16. people _____

Appendix 2
Verb Tenses

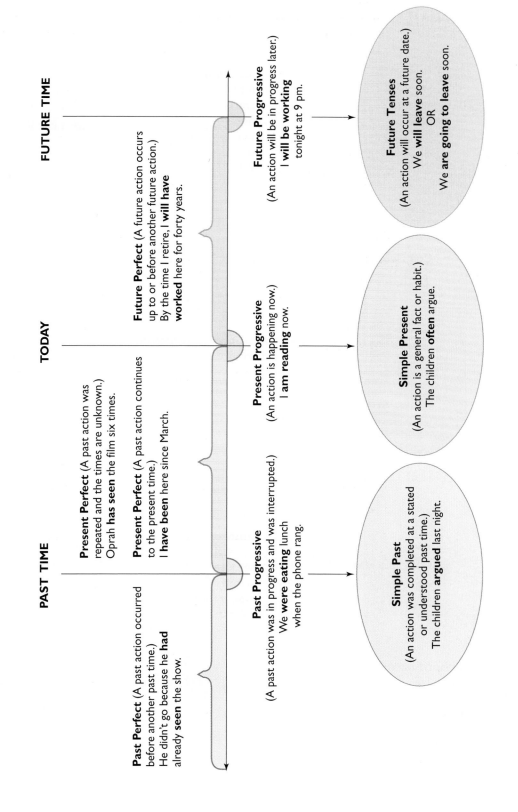

PAST TIME

TODAY

FUTURE TIME

Past Perfect (A past action occurred before another past time.) He didn't go because he **had** already **seen** the show.

Present Perfect (A past action was repeated and the times are unknown.) Oprah **has seen** the film six times.

Present Perfect (A past action continues to the present time.) I **have been** here since March.

Future Perfect (A future action occurs up to or before another future action.) By the time I retire, I **will have worked** here for forty years.

Past Progressive (A past action was in progress and was interrupted.) We **were eating** lunch when the phone rang.

Present Progressive (An action is happening now.) I **am reading** now.

Future Progressive (An action will be in progress later.) I **will be working** tonight at 9 pm.

Simple Past (An action was completed at a stated or understood past time.) The children **argued** last night.

Simple Present (An action is a general fact or habit.) The children **often** argue.

Future Tenses (An action will occur at a future date.) We **will leave** soon. OR We **are going to leave** soon.

Making Compound Sentences

A.

Complete idea

, coordinator
,for
,and
,nor
,but
,or
,yet
,so

complete idea.

B.

Complete idea

;

complete idea.

C.

Complete idea

; transitional expression,
;furthermore,
;however,
;in fact,
;moreover,
;therefore,

complete idea.

Making Complex Sentences

D.

Complete idea

subordinator
although
because
before
even though
unless
when

incomplete idea.

E.

Subordinator
Although
Because
Before
Even though
Unless
When

incomplete idea

,

complete idea.

Apostrophe (')

Use an apostrophe for the following reasons.

- To join a subject and verb

  She's tired.

- To join an auxiliary with *not*

  You **shouldn't** smoke.

- To indicate possession

  Mike's camera is new.

Comma (,)

Use a comma in the following cases.

- To separate words in a series of more than two things

  Everyone needs food, water, and shelter.

- After an introductory word or phrase

  After the election, the candidate rested.

- Around interrupting phrases that give additional information about the subject

  Isabelle, an artist, makes astonishing paintings.

- In compound sentences before the coordinator

  The job is easy, but it does not pay well.

- Around relative clauses containing *which*

  The files, which are in my office, contain important information.

- In quotations, after an introductory phrase or before an end phrase

  Durrell said, "Personality is an illusion."

  "Personality is an illusion," Durrell said.

Note: Do not join two complete sentences with a comma.

Colon (:)

Use a colon in the following cases.

- After a complete sentence that introduces a list or after *the following*

  An essay has the following parts: an introduction, a body, and a conclusion.

- After a complete sentence that introduces a quotation

    Durrell's point was clear: "Personality is an illusion."

- Before an explanation or example

    Kaitlin realized what she really needed: time alone.

- To separate the hours and minutes in expressions of time

    The college bookstore opens at 8:30 a.m.

Semicolon (;)

Use a semicolon to join two independent and related clauses.

    Many Brazilian tribes are isolated; they do not interact with the outside world.

Quotation Marks (" ")

Use quotation marks around direct speech. When a quotation is a complete sentence, do the following:

- Capitalize the first word in the quotation.
- Place the end punctuation mark inside the closing quotation marks.

    In her essay, Dorothy Nixon said, "I am the television addict."

Integrated Quotation

If you integrate a quotation into your sentence, just add quotation marks.

    Dorothy Nixon calls herself a "television addict."

"Inside" Quotation

If one quotation is inside another quotation, use single quotation marks (' ') around the inside quotation.

    Maya Angelou describes the moment: "She turned on the light and said, 'Look at the baby.' "

Citing Page Numbers

Put the page number in parentheses. Place the final period *after* the parentheses.

    In her novel, Maya Angelou says, "I didn't feel lonely or abandoned" (127).

Capitalization

Always capitalize the following:

- The pronoun *I* and the first word of every sentence

    The doctor and **I** discussed the problem.

- The names of days of the week, months, and specific holidays

    Wednesday   April 14   **L**abor **D**ay

- The names of specific places, such as buildings, streets, parks, public squares, lakes, rivers, cities, states, and countries

    Elm Street   **Mississippi River**   **Miami, Florida**

- The names of languages, nationalities, tribes, races, and religions

    Greek   **Mohawk**   **Christian**

- The titles of specific individuals

    General Smith   **President Bush**   **Mrs. Sloan**

- The major words in titles of literary or artistic works

    War and Peace   *The Last Supper*   *The Hurt Locker*

- The names of historical events, eras, and movements

    Boer War   **Dadaism**   the **Depression**

Punctuating Titles

Capitalize all of the major words in a title. Place quotation marks around the titles of short works (songs, essays, short stories, poems, newspaper articles, magazine articles, etc.).

Chopin's most famous story was called "The Storm."

Italicize the titles of longer works (television series, movies, plays, books, works of art, magazines, newspapers, etc.). If you are handwriting a text, underline titles of long works.

I read the classic novel *The Awakening*.

The goal of keeping spelling and grammar logs is to help you stop repeating errors. When you do new writing assignments, you can consult the lists and hopefully break some ingrained bad habits. The vocabulary log can provide you with interesting new terms that you can incorporate into your writing.

Spelling Log

Every time you misspell a word, record both the mistake and the correction in your spelling log. Then, before you hand in a writing assignment, consult your list of misspelled words. The goal is to stop repeating the same spelling errors.

EXAMPLE:

Incorrect	_Correct_
alot	_a lot_
responsable	_responsible_

Grammar Log

Each time a writing assignment is returned to you, identify one or two repeated errors and add them to your grammar log. Consult the grammar log before you hand in writing assignments to avoid making the same errors. For each type of grammar error, follow these steps.

- Identify the assignment, and write down the type of error.
- In your own words, write a rule about the error.
- Include an example from your writing assignment.

EXAMPLE: _Narration Paragraph (Sept. 28): Run-on_

Do not connect two complete sentences with a comma.

We hit a telephone ~~pole, the~~ pole. The airbags exploded.

Vocabulary Log

As you read, you will learn new vocabulary words and expressions. Keep a record of the most interesting and useful vocabulary words and their meanings. Write a synonym or definition next to each new word.

EXAMPLE:

Term	_Meaning_
reminisce	_to recollect in an enjoyable way_

Spelling Log

Grammar Log

Vocabulary Log

Credits

TEXT:

Page 13: *College Culture*, Veena Thomas. Reprinted by permission of Veena Thomas; **p. 23:** From *Understanding Music*, 3rd edition, by Jeremy Yudkin. Upper Saddle River, NJ: Prentice Hall, 2002; **p. 26:** *The Night Crawler*, Louis Tursi. Reprinted by permission of Louis Tursi; **p. 29, pp. 35–36, p. 40, p. 41:** "Zion Market" by Jacqueline Suh. Used by permission of the author; **p. 47:** *Freedom for Adults Only*, Mike Males. Reprinted by permission of Youth Today; **p. 52:** From "Dancing with Fear" by Bebe Moore Campbell, published in *Essence 32* (12), April 2002, p. 98; **p. 57:** Reprinted with permission; **p. 63:** Used by permission of the author; **p. 68:** From "From Pop Culture to Peep Culture," posted on http://www.arcusgroup.ca/social_media.html. Used by permission of Merril Mascarenhas, Managing Partner, Arcus Consulting Group; **p. 73:** Used by permission of the author; **p. 78:** Used by permission of the author; **p. 84:** Adapted from *Criminal Justice Today: An Introductory Text for the Twenty-First Century*, 6th ed., by Frank Schmalleger. Upper Saddle River, New Jersey: Pearson Prentice Hall, 2001; **p. 89:** Used by permission of the author; **p. 97:** "Bad Habits" by Renaud Allard. Used by permission of the author; **p. 114:** From "Yoga Y'all" by Elizabeth Gilbert, *The New York Times Magazine*, Sept. 18, 2005; **p. 209:** From *Cultural Anthropology*, 10th edition by Carol R. Ember and Melvin Ember. Upper Saddle River, NJ: Prentice Hall, 2002; **p. 224, p. 240:** Locher, David A., *Collective Behavior*, 1st edition, © 2002. Reprinted with permission of Pearson Education, Inc., Upper Saddle River, NJ; **p. 258:** From *Architectural Drawing and Light Construction* by Philip A. Grau, Edward J. Muller, and James G. Fausett. Upper Saddle River, New Jersey: Pearson Prentice Hall, 2009; **p. 271:** From *Building Construction: Methods and Materials for the Fire Service* by Michael Smith. Upper Saddle River, New Jersey: Pearson Prentice Hall, 2008; **p. 328:** From *Animal Watching: A Field Guide to Animal Behavior* by Desmond Morris. London: Jonathan Cape, Ltd, 1990; **p. 338:** From *Life of Pi* by Yann Martel (Harcourt 2001). Copyright © 2001. Yann Martel. With permission of the author; **p. 362:** Reprinted by permission of Jeff Kemp; **p. 375:** From "How to Handle Conflict" by P. Gregory Smith, from *Career World*, Nov.–Dec. 2003. Special permission granted by Weekly Reader, published and copyrighted by Weekly Reader Corporation. All rights reserved; **pp. 408–409:** "Fish Cheeks" by Amy Tan. Copyright © 1987 by Amy Tan. First appeared in *Seventeen Magazine*. Reprinted by permission of the author and the Sandra Dijkstra Literary Agency; **pp. 410–411:** From *I Know Why a Caged Bird Sings* by Maya Angelou, copyright © 1969 and renewed 1997 by Maya Angelou. Used by permission of Random House, Inc.: **pp. 412–413:** *The New Addiction*, Josh Freed, *The Montreal Gazette*, Dec. 20, 2003. Reprinted with permission of Josh Freed; **pp. 414–415:** "Fat Chance" by Dorothy Nixon. Copyright Dorothy Nixon. Used by permission of the author. Dorothy Nixon is the author of the blog "Looking for Mrs. Peel"; **pp. 418–419:** *What's Your Humor Style*, Louise Dobson, *Psychology Today*, July–August 2006. Reprinted with permission of Sussex Publishers, LLC; **pp. 420–422:** "Innocent gestures can translate poorly, traveler warns" by William Ecenbarger, Copyright *Los Angeles Times*, © 2008. Reprinted with permission; **pp. 423–425:** "The Cult of Emaciation" by Ben Barry, originally published in the *National Post*, May 17, 2007. Used by permission of the author; **pp. 426–427:** "Shopping for Religion" by Ellen Goodman, published in *The Boston Globe*, Feb. 29, 2008. Used by permission of the author; **pp. 429–431:** From *Esquire Presents: What It Feels Like*, edited by A.J. Jacobs, copyright © 2003 by Esquire Magazine. Used by permission of Three Rivers Press, a division of Random House, Inc.; **pp. 432–433:** From *A Short History of Nearly Everything* by Bill Bryson, copyright © 2003 by Bill Bryson. Used by permission of Broadway Books, a division of Random House, Inc. and Jed Mattes, Inc.; **pp. 434–435:** From *Life of Pi* by Yann Martel (Harcourt 2001). Copyright © 2001. Yann Martel. With permission of the author; **pp. 436–437:** "Is it love, or a trick?" originally published as "Why People Love Dogs" by Jon Katz, from *Slate*, © 2007, The Slate Group. All rights reserved. Used by permission and protected by the Copyright Laws of the United States. The printing, copying, redistribution, or retransmission of the Material without express written permission is prohibited; **pp. 440–441:** "The Allure of Apple" by Juan Rodriguez, from *The Montreal Gazette*, Feb. 20, 2010. Material reprinted with the express permission of Montreal Gazette Group, Inc., a CanWest partnership; **pp. 442–443:** "How to Handle Conflict" by P. Gregory Smith, from *Career World*, Nov.–Dec. 2003. Special permission granted by Weekly Reader, published and copyrighted by Weekly Reader Corporation. All rights reserved; **pp. 444–445:** *How to Remember Names*, Roger Seip. Reprinted with permission; **pp. 446–448:** "Meet the Zippies" by Thomas Friedman from *The New York Times*, © 2004 The New York Times. All rights reserved. Used by permission and protected by the Copyright Laws of the United States. The printing, copying, redistribution, or retransmission of the Material without express written permission is prohibited; **pp. 449–450:** Lindsey/Beach, *Essentials of Sociology*, "The Rewards of Dirty Work," p. 379, © 2003 Prentice Hall. Reproduced by permission of Pearson Education, Inc.

PHOTOS:

Page 3: Fertnig/iStockphoto.com; **p. 11:** © Ralph Hagen/www.CartoonStock.com; **p. 12:** © Rungroj Yongrit/epa/Corbis; **p. 30:** Photos.com; **p. 32:** Gerenme/iStockphoto.com; **p. 33, mid:** Photos.com; **p. 33, bottom:** Courtesy of www.istockphoto.com; **p. 35:** Photos.com; **p. 37:** Pixtal/Superstock Royalty Free; **p. 38:** Photos.com; **p. 39:** © Ron Niebrugge/Alamy; **p. 46:** Alexander Kalina/Shutterstock; **p. 51:** alexh/BigStockPhoto.com; **p. 56:** Ben Blankenburg/iStockphoto.com; **p. 62:** © Belinda Images/SuperStock; **p. 67:** Photos.com; **p. 72:** Images.com; **p. 77:** iStockphoto.com; **p. 83:** Radius Images/Jupiter Images Royalty Free; **p. 88:** Julie Masson/iStockphoto.com; **p. 94:** Thinkstock; **p. 95:** Photos.com; **p. 110:** iStockphoto.com; **p. 114:** Dave & Lee Jacobs/Blend Images (RF)/Jupiterimages; **p. 120:** colleen bradley/iStockphoto.com; **p. 131:** Lise Gagne/

iStockphoto.com; **p. 137:** E. Pablo Kosmicki/AP Wide World Photos; **p. 150:** Ryan Lane/iStockphoto.com; **p. 158:** AFP PHOTO/Newscom; **p. 162:** Luis Pedrosa/LuisPortugal/iStockphoto; **p. 170:** SuperStock, Inc.; **p. 180:** DNY59/iStockphoto.com; **p. 189:** CORBIS-NY; **p. 190:** ©Eros International/Courtesy Everett Collection; **p. 197:** EyeWire Collection/Getty Images—Photodisc-Royalty Free; **p. 199:** *Ta Matete: The Market*, Gauguin, Paul, 1848–1903, French, Kunstmuseum Basel © SuperStock, Inc.; **p. 207:** AFP PHOTO/Stan HONDA/Newscom; **p. 209:** Photos.com; **p. 212:** iStockphoto.com; **p. 224:** Tomasz Resiak/iStockphoto.com; **p. 235:** Photos.com; **p. 238:** Jupiter Images Royalty Free; **p. 240:** Thaddeus Robertson/iStockphoto.com; **p. 244:** Baloncici/iStockphoto.com; **p. 247:** James Steidl/Shutterstock; **p. 251:** © Wild Life Ranger/Alamy; **p. 258:** Frank Leung/Bird Images/iStockphoto; **p. 260:** Photo by Tom Vincent; **p. 269:** © Michael Doolittle/Alamy; **p. 271:** Linda & Colin McKie/travellinglight/iStockphoto; **p. 277:** Yvan Dube/iStockphoto .com; **p. 286:** Mableen/iStockphoto.com; **p. 291:** Jupiter Images; **p. 293:** AbleStock.com/Thinkstock; **p. 298:** sclbak/iStockphoto .com; **p. 302:** Bozo Kodric/bravo1954/iStockphoto; **p. 305:** iStockphoto.com; **p. 318:** Thinkstock/Getty Images/Jupiterimages/Creatas; **p. 328:** Duncan Noakes/FourOaks/iStockphoto; **p. 333:** Tom C. Amon/Shutterstock; **p. 336:** Peter-John Freeman/The_Flying_Duchman/iStockphoto; **p. 338:** Photos.com; **p. 351:** Photos.com; **p. 352:** Graeme Whittle/rohojamagic/iStockphoto; **p. 354:** Peter Kim/pkripper503/iStockphoto; **p. 362:** Jochen Tack/Photolibrary/Peter Arnold, Inc.; **p. 375:** bora ucak/khz/iStockphoto; **p. 383:** Kutay Tanir/Photos.com; **p. 385:** Kutay Tanir/iStockphoto.com; **p. 397:** Getty Images—Stockbyte, Royalty Free; **p. 405:** iStockphoto.com; **p. 413:** Polka Dot/Thinkstock; **p. 415:** Jack Hollingsworth/Valueline/Thinkstock; **p. 417:** Jack Hollingsworth/Thinkstock; **p. 429:** Photodisc/Getty Images; **p. 439:** Maria Dryfhout/iStockphoto.com; **p. 451:** quavondo/iStockphoto.com.

Index